CW00642223

Royal Air Force

COASTAL
COMMAND

A short history of the maritime air force which protected the
United Kingdom's shipping during World War I and World War II

John Campbell

Royal Air Force

COASTAL COMMAND

**A short history of the maritime air force which protected the
United Kingdom's shipping during World War I and World War II**

MEREO
CIRENCESTER

Published by Mereo

Mereo is an imprint of Memoirs Publishing

25 Market Place, Cirencester, Gloucestershire, GL7 2NX
info@memoirsbooks.co.uk www.memoirspublishing.com

Royal Air Force Coastal Command

All Rights Reserved. Copyright © 2013 John Campbell

No part of this book may be reproduced or transmitted in any form or
by any means, graphic, electronic, or mechanical, including
photocopying, recording, taping or by any information storage or
retrieval system, without the permission in writing from the copyright
holder. The right of John Campbell to be identified as the author of
this work has been asserted in accordance with the Copyright,
Designs and Patents Act 1988 sections 77 and 78.

The views expressed in this work are solely those of the author and do
not necessarily reflect the views of the publisher, and the publisher
hereby disclaims any responsibility for them.

ISBN: 978-1-909544-73-4

Printed and bound in Great Britain by
Marston Book Services Ltd, Oxfordshire

This book is dedicated to my wife Keeta, our son Jamie, our daughter Fiona, our son-in-law Colin, our grandchildren Rebecca and Dougal and to all air and ground crews of Coastal Command, its antecedents and successors.

CONTENTS

INTRODUCTION

In the decades after the Second World War I served as a Coastal Command navigator and crew captain on Shackleton aircraft in the Maritime Patrol role. Later, I converted to Nimrods. I became an Intelligence Officer at COMAIRNORLANT, finally retiring in 1984 after 31 years. Hence my desire to write this book. I hope it will show the public the serious gap in this country's defence originated by the Defence Review of 2010.

The work of Coastal Command was, and is, in conjunction with the Royal Navy, to keep the sea lanes clear. Its prime task in war time is to locate and destroy enemy submarines and enemy surface vessels and a subsidiary task is search and rescue, although Fighter Command, in the Second World War, carried out some of this work. During that War, photo reconnaissance came under its jurisdiction.

To carry out this work the Command was equipped with various aircraft. For anti-submarine work, flying boats such as Saro Londons, Southamptons, Scapas, Short Singapores, Rangoons, Stranraers and the land-based Avro Ansons were employed. For anti-shipping work, Vickers Vildebeeste torpedo bombers were used. In 1936 Coastal Command had eight squadrons, increasing in 1937 to fourteen, in response to the deteriorating situation in mainland Europe. In 1938 there were another three squadrons including the new Short Sunderland flying boat. In April 1938 the British Purchasing Commission went to the United States and ordered 200 land-based Lockheed Hudsons. On 15 October 1938 the prototype Bristol Beaufort torpedo bomber flew.

Coastal Command crews faced many problems during their flights over the seas around the United Kingdom and in overseas areas. Firstly, there was the weather. High winds caused turbulence at the low altitudes at which the aircraft flew. Fronts passing through the area brought the cloud base down to a low level and thus caused bad visibility. High sea states made detection of the enemy very difficult. In the winter there was snow and ice on the aircraft to contend with and, of course, in the higher latitudes the weather was much worse. Such weather caused airsickness, although most aircrew could cope with this. Nevertheless, it was tiring.

Further, enemy submarines were difficult to find in these conditions, as submariners would find the calmer state under the surface much more to their liking. While generally the weather was much better in the tropics, storms could be more violent and the heat brought its own problems, both in terms of aircraft performance and aircrew and ground crew fitness. Heat exhaustion, prickly heat, malaria, dengue fever and other nasties were just some of the illnesses affecting air and ground crew. Preparation for take off was always a problem, in that there was no air conditioning and the crews were invariably pouring sweat and stripped to the waist.

In addition, in hot climates dangerous animals and other creatures could be encountered. While most of these would keep away from humans, there was always the surprise element involved in the one stumbling across the other. It was always wise to shake one's shoes out before putting them on.

Secondly there was the length of sortie. Aircraft endurance was of the order of six hours until the Second World War, when the need to close the mid-Atlantic gap generated the production of aircraft such as the Consolidated Liberator with the capability of flight times of up to 18 hours. Sergeant Richard Thomas of No 86 Squadron, when describing the attack on U-43 on 20 July 1943, states: "Gone were the flights of short duration in the Lockheed Hudson, or the longer trips in the Fortress. Now we were in the air for seventeen to eighteen hours at a stretch, flying round the clock. At the height of the battle over the Bay, from May to July 1943, we had got ourselves into a steady rhythm of being airborne for some fifty hours or so in every five days, spending almost half of our waking lives within the confines of the huge Liberator which had now become our home."

Much of this book is taken from other authors and I hope that I have acknowledged them all. Without them this could not have been written. I wanted to show the public the history of Coastal Command, which is little known, and the great contribution it has made to this nation.

CHAPTER ONE

BATTLESHIP BRIGADE

There was much talk after the First World War to the effect that the aeroplane, in the form of the bomber, had rendered the battleship extinct. Temporary Brigadier General and substantive Colonel Billy Mitchell and his crews sank the obsolescent captured German Dreadnought *Ostfriesland* in 1921. This was a good feat, but there was no opposition in the form of flak or other aircraft.

Credibility was given to this achievement by the American Rear Admiral William Sims and the Royal Navy Admiral Sir Percy Scott. However, it was a fact that no armoured warship had been sunk by air attack during that war. Those officers who were opposed to air power created an imaginative Admiral to prove their case. He was the Battleship Admiral and, of course, he was a Gunnery Officer. Gunnery Officers were the backbone of the Seaman branch of the Royal Navy. It was believed that if an officer was not a gunner, he would not get on in the service.

The Battleship Admiral was sceptical of everything and in particular, of aviation. If aircraft had not performed well in the war it was his fault, as he had ignored aviation in various ways through prejudice and/or stupidity. This was partly true, as there were officers like this, but equally there were others who were much more imaginative. There were also officers who believed in aviation but did not understand it and handled it wrongly. Even today these officers exist, but in small numbers. They do not understand that a Nimrod is a weapon system in its own right and is not just a locating device for the Fleet's guns.

Rear Admiral Murray F. Sueter believed in the Battleship Admiral. He was highly critical of the Admiralty in that their Lordships refused to act on his recommendation to build some 200 torpedo aircraft. However, there is no documentary evidence for his assertion and it should be noted that Sueter was somewhat hostile to the Admiralty. He became persona non grata because he wrote to King George V seeking recognition for his work on the tank. This was a breach of professional etiquette. Nevertheless, Sueter did start development work on the Sopwith Cuckoo, but the Admiralty was late in their order. A squadron of Cuckoos was on board the carrier HMS *Argus* at the Armistice.

It must be understood that the aeroplane at that time did not have a long range or a long endurance and suffered from navigational inaccuracies, an inadequate weaponload and bad weather. A surface warship was, in these respects, preferable. On the other hand the aeroplane was much faster, could cover larger areas of sea and could see further.

In 1916 there was an Admiralty proposal to establish seaplane bases in southern Ireland to counter the U-boat. However, aircraft were unreliable at that time and Vice Admiral Sir Lewis Bayly, in command of Western Approaches, refused to have them on the grounds that his ships would waste valuable time in looking for and rescuing ditched crews. Nevertheless, when more reliable aircraft were made available he changed his mind.

An objection to having aeroplanes aboard ships was the necessity for a flight deck. This tended to get in the way of the guns. R D Layman in his *Naval Aviation in the First World War* writes of the three fixed track ramps fitted to the cruisers Aurora, *Arethusa, Penelope* and *Undaunted* in 1915. These made fire from the forward guns impossible and interfered with the capstans. On some cruisers the weight of these ramps affected the stability of the ship. These problems were solved in 1917 by the introduction of rotating platforms, often on top of a gun turret, which allowed the re-equipping of Royal Navy ships with aircraft during the last 12 months of the war. By the end of the war there were HMS *Argus,* a full flight deck carrier, the two quasi-full flight deck carriers HMS *Furious* and HMS *Vindictive* and two seaplane carriers, a total of five ships.

Admiral Sir John Jellicoe, who was C-in-C of the Grand Fleet in 1914, had become a convert to aviation after flying in a commercial Zeppelin at Potsdam in 1911. He called for the building of British airships, but this was not successful. Admiral Sir David Beatty, who succeeded Jellicoe, was equally enthusiastic about aviation and took various measures concerning reconnaissance, anti-submarine work and torpedo aircraft. He had high praise for the only British aircraft to fly at the Battle of Jutland and predicted that a future C-in-C would be based on a carrier.

There were other officers who saw the uses of aircraft, among them Commodore Sir Reginald Tyrwhitt, who despite setbacks persisted in their development. His partner at Harwich, Commodore Sir Roger Keyes, also made great use of aircraft.

Commander Mike Crosley DSC RN writes in his book *They Gave me a Seafire* that on the amalgamation of the Royal Flying Corps (RFC) and the Royal Naval Air Service (RNAS)in April 1918 into the Royal Air Force (RAF),the RAF took over 55,000 sailors, 100 shore stations and 2375 aircraft, balloons and airships. Most of the senior naval aviators left to join the RAF because there were better career prospects. Thus, in 1938, when the RN took back the Fleet Air Arm (FAA), there was a significant lack of knowledge about air matters in the Navy. The training curriculum of Naval officers did not include air power unless they volunteered to become pilots or observers, and there was little chance of that until 1935. The Navy realized in 1921 that they would lose not only administrative and material control but operational control of the FAA as well. To counteract this, it recruited observers, a new specialization, to fly in the back seat. The nearest equivalent to this profession is the RAF navigator, who undertakes a wider training. The observer would be made senior to the RAF pilot in order that the RN would then command the aircraft. The slogan was "Become a Naval Observer and command your own aircraft".

Crosley writes that the average Dartmouth-trained officer not only had little knowledge of the air threat but had to learn the slow flag and Morse communications and warning system. Naval gunnery officers believed that their anti-aircraft gunnery (AA) was the best and that no aircraft could survive it. The Japanese disproved that. Crosley goes on to say that the RN's faith in its gunnery as a means to defend against air attack was even more optimistic than its faith in its ability to hit warships. In 1916 at Jutland the Germans produced figures after the war showing that the British battlefleet's main armament caused 2.2% hits, light damage and 0.3 % hits, heavy damage. The same guns were in use in 1939.

The lack of senior aviation officers to advise on air operational matters meant also that there was nobody with experience and knowledge to write specifications for new aircraft and weapons. Some observers believe that the amalgamation of the RNAS and the RFC into the RAF in 1918 denied the army and the RN the support that was required and that this so-called intransigence continued into the Second World War. However, it must be remembered that soldiers and sailors are not aviators and that it is aviators who know best how to deploy aircraft once strategy has been decided.

The Inskip Report, produced by Sir Thomas Inskip in 1936, generated the transfer of the FAA to the RN. The report stated amongst other things that the Navy could never resist an attack on it by a large air force. If such a force was encountered the Navy must call upon the RAF. Such a comment fails to understand the nature of air power, particularly in the days of no radar and slow communications. On the other hand the report did allow the RAF to retain ownership and operational control of Coastal Command. To allow the Navy to have control, which at that time had next to no air experience, would have been a disaster. While the battleship admirals may well have been in a minority, the remainder had very little idea how to deploy anti-submarine and anti-surface aircraft. Operational control was eventually passed to the RN, but joint RAF/RN headquarters were set up.

The historian and Italian Army officer Giglio Douhet (1869-1930), writing about naval air power, divided the various options into four groups:

Group 1. This group believes that the war could be won by aircraft. Lord Trenchard and Air Chief Marshal Sir Arthur Harris probably belonged to this group. There is a suggestion that the bombing may have lengthened the war, as no one seems to have given thought to an alternative use for aircraft and crews. *Brassey's Annual* makes this point and states "It has been estimated that in its lifetime of 30 sorties a Coastal Command Liberator over the Atlantic could save three merchantmen from destruction by a U-Boat. The same Liberator over Berlin could perhaps destroy a few houses and kill a couple of dozen civilians".

Group 2. This group believes that in any surface encounter between naval units, the air above and surrounding the airfields (that is those within range of the Naval battle) should be cleared of enemy aircraft. Command of the sea could only come after command of the air above it. The battleship was relegated to night or poor visibility actions.

This idea was not popular with the Navy. The Americans and Hitler adopted this thinking. Hitler refused to risk the German army in an invasion of the UK until he had command of the air above the English Channel. He ordered *Tirpitz* away from convoy PQ17 when he heard that the carrier HMS *Victorious* was at sea. A British example was the use of aircraft in the "Harpoon" and "Pedestal" convoys to Malta. The fighter element was able to retain command of the air above the convoys. The British Naval Officers sufficiently senior to make their voices heard at that time were Dennis Boyd and Tom Troubridge.

Group 3. This group considered that command of the sea could be obtained separately from command of the air. They believed that the Fleet carrier should take her place alongside the cruiser force and be capable of fighting surface opposition with its own guns. The carrier's complement should be limited to Tactical / Strike / Reconnaissance (TSR) aircraft and a few fighters to act as escorts. The enemy fleet could then be brought under the guns of the battlefleet.

In World War 2 there were several examples of the misuse of carriers, such as when the brand new carrier HMS *Illustrious* was dive bombed off Sicily, being within range of enemy aircraft, and was then out of action for a year in a dockyard in the United States. Her replacement, HMS *Formidable*, two months later received the same treatment in the Aegean Sea. Neither carrier had more than a few Fulmar fighters on board but did have many Swordfish and Albacores. *Illustrious* Swordfish were supposed to cripple the Italian fleet, and Admiral Cunningham had refused the request of her captain to remain out of the range of the Ju87s (Stukas). *Formidable* had only three Fulmars serviceable in an area where the Germans had air supremacy.

Group 4. This group believed that guns could deal entirely with the threat from the air. After the sinking of the *Repulse* and the *Prince of Wales,* not many members of this group were left in the RN. A new form of this group is now appearing and its members believe in the missile.

Douhet published his book, Command of the Air, in 1921.

Crosley believes that the Navy had forgotten all the lessons in the Pacific War of 1944-45 and allowed Denis Healey, Secretary of State for Defence, to scrap its fixed-wing fighters in 1964. Certainly, at that time the Soviet threat loomed large, but the point about defence is that a nation must be prepared for the unexpected. This is probably the lesson that is never learned. Thus, when the Argentines invaded the Falkland Islands in 1982, the Navy had an inadequate carrier force and a poor Airborne Early Warning (AEW) force. A retired admiral wrote to the newspapers suggesting that what the RN really needed in the Falklands was more guns. In 2008 the fixed maritime force of Nimrods is lower than ever. The excuse this time is that modern electronics gives a force multiplier.

Air Marshal Sir Keith Williamson wrote in this period that while standoff missiles costing £100,000 each could become fairly effective against fixed targets, moving targets are a quite different problem. He said that we were nowhere near the stage when weapons can discriminate between friendly and enemy targets in the battle area, or between high and low value targets further back. The human brain remains the first and most flexible computer available to us.

A Naval publication sent in 1982 to retired senior Naval officers over the signature of the First Sea Lord stated that the Falklands Operation demonstrated yet again the value of maritime power, with its inherent flexibility derived from *a balanced fleet to deal with the unforeseen*. An RN weapons officer wrote in the same publication that the Argentines attacked at wave-top height and took advantage of the terrain! Well, how unusual. This should not be unexpected.

The following account is from John Wellham's book, *With Naval Wings*, published by Spellmount Ltd, The Old Rectory, Staplehurst, Kent, TN12 0AZ 1995.

The Bomba raid which was carried out by three Swordfish operating from the RAF airfield at Ma'aten Bagush on 22 August, 1940, some 100 miles west of Alexandria via a refueling stop at Sidi Barani, sank two submarines, one destroyer and one depot ship. One of the submarines was tied up to the destroyer. The C-in-C Mediterranean, Admiral Sir Andrew Cunningham, was very happy about this and other attacks as they confirmed his opinion that torpedo bombers were the answer to destroying an enemy fleet in port. Alfred Price in *Aircraft versus Submarine* states that the submarine *Iride*, the depot ship *Monte Gargano* and the torpedo boat *Calipso* were tied up together. Captain Oliver Patch, Royal Marines, dropped a torpedo which almost cut the *Iride* in two. The other Swordfish attacked the *Monte Gargano* and the *Calipso*. It was assumed that the *Calipso* had been sunk but this was not the case. The depot ship blew up and sank, but *Calipso* survived. The confusion arose because when the depot ship blew up, both she and the *Calipso* disappeared in spray. The crews had expected another submarine to be alongside *Iride*. Nevertheless it was an excellent result.

After Taranto, Admiral Cunningham recommended that all engaged should receive decorations. However the only ones awarded were a DSO each to the two squadron commanders, with a DSC to their observers and a DSC each to Captain Ollie Patch, Royal Marines, and his observer David Goodwin. Cunningham was furious and other very senior people made known their disgust. As a result of this a further list was published many months later, which bestowed DSCs on those who had confirmed hits. The remainder received a "Mentioned in Despatches". There was still no recognition for the ship's company of HMS *Illustrious*. The list arrived so late that many on it had lost their lives.

The Italians complained about the divided control of the Regia Aeronautica, the lack of maritime aircraft, particularly reconnaissance and torpedo bombers. Admiral Inigo Campioni, the C-in-C of the Italian Fleet, appreciated the advantages of an aircraft carrier, whose fighters could shoot down reconnaissance and torpedo bombers and whose own torpedo bombers could at least cause confusion in the enemy fleet, if not sink some of them. The Italians had assumed that if the British Fleet came within 180 miles of Taranto their own fleet would sally forth to engage it. However no one had told them that the British had arrived. The Fulmar fighters had shot down most of the Cant Z501 flying boats which tried to shadow the British fleet. *Illustrious* and her aircraft had proved that the vital element of any offensive operation in modern warfare was air superiority.

John Wellham goes on to say later in his book that the Royal Navy did not receive suitable aircraft from British manufacturers. In fairness, he writes that they believed they were given impossible specifications by the Admiralty. The Fairey Albacore was the successor to the Fairey Swordfish, and it was not as good. The Albacore was to be replaced by the Fairey Barracuda, and Wellham calls it a 'ghastly compromise'. It was not until the FAA was equipped with American aircraft that they had anything really suitable for the job.

The Japanese noted the implementation and the effects of the Taranto raid and mounted their own version of it on 7 December 1941 at Pearl Harbour, with similar results.

In *They Gave Me a Seafire*, Commander Crosley writes of his experiences in Operation Pedestal, one of the convoys to Malta. At the end of the first night's air battle eight Sea Hurricanes were airborne and short of fuel and trying to locate their own carrier, HMS *Indomitable*, in the darkness. The captain of the carrier, Captain Troubridge, did all he could to help his fighters by taking his ship out of line, steaming into wind and putting his masthead and deck landing lights full on. Signals from Vice Admiral E N Syfret in HMS *Nelson* told him to douse his lights and tell his fighters to ditch. This he ignored. Finally, Troubridge ordered a searchlight to be shone vertically at the clouds. He remarked "What is the good of a carrier without her fighters?" The Sea Hurricanes were fired on by their own ships, and even when the aircraft approached with their hooks down they were still fired on by their own carrier.

When in the Far East, Crosley was returning from a strike over Japan in the vicinity of Maizuru Naval Base. His carrier, HMS *Implacable*, commanded by Captain Charles Evans, was using a fogbank as cover. If the ship had remained in the bank, Crosley's Seafires, now running low on fuel, would have had to ditch in a ten-foot swell, which would have been fatal. Admiral Vian ordered Evans to turn 180 degrees away from the Japanese coast during the latter part of the land-on. Evans ignored the order, coming out of the fog and recovering all his aircraft. Evans said later that Vian never forgave him. Apparently the Americans described Vian's action as that of an "inexperienced carrier admiral".

He goes on to write that by 30 July 1945 the fleet had carried out 216 offensives, 30 Wing's share being 88 sorties. This was 34% of all sorties with 18% of the British Pacific Fleet's (BPF) aircraft. This was very good work and was greeted by a signal from the Flag Officer, Admiral Vian, stating that shipping targets had been mainly combative vessels at anchor, that airborne opposition had been nonexistent and flak not unduly severe. The hits obtained by the Avengers (torpedo bombers) had been less than expected. He continued stating that all attacks must be properly planned and deliberately executed and that formation leaders must brief subordinates either on the ground or in the air. Finally he wrote that when flak is light, press low to bomb, to hit and sink. Crosley was furious as the most "subordinate" aircrew could see that the signal was written by someone who was used to controlling battleships and was full of blunders, on the following grounds:

To believe that airborne briefing was an alternative to briefing on the ground was absurd.

The idea that the unsuitable level bombing techniques used by the Avengers could be used at low level was equally absurd.

The assumption that the amount of flak could be assessed before take off was unlikely.

Bomb release heights were strictly controlled to match the type of target, the weather, terrain, fuse settings and cloud height. The Avenger approached its target at medium height, thus giving warning to the enemy. It had neither the sophisticated bomb sight of a high-level bomber nor the agility of a dive bomber. Interestingly, *Implacable* received a congratulatory signal from Admiral Brind, who had been their admiral at Truk. The signal was repeated to the Flagship.

Another incident that Crosley quotes is when the Admiral arrived on HMS *Implacable* in a Fairey Firefly. The story was told by John Joly, one of the Seafire pilots:

"We had the usual three Seafires on deck, two warmed up and one spare with folded wings. Our Chief AA did not like the sound of my engine, so I dismounted to get into the spare. While I was doing this the tannoy told me to report to the bridge. The Admiral advanced and said: "Are you afraid of flying, young man?" "No sir". "Well get back into your aeroplane".

It should be noted that mechanics were still picking bits of Japanese destroyer out of the fuselage of his Seafire from his action two days previously.

It is probably true to say that there were, and maybe are, battleship admirals who have little understanding of aviation and believe in gunnery or missiles as the ultimate naval weapon. However, they are in a minority and there are more who have a greater knowledge of the air, due mainly to closer co-operation between the RAF and the RN brought about by courses such as those at the Joint

Anti Submarine School at HMS *Sea Eagle* at Londonderry, and after this was closed, the Joint Maritime Course at RAF Turnhouse with flying operations from RAF Kinloss.

The Long TAS (Torpedo Anti Submarine) Course and its successor the Principal Warfare Officers (PWO) Course incorporated visits to air stations where the students flew in maritime aircraft. An old joke amongst aircrew was that when working with ships the usual response to a message to the ship was a standard "Roger-Wait-Out". Not unreasonable really, when it is considered that it was a rating receiving the message and requesting the aircraft to wait while he got a decision from the officer concerned. However, the message was transmitted by an aviator actively dealing with the problem from the air. The aircrew query was "Who is Mr Roger Waitout?" The real complaint behind this was that responses should be quicker. Through the medium of the aforementioned courses this did happen.

It has to be remembered that the aircraft was in its infancy in 1914, and although progress had been made in the following four years, probably too much was expected from it. It was considered to be a reconnaissance vehicle and not an offensive weapon, so some officers thought of it as expendable. Little progress was made between the wars in technology, training and navigation techniques.

CHAPTER TWO

THE SUBMARINE AND THE AEROPLANE

The twentieth century produced probably three major weapons: nuclear weapons, the submarine and the aeroplane.

The atomic bomb was born in 1945 with the strikes on Hiroshima and Nagasaki in Japan and nuclear power followed, to generate electricity and to power submarines and surface ships. Weapons were developed further as bombs and warheads fitted to missiles, and were made smaller in size and bigger in explosive content. A nuclear depth-bomb to destroy submarines was produced.

The submarine had been in existence for some time. The first true design appeared in 1578, when the English mathematician William Bourne designed a submersible made of wood and propelled by oars. In the American War of Independence Sergeant Ezra Lee sailed a barrel-shaped submarine, called the Turtle, designed by David Bushnell, into New York Harbour and tried to sink the Royal Navy's 64-gun flagship, HMS *Eagle*. Sergeant Lee had to screw a mine onto the bottom of the ship but failed to do so. He was discovered but got away. The American engineer

Robert Fulton, in France, built in 1800 the *Nautilus*. In 1863 The Confederate Submarine *Hunley*, one of the steam powered "David" class sank the Union sloop *Housatonic* off Charleston Bar. This was a landmark in that it was the first successful sinking by a submarine. However the *Hunley* did not return, as the backwash from the explosion flooded the boat.

In 1900 the US Navy bought the 74 ton *Holland VI*, designed by the Irishman John Holland. The Royal Navy bought five. In the lead up to the First World War small submarines of around 400 tons were employed by various navies. The first all-British petrol-engined "A" class of 190 tons was introduced in 1904. This was followed by the petrol engined "C" class in 1905. This was of 287 tons and capable of a surface speed of 12 knots. The "D" class, introduced in 1909, was the first British diesel-powered boat and was 483 tons, with a surface speed of 14 knots.

The word "submarine" implies that the vessel operates under the water all of the time, but until the latter part of the century, when nuclear power became available, this was not the case. The original submarine was no more than a submersible, fitted with a steam engine. Later, petrol engines were used until diesel engines came into being with the French boat *Aigrette* in 1902. None of these would work under water. For that purpose electric motors were used, and when the batteries were exhausted, the submarine needed to surface in order to recharge them. The diesels rotated the electric motors, which then acted as generators.

By the middle of the Second World War it became a submersible snort-fitted vessel. The snort, or to give it its proper name, the schnorkel, was an air intake which was raised above the surface of the water and enabled the diesels to be used. The use of electric motors, by virtue of being under water, restricted the submarine's range and speed. The faster the submarine went, the more quickly battery power was used. Batteries could only be operated for a short time before they were exhausted and needed to be recharged. This was the weakness of the submarine.

If an aircraft sighted it, it had to submerge and go onto battery propulsion, slowing it down and preventing it attacking its target. Maximum submerged speed was around 8-9 knots, which could only be maintained for about one hour. There were improvements in batteries in terms of capacity and number carried, and the diesel submarine of the 1950s was very different to those of the First World War. In the later part of the Second World War the Germans experimented with hydrogen peroxide, which would provide a motor that needed no snort. After the war the Royal Navy experimented with another version of this namely, high test peroxide (HTP) in two submarines, HMS/Ms *Explorer* and *Excalibur*, but it proved too volatile and was abandoned. These submarines were known as the intermediate submarines.

By the 1950s the true submarines were going to sea. Powered by a nuclear reactor, they had no need to remain on the surface for the entire voyage. The reactor provided power to drive the submarine at high speeds and oxygen for the crew.

At the outbreak of the First World War, Germany had 28 boats, the United Kingdom 75, France 62 and Russia 36. The German intention had been to have a Fleet of 70 boats by 1920, 10 of which were to be for offensive use in the North Sea, 10 in the reserve and the remainder to defend German ports. This was the brainchild of Grand Admiral Alfred von Tirpitz, the founder and Chief of the Imperial German Navy. He was a battleship man, who saw no grand offensive role for the submarine and indeed worked against naval submarine enthusiasts by trying to shorten their careers. He ordered the Navy's first U-Boat, U-1, in 1904. However, the Battle of Jutland proved Tirpitz to be wrong and on 1 February 1917 unrestricted submarine warfare commenced and was Germany's last hope. In three months between 1917-18 the U-Boats sank two million tons of shipping. This caused the introduction of the convoy system, a proven technique which was several hundred years old, and the effectiveness of the boats waned. By the end of the war Germany had lost 178 out of a fleet of 374.

The types of boat in use were UB Is of 127 tons with a crew of fourteen, and UB IIIs of 516 tons, four bow and one stern tube, ten torpedoes and one 88mm gun. The UB III was an ocean-going boat, highly effective and the forerunner of the Second World War type VII. There were a number of U-cruisers of 2000 tons carrying two 88mm guns with a crew of 66. The Mobilmachungs Bootes were fleet boats which were again similar to the future type VIIc. Thus the 1939-45 boats, type IA, type II, type VIIb, type VIIc, type IX were no great advance on their predecessors. Indeed, the type IX with its broad beam was slow in submerging.

The aeroplane did not exist at the beginning of the century, although man had ventured into the air by means of balloons and there had been some attempts at winged flight. In 1903 the Wright brothers achieved this at Kittyhawk. In 1909 Blériot crossed the English Channel and the military planners, recognising the potential, formed on 1 April, 1911 the Air Battalion of the Royal Engineers. This consisted of two companies, one dealing with airships and the other with aeroplanes. Officers were appointed from any branch of the Army, but the other ranks were men already serving in the Royal Engineers.

A Royal Warrant dated 13 April 1912 authorised the absorption of the Battalion into the Royal Flying Corps which was formed four weeks later. The RFC consisted of two wings, a Naval Wing and a Military Wing. The Naval Wing carried out flying training and experimental work with seaplanes, land planes and airships and the Military Wing dealt with landplanes. The Naval Wing began to divorce itself from the RFC and called itself the Royal Naval Air Service, a term which was recognised in 1914, although it actually remained a part of the RFC until 1915. The role was reconnaissance; the aircraft were Farmans, Blériots and various others. The engines were of no greater power than 80 hp. Flying training was offered to both officers and non commissioned officers (NCOs). It was planned to have 182 officers and 182 NCOs.

In those days flying, and particularly military flying, was in its infancy. Neither equipment nor training was standardised. Operational technique, air fighting and bombing were unknown. Four squadrons went to France on 13 August 1914, nine days after the outbreak of war, with RE1's, BE2c's, Blériot Parasols, Farman Shorthorns and BE8s. The speeds of these aircraft were around

75mph, but by 1916 they had increased to, for example, the 105mph of the Sopwith Pup and a further steady increase to 130 mph had occurred by 1918.

The First Lord of the Admiralty from October 1911 to May 1915 was Winston Churchill, who took an enthusiastic interest in aviation matters. He took flying lessons but gave them up at the instigation of his wife, friends and political colleagues. It has been said that he and Sueter were the two people most responsible for anything the Navy did to help Naval Aviation before the war. British strategic air doctrine was initiated by the Admiralty and Churchill and Sueter played major roles. Churchill began a bombing offensive against the Zeppelins. At a conference of senior RNAS officers he stated the need to develop a large fleet of aircraft capable of delivering an air bombardment against the enemy.

The Admiralty formed a strategic bombing force, No 3 Wing RNAS, in May 1916 to be equipped with 55 aircraft. However, hardly had the formation started when Major General Hugh Trenchard asked for assistance in the Somme offensive. Aircraft were diverted to this task, which reduced the number available for a strategic offensive but numbers were increased gradually. Some raids were carried out and the emphasis was transferred from day to night bombing. New aircraft were added to the force, including the Handley Pages. By early 1917 the RFC had been badly depleted by the Somme offensive and asked for further assistance. The Admiralty responded, but this caused the gradual dissolution of No 3 Wing and by May 1917 it had been disbanded.

Before the First World War most major navies had

faced up to the problem of the airborne detection of submarines and their destruction. In the clear waters of the Mediterranean a submarine can be seen underwater, but as latitude increases this becomes more difficult as the sea becomes murkier. In calm seas, the periscope or snort can be seen with relative ease but as sea states increase this becomes more difficult.

Detection is also a function of aircraft altitude. The higher the altitude and the higher the sea state, the lower the detection distance, i.e. the distance at which a submarine, snort or periscope may be seen. In March 1912, Lieutenant Hugh Williamson, RN, a submariner and a qualified aviator, (at his own expense) in his paper, "The Aeroplane in use against Submarines", specified the requirements for an anti-submarine aircraft. These were good visibility, long endurance, a reliable engine and a large payload or weapon load. He then described its weapon, which was probably the forerunner of the depth charge. He also wrote that if a submarine sighted an aircraft it would submerge and wait until the danger had passed. This in the event, was how the aircraft would exert its greatest pressure on the submarine in preventing its use of the surface, thus slowing it down, causing its batteries to be used up and preventing it taking offensive action.

CHAPTER THREE

EARLY DAYS

The RNAS pioneered the art of long-distance bombing and became good at artillery spotting. The RNAS was responsible for the Air Defence of the United Kingdom, strategic bombing and the air side of the anti U-Boat campaign, whereas the RFC was responsible for support of the Army.

On 21 November 1914 the RNAS carried out the first strategic bombing raid of the war by attacking the Zeppelin works at Friedrichshafen using four Avro 504s armed with four 20lb bombs each. The raid was planned by Lieutenant Noel Pemberton-Billing, Royal Naval Volunteer Reserve (RNVR) and was mounted from Belfort in south east France. Pemberton-Billing founded the Supermarine Aviation Works in 1912, but when the company changed its name from Pemberton-Billing Limited to Supermarine Aviation Works Limited, during the course of the war, Squadron Commander Pemberton-Billing ceased to have anything to do with the company. The raid caused little damage but one bomb fell close to one airship. It was a foretaste of things to come some 30 years later.

In 1916 the Joint Air War Committee was formed. It

made a decision that the destruction of dockyards, arsenals and other centres of production, which would affect the enemy's naval productive capacity as a whole, should be carried out by the RNAS. Thus in May 1916, the Admiralty formed No 3 Wing and based it at Belfort along with the French bombardment squadrons. It was to be equipped with 15 Short Bombers, 20 Sopwith 1½ Strutter bombers and 20 1½ Strutter fighters. It was soon called upon to assist the RFC in the Somme offensive so it was not until October 1916 that the Wing was able to carry out bombing raids.

In 1915 the duties of the Royal Naval Air Service (RNAS) were to cover the troop convoys from submarine attack, spotting for the RN's guns as they bombarded German batteries and carrying out air defence of the UK with what remained. On 4 June, 1915 Sir John Jellicoe set out the true function of the RNAS, namely to reconnoitre, to fight enemy aircraft, to defend from the air all naval centres and to hunt submarines.

First Lord of the Admiralty Winston Churchill's seaplanes were certainly not perfect and were unlikely to develop into anything workable. Experiments with lighter than air aircraft had failed. Tom Sopwith addressed himself to the matter and produced the first Flying Boat just before the war. Few people showed any interest, apart from one Lieutenant Cyril Porte, RN. He had been obliged to resign from the Navy due to tuberculosis. Whilst he was a submariner, he was also very airminded and teamed up with the American, Glenn H. Curtiss. When the flying boat, *America*, took off from Hammondsport, New York, on 22 June 1914, Porte was flying it. Shortly after that he was back in uniform and was soon promoted to Commander; he became CO of Felixstowe. The Admiralty bought two Curtiss boats and, at Porte's insistence, the *America* and her sister boat. Both of these were taken to Felixstowe in November 1914. A total of 62 of these boats were bought and were known as H-4s or Small Americas. These were of course civil aircraft, but they kept the North Sea patrolled until something else came along.

Commander Porte died at the age of 36 of tuberculosis.

By the end of 1916 the RNAS had some excellent flying boats. These included the UK F-2 or Felixstowe Fury, together with some 50 of Glenn Curtiss' H12s or Large Americas. This last was considered to be the best that the Navy would have for a very long time. They were about five tons fully loaded, powered by two Rolls Royce Eagles, each of 275 hp. They had a speed of just under 100 mph and carried enough fuel to take them wherever they pleased. The endurance was about six hours. With a crew of four and three Lewis guns they could, and did, fight off any number of enemy aircraft. They carried a bomb load of 460 lbs, consisting of either four 100 pounders or two 230 pounders. Against submarines they were deadly, and their airkeeping qualities made surveillance of the North Sea possible.

This surveillance patrol was called the Great Spider Web and was established in April 1917. It was based on the Nord Hinder light vessel and had eight radial arms each of 30 miles length. There were chords linking the arms at 10, 20 and 30 miles from the centre. Similar patrols were set up at Newlyn, Fishguard, Plymouth and the Scillies.

In May 1917, Flight Sub Lieutenant C. Morrish and crew sighted a surfaced submarine. An attack with two 230 pound bombs was made and the submarine submerged. While the Official British History *The War in the Air* reports that this could have been UC-36, German records indicate that she was not sunk by this attack. On 22 September Flight Sub Lieutenant N. Magor in a Large America sighted a surfaced U-Boat. He attacked with two 230 pound bombs, the German crew dived overboard and the U-Boat heeled over and sank. This may have been the first kill in the Spider Web area. Alfred Price reports that this was probably UB-32, although the *Official British History* states that it was UC-72. However, Price states that this boat had already been sunk by HMS *Acton* two days earlier. Air Commodore Waring, then of No 246 Squadron, in August 1918, sighted a submerged submarine, apparently waiting for one of the local convoys. He dropped a 520 lb bomb, which detonated about 30 feet from the bows of the submarine. Bubbles and oil were sighted coming to the surface and it was later established that the submarine had been sunk. Waring was awarded the DFC.

There were regular anti-submarine patrols around the coast of the UK by aircraft, except off the South of Ireland, where many ships were torpedoed. The RNAS proposed the establishment of a seaplane base at Queenstown, now Cobh, near Cork. However, the local commander, Vice Admiral Bayly was against this, stating that if his ships had to "rescue or mother them" the seaplanes would be a hindrance and leave gaps in the patrols, allowing the submarines to make attacks. He did say that if they could look after themselves, they would be useful. It should be noted that the Queenstown sloops were not very effective in preventing the losses of merchant ships or in the sinking of U-Boats! Queenstown is a large harbour and would have been ideal for a Flying Boat base.

By late 1917 the convoy tactics were proving to be effective and the U-Boats were moving to British inshore waters, the most dangerous being off the South West and the North East Coasts. Admiral Beatty requested more air cover for the coastal areas but in reply Captain R. Groves, the Deputy Controller of the Technical Department of the Air Ministry, came up with an alternative. On the basis that U-Boat commanders would remain submerged during the day in those areas where continuous air cover was maintained, he recommended "Protected Lanes". If an aircraft passed any point on the lane every twenty minutes, then a U-Boat would have to submerge each time and this would render it ineffective. Further the U-Boat commander would not know if that aircraft was armed and that therefore any aircraft would suffice. Thus was borne the idea of the "scarecrow patrols" or the Special Duty Flights, which came into service in April 1918. See more of this later.

German U-Boats were now chased continually. For example in May 1918, U-98, operating in the Irish Sea, was attacked by British submarines while en route to her area. In her area she was attacked by destroyer escorts when she fired a torpedo at the ship that they were escorting. Later an attempted attack was thwarted by the appearance of a blimp. She surfaced in Cardigan Bay looking for targets, but was detected and forced to leave the area. The next day she was attacked by a British submarine. She then found a large convoy escorted by ships and aircraft. She was sighted by an observer in a flying kite balloon and had to dive.

British submarine crews had the same problem. The C-25 was attacked by a flight of five Brandenburg seaplanes when on the surface near Harwich. Ammunition exhausted, the Brandenburgs returned to base and British warships towed C-25 into Harwich, but she was damaged beyond repair and was scrapped.

The airminded Rear Admiral Mark Kerr took command of the Adriatic Squadron in May 1916. He pointed out to Mr. Balfour at the Admiralty that all enemy submarines were working out of Cattaro, that their torpedoes were made in Fiume and that Pola both built and maintained them.

He was told that no British aircraft were available to bomb them. The best that could be done was to move a small detachment of naval aircraft from Gibraltar to Otranto. Eventually a dozen Shorts and a number of 14-inch torpedoes arrived. Their station was built in February 1917 on the shore of Mar Piccolo at Taranto and was known for a long time as the "English Camp". A Torpedo School was set up in Malta at the same time. The seaplanes regularly attacked Cattaro with bombs and torpedoes but were not very effective. However, the spotters were far more effective, reporting submarines by wireless and guiding destroyers on to them, such that operations by submarines were severely curtailed. At the end of 1917, Wing Captain Arthur Longmore was appointed to command what had become No 6 Wing.

The first recognisable aircraft carrier was an old Cunarder of 20,000 tons, the *Campania*. On 16 August, 1915, Flt Lt Welsh took off in a landplane from her foredeck. Sir John Jellicoe was not impressed. He preferred the idea of an airship, as at that time they were probably more efficient than aeroplanes. On 30 May 1916, the German Fleet being at sea, *Campania* received the preliminary order to raise steam for full speed, and this she obeyed. The executive order issued at 2254 was not conveyed to her until two and a half hours later. This was a visual signal and visibility was deteriorating. Her captain discovered that the Fleet had sailed and he weighed anchor immediately and tried to catch up, but it was hopeless. Her seaplanes, which were mounted on trolleys and from which they could have been launched, were not used. Nobody can say whether or not this was decisive, but the air side of the Battle of Jutland was left to the less well-equipped HMS *Engadine* - a solitary flight by one of her seaplanes passed a message that nobody would admit to having received.

A Grand Fleet Aircraft Committee was set up in February 1917. Its unanimous conclusions, published within a few months, showed the immediate need for carriers, but there was insufficient labour to make one. The Admiralty purchased a half-finished Italian liner, the *Conte Rosso*, and renamed her the *Argus*. She was not finished in time for WW1. Beatty wanted a carrier and the Committee advised that a warship be converted to a carrier. Beatty had HMS *Furious* commissioned by July 1917.

On 1 April 1918 5378 naval officers, a slightly fewer than 50,000 ratings and almost 3000 aircraft became part of the Royal Air Force, headed by Sir Hugh Trenchard. He was a bomber man and knew little of the sea. The reorganisation was complicated. The Portsmouth Group of the RNAS at Calshot was renamed No 10 Group, Royal Air Force and was placed in the South West Area on 8 May 1918. This Group is regarded as the direct ancestor of HQ Coastal Command.

No 14 Group was formed on 1 April 1918 by renaming Milford Haven Anti Submarine Group. It was transferred to the Midland Area on 8 May 1918 and disbanded 19 May, 1919. Areas were formed on 1 May 1918. They were initially numbered but soon were given geographical names. Within the Area command, functional Groups were set up in command of bases and units. By 30 November 1918 there were ten maritime groups in the five Areas. A further change was initiated on 21 August 1919 when the Air Council proposed a reduction in the number of areas to four. These were to be Southern and Northern (as before) and Naval (Coastal) and Army (Inland). No 10 Group, which had moved to Warsash near Southampton, was included in Coastal Area and was commanded by Wing Commander (an RNAS rank) Arthur W. Bigsworth, DSO, AFC. This officer, in August 1915, when en route to Zeebrugge in a Henri Farman, sighted a U-Boat on the surface, which he attacked and apparently sank. This scheme was accepted and Coastal Area was formed on 15 September, 1919 with Headquarters at 4 Thurloe Place, Kensington, London. There were two Group HQs, one at Leuchars in Fife and the other at Lee on Solent. Headquarters Coastal Area (HQCA) later moved to the Tavistock Hotel, Tavistock

Square, London under the command of Air Vice Marshal
A. V. Vyvyan. His command was small and inadequately
equipped. In March 1920 there were four maritime
squadrons, one of which, No 238, was a cadre with no
aircraft. The remaining three were No 210 Squadron at
Gosport, equipped with the Sopwith Cuckoo, a torpedo
bomber, No 230, at Felixstowe, equipped with Felixstowes
and No 267 equipped with Short 184s, Felixstowe F2As
and F3s and Fairey IIIs. This squadron was based at
Kalafrana, Malta. It had detachments of Fairey IIIs on
board HMS *Ark Royal* and at Kilya Bay in the North
Aegean. Its Felixstowe F3s were detached to Alexandria
and to Port Said. The aircraft, flying boats, floatplanes and
landplanes were of wartime vintage and there was little
maintenance. Duties for the aircrew were protection of
UK coastal waters, the British Fleet, possible offensive
action against an enemy fleet and lastly, anti submarine.
Considering the experience of the last war with U-Boats,
this was extraordinary to say the least. No 210 Squadron
was disbanded in April 1923 and renumbered as Nos 460
and 461 Flights. No 230 Squadron was disbanded on the
same date and renumbered as No 480 Flight. No 267
Squadron was also disbanded on the same date and
renumbered as No 481 Flight

The squadrons began to be reformed at the end of the
twenties. No 201 Squadron, having been disbanded in
1919, was reformed at Calshot in January 1929 with
Southampton IIs. This was No 480 Flight, renumbered.
No 202 Squadron had been disbanded in January 1920,
reformed in April 1920 and then disbanded again in May
1921. It was reformed from No 481 Flight at Kalafrana,

Malta, with Fairey IIIDs in January 1929. No 203 Squadron was reformed at Mountbatten from No 482 Flight with Southampton IIs in January 1929. A month later the squadron moved to the Persian Gulf.

No 204 Squadron was reformed in February 1929, also at Mountbatten with Southampton IIs. In January 1930 No 209 Squadron was reformed at Mountbatten with Iris IIIs. In March 1931 No 210 Squadron was reformed at Felixstowe with Southampton IIs. In the Far East No 205 Squadron was reformed at Seletar, Singapore from the Far East Flight with Southampton IIs. On the torpedo bomber front, No 36 Squadron was reformed at Donibristle, Fife in October 1928 with Horsleys.

In September 1924 Air Vice Marshal F. R. Scarlett, CB, DSO, became AOC Coastal Area Commander and in May 1928 Air Vice Marshal C. L. Lambe, CB,CMG,DSO took over. He was relieved by Air Vice Marshal R. H. Clark-Hall, CMG DSO, in October 1931. After three years, Air Vice Marshal A. M. Longmore CB, DSO became AOC.

In 1932 HQCA moved to Lee on Solent. At this point, on 18 January, 1932, No 10 Group was disbanded. In July 1936 Coastal Area was superseded by Coastal Command.

After the First World War, or the Great War as it was then known, the Government worked on the policy that there would no war for ten years and updated it every year. The RAF was run down and a few seaplanes and flying boats were kept as winged tenders. In the Navy nobody had yet gained Flag rank by being an aviator. Admiral Mark Kerr, who was now a Major General, continued to preach that the sea and the air were not mutually exclusive.

By now it was considered that convoy protection could only be effectively carried out with air cover, and that meant carriers. Meanwhile the RAF was using Short Flying Boats. In the USA, Brigadier General William Mitchell demonstrated the vulnerability of battleships with a series of trials. In November 1920, his aircraft sank the USS *Indiana* in a demonstration. In July 1921 in a further demonstration, they sank the surrendered German battleship *Ostfriesland* with 2000 lb bombs. These were bigger than any others then in use. The US Navy regarded this as cheating. Mitchell's bombers then sank the *Alabama* and in 1923, the *Virginia* and the *New Jersey*. This last did not sink easily and gave the Navy reason to believe what all navies wanted to believe, that battleships had nothing to fear from aircraft. This of course was a great improvement on previous attempts to sink surface ships.

In 1913 during the Mexican civil war, the two attempts to sink the Federal gunboat *Guerrero* in the Gulf of California by Constitutionalists failed and rifle fire could not bring down the Glenn Martin aircraft. Japanese seaplanes at Tsingtao in 1914 could not hit their targets. An Austro-Hungarian flying boat tried to sink the French armoured cruiser *Waldeck Rousseau* in October 1914 and failed. The German battleship *Goeben* grounded in the Dardanelles in 1918. British aircraft dropped 180 bombs at her and only two scored hits, neither fatally. It should be remembered that there were no real aerial bombs and bombsights were in their infancy. However, the RNAS did possess the 20lb bomb with a seven-pound charge, which was roughly equal in explosive to a six-inch shell and a 100lb bomb with a 40 lb charge, which roughly equalled the 9.2 inch naval shell. Such bombs were deadly to small unarmoured ships.

In the summer of 1937, Admiral Tom Phillips was Director of Plans at the Admiralty and his opposite number at the Air Ministry was Group Captain Arthur Harris. They often had furious wrangles on the subject of air power over ships, Phillips being of the view that the danger was exaggerated. When the question of what would happen in the event of war with Italy was being debated for the umpteenth time, Phillips insisted that the British Fleet would have free use of the Mediterranean, however strong the Italian Air Force might be. Harris exploded "One day Tom, you will be standing on a box on your bridge (Tom Phillips was small in stature) and your ship will be smashed to pieces by bombers and torpedo aircraft. As your ship sinks your last words will be "That was a great mine". Admiral Phillips stood on the bridge of HMS *Prince of Wales* when it was sunk by Japanese aircraft.

CHAPTER FOUR

FIRST WORLD WAR

Great Britain declared war on Germany on 4 August 1914. On 5 September, Korvettenkapitän Hersing in U-21 sank the light cruiser HMS *Pathfinder* off St Abbs Head. On 22 September, Leutnant Weddigen in U-29, sank three ships - the British cruisers *Aboukir, Cressy* and *Hogue*. On 1 January, 1915 U-24 sank HMS *Formidable*. British submarines had sunk the German cruiser *Hela*, the destroyer S-116 and the Turkish battleship *Messoudieh*.

A response was soon to come. The German Zeppelin L-5 made the first-ever attack on a submarine, HMS/ME-11, but missed. On 15 May, 1915 Kapitänleutnant Heinrich Mathy in Zeppelin L-9 attacked three British submarines. None were sunk, but one of them, the D-4, was severely shaken.

The Royal Navy by now saw the value of aircraft patrols to keep down the U-boats, but in the first part of 1915 the service had only three airships and a number of small seaplanes. However, by the end of the year, at the instigation of Lord Fisher, the First Sea Lord, the RN had 29 purpose-built airships in service. These were Submarine Scouts, small non rigid airships, designated SS and generally known as blimps. Some 200 of these were built. They were equipped with wireless and one or two machine guns and could carry a small bomb load.

Aeroplanes were also making attacks on submarines. Whether or not kills were achieved was difficult to ascertain, but certainly life was being made difficult for them. Sightings of course were made visually, but frequently submarines saw the aircraft before the aircraft saw the submarine and were below the surface by the time the aircraft was on top. Even if no attack was made, part of the object had been achieved -to deny the submarine the use of the surface. The chances of an aircraft making a kill were not high, as the bombs in use at that time were not powerful enough to damage the pressure hull. However they could cause damage to the hydroplanes, causing the submarine to go out of control. Damage to the pressure gauges or the high-pressure air system could lead to the loss of a submarine. High-pressure air was used to blow water from the ballast tanks, enabling the boat to surface. There was always the danger of sea water getting into the batteries, reacting with the sulphuric acid and thus releasing chlorine gas into the boat.

In 1914 the Curtiss Company in the United States of America built a twin-engined flying boat called the *America* for transatlantic flying. Such an aircraft, with its long range, albeit with only 90 hp engines, would be ideal for maritime flying. The RN bought it and others and they came into service in 1915. It was called the Curtiss H-4. The aeroplane had an all-up weight (AUW) of 5000 pounds, carrying a small bomb load and two machine guns. It was not very successful, but the idea was on the right track.

Curtiss then built the H-8, the Large America, with an AUW of 10,000 pounds and two 160 hp engines, giving a speed of 85 miles per hour. However it proved to be as underpowered as the H-4. The RN bought 50 of these to be stationed at Felixstowe. The first machines arrived in July 1916. The station commander, Wing Commander (RNAS rank) John Porte, had one of them re-engined with two Rolls Royce Eagle engines of 250 hp each. This gave an increase in power of 50 per cent and the aircraft came into service as the H-12 Large America. However, the Rolls Royce engines were in short supply and until these problems were sorted out, the short range Short 184 seaplane carried out anti-submarine work.

At the beginning of the war, a surprise attack against a warship by a submarine was a legal act of war; against a merchant ship, it was not. The submarine had first to surface, send a boarding party and check that the cargo was prohibited. Only then was the submarine commander allowed to sink the ship, although he was still responsible for the safety of the ship's crew. The Germans did not like this as the British had mounted a blockade against Germany, and they saw these rules as unfair. In February 1915 the Kaiser ordered his commanders to ignore the rules and to sink any ship found in the war zone around the UK.

The submarine in 1914 was basically a submersible torpedo boat. It had diesel engines for use on the surface and electric motors powered by batteries for use underwater. The batteries were charged by the diesels when running on the surface. The maximum submerged speed was only 9 knots, whereas on the surface it was nearer to 15 knots. The electric motors gave a maximum range of about 60 miles, so most U-Boat commanders preferred to remain on the surface, leaving the electric motors for emergency use. When an aircraft sighted a submarine, the boat had to submerge or be attacked. In addition the submarine commander did not know when or if the aircraft had gone away, so he had difficulties giving the order to surface. Thus the aircraft could prevent the submarine from reaching its target.

As the war progressed the U-Boat became a greater menace and the United Kingdom was losing many ships. In 1917 the device used in the Napoleonic wars and previously was reintroduced - the convoy system. This had been difficult to implement as the ship owners were against the idea. The speed of the convoy was the speed of the slowest ship, increasing voyage times and reducing income. They also believed that such a large target would attract U-Boats and that sinkings would increase. The ship masters were against it, as they would be subordinate to Royal Navy Officers and their capacity for action at sea and ashore would diminish sharply. RN officers were against it as well, as it was not considered to be "offensive" but "defensive".

The Admiralty ignored the fact that troopships had been convoyed since August 1914 and that the Hook of Holland trade route had been convoyed since 1916. There had been six losses, all before mid -917. Other arguments against convoys were that large ones would be unable to zigzag, congestion would occur at the ports, masters would not be able to keep station, a separate escort would be needed for each merchant vessel and a convoy presented a larger target.

The advantages were that the ships were more difficult to find, and when they were found the U-boats were up against more escorts. While there were more ships, the U-Boat could only attack one at a time. Escorting aircraft and ships would be employed more efficiently.

A trial convoy sailed in May 1917 from Gibraltar and was a success. A further trial convoy sailed from the USA. Ten ships that stayed in the convoy arrived safely, but two which could not keep up with it were sunk. The system was instituted and an immediate reduction in losses was achieved. For example, Alfred Price in his *Aircraft Versus Submarine* states that in April 1917 834,000 tons were lost. With the introduction of the convoy in May, losses averaged 590,000 tons in May and June and 430,000 in the following three months. The submarine now, instead of waiting for individual ships, had to positively look for them. When they had found them they also met escorts, both warship and aeroplane. The aircraft, by forcing submarines to submerge, assisted in the "safe and timely arrival of the convoy".

The escorts being equipped with depth charges and hydrophonic listening devices, now began to achieve sinkings. Instead of looking for U-Boats, the U-Boats were coming to them. By the end of the war, aircraft were being equipped with hydrophone systems, although the flying boat had to alight on the sea to use it. Airships were also equipped with the systems, but they had only to hover to use them. No successes were gained, but it was useful experience for the next war.

In 1918, the U-boats, gaining no successes in the Western Approaches, now tried coastal waters around the

UK. To counteract this, it was decided to increase the number of aircraft on the strengths of the various flying boat and seaplane bases with the addition of land-based aircraft. It was well known that U-Boats submerged when sighting *any* aircraft, whether armed or not. There were about 300 surplus de Havilland DH 6's available, and these were chosen for the job. Around 220 of them were fitted with a pilot, a 100lb bomb and no observer and the remainder flew with a pilot, an observer and no bomb. Just under 4900 seaplane and landplane sorties were flown in 1918 and in that time only two ships were attacked when being escorted. However, when the weather prevented flying, then the U-Boats moved in.

On 19 April 1918 orders were given for the formation of seven DH6 flights, to be known as Special Duty Flights. The patrols they flew were known as "scarecrow" patrols. The DH6 was a trainer but had been superseded by other types, so there was a large surplus of them available. The logic of the patrol was that if a submariner sighted any aircraft he would submerge his boat, as this was certain protection. A U-Boat had at most two machine guns for anti-aircraft protection. The deck gun could not be elevated high enough to shoot at aircraft.

The flights were to be given squadron numbers, starting with No 250 Squadron. However, in practice, the DH6's were mixed with other aircraft and other squadrons.

No 250 Squadron was formed at Padstow, Cornwall on 1 May 1918 out of Nos 494, 500, 501, 502 and 503 Flights, using DH6's and DH9's. There was a detachment to Westward Ho! in May where Nos 502 and 503 Flights were formed into No 260 Squadron in August. It was disbanded in May 1919.

No 251 Squadron was formed at Hornsea on 1 May 1918 out of Nos 504, 505, and 506 Flights using DH6's and DH9's. No 252 Squadron was formed at Tynemouth on 1 May 1918 out of Nos 451, 452, 495, 507, 508, 509 and 510 Flights using DH6's, Sopwith Baby's and Blackburn Kangaroo's. It was disbanded in June 1919.

No 252 Squadron was formed in May 1918 at Tynemouth from Nos 451, 452, 495, 507, 508, 509 and 510 Flights. It was equipped with Sopwith Babys and Kangaroos until August 1918 and DH6s until January 1919. There were detachments at Seaton Carew, Redcar and Cramlington. The Squadron moved to Killingholme in January 1919 as a cadre and disbanded in June.

No 253 Squadron was formed at Bembridge, Isle of Wight in June 1918 out of Nos 412, 413, 511, 512 and 513 Flights with Short 184s, Fairey Campanias and in August DH6s. In August No 513 Flight detached to Chickerell and formed the basis of No 241 Squadron. The squadron disbanded in January 1919.

No 254 Squadron was formed at Prawle Point, Plymouth in May 1918 out of Nos 492, 515, 516, 517, and 518 Flights with DH6s and DH9s. No 492 Flight was one of the elements of No 260 Squadron. Nos 515 and 516 Flights were the basis of No 236 Squadron when they detached to Mullion. The squadron disbanded in February 1919.

No 255 Squadron was formed at Pembroke in July 1918 out of Nos 519, 520, 521, and 522 Flights with DH6s. It disbanded in January 1919.

No 256 Squadron was formed at Seahouses in June 1918 out of Nos 495, 525, 526, 527 and 528 flights with DH6s. In November it received Kangaroos when No 495 Flight was moved from No 246 Squadron. It disbanded in June 1919.

No 257 Squadron was formed at Dundee in August 1918 out of Nos 318 and 319 Flights with Curtiss H-16s, Felixstowe F2As and F3s. The Squadron disbanded in June 1919.

No 258 Squadron was formed at Luce Bay in July 1918 from Nos 523, 524 and 529 Flights with DH6s. It became a cadre in December 1918 and disbanded in March 1919.

No 260 Squadron was formed at Westward Ho! in August 1918 from No 492 Flight from No 254 Squadron, and Nos 502 and 503 Flights from No 250 Squadron, with DH6s and DH9s. It disbanded in February 1919.

No 272 Squadron was formed at Machrihanish, near Campbeltown, in July 1918 from Nos 531, 532 and 533 Flights. It was equipped with DH6s initially and in November, Fairey IIIAs. The Squadron disbanded in March 1919.

No 259 and No 261 Squadrons were authorized to form at Felixstowe but in the event this did not happen. Nos 342, 343 and 344 Flights were to be No 259 Squadron and Nos 339, 340 and 341 Flights were to be No 261 Squadron. Both units were to be equipped with Felixstowe F2As.

There were other squadrons outside the above numbering.

No 236 Squadron was formed in August 1918 at Mullion in Cornwall from Nos 493, 515 and 516 Flights with DH6s and DH9s. Nos 515 and 516 Flights were part of No 254 Squadron and had been detached to Mullion.

No 241 Squadron was formed in August 1918 at Portland with DH6s,Short 184s, Fairey Campanias and Wight Converteds from Nos 416, 417 and 513 Flights.

These squadrons were allocated to Groups as follows:

NO 9 GROUP:
No 236 Squadron
No 250 Squadron
No 254 Squadron
No 260 Squadron

NO 10 GROUP:
No 241 Squadron
No 242 Squadron
No 253 Squadron

NO 14 GROUP:
No 244 Squadron
No 255 Squadron

NO 18 GROUP:
No 251 Squadron
No 252 Squadron
No 256 Squadron

NO 25 GROUP:
No 258 Squadron
No 272 Squadron

The following squadrons were formed in the UK in August 1918:

1. No 228 Squadron from Nos 324, 325 and 326 Flights at Great Yarmouth, with Felixstowe F2As and Curtiss H16s.

2. No 229 Squadron at Great Yarmouth from Nos 428, 429, 454 and 455 Flights, with Sopwith Babies, Hamble Babies, Short 184s and Short 320s.

3. No 230 Squadron at Felixstowe from Nos 327, 328 and 487 Flights, with Curtiss H16s and Felixstowe F2As. In September Sopwith Camels, Felixstowe F3s and Short 184s were added. Fairey IIIB/Cs were also added.

4. No 231 Squadron at Felixstowe from Nos 329 and 330 Flights, with Felixstowe F2As.

5. No 232 Squadron at Felixstowe from Nos 333, 334 and 335 Flights, with Felixstowe F2As.

6. No 233 Squadron at Dover from Nos 407, 471 and 491 Flights.

7. No 234 Squadron at Trescoe, Scillies, from Nos 351, 352 and 353 Flights.

8. No 235 Squadron at Newlyn, Cornwall from Nos 424 and 425 Flights.

9. No 236 Squadron at Mullion, Cornwall from Nos 493, 515 and 516 Flights.

10. No 237 Squadron at Cattewater, Plymouth from Nos 420 and 421 Flights.

11. No 238 Squadron at Cattewater, Plymouth from Nos 347, 348 and 349 Flights.

12. No 239 Squadron at Torquay from No 418 Flight.

13. No 240 Squadron at Calshot from Nos 345, 346 and 410 Flights.

14. No 241 Squadron at Portland from Nos 416, 417 Flights and from No 253 Squadron, No 513 Flight while at Chickerell.

15. No 242 Squadron at Newhaven from 408, 409 and 514 Flights with Short 184s, DH6s, Fairey Campanias and Wight Converteds.

16. No 243 Squadron at Cherbourg from Nos 414 and 415 Flights, with Short 184s and Wight Converteds.

17. No 244 Squadron at Bangor from Nos 521, 522 and 530 Flights, with DH6s.

18. No 245 Squadron at Fishguard from Nos 425 and 427 Flights, with Short 184s.

19. No 246 Squadron at Seaton Carew from Nos 402, 403, 451, 452 and 495 Flights, with Fe2bs, Blackburn Kangaroos, Short 184s, Short 320s and Sopwith Babies. The Kangaroos came with No 495 Flight, which came from No 252 Squadron.

20. No 247 Squadron at Felixstowe from Nos 336 and 337 Flights, with Felixstowe F2As.

21. No 248 Squadron at Hornsea from Nos 404, 405 and 453 Flights, with Short 184s and Sopwith Babies.

22. No 249 Squadron at Dundee from Nos 400, 401, 419 and 450 Flights, with Sopwith Babies, Hamble Babies and Short 184s.

23. No 273 Squadron at Burgh Castle from Nos 470, 485, 486 and 534 Flights with DH4s, DH9s and Camels. There were detachments at Covehithe, Westgate and Bacton. The Squadron was reduced to a cadre in March 1919, moved to Great Yarmouth and disbanded in June 1919.

It had been intended to form No 274 Squadron at Seaton Carew in November 1918 with Vickers Vimys in the anti-submarine role, but the end of the war made that unnecessary.

Meanwhile in the Mediterranean/Aegean Seas further squadrons were formed on 1 April 1918:

No 220 Squadron at Imbros from C Squadron on No 2 Wing RNAS. These elements became Nos 475, 476 and 477 Flights. It was equipped with DH4s and then in June, DH9s. In July, Sopwith Camels came on to the inventory. Two months later, in September, the Squadron adopted the No 220 Squadron number plate.

No 221 Squadron was formed at Stavros from D Squadron of No 2 Wing RNAS. These elements became Nos 552, 553 and 554 Flights. It was equipped with DH4s and Camels and in June, DH9s were added. Again, in September, the Squadron adopted the No 221 Squadron number plate.

No 224 Squadron at Alimini from No 6 Wing RNAS. These elements became Nos 496, 497 and 498 Flights. It was equipped with DH4s and in May DH9s were added.

There was some confusion over how these units were formed. While the RAF allocated the number plates on the date of formation of the Royal Air Force (1 April 1918), these units combined with others to form other squadrons (numbered alphabetically) and the original RAF intention was not carried out. The genealogy above is probably correct. See Annex L of Wing Commander C. G. Jefford's book *RAF Squadrons*.

Further squadrons were formed in September:

1. No 263 Squadron at Otranto from Nos 359, 435, 436 and 441 Flights, with Sopwith Babies, Hamble Babies, Short 184s, Short 320s and Felixstowe F3s. It disbanded in May 1919.

2. No 264 Squadron at Suda Bay from Nos 439 and 440 Flights, with Short 184s. It disbanded in March 1919.

3. No 266 Squadron at Mudros in the Aegean Sea from Nos 437 and 438 Flights, with Short 184s and Short 320s. It had a detachment at Skyros and moved to Talikna in January 1919. The next month it went to the Caucasus on board HMS *Engadine*, thence to Petrovsk and flew operations from HMS *Aladar Youssonoff* and HMS *Orlionoch*. The Squadron withdrew in August and went to Novorossisk. It disbanded in September 1919.

4. No 267 Squadron at Kalafrana from Nos 360, 361, 362 and 363 Flights, with Short 184s, Felixstowe F2s and F3s. There were detachments at Alexandria and Port Said. Fairey IIIDs were added to the inventory in December 1920 and had detachments on HMS *Ark Royal* and at Kilya Bay. The Short 184s and Felixstowe F.3s were disposed of in 1921 and the Squadron disbanded in 1923, being redesignated No 481 Flight.

5. No 268 Squadron at Kalafrana from Nos 433 and 434 Flights, with Short 184s and Short 320s. It disbanded in October 1919.

6. No 271 Squadron at Taranto, Italy from Nos 357, 358 and 367 Flights, with Short 184s and Felixstowe F3s. It disbanded in December 1918.

No 265 Squadron was supposed to form at Gibraltar with Short 184s and Felixstowe F3s, but the project was cancelled.

The following squadrons were formed in October 1918:

1. No 269 Squadron at Port Said, Egypt from Nos 431 and 432 Flights, with BE2es and Short 184s. In December 1918 DH9s were added to the inventory and the following month it moved to Alexandria with a detachment at Port Said. The Squadron disbanded in November 1919, being absorbed by No 267 Squadron.

2. No 270 Squadron at Alexandria, Egypt from Nos 354, 355 and 356 Flights, with Sopwith Babies, Short 184s and Felixstowe F3s. In December 1919 it disbanded, being absorbed by No 269 Squadron.

It will be apparent from the above that squadron and flight numbering was somewhat confusing, in that flight numbers were retained within squadrons and some flights were transferred between squadrons.

By 1917, the Large Americas were showing signs of deterioration to the hulls. Wing Commander Porte designed a better hull, improved the tail surfaces and fitted two Rolls Royce engines. This aircraft became the Felixstowe F-2A. It was armed with two 230 pound bombs and carried fuel for eight hours.

The first land plane to be used in maritime work was the Blackburn Kangaroo. At a maximum all-up weight of 8000 pounds this aircraft weighed less than the Felixstowe but carried 920 pounds of bombs, was faster and had a better endurance. It only served with No 246 Squadron and in its six-month war service its crews sighted twelve U-boats, attacked eleven and shared in the destruction of UC-70.

The first sign of a detection device to be used with ever greater effect, in the Second World War and after, was sound. Early in the war British scientists carried out experiments with hydrophones to detect the sound of a submarine. These were successful and the device was carried on ships and on shore stations. The idea of fitting one of these to an aircraft came shortly after. However, the aircraft had to land on the water to operate it and the engines had to be switched off. This was not very appealing to crews in the middle of the ocean, or even the English Channel, as there was no guarantee that they could be restarted. The equipment was not very useful therefore, but fitted to the blimps it was more effective, as they did not have to alight on the sea. They did however, have to switch off the engines. These hydrophones were of the non-directional type but in 1918 trials using directional hydrophones were carried out and proved to be more effective. Perhaps it is worth noting that the author did not get to use directional sonobuoys until the late 1950s in Shackletons!

The Great War, as it was originally known, was the first time that submarines had been used in strength against shipping and the first time aeroplanes had been used in the antisubmarine role. A number of lessons were learned. Air cover for ships, even if the aircraft were unarmed, was vital. To be really effective, continuous cover was required. Aircraft with long endurance were better than those with short endurance. It had been shown that aircraft could sink submarines but that it was necessary for the weapon to explode very close to the target, if not on it. Speed was vital. Once the submarine had sighted the aircraft, it had to attack the boat before it was completely submerged. Aircraft crews could not see submerged submarines unless the sea was clear and the aircraft was on top. Such conditions were only found in the lower latitudes, and certainly not in the North Atlantic. They could see the "feather" of a periscope only in relatively calm conditions. A surfaced submarine could be seen, but the detection range diminished with sea state. The convoy system was probably the best countermeasure against submarines and with air cover it was even better.

The RNAS was in action in the Dardanelles in 1915 in the bombing and anti-ship roles. Commander Samson arrived with an advance party, soon to be strengthened with eighteen aircraft and crews from the RN and the army. Operations were carried in support of the British submarine E15 with bombing attacks on shore batteries, spotting for the artillery and reconnaissance. This last involved several aircraft and was on a daily basis.

The first attack on a battleship was carried out. This was the obsolete *Heireddin Barbarossa*, which was sunk by

Lt.Cdr. Nasmith in aircraft E11. In August 1915, Flight Commander Charles Edmonds, operating from the carrier *Ben-My-Cree*, attacked and sank a 5000-ton Turkish supply ship. This, the first successful torpedo attack by an aircraft, was followed up five days later when Edmonds sank three tugs. Flight Lieutenant D'Acre, having engine problems, landed on the sea and taxied towards a large tug. He launched a torpedo which sank the ship. He was then able to take off and returned to the *Ben-My-Cree*.

210 Singapore PD (Sunderland Trust)

210 Singapore PD (Sunderland Trust)

210 Southampton S1231 (Rene Thomas)

228 Stranraer PD (Sunderland Trust)

228 Stranraer PD Sunderland Trust

Curtiss Large America MOD - Wikipedia

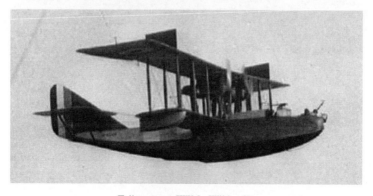

Felixstowe 1.IWM - Wikipedia

Saro Cloud (Air Ministry) - Wikipedia

Saro London (Air Ministry) - Wikipedia

CHAPTER FIVE

REORGANISATION

On 14 July 1936 Coastal Command was formed under Air Marshal Sir Arthur Longmore, KCB, DSO, RAF as Air Officer Commanding in Chief (AOC-in-C), with Headquarters at Lee-on-Solent. There were to be three groups, plus the Fleet Air Arm (FAA), but it was not possible to form all three groups immediately. Thus the Flying Boats of No 15 Group were placed temporarily under the command of No 16 Group with Headquarters at Lee-on-Solent. No 15 Group was reformed (it had been disbanded on 1 September, 1919 when it was the Aegean Group) on 15 March 1939 as No 15 (General Reconnaissance) Group under the command of Air Commodore R. G. Parry, at Plymouth. No 16 (Reconnaissance) Group, which was reformed on 1 December 1936 at Lee on Solent, under the command of Air Commodore H. M. Cave-Browne-Cave, also had under command the General Reconnaissance (GR) and Torpedo Bomber (TB) squadrons. No 17 (Training) Group was reformed on 1 December 1936, under the command of Air Commodore C. D. Breese, who also had headquarters at Lee-on-Solent and was responsible for the

training stations and FAA shore training. Air Cdre Breese was relieved in September 1938 to allow him to take over No 18 Group. His relief was Air Commodore T. E. B. Howe

It was later found necessary to form two further groups. No 18 Group had been formed on 1 April 1918 and had been renamed No 18 (Naval) Group on 26 June 1919. It was transferred to Coastal Area on 15 September, 1919. It was disbanded on 18 October 1919.

No 18 (Reconnaissance) Group was reformed on 1 September 1938 at Pitreavie Castle near Inverkeithing in Fife, under the command of Air Commodore Breese, who, as stated, had transferred from No 17 Group. It was later redesignated No 18 (General Reconnaissance) Group. No 19 Group was reformed on 5 February 1941 at Plymouth under the command of Air Commodore G. H. Boyce. Headquarters Coastal Command (HQCC) was responsible for all the Groups and the administration of the flying training of the FAA. The FAA came under the control of the Admiralty in this year. This command structure came into being in January 1937 by which time Air Marshal Philip Joubert de la Ferte was AOC-in-C. He realized that maritime work was a joint responsibility of the RAF and the RN and he set up an Area Combined Naval/Air Headquarters where RAF and RN officers worked together. At this level co-operation worked, whereas at the Whitehall level there were bitter conflicts between senior officers. Air power was a new form of warfare understood by few RAF or RN senior officers.

In the autumn of 1936 there were thirteen maritime squadrons, of which eight were in the UK:
No 201 Squadron Saro Londons at Calshot.

No 202 Squadron Supermarine Scapas at Kalafrana, Malta.

No 203 Squadron Short Singapores at Basra, Iraq.

No 204 Squadron Supermarine Scapas at Mountbatten, Plymouth.

No 205 Squadron Short Singapore IIIs at RAF Seletar, Singapore.

No 206 Squadron Avro Ansons at Bircham Newton.

No 209 Squadron Short Singapores at Felixstowe.

No 210 Squadron Short Rangoons and Singapore IIIs at Pembroke Dock, South West Wales.

No 220 Squadron Avro Anson Is at Bircham Newton, formed from No 206 Squadron.

No 230 Squadron Short Singapore IIIs. This squadron returned to Pembroke Dock from Egypt in August 1936 and set off for the Far East in October 1936.

No 22 Squadron Vickers Vildebeeste IIIs at Donibristle, Fife.

No 36 Squadron Vickers Vildebeeste IIIs at RAF Seletar, Singapore.

No 48 Squadron Avro Ansons at Manston, Kent.

The Vildebeeste Torpedo Bombers were obsolescent, being at least ten years out of date. This was a reflection of the ten-year rule and the lack of understanding of their role by Whitehall. Joubert was not a protagonist of the role, although the aircraft itself was not impressive and may well have been the cause of his bias. However, it was Joubert who later pressed for a Torpedo Bomber version of the Beaufighter. Overall little attention was given to antishipping aircraft and antisubmarine weapons.

On 18 August 1937 Joubert was succeeded by Air Marshal Sir Frederick Bowhill, who had a great deal of experience in the maritime world. He joined the Royal Navy as a midshipman in 1898 and had served in the Royal Naval Air Service (RNAS) and the RAF. One of his first acts after assuming command was to move the Command Headquarters to Northwood, Middlesex, where it has remained since. By August 1939 the Group HQs were No 15 at Plymouth, No 16 at Gillingham, No 17 at Gosport and the new one No 18 at Pitreavie in Fife. Nos 15 and 18 were responsible for antisubmarine patrols, Nos 16 and 18 for antishipping and No 17 for training. All Groups were responsible for Met flights and Air Sea Rescue (ASR). Fighter Command had a role in ASR. The Fleet Air Arm remained under the direct control of Headquarters Coastal Command (HQCC) until 1938, when the Royal Navy took it over and made it an integral part of the Royal Navy.

In the autumn of 1937 there were nineteen squadrons, of which fourteen were UK based. The new squadrons were:

No 42 Squadron Vickers Vildebeestes IIIs reformed at Donibristle from No 22 Squadron on 14 December 1936.

No 217 Squadron Avro Ansons at Tangmere, Sussex.

No 224 Squadron Avro Ansons at Thornaby, Middlesborough.

No 228 Squadron Supermarine Stranraers at Invergordon, Ross-shire.

No 233 Squadron Avro Ansons at Thornaby, Middlesborough.

No 240 Squadron Short Scapas at Calshot, Southampton.

SEARCH AND RESCUE - MARINE CRAFT UNITS

In 1935 permission was given by the Air Staff to build an experimental high-speed launch as a seagoing safety boat for coastal defence work. The boat, High Speed Launch No 100, the first of its kind, was handed over to the RAF Station at Manston, Kent in August 1936. It was a success and could carry four stretchers and was seaworthy in all but the roughest of seas. A further 15 were ordered, one of which was to be established on each of the seven GR Squadrons and one each on Malta, Aden, Basra, Ceylon, Penang and Hong Kong stations. This was the beginning of the Marine Craft Branch.

ORGANISATION - PREPARATION FOR WAR

On 18 December 1937 Air Vice Marshal C. Portal, Director of Organisation, wrote to AOC-in-C Coastal stating that the provision of combined Service Operational HQs at defended ports had been approved. Commanders at Plymouth, Portsmouth, Chatham and Rosyth were to submit proposals for bomb-proof operational HQs. Air Marshal G. R. Bromet, Senior Air Staff Officer (SASO), wrote to C-in-C Nore that under the proposed reorganization of Coastal Command, a Group HQ would be established at Chatham and that the provision of a Combined Service Operations Building at Principal Naval Ports had been approved in principle. He requested that SASO, the Chief Signals Officer (C. Sigs. O.) and the Chief Engineer should visit. On 3 January 1938 C-in-C Coastal wrote to HQ 16 (R) Group stating that there would be no RAF Group HQ at Portsmouth. On 11 January, 1938 C-in-C Nore, Admiral Sir E.R.G.R. Evans, KCB DSO LLD, wrote to AOC-in-C Coastal that he had no written instructions from their Lordships of the Admiralty. He stated that he would be pleased to see SASO and his fellow officers but a meeting would be pointless.

In these Operations Rooms, Coastal required 12 teleprinters and four Wireless Telegraphy (W/T) channels. However, these requirements would change.

On 18 January 1938 AOC-in-C Coastal wrote to Rear Admiral and Officer Commanding Coastal of Scotland, at Rosyth about the RAF Group HQ at Rosyth and requested a meeting with his SASO, C. Sigs. O. and Chief Engineer. This letter was copied to Wing Commander H. L. Macro, DFC, AFC at RAF Donibristle, Inverkeithing, under cover of a letter from the AOC-in-C stating that he, the C-in-C, would come up to meet him. There was a need to establish a Group HQ and a Group Staff in time for a combined Coast Defence exercise in July 1938. The Air Ministry Works Department was on the lookout for a large house for use as a Group Headquarters within five miles of Rosyth, ten if necessary. On 20 January 1938 AOC-in-C Coastal wrote to C-in-C Nore thanking him for a meeting. The preference for a Group Headquarters at

Chatham was for somewhere south of the River Medway. If the War Office had no objections, Fort Horsted might be suitable, at least temporarily.

Again on 20 January 1938 Rear Admiral Thomson, Commanding Officer Coastal Scotland, wrote back to AOC-in-C Coastal stating that he knew nothing of Combined HQs, that the General Officer Commanding (GOC) Army Scotland would prefer to be on the south side of the River Forth, but that problem could be overcome by the establishment of a Military Liaison Officer. On the same day Wing Commander Macro wrote to Air Commodore Bromet stating that he had seen the Admiral and agreed with him the date of the meeting. He said "The Admiral does not usually work in the afternoon and would rather have the conference in the morning at 1030". He also wrote "needless to say, the Works Directorate have not yet started on the planned accommodation at Donibristle". On 22 January 1938, AOC-in-C Coastal wrote back to Macro "I cannot help the Admiral's troubles. And as we are in a hurry to get things arranged for the exercise in July, I shall come to Scotland as stated."

The meeting was held and the minutes show the work to have been done at Donibristle. Pitreavie Castle created a favourable impression for a permanent HQ. The minutes were to be treated as secret, but bear no classification marks on them.

On 23 January 1938, HQCC wrote to Adastral House (Air Ministry) stating the teleprinter requirements, which were:

HQCC Ops Room 4

HQ 16 (R) Group 7 plus 2 in reserve.

RAF Manston 2

RAF Felixstowe 2

RAF Bircham Newton 2

RAF Thornaby 3

HQ 18(R) Group 7 plus 2 in reserve.

RAF Leuchars 2

RAF Dyce 2

RAF Tayport 2

Meanwhile full-scale temporary accommodation for the Combined Operations Room for No 16 (R) Group and No 18 (R) Group would be available in May 1938. This would be, at No 16 (R) Group, wooden buildings on the outskirts of Chatham and at No 18 (R) Group, the conversion of a suitable Building at Donibristle. A letter of 31 January 1938 discusses the possibility of Donibristle being handed over to the Navy for the use of the Fleet Air Arm. Donibristle is a few miles to the East of Inverkeithing in Fife.

On 25 January 1938 a meeting was held at the offices of the Commanding Officer, Coast of Scotland. Present were Air Commodore Bromet, Wing Commander Lang and A. R. Matheson, the Chief Engineer from Coastal. Representing GOC-in-C Scottish Command were Lt Col McLeod, Lt Col Wheeler and Major Bettington. They agreed that a Military Liaison Officer be appointed to the Combined HQ. Pitreavie Castle was up for sale and was well located, in extensive grounds and not a good bombing target (this building is now located just off the M90 at Junction 2). There was no RN presence at this meeting and copies of the minutes were sent to the Admiralty.

On 27 January 1938 C-in-C Nore had been active and had secured Army agreement to use the School of Military Engineering as a Group HQ. Fort Holsted was too far away from existing RAF and RN HQs.

On 12 February SASO at Coastal Command wrote to C-in-C Plymouth about setting up a meeting to discuss the establishment of a Combined Services HQ at Plymouth. SASO asked Group Captain Digby Johnson AFC at Mountbatten to arrange this meeting for Thursday 17 February and "explain that it does not matter if they have heard nothing about it".

Major General W. Green, Commandant South Western Area, fully agreed with all of this and suggested a temporary HQ at Hamoaze House and a permanent HQ at Mount Wise. This was agreed by C-in-C Plymouth.

The complement for the Mount Wise Ops Room was:

One Naval navigator.

One RAF navigator.

One Operations Officer.

Two plotters.

One clerk to the navigation officer.

The complement for the control dais was agreed as:

One RAF controller.

One staff officer to the controller.

One Naval Commander.

One staff officer to the Naval Commander.

One Military commander.

One GSO.

The Meteorological Office was to be established as:

One Met Officer.

One assistant.

SASO at HQCC wrote to Adastral House stating that there was a rumour that No 18 Group would be planned in peace but formed in war. This was wrong, he stated; No 18 Group was to be formed now. Pitreavie was a lucky find.

Amongst the papers concerning Coastal Command War Plans, including the Tactical Employment of Squadrons, there is a draft letter which states that there were suggestions that General Reconnaissance (GR) aircraft should be slow so that they can shadow enemy raiders, protect convoys and carry out anti-submarine work. The writer of the letter did not agree with this. He wrote that they might need to fight for their information, and speed was essential as it was for the wider areas to be covered and for the secondary role of bombing. Considerable range was essential and the aircraft should be well fitted with armament. The highest degree of efficiency was required and the aircraft must be soundproofed to allow the navigator to work.

The C-in-C stated that GR squadrons may be called upon to:

Bomb military targets in foreign countries.

Bomb battleships and cruisers.

Bomb armed merchant cruisers.

Bomb submarines.

The letter stated that it would perhaps be better concentrating on low-level bombing.

The minutes of a meeting at the office of the Deputy Chief of the Air Staff (DCAS) on 4 January 1938 discussed co-operation of Coastal Command with the Royal Navy. Present were AVM Peirse, AVM Portal, AVM Douglas, Group Captain Stevenson, Mr M J Dean, Wing Commander A C Collier, AM Sir Frederick Bowhill, Air Commodore Bromet and from the Admiralty, Vice Admiral Sir William James and two Captains. DCAS recapitulated the staff proposals for placing RAF Group HQs at Plymouth, Chatham and Rosyth and a Wing HQ in the Stranraer/Lough Swilly area. DCAS explained a point that he thought was not quite clear to the Admiralty, that it was not the Air Staff intention that one RAF group should have the specific function of carrying out extended reconnaissance while another group would be responsible for trade defence. He also pointed out that RAF group facilities, ops rooms and communications could not be improvised easily. DCNS said the main problem was commerce raiding and that the new types of German ships were almost ideal for this purpose.

On 25 October 1938 DCAS stated that there was an inability to train in torpedo work at Wick. There was a need to concentrate torpedo squadrons at RAF Thorney Island in peace. Nos 42 and 48 squadrons were mentioned.

On 1 April 1939 it was admitted that the Royal Navy would only have sufficient escorts to undertake convoy escort every other day.

Due to the difficulties of assembling merchant vessels at the outbreak of war without serious delay and possible dislocation of the food supply, the convoy system would not be instituted at the outset but controlled routing would, except for East Coast trade, where the convoy system would be instituted.

The probable convoys were:

Norwegian Convoy.

West coast of Scotland (Minch) Convoy.

East Coast of England Convoy.

Western Approaches Convoys by way of the English, Bristol and St. George's Channels.

Convoys would not assemble at Lerwick or Plymouth.

Aerodromes were to be built at Jamaica and Sierra Leone.

At the end of 1938 there was a problem with the supply of Cheetah IX engines for the Avro Ansons. There was a need to conserve the life of the Vildebeeste IVs and an urgent need of spares for the Stranraers and for Pegasus IX engines for the Londons and the Stranraers.

At the end of 1938 there were 10 Stranraers, 17 London IIs, 12 Singapore IIIs and 10 Sunderlands. The supposed Sunderland replacement, the twin-engined SARO Lerwick, would not be available until April 1939. Some of these aircraft might well not be fitted with engines. At MAEE there were three London IIs, two Stranraers, two Sunderlands and four Singapores.

Coastal Command provisional Battle Instructions 1938 stated that coastal aircraft would provide reconnaissance and trade protection in co-operation with the Royal Navy. If there was little or no interference with UK seaborne trade, then these aircraft might be called upon to assist in implementing the main offensive. The readiness states were to be:

Released until ..... Hours. All personnel within two hours of recall.

Available. All personnel on the station and ready for duty.

Ordered to Standby. Pilots and navigators to the Ops Room to collect all information on the General Situation Map (GSM) and other boards and weather information.

At Standby. Pilots and navigators in the Ops Room awaiting final instructions. The remainder of the crew to be in aircraft.

Ordered to leave ground. Pilots and navigators to receive final instructions from the station controller and to proceed to aircraft by transport. The remainder of the crew to start up aircraft. Aircraft to take off within 10 minutes of receiving the order for landplanes and 20 minutes for flying boats.

The tasking of aircraft was achieved by signal in a prescribed format. These signals or forms were given the names of colours:

Form Pink was a plain language version of enemy reports from aircraft.

Forms Green:

Form Green 2: Records the Dead Reckoning (DR) position of own aircraft and for transmission of this information to MHQs.

Form Green 3: Broadcast of all information regarding

our own forces from MHQ to other MHQs and to Station Ops Rooms.

Form White: Broadcast of all information regarding enemy from MHQ to other MHQs and to Station Ops Rooms.

Form Blue: Records all attack reports.

Form Blue 2: Records messages received or issued by Staff Officer to the Controller in MHQ and which are not covered by any other form.

AIR ASPECTS OF VISIT AND SEARCH

This was the subject of a Secret signal from the Air Ministry 26 August, 1939 which gave the following information:

Enemy warships, troopships and auxiliaries in direct attendance on the enemy fleet may be attacked without warning provided they have been identified beyond doubt. Suspect enemy raiders to be directed to nearest port or HM ship for investigation. May be ordered to heave to and await HM ship. Only sufficient force to make ship comply can be used. If vessel fails to comply then bombs or guns may be dropped or fired ahead of her. If this fails a non-vital part of the ship may be attacked. Neutrals should not be alienated. Even if fired on, do not retaliate.

This was incorporated in Coastal Command Tactical Instructions (CCTIs).

The AOC 16 Group argued about this. He stated that 16 group stations were not provided with 20lb bombs. Anson and Vildebeestes would not have anything lighter than 100lbs bombs. What was a non-vital part of the ship?

It was stated that where a pilot finds a ship in approximate position of a briefed raider and tallies with information given, he:

Reports the situation to base.

Signals ship with Aldis to heave to or to steer a specific course.

If no compliance, a short burst of machine gun fire should be made ahead of her and the signal repeated.

If still no compliance, a short burst of machine gun fire should be made into the bridge. If still no effect, bomb until one hit is registered. If still no compliance continue to bomb and then machine-gun the deck.

No attention is to be paid to signals from the ship.

If ship opens fire, bomb for destruction.

This order applies where aircraft has been sent specifically to locate raider and position found ties in closely with briefed information.

On other occasions, machine guns may be fired or a bomb dropped ahead. If no reaction, shadow and report.

If however, there has been a positive identification as enemy, then treat as enemy and destroy.

No 200 Group at Gibraltar was part of RAF Mediterranean, but in 1941 it was decided to strengthen Gibraltar. Consequently the Group was abolished but re-established as RAF Gibraltar under Air Commodore S. P. Simpson and responsible to HQCC, in December 1941. An Area Combined Headquarters was set up, thus improving the liaison between the Royal Air Force and the Royal Navy.

In March 1943 Portugal gave the UK basing rights in

the Azores and No 247 Group was set up. In August 1943 Nos 172 and 179 Squadrons operating Leigh Light equipped Wellington XIVs were detached there, followed in October 1943 by Nos 206 and 220 Squadrons operating Fortress IIs. Interestingly, No 233 Squadron and its Hudsons had been detached to the Azores since July 1942.

CHAPTER SIX

MARITIME AIRCRAFT

FIRST WORLD WAR

Aircraft used in the maritime role, be it anti-submarine, anti-shipping or general reconnaissance, are listed below. Speeds are given but these figures must be regarded as for illustration and comparison only. Maximum speed normally should be given for an appropriate height, and heights vary on a patrol according to weather conditions and the tactical situation. The speed used by the crew could be range speed, the speed which gives the maximum range, or endurance speed, the speed which can give the longest time in the air. Range speed would have been used for transit to and from the patrol area and endurance would have been used in the patrol area.

Speed of aircraft used to be measured in statute miles per hour (mph), i.e. 1760 yards to the mile. This was changed to nautical miles per hour (knots) i.e. 2000 yards to the mile. Thus one knot is 2000 yards per hour and one mph is 1760 yards per hour. One knot is faster than one mph. It should be noted that the measurement is not expressed as knots per hour.

Speed is shown on an air speed indicator (ASI). Being

an instrument, it is subject to error and the speed shown is known as indicated air speed (IAS). When this is corrected for position (of the sensor) and instrument error it is known as rectified air speed. The speed is calculated by the difference between the pitot or the pressure of the airflow at the pitot head and the static pressure at the static vent. If the pitot head and/or the static vent are in positions where the air is disturbed by other parts of the aircraft, then there is a position error. This can be found by calibration. Instrument error lies in the manufacture of the instrument itself. The formula used for this difference is valid at sea level. There is therefore a height error which is calculated on the handheld computer (not a digital computer). There are other smaller errors and when these are taken into account true air speed (TAS) is found. TAS is the speed at which the aircraft flies through a parcel of air. This air is itself moving due to wind and the final speed is then known as groundspeed. The speeds given below are TAS.

AIRCO- later de Havilland (UNITED KINGDOM)
DH6

- Wingspan: 35 feet 11 inches
- Maximum Speed: 66 mph
- Engine: 100 hp RAF 1a (Royal Aircraft Factory, became Royal Aircraft Establishment)
- Endurance: 28 gallons
- Role: Training, later maritime patrol.

AIRCO (UNITED KINGDOM)
DH9

- Wingspan: 42 feet 4 5/8 inches
- Maximum Speed: 110 mph at 10,000 feet
- Engine: Beardmore-Halford-Pullinger,
  or BHP 240 hp
- Endurance: 74 gallons
- Role: Bomber, later anti submarine

BLACKBURN (UNITED KINGDOM)
Kangaroo

- Wingspan: 74 feet 10 ¼ inches top wing, 47 feet 9 ½
  inches bottom wing
- Maximum Speed: 87 knots
- Engines: Two Rolls Royce 250 hp Falcons
- Endurance: 8 hours
- Role: Anti submarine
- Armament: 920 pounds of bombs

CURTISS (UNITED STATES OF AMERICA)
H 12 Large America Flying Boat

- Wingspan: 96 ½ feet
- Maximum speed: 95 mph
- Rate of climb: 4000 feet in 10 minutes
- Engines: Those used by the RNAS were fitted with
  two Rolls Royce Eagle engines. Maximum range at
  economic speed: 675 miles
- Curtiss H16 was a larger derivative of the above.

FAIREY (UNITED KINGDOM)
Campania
There were three versions of this seaplane, the F16, F17 and F18.

- Wingspan: 61 feet 7 ½ inches
- Engines: The F16 was fitted with a Rolls Royce Eagle of 250 hp and the F17 with an Eagle of 275 hp. There being a shortage of these engines, the F18 was fitted with a Sunbeam engine.
- Maximum speed: F16 - 72 knots, F17 - 78 knots, F22 - 74 knots.
- Rate of climb: F16 - 5000 feet in 14 minutes. F17 - 5000 feet in 12 minutes. F22 -5000 in 18 minutes.
- Role: Patrol
- Crew: Two.

Fairey III

This was a biplane configured as either a landplane or a seaplane.
There were several marks of this aircraft: N10, IIIA, IIIB, IIIC, IIID, IIIF I, IIIF II, IIIF III and the IIIF IV. The following refers to the IIIF IV.

- Wingspan: 45 feet 9 inches
- Engine: One 570 hp Napier Lion water cooled
- Maximum Speed: 120 mph
- Range/Endurance: 1520 miles
- Role:General Reconnaissance
- Crew: Pilot and gunner. In the three seat version a wireless operator was seated between the pilot and the gunner

■ Armament: One fixed forward firing Vickers and a
Lewis gun aft. Bombs were carried under the wings
and were aimed from a prone position in the fuselage.
The aircraft first flew in 1917.

Hamble Baby (Fairey Aviation) (UNITED
KINGDOM)
This was a small seaplane.

■ Wingspan: 27 feet 9 inches
■ Rate of climb: to 5000 feet in eight minutes
■ Endurance : 3½ hours
■ Role: Reconnaissance

SHORT (UNITED KINGDOM)
Felixstowe F3 Flying Boat

■ Wingspan: 102 feet
■ Engines: Two Rolls Royce Eagle 8s
■ Maximum speed: 85 mph
■ Endurance: Around nine hours
■ Role: Anti-submarine
■ Crew: Two pilots and two gunners.

Short 184 Seaplane

■ Wingspan: 63 feet 6 inches
■ Rate of Climb: 300 feet per minute initially
■ Engine: Sunbeam 225 hp, then 240 hp Renault
Mercedes, then 250 hp Rolls Royce, then 260 hp
Sunbeam Maori. The aircraft was sometimes known
as the Short 225 in recognition of the 225 hp

Sunbeam engine.

- Maximum Speed: 84 mph with a 260 hp engine
- Endurance: 4 ½ hours
- Role: Torpedo Bomber
- Crew: Two
- Remarks: Lewis gun in rear cockpit. Aircraft could carry one torpedo or 400 lbs of bombs.

Short 320

- Role: Torpedo Bomber and patrol.

SOPWITH (UNITED KINGDOM)
Sopwith Baby This was a small seaplane.

Sopwith Cuckoo
Land plane

- Wingspan: 48 feet 9 inches
- Rate of climb: 26 minutes to 10,000 feet
- Engine: Production model 220 hp Sunbeam Arab
- Maximum Speed: 90 knots
- Endurance: 4 hours at maximum speed
- Role: Torpedo Bomber.

VICKERS (UNITED KINGDOM)
Vimy
Land plane

- Wingspan: 67 feet 2 inches
- Rate of climb: To 5000 feet, 21.9 minutes
- Engines: Two 350 hp Rolls Royce Eagle Mark VIIIs. Some models were fitted with Fiat engines and others

with Hispano Suizas.
- Maximum Speed: 98 mph at 5000 feet
- Endurance: 452 gallons
- Role: Bomber or anti submarine
- Crew: Pilot and two gunners.

J. SAMUEL WHITE (UNITED KINGDOM)
Wight 840 seaplane

- Wingspan: 61 feet
- Engine: Single 225 hp Sunbeam
- Maximum speed: 81 mph
- Endurance: 4 hours
- Role: Anti submarine
- Crew: two.

BETWEEN THE WARS

AVRO (UNITED KINGDOM)
Anson Mark I

- Land plane
- Wingspan: 56 feet 6 inches
- Engines: Two 350 hp Armstrong Siddeley Cheetah IXs
- Maximum Speed: 188 mph
- Range/Endurance: 800 miles
- Role: Reconnaissance
- Crew: One pilot, one navigator and one wireless operator/air gunner
- Armament: One fixed forward firing pilot operated Vickers .303 machine gun in the nose and one in a

dorsal turret. Two 100 lb bombs could be carried internally and eight 20 lb bombs, flame floats or flares on external racks.

BLACKBURN
Iris
Long Range Flying Boat

The marks were I to V, the Mark II (of which there was one) being a conversion from a Mark I and the Mark IV (of which there was one) being a conversion from the Mark II.

- Wingspan: 95 feet 6 inches
- Engines: Three 650 hp Rolls Royce Condor IIIs mounted between the wings
- Maximum Speed: 115 mph
- Range/Endurance: 560 miles
- Role: General Reconnaissance
- Crew: Two pilots and three gunners all in open cockpits, although there was a large cabin.
- Armament: One Lewis forward and two aft. Bomb load was 1040 lbs.
- Remarks: The aircraft first flew in 1926. Ten were built and served with No. 209 Squadron at RAF Mountbatten. They were replaced by the Blackburn Perth.

Perth
Long Range Flying Boat

- Wingspan: 97 feet
- Engines: Three 825 hp Rolls Royce Buzzard IIMS mounted between the wings

- Maximum Speed: 132 mph
- Range/Endurance: 1500 miles
- Role: General Reconnaissance
- Crew: Two pilots in an enclosed cockpit. One open cockpit forward and two aft.
- Armament: One Lewis gun in each of the open cockpits and one 37mm in the nose. Bomb load was 2000 lbs.
- Remarks: The aircraft first flew in 1933. Four were built and served with No. 209 Squadron at RAF Mountbatten.

BRISTOL
Blenheim Mark I
Land based

- Wingspan: 56 feet 4 inches
- Engines: Two Bristol Mercury XVs
- Maximum Speed: 295 mph
- Range/Endurance: 1900 miles
- Role: Anti shipping
- Crew: One pilot, one navigator/bombaimer and one WOP/AG
- Armament: One .303 machine gun in port wing and two in a dorsal turret. A bomb load of 1000 lbs was carried.

HANDLEY PAGE (UNITED KINGDOM)
Hampden
Land based

- Wingspan: 69 feet 4 inches.

- Engines: Two 1000 hp Bristol Pegasus XVIII
- Maximum Speed: 265 mph
- Range/Endurance: 1100 nautical miles
- Role: Anti shipping
- Crew: One pilot, one navigator, one wireless operator and one gunner.

HAWKER (UNITED KINGDOM)
Horsley
Land based

- Wingspan: 56 feet 6 inches
- Engine: One 665 hp Rolls Royce Condor IIIA
- Maximum Speed: 125 mph
- Range/Endurance: 10 hours
- Role: Torpedo Bomber
- Crew: One pilot and one gunner aft
- Armament: One forward firing Vickers and one Lewis gun for the gunner. One torpedo or 1500 lbs of bombs.

SAUNDERS-ROE (SARO) (UNITED KINGDOM)
Lerwick
Flying Boat

- Wingspan: 80 feet 10 inches
- Engines: Two 1375 hp Bristol Hercules
- Maximum Speed: 214 mph
- Endurance/Range: 1600 nmls
- Role: 1540 miles
- Crew: Six
- Armament: Three power-operated turrets, one in the

nose, one midupper and one in the tail. The aircraft could carry four 500 lbs bombs or depth charges.

- Remarks: The aircraft looks like a twin-engined Sunderland. It first flew in 1938.

London
Biplane Flying Boat

- Wingspan: 80 feet
- Engines: Two 1000 hp Bristol Pegasus X (Mark II aircraft)
- Maximum Speed: 155 mph
- Endurance/Range: 1700 miles
- Role: Reconnaissance
- Crew: 6
- Remarks: Machine guns in the nose, amidships and in the tail.

Cloud
Navigation Trainer Flying Boat

- Wingspan: 64 feet
- Engines: Two 340 hp Armstrong Siddeley Serval IIIs
- Maximum Speed: 118 mph
- Endurance/Range: 360-400 miles
- Role:
- Crew: Two pilots and six navigation students.

SHORT (UNITED KINGDOM)
Singapore
Flying Boat

- Wingspan: 90 feet

- Engines: Two 675 hp Rolls Royce Kestrel IX tractors and two 700 hp Rolls Royce Kestrel VIII pushers mounted between the wings in pairs.
- Maximum Speed: 136 mph
- Endurance/Range: 1235 miles
- Role: General Reconnaissance
- Crew: Six in an enclosed cabin
- Remarks: Gun positions in the nose, amidships and the tail with a single Lewis gun in each position.
- Armament: 2200 lb bomb load.

Rangoon
Flying Boat

- Wingspan:93 feet
- Engines: Three 540 hp Bristol Jupiter XIF mounted between the wings
- Maximum Speed: 115 mph
- Range/Endurance: 650 miles
- Role: General Reconnaissance
- Crew: Five in enclosed cockpit and three gun positions
- Armament: Gun positions in the nose and two amidships. Bomb load of 1000 lbs.

Sunderland Mk I
Flying Boat

- Wingspan: 112 feet 9 ½ inches.
- Engines: Four Bristol Pegasus 22.
- Maximum Speed: 210 mph.
- Endurance/Range: Normal 1780 miles, Overload 2900 miles.

- Role: Reconnaissance/Anti submarine.
- Crew: Was accommodated on two decks. The flight deck contained two pilots, a navigator, a radio operator and a flight engineer. There were gunners and later, radar operators. In the nose there was the bomb aimer's position and the nose turret. Aft of the turret there was the mooring compartment, a lavatory, a wardroom, a galley, the bomb compartment and crew's quarters. The inflatable dinghy, a work bench and flares and markers were contained further aft.
- Armament: There was a gun turret in the nose with two guns, two amidships positions but not in turrets with one gun each and a turret in the tail with four guns. Depth charges and bombs were carried internally on racks which were wound out to the underneath of the wings inboard of the engines.
- Remarks: The aircraft was developed from the Empire class of commercial flying boats. Around 40 aircraft were operational by the outbreak of the Second World War.
- The Pegasus engine did not have feathering propellers. Thus losing an engine could mean exactly that - it left the aeroplane.
- A total of 75 aircraft were built.

SUPERMARINE (UNITED KINGDOM)
Southampton
Biplane Flying Boat

- Wingspan: 75 feet
- Engines: Two 470 hp Napier Lions or Bristol Jupiter

VIIs or Armstrong Siddeley 425/450 hp Jaguars or
Rolls Royce "F" Type

- Maximum Speed: 108 mph
- Endurance/Range: 800 miles
- Role: Reconnaissance
- Crew: Gunner/Bomb aimer in the nose, two pilot
  cockpits in tandem with dual controls, wireless
  operator below the wings and two cockpits aft of that
  each with guns. A crew of five was normally carried.
- Remarks: Two 18 inch torpedoes could be carried,
  one each side of the hull.

Stranraer
Biplane Flying Boat

- Wingspan: 85 feet
- Engines: Two 1000 hp Bristol Pegasus X
- Maximum Speed: 165 mph
- Endurance/Range: 1000 miles
- Role:Reconnaissance
- Crew: 6-7
- Remarks: Machine guns in the nose, amidships and in
  the tail.

Walrus
Biplane Amphibian

- Wingspan:45 feet 10 inches
- Engine: One 775 hp Bristol Pegasus
- Maximum Speed: 135 mph
- Endurance/Range: 600 miles
- Role: Search and Rescue

- Crew: 3-4
- Remarks: Machine guns in the nose and aft. This aircraft was known in the Royal Australian Air Force as the Seagull V.

VICKERS (UNITED KINGDOM)
Vildebeeste
Land based

- Biplane Marks I, II, III and IV
- Wingspan: 49 feet
- Engine: One 635 hp Bristol Pegasus IIM3
- Maximum Speed: 143 mph
- Endurance/Range: 1250 miles
- Role: Torpedo Bomber
- Crew: One pilot, one navigator and one gunner in tandem seating
- Armament: One Vickers forward and one Lewis gun aft. One 18 inch torpedo.

SECOND WORLD WAR

Some pre-war aircraft remained in service for a short period, such as the Vildebeeste, Anson Mk I, Blenheim IV, Hampden, London II, Singapore III, Sunderland I, Stranraer, Hudson I, Lerwick and Walrus.

Towards the end of the war, with the advent of more sophisticated maritime reconnaissance aircraft such as the Liberator, two navigators were in each crew. They were known as the first and second navigators depending on their experience. They generally filled the roles of the routine, i.e. the geographical navigation and the tactical navigator, i.e. the control of the aircraft in a fighting situation. Some navigators became captains of their crews.

ARMSTRONG WHITWORTH (UNITED KINGDOM)
Whitley VII

- Wingspan: 84 feet
- Engines: Two 1000 hp Rolls Royce Merlins
- Maximum Speed: 230 mph
- Range/Endurance: 2400 miles
- Role: General Reconnaissance (GR)
- Crew: Two pilots, one navigator and three WOP/AGs
- Armament: Gun turrets in the nose and tail. Depth charges carried.

BOEING (UNITED STATES OF AMERICA)
Flying Fortress Mark I (B17C)
and Mark II (B17E & B17F)

- Wingspan: 103 feet 9 inches
- Engines: Four 1200 hp Wright R-1820-97s
- Maximum Speed: 295 mph
- Endurance: 1100 miles
- Role: General Reconnaissance
- Crew: Six to ten
- Remarks: Used by the RAF initially as a bomber and found unsatisfactory and transferred to Coastal Command. No 220 Squadron was the first to use the aircraft, followed by Nos 59, 206 and 521 Squadrons.

BRISTOL (UNITED KINGDOM)
Beaufort Mark I and II

- Wingspan: 58 feet
- Engines: Two Bristol Taurus II or VI in the Mark I and two Pratt & Whitney Twin Wasps in the Mark II
- Maximum Speed: Mark I with torpedo 225 mph. Mark II with torpedo 230 mph
- Range/Endurance: Mark I 1600 miles. Mark II 1450 miles
- Role: Torpedo Bomber
- Crew: One pilot, one navigator and wireless operator gunner (WOP/AG)
- Armament: Originally one .303 in the nose and one in the turret but later updated to two nose guns, two in a power operated dorsal turret, two side guns and in some aircraft a rear ward firing gun under the nose.

Beaufighter Mark IC, IIF, VIC, X, XI

- Wingspan: 57 feet 10 inches
- Engines: Mark IC Two Bristol Hercules IIIs or IXs. Mark IIF two Rolls Royce Merlin XXs. Mark VIC two Bristol Hercules VIs or XVIs. Mark X two Bristol Hercules XVII or XVIIIs. Mark XI two Bristol Hercules XVIIs.
- Maximum Speed: 320 mph
- Range/Endurance: 1450 miles
- Role: Anti shipping
- Crew: Pilot and Navigator
- Armament: Four 20 mm cannon in the nose, two .303 machine guns in the port wing and four in the

starboard wing. One Vickers .303 in the navigator's station amidships. Torpedo version carried an 18-inch torpedo externally under the fuselage. Four rockets under each wing could be carried instead of the wing machine guns.

Blenheim Mark IVF

- Wingspan: 56 feet 4 inches
- Engines: Two Bristol Mercuries
- Maximum Speed: 295 mph
- Range/Endurance: 2000 miles
- Role: Anti shipping
- Crew: As in Mark I
- Armament: As in Mark I
- Remarks: The Canadian version of this aircraft was called the Bolingbroke and was fitted with two Pratt & Whitney Wasp Juniors. It was gradually replaced by the Beaufighter.

CONSOLIDATED (UNITED STATES OF AMERICA)
Catalina

- Wingspan: 104 feet
- Engines: Two 1200 hp Pratt & Whitney Twin Wasps
- Maximum speed: 196 mph
- Range/Endurance: 3100 miles
- Role: Maritime reconnaissance and anti-submarine
- Crew: Two pilots, one navigator, one flight engineer and two gunners in blister turrets aft of the wing.
- Remarks: The US Navy designation was the PBY. The amphibious version known by the RAF as the

Catalina Mark III was known by the USN as the PBY 5A and by the RCAF as the Canso. Some versions of this aircraft could remain airborne for 24 hours.

Liberator Mk I, II, III, GR V and GR VI.

- Wingspan: 110 feet
- Engines: Four 1200 hp Pratt & Whitney R-1830-43s
- Maximum Speed: 297 mph
- Range/Endurance: 1540 miles
- Role: Maritime Reconnaissance, anti submarine
- Crew: Power turret in the nose above the bomb aimer. Navigator in the nose with astrodome in the roof. Two pilots, one flight engineer, midupper gun turret, two side gunners and a tail turret.
- Armament: Maximum bomb load was 8000 lbs. The Mark II was the first model to carry two 4000 lb bombs on external carriers one under each wing.
- Remarks: The US Army Air Force designation was B24 and the US Navy designation was PB4Y. The Mark I had a tray of four 20 mm cannons under its belly, two .303 waist guns, one .303 tunnel gun and two .303 tail guns. The Mark II had four .303 guns in each of the dorsal and tail Boulton Paul turrets, one .303 in the nose and two .303 waist guns. The Mark III and the GR V had one .303 or .50 gun in the nose, two .50 guns in the upper turret, either four .303 or two .50 guns in the waist and four .303 guns in the tail. The GR VI had six .50 guns, two in each of the nose and dorsal turrets and in the waist and four .303 guns in the tail.

DE HAVILLAND (UNITED KINGDOM)
Mosquito Mark II, FB Mk VI, XVIII.

- Wingspan: 54 feet 2 inches
- Engines: Two Rolls Royce Merlins 21, 23 or 25s
- Maximum Speed: 400+ mph
- Range/Endurance: 1500 miles with 4000 lb bomb load
- Role: Anti Shipping
- Crew: Pilot and Navigator
- Armament: Four rocket projectiles under each wing. Four .303 machine guns in the nose. In some models these were replaced by a 57 mm gun known as the Tsetse.

HANDLEY PAGE (UNITED KINGDOM)
Halifax GR VI.

- Wingspan: 104 feet
- Engines: Four Bristol Hercules 100s
- Maximum Speed: 282 mph
- Endurance/range: 1860 miles
- Role: General Reconnaissance
- Crew: Seven
- Remarks: This aircraft remained in service with Nos 202 and 224 Squadrons until the early 1950s.

LOCKHEED (UNITED STATES OF AMERICA)
Hudson III

- Wingspan: 65 feet 6 inches
- Engines: Two Wright R-1820-G205As
- Maximum Speed: 275 mph

- Range/Endurance: 1700 nmls
- Role: Reconnaissance
- Crew: One pilot, one navigator and three WOP/AGs
- Armament: Two .303 machine guns on fuselage in front of the pilot, two .303 machine guns in a dorsal turret, one .303 in each side of the fuselage and one .303 (retractable) beneath the fuselage.

SHORT (UNITED KINGDOM)
Sunderland Mark II

- Engines: Four Bristol Pegasus XVIIIs
- Remarks: Similar to the Mark I but later versions were fitted with a two gun dorsal turret. Only 43 aircraft were built.

Sunderland Mark III

Remarks: Similar to the Mark II but with a streamlined front step. The aircraft was equipped with ASV Mark2 radar although ASV Mark 6C equipped later models. A total of 461 Mark III and IIIA aircraft were built.

Sunderland Mark IIIA

The only difference between this and the Mark III was the replacement of ASV Mark 2 with ASV mark 3 radar.

Sunderland Mark IV

This version had a stronger wing, a longer fuselage and a bigger tailplane. The nose turret now had two 12.7 mm machine guns in place of the 7.7 mms, two fixed 12.7 mms in the nose, two 20mm Hispano cannons in the dorsal turret, twin 12.7 mms in the tail turret and a handheld 12.7 mm either side of the fuselage. The engines were four Bristol Hercules XIXs. The aircraft was so different to previous models that it was named the Seaford. Only eight were built and it did not become operational.

Sunderland GR 5

This version was fitted with four Pratt & Whitney Twin Wasps. Four fixed .303 guns were added to the nose. ASV Mark 6C radar was fitted. A total of 155 Mark Vs were built and 33 Mark IIIs were converted to GR V.

VICKERS (UNITED KINGDOM)
Warwick GR Mk 1 and ASR Mk 1

- Wingspan: 96 feet 8 ½ inches
- Engines: Two Pratt & Whitney R-2800-S1A4G or 2SBGs
- Maximum Speed: 260 knots
- Range/Endurance: 2075 miles
- Maximum All up weight (AUW): 45000lbs
- Armament: 2x .303 machine guns in a nose turret, two in a midupper turret and four in a tail turret. Bomb bay carried bombs, mines or depth charges. The ASR Mk 1 had a modified bomb bay to allow it to carry an airborne lifeboat.
- Role: Search and rescue
- Crew: One pilot, one navigator, one WOP and three gunners
- Remarks: This aircraft was a development of the Wellington.

Warwick GR Mk II

This was similar to the Mark 1 except that it had two Bristol Centaurus VII engines.

Warwick GR Mk V

This was similar to the Mark 1 except that it had two Bristol Centaurus VII engines and the nose and midupper turrets were removed and replaced by a .5 machine gun in the nose and one .5 machine gun in each beam. The tail turret was retained.

Wellington Mk VIII

- Wingspan: 86 feet 2 inches
- Engines: Two Bristol Pegasus XVIII
- Maximum Speed: 235 mph
- Max range: 2550 miles
- Maximum all up weight: (AUW) 25800 lbs
- Armament: One Frazer-Nash turret in the nose and one in the tail with two .303 machine guns in each. The bomb bay carried depth charges, mines or two 18-inch torpedoes up to a weight of 4500 lbs.
- Role: General reconnaissance
- Crew: Two Pilots, one Navigator and three WOP/AG's.
- Remarks: This aircraft was the first to be equipped with the fitted with a Leigh Light.

Wellington Mk XI

This had two Bristol Hercules VI or XVI engines. It was

the GR version of the Mark X and could carry the same weapon load as the Mark VIII. It was fitted with a Leigh Light. The maximum speed was increased to 255 mph and the AUW to 29500 lbs. The maximum range was reduced to 2085 miles.

Wellington XII

This had two Bristol Hercules VI engines and carried 5100 lbs of bombs, mines or depth charges but at the price of a reduced range. It was Leigh Light fitted and carried six .303 machine guns. The AUW was increased to 36500 lbs and the speed to 256 mph. The maximum range was now 1810 miles.

Wellington XIII

This was fitted with two Bristol Hercules XVII engines giving a speed of 250 mph and a range of 1760 miles. The weapon load was 5000 lbs of bombs, mines or torpedoes. This aircraft carried a four-gun tail turret. Maximum AUW was 31000 lbs.

Wellington Mk XIV

This version was similar to the Mark XIII. There was no nose turret but it had one .303 machine gun in each beam and four in the tail turret. The Leigh Light was retractable and fitted in the rear of the bomb bay.

PHOTOGRAPHIC RECONNAISSANCE

The photographic reconnaissance units were part of Coastal Command although their tasks were undertaken for the benefit of all. Their aircraft are listed below.

De HAVILLAND (UNITED KINGDOM)
Mosquito PR Mk I

- Engines: Two Rolls Royce Merlin 21s
- Crew: Pilot and Navigator
- Remarks: Performance to other types as above. Four cameras were fitted. Ten aircraft were built. Aircraft was unarmed.

Mosquito PR Mk IV

- Engines: Two Rolls Royce Merlin 21s or 23s.
- Remarks: This was a version of the B Mk IV. It was unarmed.

Mosquito PR Mk VIII

- Engines: Two Rolls Royce Merlin 61s
- Remarks: This was the first high altitude Mosquito and was a conversion of the Mk IV.

Mosquito PR Mk IX

- Engines: Two Rolls Royce Merlin 72s
- Range/Endurance: 2000 miles
- Remarks: This was a conversion of the B Mk IX. It was also used as a meteorological reconnaissance aircraft before day and night bombing raids.

Mosquito PR Mk XVI

Engines: Two Rolls Royce Merlin 72 or 76 on the starboard side and 73 or 77 on the port side. The port engine drove a cabin super charger.
Remarks: The aircraft was fitted with an astrodome to allow the navigator to take star sights.

MARTIN (UNITED STATES OF AMERICA)
Maryland

- Wingspan: 61 feet 2 inches
- Engines: Two Pratt & Whitney R-1830-S3C4-Gs
- Maximum Speed: 316 mph
- Range/Endurance: 1000 miles
- Role: Photo reconnaissance
- Armament: Four .303 machine guns in the wings and a Vickers in each of the dorsal and ventral positions. It carried a bomb load of 2000 lbs.
- Crew: One pilot, one navigator and a WOP/AG
- Remarks: The aircraft was used mainly in Malta. Its best-known pilot was Wing Commander Adrian Warburton.

NORTH AMERICAN
(UNITED STATES OF AMERICA)
Mustang III

- Wingspan: 37 feet 5/16 inches
- Engine: Packard Merlin V-1650-7 (i.e. Merlin 69)
- Maximum Speed: 445 mph
- Range/Endurance: Six .50 machine guns in the wings. It was possible to carry one 1000 lbs bomb under each wing.
- Role: Photo reconnaissance.

SUPERMARINE (UNITED KINGDOM)
Spitfire PR IV

- Wingspan: 36 feet 10 inches
- Engine: Rolls Royce Merlin 45 or 46
- Maximum Speed: 372 mph
- Range/Endurance: 1460 miles
- Armament: Nil
- Role: Photo Reconnaissance.

Spitfire IX

- Wingspan: 36 feet 10 inches
- Engine: One Rolls Royce Merlin 61, 63, 63A, 66 or 70
- Maximum Speed: 400 to 416 depending on engine
- Range/Endurance: 434 miles
- Armament: Two 20 mm cannon and four machine guns
- Role: Photo Reconnaissance.

Spitfire X

Similar to the above except no armament and fitted with a Rolls Royce Merlin 64 or 71 engine, giving a maximum speed of 416 mph and a range of 1370 miles.

Spitfire PR XIX

Similar to the above except it was fitted with a Rolls Royce Griffon 65 or 66 engine giving a maximum speed of around 450 mph and a range of 1500 miles. The armament was two 20 mm cannon and two .50 machine guns.

Spitfire PR XI

- Wingspan: 36 feet 10 inches
- Engine: Rolls Royce Merlin 61, 63, 63A or 70
- Maximum Speed: 422 mph
- Range/Endurance: In excess of 1200 miles
- Armament: Eight .303 machine guns
- Role: Photo Reconnaissance.

VICKERS ARMSTRONG
Wellington Mark IV

- Wingspan: 86 feet 2 inches
- Engines: Two 1200 hp Pratt & Whitney R-1830-83C4G's (Twin Wasps)
- Maximum Speed: 229 mph
- Range/Endurance: 2180 miles
- Armament: Two gun nose and tail turrets and beam guns were fitted. The bomb load was 4500lbs.
- Role: Used as a photo reconnaissance aircraft as well as a medium bomber.

POST WAR

The Handley Page Halifax continued in service, as did the Sunderland GR5. The Halifax eventually transferred to meteorological reconnaissance duties. The Lancaster GR3 was transferred to Coastal Command.

AVRO (UNITED KINGDOM)
Lancaster GR3

- Wingspan: 102 ft

- Engines: Four Rolls Royce Merlin
- Maximum Speed: 282 mph
- Range/Endurance: 2350 nmls
- Crew: 7
- Role: Reconnaissance. When the Shackleton came into service, the Lancaster reverted to a training role at the School of Maritime Reconnaissance at RAF St Mawgan.

Shackleton MR Mk 1, 2, 2c, 3 and T4

- Wingspan: 120 ft
- Engines: Four Rolls Royce Griffin 57s.
- Maximum Speed: 260 knots
- Range/Endurance: 24 hours at endurance speed but a more practical figure was 18 hours.
- Crew: Two pilots, two navigators, one flight engineer and five signallers to operate the radio, radar, sonics and illuminants. Later these five became one air electronics officer and four air electronics operators.
- Role: maritime reconnaissance.

HANDLEY PAGE (UNITED KINGDOM)
Hastings Met 1

- Wingspan: 113 feet
- Engines: Four Bristol Hercules 106s
- Maximum Speed: 303 knots
- Range/Endurance: 1700 miles
- Crew: Two pilots, one navigator, one flight engineer, one signaller and a meteorological observer.
- Role: meteorological reconnaissance. The only squadron to use it was No.202 Squadron.

HAWKER SIDDELEY (UNITED KINGDOM)
Nimrod MR1 and MR2

- Wingspan: 114 feet 10 inches
- Engines: Four Rolls Royce Spey turbo jets
- Maximum Speed: 500 knots
- Range/Endurance: 10 hours. About 19 hours with in flight refuelling.
- Crew: Two Pilots, two navigators, one flight engineer, one air electronics officer and six air electronics operators.
- Role: maritime reconnaissance.
- Armament: Nine Mark 46 or Stingray anti submarine torpedoes in the bomb bay and Sidewinder or Harpoon or Sea Eagle anti ship missiles on the under-wing strong points.

LOCKHEED (UNITED STATES OF AMERICA)
Neptune P2V5

- Wingspan: 103 feet 10 inches
- Engines: Two Wright R-3350-32W Turbo Compounds
- Maximum Speed: 345 knots.
- Range/Endurance: 3685 miles
- Crew: Two pilots, two navigators, one flight engineer and five signallers to operate the radio, sonics and the APS 20 radar.
- Role: maritime reconnaissance
- Remarks: The Neptune was used by Coastal Command until 1957.

CHAPTER SEVEN

NAVIGATION OF COASTAL AIRCRAFT

The navigation of a maritime reconnaissance aircraft, and indeed of any other aircraft, particularly in the early part of the 20th century, was very much 'Dead', meaning deduced reckoning or DR. This is based on what is known as the triangle of velocities. One side of the triangle represented the track, marked with two arrowheads, another the heading, with one arrowhead and the third the wind velocity (W/V) with three arrowheads. The track is a line on a chart representing the path which the aircraft should take. Track made good (TMG) is the path the aircraft has taken. Heading is not the same as track. If it is imagined that the wind is coming from the left, then the aircraft will be blown to the right. Therefore the aircraft must point to the left of its intended direction to compensate. This is heading, which used to be called course. The difference between heading and track is "drift" and is called "port" or left when the aircraft is blown to the left and "starboard" or right when the aircraft is being blown to the right. It is measured in degrees and relative to heading. Wind velocity is the direction FROM which the wind is coming and its speed. Heading and track is the direction TO which the aircraft is going. All speeds are measured in knots. One knot is defined as one nautical mile per hour and therefore cannot be called a "knot per hour". A nautical mile is 6080 feet. It also equates to one minute of latitude. Direction is measured in degrees of the compass.

The triangle can be solved graphically on a piece of graph paper or on a chart where a constant scale is available. The following example will illustrate the problem. The track AB, 060 degrees, is drawn. From A the wind direction is drawn downwind, 340 degrees. The length of this vector, 20 knots (kts) is measured against the constant scale-20 units and arced off along the wind vector. At the end of this vector, with a compass or dividers, arc off on the track the true air speed (TAS) 150 kts using the same constant scale, 150 units. Join the end of the wind vector to where the compasses cut the track. This line is the heading.

As wind speed and direction go together, so do track and groundspeed and so do heading and airspeed. Airspeed is the speed at which the aircraft passes through the air. Groundspeed is the speed of the aircraft over the ground or sea. If for example, there is a headwind of say 20 kts the speed of the aircraft over the ground is reduced by the wind of 20 kts. Thus if the true airspeed (TAS) is 150 kts then the groundspeed will be 130 kts. Equally if it was a tailwind, then the groundspeed will be 170 kts.

The navigator did not have to go through this procedure when doing his calculations. He had a hand-held computer on which he drew out the triangle and on the other side he had a circular slide rule with which he made his calculations of time, distance and TAS. This was not a computer of the modern electronic variety. It was originally known as the Dalton computer.

This is all very well in flight planning when the navigator has access to forecast winds from the weather forecaster, but what about in flight? It can be seen from the description of the triangle of velocities above, that if any four of the quantities are known, then the remaining two may be found easily. Thus, if a drift is taken and then the aircraft heading is changed, say sixty degrees starboard and another drift is taken, what is called a double drift wind velocity can be found. If the aircraft heading is then altered 120 degrees port and another drift is taken, then a more accurate multi drift wind can be found. The aircraft heading is then altered sixty degrees to starboard to the original heading. Each leg is flown for two minutes, so the aircraft should be on the original track. The navigator would increase his Estimated Time of Arrival (ETA) by the amount of time spent on one leg, that is, two minutes.

A track and groundspeed wind can be calculated when a fix is obtained, assuming that no material change of heading has occurred. A line is drawn from the last known position to the fix. The distance is measured and, knowing the time elapsed between the two positions, the groundspeed can be calculated. The track can be measured. The heading is known from the compass and the true airspeed (TAS) is known from the airspeed indicator (ASI). Four components of the triangle are now available and the remaining two may be calculated. This is what is known as a track plot.

The disadvantage with this method of plotting as opposed to the air plot method described below is that drift has to be applied to the heading in order to ascertain track. Groundspeed has to be estimated in order to calculate a DR position. This applies to every heading flown, and where many headings have been flown, this can be time consuming.

As stated above, the heading is what is flown to make good a track. Thus any point in time along this heading, known as an air position, is where the aircraft would be with zero wind. Therefore if a fix is found at the same time as an air position is calculated, the vector joining the two represents the wind. This method of finding the wind velocity (W/V) is called the air plot method and is more flexible than the track and groundspeed method.

There are a number of instruments available to the navigator in the aircraft. The airspeed indicator (ASI) measures the airspeed. The instrument is built according to the ICAO standard which says that the mean sea level pressure is 1013.2 millibars, the temperature at sea level is plus 15 degrees centigrade and that it decreases by 1.97 centigrade degrees per 1000 feet. This standard is of course an average and means that the ASI has an in-built error. However, this was easily solved on the navigator's computer with a knowledge of the outside air temperature (OAT) which was shown on a thermometer in the aircraft. The ASI had its own instrument error caused during manufacture. It was calibrated at the factory and the error, which only amounted to a few knots, was shown on a small chart located by the instrument.

The altimeter is in effect, a barometer, but shows

altitude. The local atmospheric pressure is set on the instrument and altitude is then presented. Like the ASI, the altimeter is built according to ICAO standard and suffers from similar errors. The problem over the open sea is that there are no stations reporting pressure or indeed any other weather, although there used to be Ocean Weather Ships. Other ships and aircraft would report weather while in transit, but not in wartime. The local pressure would be found by flying at what was believed to be say, 500 feet and setting that height on the altimeter. The advent of radio and radar altimeters eased this problem considerably and the two instruments, radio/radar and pressure, could be synchronized. The pressure would then be revealed and the aircraft could be flown at higher altitudes with some confidence. In later times the Meteorological Office's forecast pressure for defined areas was broadcast to all aircraft. This is called the QNH (part of the "Q" code) and means the pressure setting on the altimeter, which will then record the height above sea level. This was vital if two aircraft were operating in adjacent areas, in order to avoid collisions.

From about 1942 onwards air plot became automatic, with the fitting of an air position indicator (API). This received inputs from the gyro magnetic compass and air distance from the air mileage unit (AMU) and presented the air position to the navigator. A device called the variation setting counter was incorporated so that true heading was displayed by the compass and input to the API. This saved much work in plotting the headings, particularly when multi headings had been flown, such as when orbiting ships or submarines under attack.

A further development of this was an instrument mounted above the chart table, the ground position indicator (GPI), which took the input from the API and a manually-set wind velocity and projected an illuminated arrow down onto the navigator's chart, which was pinned to the chart table.

Drift could be measured by various methods. The Drift Recorder Mk II, which was a small periscopic device which protruded out of the side of the aircraft, was the main instrument. Over land the navigator, looking through it, could follow objects passing underneath him and by aligning a scale he would measure the drift. Over sea it was slightly more difficult, in that he had to align the scale with the motion of the aircraft, but with practice accurate drifts could be found. The bombsight and the rear gunner's bearing plates were other methods. Not to be forgotten was the astro compass, which was really an instrument for measuring heading, using celestial objects such as stars, planets or the sun. This was used to check the serviceability of the magnetic and gyro compasses.

Aircraft compasses were of two types, namely the magnetic compass, which contained a bar magnet which aligned itself with the Earth's magnetic field, thus indicating magnetic north, and the gyro magnetic compass. This latter had a gyro, which made use of one of the properties of such an instrument, "rigidity in space" to give a steady heading. However, another of a gyro's properties is "precession" i.e. it will gradually drift off that heading. Accordingly, it was combined with a flux valve in the wing tip or fin which defined magnetic north. Thus it was easier to make accurate turns and to maintain a heading.

True north lies at the geographic North Pole, but this is not coincident with the magnetic North Pole, which moves, over a considerable number of years, very slowly around the geographic pole. The angular difference between the two is called variation. It is called west at any particular point on the Earth's surface when magnetic north is west of true north and east when the converse applies. As stated above in connection with the API, with a gyro magnetic compass there is a device, a variation setting counter (VSC), by which the variation can be set and true heading shown on the compass repeaters and master indicators.

Every compass, be it gyro or magnetic, suffered from an effect called compass deviation. This is caused by the metal components of the aircraft. This was calculated and to an extent compensated by "swinging" the compass. This could be done in the air or on the ground. The aircraft would be towed to the compass base, an area in a remote part of the airfield and relatively free from magnetic influences. It would be lined up on the points of the compass and the heading of the aircraft measured by an outside compass. Some of the deviation could be taken out and the remainder left as a correction to be applied to the heading flown.

The magnetic compass always showed compass heading, as no variation could be applied to it. In high northerly latitudes (and southern for that matter) the compass needle tends to point downwards towards the magnetic pole, thus losing accuracy. Thus the use of a gyro is vital. Again in these high latitudes there is a problem with the charts. On a Mercator the meridians of longitude are parallel to each other and the scale expands very rapidly in high latitudes. The chart then becomes unreliable. The alternative is to use a chart with a conical projection such as a Lambert's Conformal. This however, has the disadvantage that meridians converge quickly, creating a problem in the plotting of a position. The solution is to superimpose a rectangular or square grid on the chart and to measure from grid north instead of true north. The angular difference between grid and magnetic north is called grivation, and this value may be set on the variation setting counter. This takes into account variation and convergence, the difference between grid and true north.

An outside air temperature thermometer was also fitted to the aircraft.

The navigator would carry with him a chronometer in the form of a wristwatch, a sextant, dividers, a Dalton computer, a Douglas square-sided protractor, a ruler known as a straight edge, pencils and a rubber. He would also carry a variety of maps and charts and astronomical tables.

The atmospheric pressure distribution over the Earth is a low-pressure band at the equator, then a subtropical high pressure, a mid-latitude low pressure then the polar high pressure. The main area of North Atlantic operations is governed by the Azores High and the Icelandic Low Pressure areas. The bad weather created by the Icelandic lows causes turbulence and low cloud and maritime aircraft flew in this most of the time. It was necessary to see the sea in order to take drifts, to estimate the wind velocity and for tactical considerations.

The navigator needed to find a fix, which is a ground position calculated from visual, astronomical, radio or radar observations. Apart from astro and visual (the latter only applying when in sight of land), navigation aids were sparse indeed. Astro required a stable platform, sight of the sky and space in the aircraft to enable the navigator to work his calculations. Sight of the sky in the North Atlantic was, and is, rare at the lower levels. He needed an air almanac and sight reduction tables for the calculations, along with a bubble sextant. A bubble sextant differed from a naval sextant in that an air bubble was introduced such that it represented the horizon so that the angle of the celestial object above the horizon could be measured. It was something like a spirit level.

As the Second World War progressed, so further navigation aids came into use. Gee was a radar aid operating around 80 megacycles (m/cs) in the VHF band, now known as megahertz (m/htz). It worked on the principle of "measurement of time difference by pulse technique". It was a ground system consisting of a master and three slave aerials. These three were known as the "B,"C" and "D" slaves and on the Gee chart as the red, green and purple hyperbolae respectively. A master and its slaves were known as a chain. The system was shown on a cathode ray tube (CRT) with a split horizontal time base.

The master station transmitted a pulse and after a short delay, different for each, the slaves would transmit their own pulses. The aircraft receiver then measured the time differences and presented them on the time bases on the indicator. The time differences were shown on a chart in the colours mentioned above and the navigator plotted his received signals. He needed to transcribe the latitude and longitude from this chart to his plotting chart. The system gave a good fix, depending on where the aircraft was located in relation to the various stations. Being VHF it was limited to line of sight, but to compensate for this a number of chains were set up which covered the whole of the UK and Ireland out to about 10 degrees west and eastwards to Denmark. In the south it covered northern France and to the north to Shetland.

Another system which gave only single position lines was Loran, standing for LOng RAnge Navigation. Its principle was the same as Gee, that is measurement of time difference by pulse technique. A position line is defined as a line on a chart on which an aircraft is at a given time.

This was an American system and operated in the MF range, i.e. 1750, 1850, 1900 and 1950 k/cs. It was almost worldwide in use. Its disadvantage was that two different chains had to be used to obtain a fix, but nevertheless, like Gee it was reasonably accurate.

Consol was a radio aid operating in the MF range, from 200 k/cs to 400 k/cs. This was originally of German design for the use of the German Navy and was called by them "Sonne". It was discovered during the Second World War by the Allies, but instead of bombing the stations, they made use of them. The stations were in Spain and France. After the war the number of stations was increased and were in Lugo and Seville in Spain, Ploneis in Brest, northern France, Bush Mills in Northern Ireland and Stavanger in Norway. The Russians had two stations and the Americans also had two, but called them Consolan. The principle was to gain "a bearing by phase comparison". The ground station consisted of three aerials in line.

Interchanging the phases of the outer aerials caused the polar diagram to rotate, thus giving a number of equisignals. The station transmitted 60 symbols as either dots or dashes, or a combination of both. The navigator had to count the number of dots and dashes over a period of one or in some cases, two minutes and plot them on a prepared chart. In the early hours of the morning it could be like counting sheep! A single position line only was obtained and to obtain a fix another station had to be listened to, or a line obtained from another source.

A further aid was MF direction finding (MFDF). A ground station operated on a frequency of around 300 k/cs and the navigator or signaller took a bearing on it with the DF loop in the aircraft. This was a loop bearing relative to the fore and aft axis of the aircraft. The true heading of the aircraft was added to it to obtain the true bearing, which was then plotted to give a single position line. This all sounds very easy, but all navigation suffered from errors of some sort and the skill was to interpret them. Loran, Consol and MFDF suffered from night effect, making the signal difficult to hear or in the case of Loran, see, and to take a bearing. In the case of Loran it caused the signals to break up. Later on the navigator was provided with a radio compass with which he could take his own bearings and listen to Consol stations. It should be noted that a radio compass was not a compass! It was a radio with a direction-finding capability.

The navigator was required to log everything that he observed on a special log form. Before take-off, he was required to draw up his tracks on a chart, apply the forecast wind velocities and from all that, complete a flight plan. At the end of the flight he had to submit his logs and charts to his squadron navigation leader for assessment.

The charts used were a mixture of Mercator, scales 1:1,000,000 or 1:2,000,000, known as one million and two million charts. If a ground position indicator was fitted to the aircraft a 1:500,000 or half million Lambert Conformal chart was used for tactical purposes. A Mercator chart is one where the parallels of latitude and meridians of longitude are straight and intersect at right angles, whereas a Lambert Conformal is closer to a true picture of the round earth in that the parallels are curved and the meridians converge towards the poles. This has consequences in plotting. A great circle is a line on a chart where the plane of the circle passes through the centre of the earth. A rhumb line is a line drawn on a chart which cuts all meridians at the same angle. Thus a straight line drawn on a Lambert is very close to a great circle, whereas a straight line drawn on a Mercator is not and is a rhumb line. A radio bearing follows a great circle, which means that to plot it correctly on a Mercator, a correction called conversion angle has to be applied.

It can be seen that the navigator had much to consider. In the early days of maritime flying the second pilot was the navigator and indeed the teaching of navigation to pilots continued until 1956. The pilots the author trained with hated it! It became obvious at the outset of the Second World War that navigation was a specialized profession. Indeed he had to know and understand meteorology, maritime operations and tactics, radio, radar, sonics and maps and charts. As time progressed so the navigator became the tactical coordinator. This paved the way for him to become a captain of aircraft. Unlike other Commands, in Coastal the Captain is the most experienced person in the crew regardless of aircrew category. Members of the crew worked together, pilots, navigators, signallers and flight engineers. A failure by any one of them could put them all in jeopardy.

CHAPTER EIGHT

COASTAL COMMAND WEAPONS

At the beginning of the Second World War the only anti-submarine weapons available to maritime aircraft were the 100lb, 250lb and 500lb antisubmarine bombs, and these were not very satisfactory. The situation in respect of both aircraft and weapons was such that it was considered that the Blackburn Kangaroo and its 230lb anti submarine bombs in the First World War was probably a more effective weapon than anything that Coastal Command had in its inventory in 1939. However, the Naval 450lb depth charge was available and trials were carried out to see if this weapon could be dropped from an aircraft. The Naval Depth Charge Mark VII was finally selected with a fairing fitted to the nose and fins to the tail. This weapon had a hydrostatic pistol, which meant that the charge exploded at a preset depth. This was more reliable and did not explode on the surface, causing a risk to the aircraft. There was more explosive in this weapon than in the anti-submarine bombs, making it more effective. While there were more advantages than disadvantages to the depth charge, it had to be remembered that they could not be released from a height greater than 100 feet nor a speed greater than 115 mph. Outwith these parameters the depth charge could be damaged on contact with the sea. The 100lb and 250lb antisubmarine bombs were eventually replaced by the Mark VIII 250lb depth charge.

Sonic detection was in its infancy in the First World War. There was a hydrophone available, but the flying boat that carried it had to land on the sea in order that it could be lowered into the water. By the start of the Second World War ASDIC was available to warships, but aircraft had to wait until 1942 before sonobuoys became available to the crews. Even ASDIC had its limitations. It was mounted below the hull of a warship and above about 15 knots it was useless. It could not detect submarines which were below 750 feet. However, it was a very useful device and tactics were devised to maintain contact. Captain Walker RN used a tactic whereby one ship held contact and it directed the attack by other ships. This was probably the forerunner of today's Vector Tactic (Vectac).

BOMB 100LB ANTI SUBMARINE

This weapon could cause damage, but not necessarily sink a U-Boat. On 25 August 1940 three Hudsons of No 233 Squadron found and attacked U-46, commanded by Kapitänleutnant Endrass. Pilot Officer Maudsley straddled the U-Boat with ten 100lb bombs. One bomb scored a direct hit, causing a 10-foot hole in the outer casing, but U-46 made it back to port safely.

BOMB HE AS35lb MARK I AND MARK II

These weapons were carried by the Liberator and the Halifax. The Liberator carried 48 or 72 Mark I bombs and the Halifax carried 54 Mark II bombs.

The bomb was a thin-cased weapon of seven inches

maximum diameter. The fuse was attached to a conical snout at the forward. The length without the fuse was 29¼" and width was 33 5/8". The weight without the fuse was 33½ lbs and with 35lbs. It contained 16lbs of RDX or TNT with a charge/weight ratio of 45%.

The Mark I had no lug or suspension device but it had a semicircular projection at the end of the tailtube to guide the bomb in its carrier. It could only be loaded into the aircraft with a magazine, or in a chute as in the Liberator.

The Mark II did have a fixed suspension lug and could be retained through its lug on a bomb carrier.

The fuse was a direct acting contact No 866 percussion fuse with a vaned cap for arming and four forward-projecting firing plungers, bearing on a swash plate which transmitted their thrust to a single central firing pin held in place by a steel shear wire, shearing at 150lbs pressure.

The terminal velocity was 370 feet per second, the trail angle 40 degrees. Water entry without ricochet occurred when released from 100 feet or higher at 215 knots.

The shape of its underwater path was not determined, but for entry at 30 degrees and at terminal velocity in air, the bomb advanced about 27 feet underwater, attaining a vertical path at a depth of 40 feet. The terminal velocity underwater was 17 feet per second and the fuse functioned on contact at any depth. The underwater advance would have been accommodated by the number of bombs at any one time, known as the stick, and the length of that stick. The usual stick was of 24 bombs.

The parameters for dropping the bombs were:

No restriction on maximum height and speed.

Minimum height was 350 feet.

Minimum Speed no restriction.

BOMB-BAY LOADING OF BOMB HE AS35lb

Liberator

When 48 bombs were carried they were loaded in eight cage-type racks, six bombs per rack. Four racks were carried in the starboard rear bomb-bay and four in the port rear bomb-bay. When 72 were carried the other 24 were carried in the front bomb cell. There were two racks abreast each side of the catwalk. The release unit was an Electro Magnetic Release Unit (EMRU) Type L Mark1.

Halifax

They were carried on nine special bomb carriers with six bombs on each. The bomb carrier was a fabricated beam with a special EMRU. The bombs were released through the master switch, the bomb door control switch, the bomb release switch and a thermionic valve bomb distributor. The bomb stations used in the bomb bay were Nos. 1, 4, 6, 10, 11, 12, 13, 14 and 15.

(National Archives AIR15/393)

MARK XI DEPTH CHARGE

This contained an explosive charge of 180 lbs of Torpex. It had a lethal range of 19 feet against a submarine and was set to explode at 25 feet depth. Its serious damage range was 30 feet. Depth charges were dropped in sticks, usually of six but it depended on the war load of the aircraft. A 100 yard stick gave five spaces of 20 yards or sixty feet, meaning that at least serious damage would be caused if the stick was dropped accurately. Where the stick consisted of four DCs the spacing was 100 feet. This also applied to a pilot-dropped stick (that is, dropped by eye). The DC sank at a rate of around 8 feet per second and had a forward travel underwater of 35 to 40 feet. It could be released at a maximum height of 1000 feet and a maximum speed of 250 knots. The weapon was set to explode at 25 feet below water. Switching distributor settings to allow for different stick spacings was difficult in sudden attacks. By the time the author joined to fly Lancasters and Shackletons, the spacings were standard and set on the "crossing the coast" checks.

MARK 24 HOMING TORPEDO

This was an American weapon and was a 19-inch acoustic torpedo, introduced in mid 1943, designed to home onto the cavitation of a ship's screws, in this case a submarine. It was called Fido or Zombie but in all reports, to protect its secrecy, it was called a mine. It had a weight of 680 lbs and a Torpex charge of 92 lbs. Its length was seven feet. It had a range of 4000 yards at 12 knots and was battery powered. Homing was by means of four crystal hydrophones around the body with a simple steering mechanism. Use of this weapon caused the destruction of 68 submarines and damage to a further 33. To sink a Type XXI U-Boat, it was necessary to drop it ahead of the boat as it was too slow for that particular target. It was of no use against a very deep target. It is believed to have been first used by a No 86 Squadron Liberator on 12 May 1943.

To drop weapons accurately bomb sights were used. There were a number of these, among them the Mark 4 and T.I. sights suitable for use from 800 feet to 2500 feet. There was a radar sight, but this depended on the submarine remaining partly surfaced, which was highly unlikely! The pilot could carry out a visual drop which required practice. More than likely he would make a mark on his cockpit Perspex which would be his dropping point. Many became expert at this. However, the main sight which was for use by the bombaimer or navigator was the Mark III Low Level Bomb Sight.

MARK 30 HOMING TORPEDO

This was a passive homing torpedo, that is it emitted no signals, and homed on to the acoustic noise of the target at a speed of 30 knots.

MARK III LOW LEVEL BOMB SIGHT

This was a bomb sight that was based on the angular velocity principle. Simply explained, consider a man in a moving train looking at the telegraph poles coming towards him. Initially they appear to move slowly then, as they come alongside, they move very rapidly. If the speed at which an object is approaching and the perpendicular distance between the tracks of the observer and the object are known, the angular velocity can be calculated exactly in degrees or radians per second for any instant during its approach. The sight consisted of a sighting head, a computer box and a control panel. The groundspeed and height were entered into the computer box and this automatically adjusted the sighting head. The bombaimer was presented with a ladder like graticule in the sight which moved towards him and he adjusted the head for drift. When the target entered his field of view it would appear to move more slowly than the graticule. Eventually, the two movements would coincide and this was the release point. The sight was intended for use below 1000 feet. It gave good tactical freedom as it was possible to bomb in a descent or climb and large errors in height setting did not give large bombing errors.

MARK 4 AND T.I. BOMB SIGHTS
These were used for attacks of between 800 and 2500 feet. Thus the target had to be known before take off to allow the sight to be fitted and calibrated.

MARK XIV BOMB SIGHT
This was a sight normally used by Bomber Command, but was used by Coastal when the 600lb anti-submarine bomb was carried.

MARINE MARKER No 3 Mark 2
A marine marker was used to mark the position of sonobuoys, dinghies or any other position. It was released from the flare chute at heights of between 200 and 500 feet at a maximum speed of 174 knots. It was 37 inches long and had a diameter of 6 inches. It burned for two hours and could be fitted with a clockwork valve which allowed a delay of up to six hours before the marker functioned. This allowed a position to be marked for eight hours without the aircraft revisiting the position.

MARINE MARKER No 4 Mark 1

This marker could be dropped from the bomb bay or through the flare chute and had the ballistics of a sonobuoy. It was 36 inches long and 5 inches diameter and was released between 150 and 1000 feet at a maximum speed of 200 knots. It burned for 50 to 60 minutes.

FLARE ILLUMINATOR 1.7 INCH
A flare chute-launched illuminant, this had a two second delay and burned for three seconds at 3 million candlepower. It was hand launched at one to three quarters of a mile from the target.

FLARE ILLUMINATOR 1.75 INCH
These flares were fired from a multi-barrel discharger at a range of one mile from the target. They had a delay of three seconds and a burning time of three seconds at 3.75 million candle power. They were fired in succession from a multi discharger.

ANTI SUBMARINE 4 INCH FLARE
This was a parachute flare of two million candlepower that burned for between 50 and 70 seconds. It could be dropped from a flare chute or the bomb bay at a range of between 1.5 and 1.25 miles from the target. Minimum height of release was 500 feet.

RECONNAISSANCE FLARE 4.5 INCH
This had a minimum height of release of 3000 feet and was bomb bay carried.

SONOBUOYS

Professor P. M. S. Blackett, the head of an Admiralty committee, had an idea for an expendable sonar buoy, as it was then called. The idea was to drop it from ships to detect trailing submarines. However the USN tested it as an airdropped buoy in March 1942. It was successful and the first operational sonobuoy was the AN/CRT-1, which entered service in June 1942. It had six radio frequencies which were colour coded for the operator, namely purple, orange, blue, red, yellow and green or POBRYG for short.

The buoy consisted of a flotation chamber, a hydrophone and its connecting cable, a transmitter and aerial and a small parachute to stabilize and control the descent.

Sonobuoys are classified by size, namely A, B, C etc and by type, namely active, passive or measurement. A bathy thermo buoy is a measurement buoy and measures the water temperatures through selected depths. The USN uses mainly the "A" size and was the size of the "POBRYG" series, which was also used by Coastal Command. It is small enough to be hand dropped.

The RAF went on to develop the "C" size buoy, which was bomb bay launched and much bigger. This initially was a passive directional buoy and a bearing was displayed on a screen in the aircraft. It came into service in 1959. Depending on water conditions, ranges of up to 4000 yards could be obtained. The next development was the active "C" size buoy, which gave a range up to 2000 yards. These buoys were combined into the Mark 1c Sonics system and which was used by the Shackleton and the Nimrod Mark 1.

Meanwhile the Americans developed the "A" size buoy into passive directional and active buoys. These were used by the Lockheed P-3 Orion and the Nimrod Marks 1 and 2. Initially the cable length was fixed, which meant that if there was a layer below that depth nothing could be heard. Eventually a way was found to tie up an extended cable and to it cut remotely from the launching panel if bomb bay released, as in the Shackleton and Nimrod. This gave a longer cable length. Thus two lengths were available, typically, 60 feet or 140 feet. The "A" size buoy is usually released from a launcher inside the aircraft and could be loaded while airborne. The cable length can be selected at this point.

The use of sonobuoys was to locate a submarine after a visual or radar detection and was not considered to be a detection device due to its short range. Sonobuoys have now developed to such a degree that they can now be considered to be detection devices. The transmitter of the buoy operates on a number of channels far greater than the early days of the POBRYG system. There is one channel for each buoy. Thus a field of buoys may be laid, the buoys spaced at about one and a half times the detection range for a submarine in the prevailing water conditions. This could be around two miles. Once a submarine is heard, Doppler frequencies would be calculated and efforts made to establish the centre frequency, that is, the frequency when the boat is abeam the buoy. Once that is known, frequencies approaching and departing from the buoy are known and a reasonable fix made. However, that would not be sufficiently accurate for an attack. Buoys may now be laid much closer together, perhaps in the form of a chevron, and accuracy achieved. The use of the MAD in the final stages would give much greater accuracy, assuming that the boat was not too deep.

MAGNETIC ANOMALY DETECTOR (MAD)

Metallic objects cause a slight change in the magnetic field of the Earth. The magnetic anomaly detector senses this. The maximum range is about 1500 feet, which means that the aircraft has to fly low. It also means that a very deep submarine might not be detected, however the accuracy is good. In the Second World War Catalinas flew MAD patrols over the Straits of Gibraltar. The detection equipment is housed in the "sting tail" of the aircraft.

CHAPTER NINE

TORPEDOES

Rear Admiral Sir Christopher Cradock, one of the last captains of the old Britannia before she was condemned and supplanted by the College (Dartmouth), wrote of torpedoes in 1908: "A boat once fired a torpedo. It was considered lost. For the whole day they searched and then returned to harbour sorrowfully. Then they found it had never left the tube; and Whale Island whispered, "I thought your Service never had misfires". After that we sent them the motto of the Submarine Service worked in silk on a cloth of gold. "Guns is Dead". They were not; not yet. It was the guns of von Spee's squadron that sent Sir Christopher and most of his old ships to the bottom off Coronel. For years to come, navies reckoned their battleships as the visible sign of their power.

(the above information from A. J. Smithers' book Taranto 1940. *Published by Leo Cooper 1995. 190 Shaftesbury Avenue, London WC2H 8JL; an imprint of Pen & Sword Books Ltd, 47 Church St., Barnsley, South Yorkshire. S70 2AS.)*

The flying machine, be it aeroplane, seaplane or flying boat was quickly perceived as something with a future, even if the nature of it was a little obscure. One purpose was obvious. Battleships, even Fisher's dreadnoughts, did not shoot very well. When eight of them, anchored, had bombarded Alexandria in 1882, they fired 3000 rounds at the Egyptian forts. Only ten hit. As ranges grew longer the difficulties of observing the fall of shot were increased. This was a job for airmen. If they spotted effectively and reported back, the big gun would be king again.

For a service whose whole history had been devoted to attack in all circumstances, it might be thought that it would have been the first to study how the torpedo might have been launched from the air. It was not.

In 1911 or so aircraft were barely capable of carrying the pilot, let alone a half-ton torpedo. The intricate propulsion system of the torpedo was easily damaged and it demanded launching at a precise angle in order to do its job. However in 1911 Captain Guidoni of the Regia Aeronautica, flying a Farman with an 80 hp Gnome rotary engine, carried out a successful launch. This would have been a worry to the Admirals.

Commander Murray Sueter was instructed to enquire into the matter. In 1913 he persuaded Sopwith to build an aircraft that would do the same thing as the Italians and this was achieved at Calshot at the end of the year. Few people took much notice. It was the era of the Dreadnought and the battlecruiser. Navies remained masters of their seas because their lines of great ships and great guns were more than a match for their enemies. Everything else was there only to make possible bigger Trafalgars. Aircraft, it was grudgingly admitted, might have some function analogous to the frigate in working ahead and telling the battle line where to form, but they were no more expected to take part in the battle than the scorers in a cricket match.

However on 3 April 1915, 22 days before Gallipoli, Winston Churchill minuted his Director of the Air Division that "The torpedo seaplane must be strenuously pressed forward, the object being to use at least ten machines carrying torpedoes for a night attack on German ships of war lying at anchor."

In the Mediterranean, the old 350-foot Isle of Man ferry *Ben-My-Chree* had been transformed into a seaplane carrier. She carried four Short 184s, each powered by a 225 hp Sunbeam Mohawk engine and carrying a 14-inch torpedo between the floats. The British submarine E-14 had attacked a Turkish merchantman and left her dead in the water. Flight Commander Edmonds sank her with one torpedo. Flight Lieutenant Dacre had force landed his Short on the water due to engine trouble. Having been repaired, he was taxiing for take off when he sighted a Turkish tug. He turned towards her and sank her with his torpedo. This opened up the possibility that aircraft could equally well sink much larger ships and that further study and money were required. However, Churchill left the Admiralty and the Admirals took another view.

In 1915 RNAS aircraft joined submarines during the Gallipoli campaign, interdicting Turkish supply lines to the peninsula. The aircraft probably made seventy attacks, spotted for gunfire from warships and guided a submarine to a concentration of shipping. This was a preview of the activities of the German Focke Wulf Kondor (FW200) against Allied convoys in the Second World War. This airborne campaign was the first use of torpedo bombers in combat and caused the Turkish and German commands some serious concern.

Another example was in 1917, when German torpedo-armed seaplanes from Zeebrugge instigated a series of attacks against British shipping in the Straits of Dover. As in Gallipoli this caused serious concern, this time to the British, and anti-aircraft guns were mounted on the merchantmen and a unit of fighters was based at Walmer to fly patrols over the convoys. These attacks lasted until September, three ships being sunk and three torpedo bombers shot down.

These examples showed the problems with the torpedo bomber. The major one was the ability to carry only the smaller types of weapon, that is the 18-inch torpedo, or in the case of the Germans, the 450mm version. The British used a single-engine floatplane which had difficulty taking off, even with only the one crewman and a low fuel load. The Germans used the twin-engine aircraft but these were difficult to fly. The attacks also demonstrated that to be successful the aircraft had to fly at low level where all shipboard guns could be brought to bear. In August came a preview of the Mosquito and Beaufighter Strike Wings in the Second World War, when a squadron of six British motor torpedo boats was wiped out by German seaplanes with machine gun fire. However, before the Strike Wings there were the Swordfish of the Fleet Air Arm and the Beauforts of Coastal Command.

Interestingly, apart from a number of Torbeaus-Beaufighters carrying torpedoes, the favoured anti-shipping weapon became a combination of cannon and rockets. These aircraft were reckoned to have the punch of a broadside from a cruiser. The depth charge was the favoured weapon for an attack against a submerging submarine which could still be partly seen, but for an attack later than this, the favoured weapon became the torpedo. Late in the Second World War an aircraft-carried anti-submarine torpedo came into use. This was the passive Mark 24 torpedo, which homed on cavitation and other noises. It was called a mine for security purposes. After WW2, the Mark 30 or Dealer "B" anti submarine torpedo, another passive weapon, came into service followed later by the Mark 44 active torpedo.

CHAPTER TEN

COASTAL – CONVOY PATROLS AND SEARCHES

On joining a convoy for escort duties, the Maritime Patrol Aircraft is given a patrol by the Surface Escort Commander, sometimes known as the Senior Naval Officer (SNO) or the Officer in Tactical Command (OTC). It is he who knows where the threat comes from. To define an area by latitude and longitude or bearing and distance from the convoy would take up valuable radio time and therefore standard patrols to cover all circumstances were devised and given names. The following were the patrols used in the Second World War:

ADDER "Y". To patrol ahead or astern or on any bearing from the convoy at between eight and fourteen nautical miles, given as "Y", on a patrol line of 30 nautical miles, ie 15 nautical miles either side of the intended movement of the convoy.

ALLIGATOR. (PORT or STARBOARD). To patrol on the side indicated at 10 nautical miles from the convoy on a line parallel to the intended movement of the convoy. The line was to be 20 nautical miles in length, ten nautical miles ahead and astern abeam of the convoy.

COBRA "Y". "Y" is the distance from the convoy. To patrol around the convoy in a box, where "Y" is the distance to the centre of each side of the convoy. The patrol was relative to the convoy's mean line of advance (MLA) and thus moved with the convoy's speed. It was used to provide a defensive perimeter patrol around a stationary or slow moving object, i.e. one moving at less than five knots.

CROCODILE "Y". To patrol ahead of the convoy from one side to the other of the intended movement of the convoy at the given distance, "Y" nautical miles.

FROG "Y". To patrol astern of the convoy at a distance "Y" nautical miles. The length of the patrol line was "Y" nautical miles either side of the convoy's intended movement extended astern.

VIPER. To patrol around the convoy at the visibility distance.

"X" PYTHON "Y". Where X equals a bearing and "Y" equals a distance. This would have been used when a U-Boat had been reported either visually or by HF/DF and the operator was confident of the estimated range. Bearings do not give a range, but a good operator can give an estimate by strength of the signal. A square search would have been carried out at the end of the bearing for around twenty minutes. HF/DF means High Frequency Direction Finding and was a method of detecting the presence of a submarine when that submarine transmitted a message on HF radio.

"X" LIZARD "Y". Similar to the Python but without the square search.

"X" MAMBA . Search along bearing "X" for twenty nautical miles and then return for further instructions.

TOAD. This was used when the direction from which the threat might come was not known and was suitable for up to two aircraft. It provided all-round protection to a convoy and was intended to give advance warning of a submarine approaching within radar or ASDIC range. The U-Boat was assumed to have a maximum speed of 17 knots and the aircraft are assumed to cruise between 120 and 150 knots. Toad Able provided cover for a force moving at 5-10 knots with one aircraft, Toad Baker for a force moving at 11-15 knots and Toad Charlie was designed for two aircraft protecting a force moving at between 5-15 knots.

TORTOISE PORT OR STARBOARD. This could be flown by one aircraft alternating between port and starboard or two aircraft, one on the port and the other on the starboard of the convoy's MLA. It was designed to hamper submarines within the leading lines of submerged approach by forcing them to exercise caution in the use of periscope, snort and radar mast.

RATTLESNAKE PORT OR STARBOARD. This was designed to hamper submarines using speed on the surface to enter the leading lines of submerged approach.

SEARCHES

When intelligence was gained about submarines in the vicinity of the convoy in the form of a radar fix or a High

Frequency Direction Finding (HF/DF) bearing, the escorting aircraft would be sent on a search.

BUZZARD. This was used when a bearing only had been obtained. The aircraft would be sent to search the bearing and then return. If the aircraft used its radar the U-Boat would stay down and thus fall behind the convoy.

KESTREL. This was used when a bearing and distance had been obtained. The aircraft would fly along the bearing to the distance of the fix and then commence a square search for 20 minutes and then return to the force. If the fix was good then the aircraft could fly directly to it.

FALCON. This was used when the Escort Commander wished to examine a sector of 60 degrees on any bearing from the convoy to a shallow depth. The search was ordered by giving a bearing and the distance in nautical miles to be searched. The aircraft would fly tracks at right angles to the bearing with a track spacing of six nautical miles. A depth of 36 nautical miles could be searched by a 150-knot aircraft in one hour.

CHAPTER ELEVEN

MARITIME PATROL
OPERATING AREAS

A number of predesignated operating areas were set up for Maritime Patrol Aircraft. These were:

Enclose I and II in March 1943.

Derange: 4500N to 4900N and 01000W to 01200W, 13 April to 6 June 1943.

These were changed to Musketry and Seaslug.

Musketry: 4330N to 4730N OO930W to 01130W. To be swept by seven aircraft at a time on parallel tracks and carried out three times daily during daylight. It was assumed that U-Boats would submerge at night to avoid Leigh Light aircraft and would therefore surface at first light and reform into their groups. The first sweep aircraft had to be well into the area by dawn. During daylight, Leigh Light Wellingtons were to be used. On 14 June 1943 the area was 4345N 01130W/4730N 001130W/4730N 00945W/4345N 00945W. On 27 June it was 4345N 01200W/4800N 01200W/4800N 00945W/4345N 00945W. In July 1943 the area became 4345N 01200W/ 4800N 01200W/4800N 00930W/ 4345N00930W/. It was extended 4310N to 4500N and

00830W to 01000W avoiding the Spanish coast. A further area 4230N to 4430N and 01000W to 01200W was established.

Seaslug: 4400N to 4730N 01300W to 01500W. To be patrolled by VLR (Very Long Range) aircraft and/or LR (Long Range) aircraft from 15 Group during the day when convoy situations permitted. The patrols were to be co-ordinated by AOC 19 Group in conjunction with his own aircraft. During daylight, Leigh Light Catalinas were to be used. This area was moved further east on 27 June when it was realised that Ju88s had not interfered too much with Coastal Command aircraft. The area became 4300N to 4730N and 01200W to 01400W.

In June 1943 it was realised that U-Boats could detect ASV Mk II transmissions. Aircraft fitted with this radar were to keep their radars on continuously in order that aircraft fitted with centrimetric radar would have a better chance of detection, surprising the U-Boats.

Percussion: There was a conference at Plymouth where it was agreed that Captain Walker, commander of the 2nd Escort Group would have an aircraft allocated to him, under his personal control, to provide a direct link with sightings within his range. At debriefing the crew would give MHQ knowledge of the group's location, the commander's intentions and any other information. Because of the need for radio silence this would have been passed to the crew by Aldis. No 19 Group would also pass to the group confirmation of all positive sightings to avoid wasting time and resources chasing after suspected U-Boats or any swirls that could, for example, be whales.

In April 1944 Operation Pitchbown was established

in the North West Approaches and in August 1944 operation CX was set up in the same area. Operation Dredger was set up in the Bay of Biscay in July 1944.

CHAPTER TWELVE

COASTAL SEARCH AND PATROL

◉

It should be noted that looking for submarines and surface ships does not mean flying around the ocean aimlessly. First, it is useful to have some intelligence of the whereabouts and intentions of the target. Second, there are specific search forms that may be undertaken. Third, the weather and specifically the visibility are important. Fourth, the size of the target is important. A submarine periscope is less likely to be seen visually or on radar than a surfaced submarine.

A search is the systematic examination of an area to either confirm or deny the presence of a target.

A patrol is the systematic movement along a track or tracks to detect a target which is expected to cross that track.

SEARCHES

PARALLEL TRACK SEARCH
This may be used when plenty of aircraft are available. A number of aircraft fly parallel tracks spaced 2D apart, where D equals the detection distance, in perfect line abreast. Good visibility to avoid collisions is vital and quick fixing is necessary. It is suitable for a quick search of a large area.

CREEPING LINE AHEAD SEARCH (CLA)

Here the aircraft flies a series of parallel tracks joined at the ends by short legs whose length equals twice the detection distance, (D). This is used usually when the target is stationary but can be used against a moving target provided the direction of the creep is the same as that of the target and that the speed of the creep is greater than the speed of the target. This search is most useful for search and rescue sorties.

MODIFIED CLA

In a search and rescue creep where the target is a dinghy, the detection distance will be very small. The track spacing may be as little as half a mile. In this case a modified CLA is used and it is impossible to turn the aircraft on to the next track due to its close proximity. The tracks are drawn on a chart parallel to each other at twice the detection distance apart (2D) and numbered. Track number one is flown and the aircraft turned on to track seven. When that track is flown the aircraft is turned onto track two and then eight and so on. Tables are available to calculate the rate of turn required to go from one track to another but more commonly the navigator's Ground Position Indicator (GPI) is used to "con" the pilot round.

SQUARE SEARCH

This is the search used when at the Estimated Time of Arrival (ETA) nothing is sighted, or, against a submarine known to have dived at a certain time and the direction of movement is unknown. The tracks are at right angles to each other and orientated into wind, down wind and cross wind to simplify the track keeping. The length of the legs is 2D for the first two, 4D for the next two, 6D for the next two and so on.

PATROLS

LINE PATROL

This is the simplest of all and is usually near a point of land at each end. It is secure, but wasteful in that the centre point is covered frequently.

CROSSOVER PATROL

This is more efficient than the line patrol. It has the look of a bow tie with the ends aligned with the probable direction of approach of the target.

BOX PATROL

This is exactly what it says, a box, and is used when the direction of approach of the target is unknown. It is not particularly suitable for one aircraft. Such patrols were flown in the English Channel during the invasion of Normandy in 1944, when sufficient aircraft were available to saturate the Channel with air cover.

PERIMETER PATROL

This patrol isolates a given area and is designed to detect a target either leaving or entering it.

In addition to the above searches and patrols there were a number of screening plans which the Officer in Tactical Command (OTC) of a convoy could direct an escorting aircraft to use. The choice depended on the threat and the direction of the threat. There were specific ones that could be used to investigate HF (High Frequency) radio bearings (HFRF), sometimes called Huffduff, obtained from a submarine's radio transmission. Such a search might be along the bearing for a judged distance when the radio operator could make an estimate, or it might be along the bearing for a known distance. The aircraft crew would investigate and perhaps loiter in the area for a time.

TACTICS

In the early days, of the First World War, tactics used by crews would have been a simple visual search, either for a submarine known to be in an area or to sanitise an area to keep a possible submarine submerged. If a submarine was found it would have been attacked. If the attack missed or perhaps the aircraft arrived too late to make an attack and the boat had submerged, then Gambit or Baiting tactics were used. This meant that the aircraft would leave the area and return, say between 45 and 90 minutes later, and hope to catch the boat on the surface. It must be remembered that the submarine commander preferred to be on the surface, where he could make best speed and keep his batteries charged. Once submerged the speed dropped and the batteries started to discharge with use, and the boat might not catch its target. A submariner does not like aircraft.

Later in the war hydrophones were used, but this meant that the flying boat had to land and switch off its engines. Not a satisfactory position.

Nothing much had changed by the start of the Second World War. However, by the early 1940s radar had arrived and this improved the detection opportunities. Then the

Germans found that that they could detect radar transmissions using an equipment called Metox and the U-Boat dived before the aircraft arrived on top. This was useful, because it delayed the boat as before. The aircraft would then use a Gambit and hopefully find the submarine again. Better weapons came on the scene, in particular what was then called the Mark 24 mine to fool the Germans, but was in fact a passive homing torpedo. Passive meant that the weapon did not transmit sound, unlike the 1950s and 1960s torpedoes.

Captain John Walker, the Escort Group commander, devised a surface tactic whereby one vessel would hold a U-Boat in contact on ASDIC and direct other vessels on to the contact. This was similar to the Vectac, or Vector Tactic, used years later by aircraft co-operating with ships or helicopters. The ship or helicopter would hold contact and direct the aircraft to the target either visually or by radar.

Sonobuoys were developed in the Second World War. These were passive and non-directional, did not transmit a sonar pulse and were limited in frequency. Each frequency was given a colour name, namely purple, orange, blue, red, yellow and green. A five-buoy pattern, POBRY, after the initials of the colours, was dropped on a dived contact, one on the datum and the other four at 2500 yards and 90 degrees removed from each other. A sonics operator listened to each buoy in turn and reported the strength of signal received to the Navigator. He would plot his buoys on a chart and draw concentric circles around each plotted buoy at 500, 1000, 1500, 2000 and 2500 yards. Each increment of 500 yards was a signal strength. The first 500 yards was strength five, 1000 was strength four, 1500 was strength three, 2000 was strength two and 2500 was strength one. These strength indications would then provide a fix which the navigator would plot and an attack mounted. The green buoy was available for an extension to the pattern.

The UK developed its sonobuoys into the type "C" active and passive directional buoys. These were large and heavy and were carried in the bomb bay. They were really a localisation system as opposed to a detection system. In other words a detection by another system, eg visual or radar, had to be made before the Mark 1c sonics system could be used. Despite that, it was very effective.

The US Navy meantime developed the above non-directional or "A" sized buoy system. By dropping a small explosive charge alongside a passive buoy in the water the buoy became in effect, active, and was called Explosive Echo Ranging (EER). This system of passive and EER buoys was the Jezebel system. Eventually a field of 12 or 24 buoys could be laid in an area through which a submarine would be expected to pass and thus it became a detection system. Measuring the Doppler shift in the frequency of the target being tracked and the dropping of buoys close together meant that submarines could be tracked closely and attacked.

The Magnetic Anomaly Detector (MAD) is a device for detecting a change in the earth's magnetic field. This change could be caused by the presence of a submarine or a wreck. The detection range is about 1500 feet and can be used to refine the sonobuoy tracking. An aircraft carrying such equipment is recognised by the characteristic "sting tail", a pointed boom sticking out of the rear of the aircraft.

Submarine/air barriers were a means of co-ordinating the abilities of the submarine and the aircraft to detect other submarines. Such a barrier would be laid in areas like the Iceland/Faeroes, Faeroes/Shetland and Shetland Norway gaps. The aircraft would flood the area with radar, causing the enemy boat to dive and use batteries to exhaustion. The submarine would eventually be forced to snort and use his diesels, creating noise and providing a detection opportunity for the allied boat lying in wait with a passive acoustic watch.

At first radar was used continuously, but with the advent of the search receiver, the Metox, intermittent scan was used. This would confound the search receiver operator in that he knew that an aircraft was present but did not know if it was an immediate threat. Thus the submarine commander might well take the risk and remain on the surface or snorting. If he did not then he was slowed down and forced to use battery power. If the aircraft track was made random the enemy operator could be confused even further.

CHAPTER THIRTEEN

COASTAL NOTES

ASDIC
This name was derived from the initials of the Anglo-French Anti-Submarine Detection Committee, which was set up in 1917 to find a counter-measure to the U-Boat. A beam of sound is transmitted from a transmitter encased in a dome below the ship's hull. When the beam hits an object an echo is returned. From this the range and bearing of the object can be determined but not the depth.

When it was first used in 1918, it was announced that never again would the submarine be a threat. But Otto Kretschmer used a tactic of surfacing inside a convoy and torpedoing merchant ships as they sailed past him. ASDIC did not discover him.

LIMITATIONS
Range 1500-2000 yards at 15 knots in a moderate sea. As speed increased the range was reduced.

Performance deteriorated as swell and sea state increased.

Wrecks, tidal rips, shoals, rocks, other ships in the vicinity operating ASDIC and artificial decoys transmitted from U-Boats could send back echoes.

In some water conditions, layers at different temperatures could bend the transmissions, thus hiding the target. This is called layering.

ASDIC lost contact with a deep target at around 750 yards and around 150 yards with a shallow target. This could give some idea of the depth of the target. It was also a "blind period", which meant that the U-boat could be taking evasive action, unknown to the attacker.

The course and speed of a target was estimated by the rate of change of angle combined with Doppler effect.

There were about 200 escorts equipped with ASDIC at the outbreak of war.

A U-boat could dive below the maximum depth of a depth charge.

The system had not been thoroughly tested in peacetime in convoy conditions. No exercises had been carried out between the wars.

When the Germans introduced the acoustic torpedo (Gnat), escorts were equipped with Unifoxer to distract the torpedoes. In so doing they interfered with ASDIC.

CREEPING ATTACK

The directing ship took station behind the U-Boat at a suitable range for maintaining ASDIC contact, roughly 1500-2000 yards, and remained there. The attacking ship under the director's orders proceeded at about 5 knots, taking station about 1000 yards ahead of the director and attacked at this speed. She did not use ASDIC. The director passed continuous ranges and bearings by R/T and told her what course to steer. At the appropriate point the director ordered the attacker to fire. She fired 26 depth charges (DCs) at a previously-ordered setting at 25-yard intervals. When fired, the attacker reported and cleared the area at full speed. The director then went to full speed, dropping 22 DCs over the U-Boat or over the area of the first attack. The pattern was of 18 DCs from the rails and four from the throwers.

The depth charge was developed at the end of the First World War. It contained 300lbs of Amatol and was hydrostatically fused by the crew to fire at a pre-set depth. It could be dropped over the stern, thrown sideways or later, ahead.

INCREASED ARMAMENT ON U-BOATS

On 20 May 1943 Dönitz ordered 10 U-Boats to carry much heavier AA armament. On 29 May 1943 he ordered his commanders to cease diving when detected and to remain on the surface and fight their way through, travelling in groups to achieve maximum fire power. Coastal retaliated by calling up more aircraft and attacking simultaneously.

On 14 July Dönitz had given up this idea and reverted to transiting the Bay submerged, and surfacing to recharge batteries at night.

CONVOYS

A convoy was organised into columns and rows, ships at about half a mile spacing. The position of a ship in the convoy was given according to which column and row it was in. The numbering started at the left front of the convoy. The ship in that position was in column one, row one and was given the number 11. The ship behind was in column one row two and was given the number 12. The ship next to the front left was in column two row one and was given the number 21 and so on. The convoy would be in a rectangular pattern because it is compact and escorts can get round it satisfactorily. Flag signals can be seen more easily and the pattern is manoeuvrable. The risk of collision is minimised and the ships provide support against aircraft attack.

The Commodore was in the ship in the middle of row one and in the centre column, that is, the lead ship of the centre column. If there were an odd number of columns then he would be in the ship to the right of the centre. The proximity of each ship to the next made for difficult station keeping, for which Merchant Masters were not trained. The speed of the convoy was the speed of the slowest ship and while the Naval Control of Shipping Officer (NCSO) tried to match ships with similar speeds, this was not always possible. Thus, masters of faster ships could have difficulty in controlling their vessels at slow speeds. At night, ships would be darkened, which added to the difficulties of station keeping.

The Commodore was the officer in command of the merchant ships. He was usually a retired Naval Flag Officer in the rank of Commodore or above, or he could be a Merchant Navy captain in the rank of Captain Royal Naval Reserve (RNR). He had with him a Yeoman of Signals and several, probably three, signalmen. This caused a problem in accommodation in the merchant ship to which they were assigned, as there was little available. The Commodore was responsible for the navigation of the convoy, course changes, zigzags and so on. He would be supported by a Vice Commodore and sometimes by a Rear Commodore.

The officer in command was known as the escort commander, the Senior Officer Escort (SOE) or the Officer in Tactical Command (OTC). He was responsible for the "safe and timely arrival of the convoy." He would give the order to change the course of the convoy and the Commodore would implement that order. However, it should be noted that it would be a foolish man who ignored the advice of the Commodore, who probably had more seatime than the SOE.

Coastal convoys were different from ocean convoys. These sailed the Channel and the North Sea, where minefields were laid. Consequently, the convoys sailed in narrow swept channels and thus were long and thin as opposed to short and wide and therefore difficult to escort. Ships were expected to double the number of lookouts, but the ship owners were not keen to provide the extra sailors as this was a competitive trade. These convoys were numbered FN1 (north going) and FS1 (south going) to FN100 and FS100. At this point the numbering was restarted.

Coastal convoys came under attack not only from submarines, but aircraft and E-boats. This last was a kind of torpedo boat. On occasion they came under fire from long-range shore batteries. Then in common with ocean convoys, once in port, they were subject to further bombing attacks but with no chance of taking avoiding action.

The commodores of these convoys came from the lieutenant commanders or commanders of the RNR. These were experienced masters of merchant ships who had undergone annual training with the Royal Navy. If there was a problem finding accommodation for ocean commodores, it was greatly accentuated on the coastal convoys as there, the ships were in the main small coasters. The masters of these ships were not keen on having someone telling them what to do.

Before sailing there was a convoy conference which the masters and their radio officers attended. The convoy route, speed, special signals and expected threats from U-Boats, surface warships and minefields were briefed. Each ship was given a particular place in the convoy. A Meteorological Officer would brief the expected weather. Warnings about straggling and making too much smoke were given. Once at sea radio silence was imposed making this briefing very important.

The advantages of the convoy system are:

The number of targets is reduced in a given time.

Escorts may be placed where they are most effective, defending many ships and in an area where submarines could appear.

Good for the morale of merchant ship crews.

The disadvantages are:

The speed of the convoy is the speed of the slowest ship.

Congestion of shipping at the arrival port giving the enemy a large target. It is also a cost to the shipowner and is one of the reasons why they do not like the system.

Delays in turn round when forming the convoy. Again another reason why the shipowners do not like it.

Problems in station keeping and the consequent risk of collision.

It provides a larger target when found.

TYPES OF CONVOY
One or more ships sailing together forms a convoy. Some definitions state that an escort must be present.

TRADE CONVOY
Speed is about 7-10 knots and carries food and materials.

TROOP CONVOY
Speed is 12-20 knots carrying troops and military equipment. It will zigzag to avoid being hit.

TANKER
Speed again is about 12 -20 knots and size is small. It was sailed separately from a trade convoy because of its high strategic value. It will zigzag.

MONSTER
This consists of probably a single large ship such as one of the "Queens" sailing independently at around 26 knots. It relies on its speed to avoid attack.

A convoy would have been subject to several alterations of course during its voyage. Some of these would have been ordered by MHQ to meet a strategic situation, in which case it would have been made known to a maritime patrol aircraft (MPA) going out to meet it. However, the OTC would also have ordered alterations to meet a tactical situation, in which case the MPA would be unaware of it due to radio silence. Thus there were many times when the MPA could not find the convoy. The captain would then transmit a "Not Found" or "Not Met" message and request instructions. The aircraft would probably carry out a suitable patrol.

Before joining a convoy the aircraft crew would check in with the OTC, giving their details and ensuring that "guns were tight" ie would not fire on the aircraft. Naval gunners were notoriously trigger happy and had reason to be. The OTC would then give the crew an area to search, usually outside the leading lines of submerged approach. His own ships would take care of the area inside those lines.

Convoys were identified by combinations of letters and numbers:

HX plus a number was a Halifax convoy.

SC plus a number was a slow Atlantic convoy.

ON was Outbound North.

ONS meant Outbound South.

HX-BX was Halifax to Boston.

UGF, UGS: New York to Gibraltar and back.

GUF, GUS: Fast, Slow

CU-UC: Fast Caribbean to UK and Return.

OT-TO: Tanker convoys Caribbean to Gibraltar and return.

KMF, KMS, MFK, MKS: UK to Mediterranean.

WS: Military convoy.

OS, SL: Slow UK - Sierra Leone and other West African ports.

UR and RU: UK to Iceland and return.

PQ and QP, JW and RA: UK to Russia and return.

RADAR AND DETECTION AIDS

There was no radar fitted to Coastal aircraft at the outbreak of War in 1939, although experiments were in progress. The hunting of enemy submarine and surface forces depended on reliable intelligence, visual lookout and accurate navigation. As flying had to be over water at low level and with no fixing aids available, the navigation was Dead Reckoning (DR). In reasonable weather when the sea is visible and winds can be measured, good results will be obtained. However, if this is not the case, position information can be well out.

Radar (Radio Detection And Ranging) is the means of finding something by the transmission of radio energy. Radio waves travel at a speed of 300,000 kilometres per second. Nowadays there are primary, secondary and Doppler radars employing the pulse technique. In the beginning there was only primary radar. This is a system where the transmitter sends a pulse at regular intervals. Each pulse is of a defined size and is called the pulse width or pulse length. The pulse width decides the minimum range of the radar. The interval in time between two pulses is called pulse recurrence period (PRP) or interval (PRI).

The number of pulses transmitted in one second is called the pulse recurrence frequency (PRF) or rate (PRR).

Early radars were of metric wavelength and worked on the principle or formula (as they still do) $t = s/v$, where t = time, s = distance and v = velocity. In radar the energy travels twice the distance from radar to reflector or target, so the formula becomes $t = 2R/c$ where t = time between transmission and reception, R = range from radar to reflector and c = speed of propagation of radio energy. By confining the radio energy to a narrow beam and rotating the scanner, the bearing of the reflector can be determined. A wavelength of 10 metres corresponds to a frequency of 30 megahertz. A wavelength of 10 centimetres corresponds to a frequency of 3000 megahertz. The early maritime surveillance radars, ASV Mark I and Mark II, used a wavelength of one and a half metres and a valve called a Klystron. ASV Mark III used a wavelength of 10 centimetres, but a Klystron was inadequate for the purpose. One of the greatest secrets of the war was the Magnetron, which was the valve to handle these wavelengths.

The first radar to enter Coastal Command service was designated ASV (Air to Surface Vessel) Mark I, operating on a frequency of 214 megacycles (m/cs), now called megahertz (mhz) which is a wavelength of 1.4 metres.

The first production sets started trials in November 1939. A dipole transmitter antenna with a reflector gave a beam forwards. The two receiver aerials were fitted to the wings of the aircraft, the polar diagrams overlapping. Thus direction was found by the comparison of the two received signals. The maximum range was found to be five and a half miles at 3000 feet. However, sea returns were present up to four and a half miles. Reducing height minimised the sea returns and gave a maximum range of three and a half miles at around 200 feet and the ability to hold the contact down to half a mile - assuming that the submarine did not submerge!

By the beginning of 1940 twelve Hudsons of Nos 220, 224 and 233 squadrons had been fitted with these sets. ASV Mark I was not a very good radar. It was unreliable and not very effective against submarines. However, it was useful in achieving rendezvous with convoys and for fixing on coastlines. A variation of this set was Long Range ASV, which was a sideways-looking system. Ten transmitter dipoles were arranged in pairs on top of the fuselage and the receivers were fitted to the side of the fuselage. This system could detect submarines at 12 miles.

Work now began on the Mark II version. This had a more powerful transmitter and a more sensitive receiver, giving a better detection range and operating on a slightly lower frequency of 176 m/cs (1.7 metres wavelength) to avoid interference with other radio devices. The aerial system used by ASV Mark I, as stated above, consisted of a forward-looking transmitter and a receiver aerial under each wing. The result was presented on a vertical timebase calibrated in nautical miles, the lowest at the bottom. The contact was shown as a deflection on this timebase. If it was to the left, then the operator would direct the pilot to turn left until the signal was equal on both sides of the timebase. If it was to the right, then the converse applied. In the ASV Mark II the aerials were somewhat different. A sideways looking, Long Range ASV aerial system of eight radiating elements on each side of the fuselage was fitted, the aircraft skin acting as a reflector. On top of the fuselage were four posts, each four feet high, supporting eight reflectors. The forward-looking transmitter aerial was fitted to the nose of the aircraft with the receivers fitted to the wings. The presentation in the aircraft was similar to the ASV I.

The operator could select either the forward or the sideways looking aerials, but not both at the same time. Thus the method of search was to scan at 90 degrees to track and when a contact was gained the aircraft turned on to it and homed in using the forward-looking aerials. At 2000 feet detection range on a beam-on submarine was around 20 miles, 12 miles on an end-on target with sea returns out to five miles depending on sea state. At 1000 feet these distances were reduced by about half. By the end of 1942 the Germans were able to detect ASV II by the use of a radio receiver which was called "Metox". While this reduced the number of detections it forced the U-Boat to dive, thus slowing the speed of advance.

The frequency used at this time was limited, because the valves used could not generate sufficient power at frequencies beyond 200 MHz. If a higher frequency could be used, a smaller aerial system could be employed and indeed rotated. In February 1940 Professor J. T. Randall and Dr. H. Boot built a high power magnetron which generated 500 watts and 3000 mhz. This frequency corresponds to a wavelength of 10 centimetres, which gave the name centrimetric radar to future radars and metric radar to all previous radars.

An airborne version was flown in March 1941. Coastal

Command liked the look of this, but there were other priorities. Fighter Command needed a centimetric radar for their nightfighters as the Luftwaffe were still bombing at night and Bomber Command needed a radar for night bombing. The Coastal version of this radar was ASV III and the Bomber version was H2S, both of them essentially the same equipment, and they came into service at the end of 1942. There was much argument between Bomber and Coastal Commands as to which Command should have the first use of the new radar, H2S in bombers or ASV III in Coastal reconnaissance aircraft. At the end of 1942 Sir Robert Watson-Watt was invited to negotiate, and he wrote a paper on what would happen if the Germans captured an H2S radar. He wrote that there was no substantial evidence that the Germans were aware of the Allied work on centimetric radar.

The worry was that if Bomber Command used it first, it only being a matter of time before an H2S equipped aircraft was shot down, the magnetron secret would be exposed and the Germans would build a search receiver to detect ASV III. This proved to be the case when a Stirling was shot down by a nightfighter, crashing near Rotterdam. German engineers found the magnetron, recognising it for what it was and its wavelength and called it Rotterdam. The centimetric ASV was now compromised, but it took the Germans a long time to build the appropriate search receiver.

The magnetron came as a complete surprise to the Germans. They had no advance warning and had not monitored the frequency spectrum at the centimetric end. The German scientists had calculated that such a radar would not work because radar signals would bounce away from the radar equipment after hitting the target. This is known as super reflectivity. They were partly correct. The phenomenon existed but not to any great degree.

A radar transmitter sends out a pulse which can be detected by a search receiver. A search receiver is not a radar, because it does not transmit pulses. Given the right equipment the direction from which this pulse has been transmitted can be measured. The pulse will decrease in intensity over distance and this means that range can be measured. This is not precise but more in terms of close, medium and far off. However, provided the equipment is calibrated before departure, a competent operator can produce a reasonable plot of the path of the transmitting aircraft. Against that, if the aircraft adopted an intermittent policy of radar transmission the submarine operator can be confused.

The Germans had radar on their surface ships before the British, so it was no surprise to them to find that their opponents had radar on their aircraft. However, it was not until 1942 that Befehlshaber der U-Boote (BdU) felt that the threat was sufficiently serious and that a countermeasure was needed. ASV Mk I had been fitted to aircraft since 1940, but large numbers of aircraft so equipped did not appear until 1942. The Naval Type 286 radar was developed from ASV Mk I and was fitted to surface escorts. This was not much of a threat to U-boats as the number of escorts was low. It was large numbers of ASV-equipped aircraft that worried BdU.

The first radar detector was based on a French set and became the FuMB (Funkmessbeobachter) 1 Metox

R.600, named after the French company. This was fitted to U-Boats from July 1942, but a major problem was that there was no adequate aerial system for the Type VII boats. An aerial made from bits of wood and two lengths of antenna cable was built. The wood formed a cross and the cable was strung over it to form horizontal and vertical receivers. This was known as the Biskayakreuz. This was mounted on a bracket welded to the periscope stanchion. It was normally kept below and brought on deck when the boat surfaced. When the boat had to dive the antenna was thrown down the conning tower, which meant that it was liable to break. This was repairable, but a more serious problem occurred if the cables were caught in the hatch during a dive. This meant that the boat had to resurface, probably in the path of an attacking aircraft. When in operation the cross had to be rotated by hand.

The Metox was connected to the boat's loudspeaker system. An intercepted radar signal caused an audible note to be heard throughout the boat. The higher the radar's PRF, the higher the note. However, some PRFs in the ASV Mk I were so high that an audible note could not be heard. This was solved by the use of a magic eye detector, which lit up depending on the signal strength.

While this may seem to negate the advantage of radar because the U-Boat had dived, and indeed it meant that no visual sighting of the boat was gained when the aircraft came on top, it also meant that the boat now had to use battery power which could only be topped up by coming to the surface and using diesel engines to charge the batteries and propel the vessel. Importantly it also meant that the speed of the boat was reduced. This in turn, meant that the boat was possibly prevented from reaching or keeping up with a convoy. This was one of the objects of the operation, the other of course being to sink U-Boats.

The new ASV III could not be detected, and neither could the American SCR 515 centimetric radar. With the introduction of Metox as a counter to ASV II to U-Boats, Coastal Command and its Allies had little success. However in February 1943, No 19 Group established Operation Gondola, an all-out operation for 12 days, in an area of the Bay of Biscay laid across the U-boat transit routes. The USAAF Liberator Nos 1 and 2 Squadrons were on loan to the Group and were fitted with SCR 517 but not long-range tanks. The Group flew some three hundred sorties and gained 19 sightings and eight attacks. No 2 USAAF Squadron claimed one kill, that of U-519.

The first RAF squadron to operate with centimetric radar was No 172, the original Leigh Light squadron, and that was not until the following month, March. Air Vice Marshal G. Bromet, the AOC No 19 Group, decided to mount a further intensive operation in March called Operation Enclose. He had lost control of the two USAAF Liberator squadrons, which had gone elsewhere, but he did have 32 Leigh Light Wellingtons equipped with ASV III from Nos 172 and 407 Squadrons. This operation yielded 26 sightings and 15 attacks. One boat, U-665, was sunk, and that was by No 172 squadron. The operation was repeated in April and this time 11 sightings were gained and four attacks were made. Once more only one sinking, U-376, was achieved and again it was No 172 squadron that caused it. Operation Derange was mounted after the second Operation Enclosure in a different part of the Bay and this time with ASV III fitted Liberators and Halifaxes. Now the Germans were very worried, and Dönitz ordered his boats to submerge at night and to surface only by day to recharge batteries.

In 1940 Squadron Leader Humphrey de Verde Leigh was working as an administrative officer at HQCC. By chance, the AOC-in-C was Air Chief Marshal Sir Frederick Bowhill, who had been his squadron commander in the First World War when he had been a pilot and had flown anti-submarine sorties. He learned from a fellow officer about ASV and that although it could detect a target and could home to it there was a great difficulty in the last mile or so due to sea clutter in which the target could not be distinguished. He realised that an illuminant was required and he thought of a searchlight mounted on the aircraft. Such a device needed a lot of power to be generated and the only aircraft available was the DWI (Directional Wireless Installation) Wellington which was used to explode magnetic mines. This carried a generator sufficient for the searchlight.

Leigh received the support of the AOC-in-C, but from other sources there was the usual negative attitude. It was "thought" that the light would be too big for the aircraft and a smaller Mercury light was suggested, but it was not certain that it could be obtained. A trial of 1928 was referred to whereby two aircraft would be towing a flare! Leigh rebuffed this decisively.

By May 1941 his searchlight was proven, but then an alternative appeared on the scene. Group Captain Helmore had designed a massive light for airborne use, to be carried by a large aircraft. The power source was so large that it occupied the whole of the bomb bay and it was a fixed beam. Air Chief Marshal Joubert, who had become AOC-in-C Coastal, was in favour of the Helmore Light and sent Leigh back to his administrative duties. He realised his mistake when he found that the light was too brilliant and ordered Leigh back to his project. Leigh's light proved to be a great success. No 172 Squadron was the squadron which put it through its trials and was the first to use it operationally.

After the war the searchlight dropped out of use by British maritime aircraft in favour of flares. The author has some considerable experience of attacking submarines at night (not in the war) and in his view these caused a lot of reflection and the light was to be preferred.

The searchlight came back into Coastal Command with the advent of the Hawker Siddeley Nimrod (HS 801) in 1969. The flares used were 1.75 inch calibre and the dischargers were mounted on the starboard side of the Shackleton near the rear spar. In the roof nearby was a 1.5 inch flash discharger to provide illumination for a photograph.

The Germans introduced the "Naxos" system to counter the ASV III and, in anticipation of this, the British developed ASV VI, a three centimetre radar. It was fitted with an attenuator called "Vixen" which reduced the power when the submarine had been detected, thus giving the impression that the aircraft was flying away from the target. However, all 3 cm radars were allotted to Bomber Command, except for ASV X which was the American-built AN/APS-15. ASV Mk VIA allowed an aircraft to lock onto a U-Boat and also aim the Leigh Light. ASV Mk VIB made blind bombing possible. ASV Mk VII was not fitted to Coastal Command aircraft until after the war. ASV Mk XI was intended for the Fleet Air Arm's torpedo bombers and reconnaissance aircraft. ASV Mk XIII was fitted to the post war Shackleton force which was later re-equipped with ASV21. The Nimrod force was fitted with Searchwater.

CHAPTER FIFTEEN

COASTAL SIGNALS ORGANISATION

In maritime operations a signals organisation is required for passing orders and information:

Between controlling units on the ground, in the air and at sea.

Between ships and aircraft.

Between aircraft.

And for providing:

Navigational aids.

Distress facilities.

Air Traffic Control facilities.

Such channels of communication are:

Land lines for passing operational orders, briefings and debriefings, meteorological information and administration matters.

VHF/UHF/HF frequencies for air to air, air to sea, sea to air, air to ground, ground to air, sea to land and land to sea channels.

Central control of maritime aircraft by a maritime headquarters is essential because:

A standardised procedure adopted by all maritime participants is necessary. Various units taking part using their own procedures would lead to chaos.

The operating authority would be in immediate contact with the Naval operating authority.

It would simplify radio channel allocation.

No individual commander, except at the MHQ, would know the whole operational situation at any one time.

An operating authority would have access to weather information and thus be in a position to divert aircraft in a deteriorating weather situation.

The methods of communication are of three types, depending on whether or not the communicators need to keep their location or identity secure. First is the direct method whereby neither communicator needs to conceal its location. Second is the intercept method, where the originator passes a message to an address and does not need to keep its location concealed or secure. The preamble in the message contains a message to the true addressee to intercept. The message is read back by the receiving addressee, thus providing two opportunities for the true addressee to receive it. Third is the broadcast method, where the receiving addressee's location and/or existence must be concealed. The broadcast method can be used routinely in order to pass area QNHs, that is, the atmospheric pressure at sea level in a given area in order that crews can set this on their aircraft's pressure altimeter to give a true height. Modern aircraft carry a radio/radar altimeter which will give the true height, but there may be occasions when this cannot or may not be used. Such broadcasts will contain Terminal Aerodrome Forecasts (TAFs) and possibly tactical information.

There were four signals organisations. No 1 was used to allow what was then called the Area Combined Headquarters, now the Maritime Headquarters, to exercise control of aircraft except those on convoy escort duties. Aircraft using this organisation transferred to Organisation No 2 during their transit.

Organisation No 2 was used by aircraft operating under the control of their local bases and aircraft in transit to and from operating areas.

Organisation No 3 was designed to be used to link up all maritime forces and controlling units concerned with convoy escort duties and anti-submarine operations.

Organisation No 4 used radio telephone on very high frequencies (VHFRT) and was used for short-range communications with ships and aircraft, fighter direction by ships, communication between aircraft, navigational aids and Air Traffic Control.

Three homing procedures were established. Homing "A" was used where an aircraft wished to home on to a ship. The ship concerned, when permitted to do so, would transmit on medium frequency (MF) and the aircraft would measure the bearing by way of its direction finding loop aerial and then fly down the bearing.

Homing "B" was used when an aircraft wished to home to a ship when it was inadvisable for that ship to transmit on MF. It could also be used by an air strike force, not equipped with DF loops needing to home to a shadowing aircraft. The ship would set a DF watch on a prearranged frequency when so ordered. The homing aircraft would transmit its callsign followed by a ten-second dash and the ship would measure the bearing and pass it to the aircraft on HF. The aircraft would read back the bearing and the ship would confirm or amend accordingly.

Homing "C" was used where an aircraft or ship that could not break radio silence wished to home to an aircraft that was able to transmit. This aircraft, having been ordered to carry out this procedure, would transmit on a prearranged frequency its callsign and a ten-second dash. The ship or aircraft under radio silence would then DF these transmissions and home in. The risk with an air-to-air homing was that of collision, and it was necessary to arrange height separation and a common QNH so that both aircraft could measure height on the same basis. It was suggested that the collision between two No 42 Squadron Shackletons in 1955, off southwest Ireland, was a consequence of such a homing.

CHAPTER SIXTEEN

OUTBREAK OF WAR

◉

On 6 December 1939, Air Chief Marshal Bowhill, Air Officer Commanding in Chief Headquarters Coastal Command, now at Northwood, wrote to the Air Ministry agreeing with the rules of engagement specified in a signal in August 1939. This was the subject of a conference on 30 December 1939. Representatives from the Foreign Office, the Admiralty and the Air Ministry were present. Air Marshal Sir Phillip Joubert de la Ferte was chairman.

At Annex C on the agenda was a report of the bombing of ships by Wellingtons on Christmas Eve 1939. One section of three aircraft sighted four ships of around 1000 tons each in two pairs, in position 5553N 00611E steering due south. The ships were challenged and the aircraft sent the recognition signal. One pair of ships opened fire. The section leader decided to attack. No results were observed and photographs were taken. The Leader, on return was placed under arrest! The matter was currently under investigation by Bomber Command. Seventeen Wellingtons took part, in five sections of three and one of two.

AOC No 16 Group had raised some queries as to what

constituted a vital part of the ship and the lack of adequate bombs. The conference agreed with him and stated that there must be three repeats of the order to stop or alter course. The aircraft were allowed to attack on sight without challenge in a special zone. This was defined as a northern limit of 5630N, an Eastern limit of 00430E thence to 5335N 00430E then due south to Dutch territorial waters, then south east along that part of the Ems estuary to the coast at the German/Dutch frontier, thence along the German coast.

On 23 February 1940 ACM Bowhill wrote to the Air Ministry stating that he agreed with the conference but the revised rules were different and once again confusing. The rules of 30 December 1939 left a little loophole for the escape of suspicious vessels, which were practised in the art of deception and prevarication. The Air Council did not agree but would allow some discretion to captains of aircraft.

Further aircraft should not be ordered to challenge vessels at sea unless engaged in contraband control in co-operation with HM ships or a contraband base.

On 11 April 1940 Air Ministry informed Coastal and Bomber Commands that aircraft may attack without warning any ships, merchant or otherwise, underway within ten nautical miles of the Norwegian coast south of 61N and east of 006E down to 54N. Ships at anchor, if definitely identified as enemy, could also be attacked.

On 21 April 1940 it was announced that all military aircraft East of 10W wearing Danish markings were to be treated as enemy. Faeroese ships, pending new flags, would have "Faeroes" painted on the side. The Germans gave notice of 64 small vessels marked with the Red Cross and detailed for rescuing airmen from the sea. This was rejected by the United Kingdom.

On 16 July 1940 it was decided that ships in Swedish territorial waters could only be attacked if underway. Ships in a defined channel could be attacked at night. In September these types of instructions now spread to cover the South West Approaches and the Bay of Biscay. By February 1941 there was an area in the English Channel where all ships could be bombed, and this was in the vicinity of Dungeness. In March 1941 a signal from HQCC to Nos 15, 16, 17 18 and 19 Groups defined areas in the North Sea, the Bay of Biscay and the English Channel where aircraft might attack ships at sight. In April 1941 some concern was expressed about attacking Dutch fishing vessels, as they carried German wireless telegraphy (W/T) operators. The Dutch government in exile warned their fishermen that they might be attacked. In May 1941 there was some correspondence about the prevention of scuttling enemy warships.

In August 1941 the Admiralty requested that no attacks be made on French sailing fishing vessels in the Western Approaches, as they were a valuable link for intelligence. They should however remain liable to visit and search, as some were known to be made use of by the Germans. There was some correspondence about attacking fishing vessels off Norway, but Military Branch, Admiralty pointed out that regular courier services between Scotland and Norway (the 'Shetland Bus') was bringing an ever-growing stream of refugees. At that time it was around 130 per week and was a very important source of intelligence. It was said that the craft were navigated by desperadoes who required a great deal of latitude in their comings and goings. Effective control of them was not possible. They departed anywhere between Stavanger and Aalesund and arrived anywhere between Aberdeen and the Faeroes. There were some 113 observation posts on the coast of Norway. No attacks were authorised.

On 2 October 1941 the Chief of Staff at HQCC wrote a memo to AOC 19 Group classified Secret, stating that he had been keeping a detailed record of all fishing vessels sighted in the Western Approaches and the Bay of Biscay. A great many were genuine and innocent, but it was a safe assumption that a number were used for intelligence and to assist the safe passage of U-boats to and from Biscay ports. There was definite evidence of this the previous day in the case of two Spanish trawlers off South West Ireland. He believed that they might also compromise "our special equipment", words used to put the Germans off the scent that the Allies were using radar. Two Forms Orange (debriefing reports) by crews of No 221 Squadron in August 1941 mentioned large numbers of tunnymen, which, in the prevailing weather conditions, made the operation of special equipment (radar) difficult. The numbers of contacts and the subsequent homings carried out would signify the presence of radar on board the aircraft. The Chief of Staff recommended the establishment of protected fishing areas.

On 12 November 1941 Sir Phillip Joubert de la Ferte wrote to Brigadier S. G. Menzies, DSO MC (Head of SIS), about French and Spanish fishing vessels, recommending a declared area and if they were outside this they would be sunk (presumably excluding transit lanes). What thoughts did he have on the subject? On 22 November 1941 Menzies agreed.

On 30 December 1941 the Admiralty wrote stating that Coastal's problems were appreciated but they did not want to antagonise the fishermen, who were mostly anglophile, until a sufficient surface force was available to make them powerless to do any harm. This did not exclude the possibility that fishing vessels might have acted for the Germans. Reports from submarines did not show this.

CHAPTER SEVENTEEN

WORLD WAR TWO - 1939

At the outbreak of the war in Europe on 3 September 1939 (although for the Poles it was 1 September) Coastal Command was well organized. Liaison with the Royal Navy was very close and there were joint staffs at the Command Headquarters and at No 15 Group HQ at Plymouth, No 16 Group HQ at Chatham and at No 18 Group HQ at Pitreavie Castle near Rosyth. Initially there was a temporary operations room at RNAS Donibristle. An underground operations room was built at Pitreavie. No 17 Group was responsible for training. In the middle of September an air headquarters (AHQ) was set up at Gibraltar. However, the Command was not well equipped. There existed the following maritime patrol squadrons:

In the United Kingdom:

No 10 Squadron Royal Australian Air Force was formed at Point Cook, Australia in July 1939. It was equipped with Seagulls Mark V, Southamptons, DH60 Moth Floatplanes, Catalinas and Walrus aircraft for training. Air and groundcrew were sent to the UK to convert to the Sunderland flying boat. The UK Government requested that the squadron be allowed to stay, and this was granted by the Australian Government. It was based at Pembroke Dock in South Wales. An aircraft was detached to Tunisia in October.

No 48 Squadron - Anson Mark I based at RAF Thorney Island, Hampshire with detachments at RAF Bircham Newton, Detling, Guernsey and Carew Cheriton. This was the first squadron to be equipped with Ansons, and it trained other squadrons.

No 201 Squadron - London Mark II at RAF Sullom Voe, Shetland.

No 204 Squadron - Sunderland Mark I at RAF Mountbatten, Plymouth.

No 206 Squadron - Anson Mark I at RAF Bircham Newton.

No 209 Squadron - Stranraer at RAF Invergordon, Ross-shire with a detachment at Falmouth.

No 210 Squadron - Sunderland Mark I at RAF Pembroke Dock, South Wales.

No 217 Squadron - Anson Mark I at RAF Warmwell, Dorset.

No 220 Squadron - Anson Mark I at RAF Thornaby.

No 224 Squadron - Hudson Mark I at RAF Leuchars with a detachment at RAF

Aldergrove, Northern Ireland.

No 228 Squadron - Sunderland Mark I, was at Alexandria but returned to RAF Pembroke Dock on 10 September, 1939 only to go back to Alexandria on 10 June 1940.

No 233 Squadron - Anson Mark I and Hudson Mark I at RAF Leuchars, Fife.

No 240 Squadron - Lerwick Mark I and London Mark II at RAF Invergordon with a detachment at RAF Falmouth.

No 269 Squadron - Anson Mark I at RAF Montrose, Angus.

No 500 Squadron Auxiliary Air Force (AAF) - Anson Mark I at RAF Detling.

No 502 (Ulster) Squadron AAF - Anson Mark I at RAF Hooton Park.

No 608(North Riding) Squadron AAF - Anson Mark I at RAF Thornaby.

No 612 Squadron (County of Aberdeen) AAF - Anson Mark I at RAF Dyce, Aberdeen with detachments at RAF Stornoway and RAF Wick.

Coastal Patrol Flights, known as "scarecrow flights", equipped with De Havilland Tiger Moths, except for No 6 Flight which was equipped with Hornet Moths, were established at various airfields:

No 1 at Dyce, Aberdeen.

No 2 at Abbotsinch, Renfrewshire.

No 3 at Hooton Park, Cheshire.

No 4 at Aldergrove, Belfast.

No 5 at Carew Cheriton, Pembroke, South West Wales.

No 6 at St Eval, Newquay, Cornwall.

Each flight was established with nine aircraft and six pilots.

The only armament was a signal or Verey pistol which enabled the pilot to alert any Royal Navy ship in the vicinity to any sighting he may have made. The first sighting was made on 17 December, 1939 when a pilot saw a periscope and dived towards it. The submarine submerged but the Tiger Moth had achieved its purpose, which was basically to force U-Boat commanders to use up their battery strength.

In the early months of the war destroyer escort of convoys went no further than 13 degrees west, which is no more than 100 miles west of Ireland. Coastal Command did its best to provide convoy escort west of the UK, but most of its effort was required in the North Sea. In any event escort could be provided no further than the destroyers, due to the short-range aircraft then in service. However there was an outstanding rescue. The SS Kensington Court, a tramp steamer with 8000 tons of grain, was torpedoed 70 miles west of the Scilly Isles. Two Sunderlands, one from No 204 Squadron and another from No 228 Squadron, intercepted the distress signals. The first aircraft to arrive found an overcrowded lifeboat with a number of the crew hanging on to the outside of the boat. The flying boat crew checked for U-Boat activity and then landed in a heavy swell. The second flying boat arrived, checked for U-boats and also landed. The boats picked up all 34 of the crew and took them back to dry land. A third was also on the scene and provided top cover. The crew of this sighted a surfacing U-Boat, which they attacked. Unfortunately, the bombs hung up (the bomb would not release) and the U-boat dived and escaped.

The North Sea patrols, laid on to locate surface

warships, were also proving successful in locating U-Boats en route to the Atlantic transiting around the north of Scotland. By November 1939 anti-submarine patrols were rated as important as anti-surface patrols. However the aircraft did not have a successful weapon. The 100lb bomb proved to be harmless even when a direct hit was scored and the 250lb A/S bomb could only cause serious damage when it exploded within six feet of the target. Only the Hudson had a distributor in its weapon system to enable it to drop an evenly-spaced stick. The Mark IX bombsight, which could only be used at a height above 3000 feet, was basically for use against stationary targets and of no use whatever against submarines.

In December 1939, after HMS/M *Snapper* had received a direct hit in error by a 100lb bomb dropped by an Anson, the Admiralty began to develop depth charges for air drops. Maritime aircraft may not have had the ability to sink U-Boats but they could, and did, find them. The U-Boats did not know that the aircraft could not sink them and they dived when they were sighted. This slowed them down and caused them problems in gaining contact with convoys and even ruining their attacks.

AIR SEA RESCUE

Search and rescue consisted of high-speed launches of Coastal Command, MTBs from the Royal Navy plus any aircraft that could be spared from the parent unit of the ditched aircraft or any other unit.

TORPEDO BOMBER AND ANTI SHIPPING

There existed the following torpedo anti-shipping strike squadrons:

No 22 Squadron-Vildebeeste Mark IV at RAF Thorney Island, Hampshire.

No 42 Squadron-Vildebeeste Mark IV at RAF Bircham Newton.

Basically the Command was equipped with out-of-date aircraft and virtually no effective weapons. Its main job was to patrol the North Sea looking for surface raiders, which were considered to be main threat. This was a line from Montrose to the South West tip of Norway and was carried out by Ansons. After that the flying boats took over. The *Graf Spee* passed through this area before the patrols started which was on 24 August. The *Deutschland* slipped through before the outbreak of war when all aircraft were grounded by fog. In October, a No 224 Squadron *Hudson* located a battleship, a cruiser and four destroyers off south west Norway. The bomber force sent to attack the ships was unable to carry out its mission due to low cloud. Other sea areas to patrol were the Skagerrak and of course the coastline from Denmark to western France, not forgetting the East Coast convoys. Fighter Command assisted with the latter. The enemy's minelaying efforts had to be watched and damaged shipping had to be escorted back to port.

MIDDLE EAST AIR SEA RESCUE

There was little flying in the Mediterranean area and thus there was little rescue work. There were only four high-speed launches and these were based at Malta, Aden, Basra and Singapore. A launch was sent to Gibraltar later.

No 202 Squadron was equipped with Saro London Mark IIs and was sent from Kalafrana to Gibraltar in September 1940.

TORPEDO BOMBER AND MARITIME PATROL

No 8 Squadron was at Khormaksar with detachments at Riyan, Berbera and Sheikh Othman operating Blenheim Is. No 203 Squadron was at Isthmus, Aden with Singapore IIIs.

FAR EAST AIR SEA RESCUE

A similar situation prevailed here as in the Mediterranean area.

FAR EAST TORPEDO BOMBER AND MARITIME PATROL

No 36 Squadron had reformed at Donibristle, Fife, from the redesignated Coastal Defence Torpedo Flight and was equipped with Horsleys. In October 1930 the squadron was moved to the Far East via Leuchars, arriving in Seletar in November 1930. In July 1935 it re-equipped with Vildebeeste IIIs.

No 100 Squadron was one of those squadrons which had been existence since February 1917 and had not been disbanded after the First World War. In December 1933 it was sent to the Far East, arriving in Seletar in January 1934 equipped with Vildebeeste IIs. In December 1937 it added Mark IIIs to its inventory.

No 205 Squadron had reformed at Seletar from the Far East Flight in January 1929 equipped with Southampton IIs, which it retained until February 1936. In April 1935 it received Singapore IIIs.

TYPES OF AIRCRAFT

The Anson Mk I was fitted with two 320 hp Armstrong Siddeley Cheetah Mk IX engines giving a maximum sea level speed of around 170 mph and a range of about 600 miles. It was armed with one fixed forward-firing Vickers .303 machine gun in the port side of the nose and another in a midupper turret. There was internal stowage for two 100lb bombs and racks for eight 20lb bombs.

The Lockheed Hudson was a derivative of the civilian Lodestar. It was fitted with two Wright GR1820-G102A engines giving a maximum speed of 275 mph. It carried a crew of five, two pilots, one of whom acted as navigator, wireless operator and two gunners. One of these gunners could have been the WOP/AG, in which case the crew was four. It carried two .303 Browning machine guns in the top of the fuselage in front of the pilot, two .303 waist machine guns, one .303 in a retractable prone position beneath the fuselage and a midupper turret fitted with two .303 machine guns. The bomb bay carried up to 1400lbs of bombs or depth charges.

The Supermarine Stranraer was a biplane flying boat fitted with two 1000hp Bristol Pegasus X radial air cooled engines. It had a maximum speed of 165mph and a range of 1000 miles. There was a machine gun and a bomb aiming position in the nose, one gun position amidships and another in the tail.

The Saro Lerwick was a flying boat looking very similar to the Sunderland. It had two Bristol Hercules engines of 1375 hp. It was armed with three power-operated turrets, one in the nose, another in the midupper and the third in the tail position.

The Saro London was a biplane flying boat fitted with two 1000hp Bristol Pegasus X engines giving a range of 1700 miles at around 109 mph, cruising speed of 137mph and a maximum speed of 155mph.

The Short Sunderland Mark I was a development of the Empire Flying Boat. It was fitted with four Bristol Pegasus 22 engines. Armament consisted of a Frazer Nash front turret with twin .303 machine guns, a tail Frazer Nash turret with four .303 machine guns and two hand operated .303 mountings in the upper part of the hull aft of the wings. Bombs and/or depth charges were stored in the hull and wound out to a position underneath the wings. Maximum speed was around 210 mph at 6500 feet. The crew consisted of two pilots, a navigator, an engineer, a wireless operator and three gunners.

The Vickers Vildebeeste was a torpedo bomber.

Apart from the Sunderland, and perhaps the Hudson, these aircraft were inadequate for the conflict to come, and a consequence of Government failure.

Armstrong Whitworth Whitley (RAF) - Wikipedia

Bristol Beaufighter, Canadian Govt - Wikipedia

Bristol Bolingbroke, Canadian Govt - Wikipedia

Handley Page Halifax, UK Govt - Wikipedia

Liberators 120 & 86 Squadrons Aldergrove, IWM - Wikipedia

Mosquito with Molins Gun, IWM, Fg Off Forward - Wikipedia

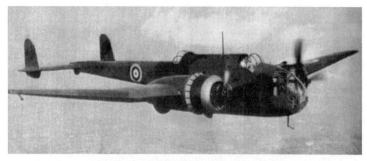

Handley Page Hampden, IWM - Wikipedia

HSL rescuing Halifax crew, IWM, UK Govt - Wikipedia

Saro Lerwick, IWM - Wikipedia

Vickers Warwick UK - Wikipedia

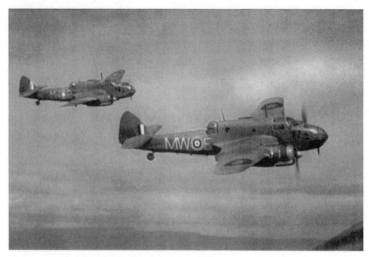

Beauforts of 217 Sqn IWM, Canadian Govt - Wikipedia

Hudson V 48 Squadron, IWM - Wikipedia

U-534 at Liverpool (author)

WW2

Sunderland by Geoff Kirkman

USN Catalina (courtesy Nev Feist)

USN Catalina (courtesy Nev Feist)

Loch Ewe defences (author)

Loch Ewe Gun Defence (author)

USN Catalina (courtesy Nev Feist)

CHAPTER EIGHTEEN

1940

The fall of France meant that the Biscay ports were useable by the Germans. This allowed the U-Boats to transit easily to the North West Approaches. This in turn caused C-in-C Western Approaches, Royal Navy to move to Liverpool and No15 Group moved with it. A new Group, No 19, was formed at Plymouth and was responsible for all Coastal Command bases in South West England and Wales while No 15 was responsible for all Coastal bases in Northern Ireland plus two Scottish bases at Tiree and Benbecula. The Command's aircraft began to operate from Iceland.

DISPOSITION OF SQUADRONS
31 DECEMBER 1940

Sixteen months into the war the number of maritime squadrons had increased, the equipment had improved a little and dispositions had changed.

TORPEDO BOMBER/ANTISHIPPING

No 22 Squadron moved to North Coates with Beaufort Is in April. Detachments were at Manston, St Eval and Wick.

No 42 Squadron gave up its Vildebeeste IIIs in April 1940 in exchange for Beaufort Is and moved to Thorney Island. In June it moved to Wick, leaving a detachment at Thorney Island.

No 48 Squadron equipped with Beauforts Is in exchange for its Ansons in June, still based at Thorney Island with detachments at Bircham Newton, Detling, Guernsey and Carew Cheriton and St Eval. In July it moved to Hooton Park, maintaining the Detachment at Carew Cheriton but changing the others to Aldergrove, Port Ellen, Limavady and Stornoway.

No 53 Squadron had transferred from Fighter Command with Blenheim IVs on 3 July 1940. It was based at Thorney Island with detachments at Bircham Newton and St Eval.

No 59 Squadron transferred from Fighter Command on 5 July 1940 with Blenheim IVs. It was also at Thorney Island with detachments at Manston, Bircham Newton and Detling.

No 217 Squadron exchanged its Ansons for Beaufort Is at St Eval in September 1940 with a detachment at Carew Cheriton.

No 235 Squadron transferred from Fighter Command on 27 February 1940, adding Blenheim IFs to its inventory. In April it moved to Bircham Newton, in May to Detling, early June to Thorney Island and in late June back to Bircham Newton with detachments at Thorney Island and Aldergrove.

No 236 Squadron transferred from Fighter Command on 29 February 1940 and moved to North Coates with Blenheim IFs. In April it went to Speke, in May to Filton, in June to Middle Wallop and in July to Thorney Island, where it exchanged its Blenheim IFs for IVFs. It sent a detachment to St Eval and in August the squadron moved to St Eval.

No 248 Squadron transferred from Fighter Command 26 February 1940 and moved to North Coates. In March it converted to Blenheim IVFs and in early 1940 moved to Thorney Island, only to go to Gosport eight days later. The Blenheim IFs were disposed of in May when the squadron moved to Dyce with a detachment at Montrose. In July the squadron moved to Sumburgh.

No 254 Squadron transferred from Fighter Command on 28 January 1940. It was equipped with Blenheim IFs which were disposed of in April. In January it re-equipped with Blenheim IVFs and was based at Bircham Newton and had a detachment at Lossiemouth. In April it moved to Hatston and in May to Sumburgh. In August it moved to Dyce with detachments at Aldergrove and St Eval.

No 272 Squadron had formed from No 235 and No 236 in November 1940 with

Blenheim IV Fs at Aldergrove.

The year 1939 opened with two Vickers Vildebeeste squadrons allocated to

the antishipping role in the UK. Overseas, No 36 Squadron was in Singapore with Vildebeeste IIIs. This was not a very effective force. However, as 1940 came in, events changed. Both Nos 22 and 42 squadrons re-equipped with Bristol Beauforts and Nos 48 and 217 Squadrons changed role from Maritime Patrol to torpedo bomber and exchanged their Ansons for Beauforts.

Squadrons were sent on what were known as Rover

Patrols. These were patrols on the enemy shipping lanes seeking targets on an opportunity basis. German convoys were protected by surface ships and, inshore, by fighters. They were therefore difficult targets. The method of attack was a single aircraft at a time. They flew at low level at a precise height and at a low speed, otherwise the torpedo would malfunction.

The torpedo bombers were not alone. Bomber Command Blenheims of No 2 Group attacked ships in ports and at sea with bombs, as Coastal Command could not mount an intensive anti shipping offensive in these waters. By June the offensive had intensified to the extent that German convoys had stronger escorts, dedicated flak ships and fighter escorts.

On 21 June 1940 nine Beauforts of No 42 Squadron attacked the *Scharnhorst* with bombs as she steamed along the coast of Norway after she had sunk the carrier HMS *Glorious*. The squadron had equipped with Beaufort Is in April and this was the first attack carried by Beauforts. Unfortunately the crews were not fully trained in torpedo tactics, nor were there any torpedoes at Wick from whence they had come. They therefore had to use bombs. It was a dive-bombing attack on an armoured deck and the bombs were of no use against such a target. There were near misses, but even a direct hit would have made no difference. The *Scharnhorst* had a fighter escort of Messerschmitt bf109s and they shot down three Beauforts.

By October the Government had relaxed the regulations governing attacks on merchant ships and "sink at sight" areas were declared in the North Sea, the English Channel and Biscay.

ANTISUBMARINE/SURFACE SURVEILLANCE 1940

No 10 Squadron Royal Australian Air Force had arrived at Pembroke Dock, South West Wales, in September 1939 and trained under RAAF control on Sunderland Is. It was placed under Coastal Command control in October 1939. The squadron was declared operational in February. In April 1940 the squadron moved to Mountbatten, near Plymouth. On 1 July 1940, the SS *Zarian* in convoy was torpedoed. Flt Lt W. Gibson and crew on convoy escort saw this and a quarter of an hour later found U-26, a type 1A boat commanded by Kapitänleutnant Heinz Scheringer, on the surface. It dived on the approach of the Flying Boat which dropped four 250lb A/S bombs on it. It resurfaced and Flt Lt Gibson dropped a further four bombs. The U-Boat went down and her entire crew was rescued by HMS *Rochester*. After her attack on the convoy she had been depth charged and damaged by the Flower class corvette HMS *Gladiolus*. She was trying to escape on the surface when the Flying Boat crew found her. Gibson was awarded the DFC.

The squadron went to Gibraltar in July 1940, but after a few days it returned to Pembroke Dock. It detached to Oban, Argyll in August and returned to Pembroke Dock in November 1940.

No 201 Squadron with Sunderland Is was at Sullom Voe.

No 204 Squadron with Sunderlands Is was at Sullom Voe.

No 209 Squadron equipped with Lerwick Is was at Pembroke Dock.

No 210 Squadron with Sunderland Is was at Oban,

Argyll with detachments at Reykjavik, Iceland, Sullom Voe and Stranraer. On 16 August 1940 Fg. Off. E. Baker and crew were escorting convoy OA198. The Senior Naval Officer (SNO) tasked them to look for a Norwegian straggler, 20 miles astern of the convoy. Nothing was found but later the SNO advised that the SS *Empire Merchant* had been torpedoed in position 5521N 01340W and tasked them to look for a U-Boat. After some five hours a semi-submerged submarine was sighted and a depth charge dropped on it. The boat was blown to the surface, and a further charge dropped. The boat heeled over and went down, Baker dropping a further four charges. Oil was seen but nothing else. The SNO was informed and a destroyer investigated, again finding nothing. The boat was U-51, commanded by Kapitänleutnant Dietrich Knorr. She was on her fourth patrol and had been damaged. On 20 August 1940 she was sunk by HMS/M *Cachalot*.

No 221 Squadron had reformed in November 1940 with Wellington Ics at Bircham Newton and detachments at Limavady and St Eval.

No 228 Squadron was still at Pembroke Dock with its Sunderland Is. On 30 January 1940, Fg. Off. Edward Brooks and crew were called out and briefed about a U-boat in the vicinity of the Scilly Isles. On arriving in the area the crew received an updated position. Shortly after, the sloop HMS *Fowey* and the French destroyer X.32 were sighted rescuing survivors from a torpedoed ship. Half an hour later a surfaced U-Boat was sighted. A bomb was dropped and then the U-Boat's gunners opened fire. It was believed that the boat was unable to submerge and the Allied ships were called to assist. A bright flash was seen at the stern of the U-boat which then sank. HMS *Fowey* picked up survivors. This was U-55 under the command of Kapitänleutnant Werner Heidel and was on its first patrol, having sunk four ships. On this day she had torpedoed the tanker *Vaclita*, which had been in convoy. The escort, HMS *Whitshed*, had depth charged and damaged her. U-55 was the first U-boat sunk with the help of a Coastal Command aircraft.

No 240 Squadron had Supermarine Stranraers at Stranraer.

No 320 Squadron (basically Royal Netherlands Navy) had Anson Is and Hudson Is at Leuchars with a detachment at Silloth.

No 321 Squadron (again basically Royal Netherlands Navy) had Anson Is at Carew Cheriton. By 18 January 1941 this squadron was absorbed into No 320 Squadron.

No 500 Squadron had Anson Is at Detling.

No 502 Squadron had Whitley Vs at Hooton Park.

No 608 Squadron was at Thornaby with Anson Is.

No 612 Squadron was at Dyce with Whitley Vs, with detachments at Stornoway and Wick.

In January 1940 two Tiger Moths took off from Dyce on a joint patrol. Flying Officer Hoyle sighted a moving oil slick. He contacted nearby destroyers by using his Very pistol and orbited the head of the slick. The destroyer depth-charged the area but no results were seen. The Scarecrow Flights were disbanded in June 1940.

THE HUDSON SQUADRONS

No 206 Squadron with Hudson Is and IIs at Bircham Newton with a detachment at St Eval.

No 220 Squadron had Hudson IIs at Thornaby.

No 224 Squadron now had Hudson IIs at Leuchars with a detachment at Aldergrove.

No 233 Squadron re-equipped with Hudson IIs in October 1940. On 25 October 1940, three Hudsons captained by Plt Off A. Maudsley, Plt Off Winnicott and Plt Off Walsh were 10 miles off Stavanger, South Norway when they sighted U-46, a type VIIB commanded by Kapitänleutnant Engelbert Endrass. Plt Off E. Baudoux was flying Maudsley's aircraft and attacked with 100lb bombs, which fell in a straddle. The U-Boat returned fire, hitting the Hudson. Winnicott then attacked again straddling the target. Walsh made an attack but the bomb release mechanism failed. All three Hudsons returned to base, although Baudoux had problems as his elevators had been shot away. U-46 had been damaged. The squadron moved to Aldergrove in December 1940.

No 269 Squadron had Hudson IIs at Wick with a detachment at Kaldadarnes near Reykjavik in Iceland.

AIR SEA RESCUE

Two pre-war orders for high speed launches were followed by another order in December 1940 but it was not believed that these would be available until late 1941. This order brought the number of launches in use and under production to 66.

MEDITERRANEAN 1940 AIR SEA RESCUE

As there was an increase in reconnaissance over the sea, it was decided to build up the rescue facilities in the Mediterranean area. The initial step was to move the launch at Basra to Hurghada at the entrance to the Gulf of Suez. However, it was felt that there was no need to increase the facilities any further until Italy entered the war in June 1940, when the situation was reviewed. In August, anticipating the campaigns in the Western Desert, HQ Middle East moved the High Speed Launch to Mersa Matruh. Assisted by a suitably modified cabin cruiser, it remained there until autumn 1941.

There were no dedicated rescue aircraft. The Command relied on operational and training units for the first two years of the war.

MARITIME PATROL

No 202 Squadron was at Gibraltar. In October 1940 some Swordfish Seaplanes were added to the squadron. On 18 October 1940 two Londons captained by Flt. Lt. N. F. Eagleton and Flt. Lt. P. R. Hatfield sighted air bubbles and attacked them. The submarine *Durbo*, an Italian Adua class boat commanded by *tenente di vascello* Armando Acanfora, was forced to the surface and attacked by the destroyers HMS *Firedrake* and *Wrestler*. The boat was captured by them.

No 228 Squadron was at Kalafrana, Malta with Sunderland Is and a detachment at Alexandria, Egypt.

No 230 Squadron was at Alexandria with Sunderland Is and detachments at Kalafrana, Malta, Aboukir, Egypt and Scaramanga, Athens. On 28 June 1940 Flt. Lt. W. W. Campbell and crew sighted a periscope, which Campbell attacked with two 250lb anti-submarine bombs. The bow of the boat was seen to rise and then slide vertically down. Oil, bubbles and wreckage were seen. This was the Italian boat *Argonauta*, the lead boat of its class, commanded by Tenente di Vascello Vittorio Cavacchia Scalamonti. It was commissioned on 10 June 1940 and was sunk in this attack. On 29 June 1940 Flt. Lt W. W. Campbell and crew sighted a partly-surfaced submarine from 1000 feet and attacked with two 250lb anti-submarine bombs, achieving a straddle. A follow-up attack was made with two more bombs. Survivors were seen in the sea and Campbell landed the Sunderland and picked up four of them despite deteriorating weather. The boat proved to be the Italian *Rubino*, a class Sirena submarine commanded by Tenente di Vascello Luigi Trebbi. On the return to Malta another boat was seen, but with no more bombs the crew could make only a machine gun attack. With two sinkings in two days Campbell was awarded the DFC.

On 30 September 1940 Flt. Lt. P. H. Alington and crew arrived in position 3135N 02843E, where the Australian destroyer HMAS Stuart had engaged the *Gondar*, an Italian Adua class submarine commanded by Tenente di Vascello Francesco Brunetti. Contact had just been lost, but the Sunderland crew sighted air bubbles two miles from the destroyer and dropped three anti-submarine bombs, one on each bubble, one of which failed to explode. The boat surfaced and Alington made another attack with three A/S bombs. HMAS *Stuart* and an armed trawler opened fire, and the crew abandoned the boat, which then sank.

FAR EAST 1940

No 36 Squadron was still at Seletar with Vildebeeste IIIs with detachments at Kota Bahru, Gong Kedak and Kuantan, Malaya.

No 100 Squadron was still at Seletar with Vildebeeste IIs and IIIs.

No 205 Squadron was still at Seletar with Singapore IIIs.

MIDDLE EAST 1940

No 8 Squadron was at Aden. On 19 June 1940 Flt. Lt. Goodwin and crew gained a visual sighting of *Galileo Galilei*, an Italian Archimedes class boat commanded by Capitano di Corvetta Nardi 10 miles off Aden harbour. The boat opened fire and the aircraft dropped two anti-submarine bombs. The boat dived. It was also seen by a Gladiator pilot of No 94 Squadron. The next day an armed trawler, HMS *Moonstone*, sighted the boat's periscope and attacked with depth charges. The boat then surfaced and opened fire with guns and a torpedo. The boat eventually surrendered and was towed into Aden. The squadron added Maryland Is to the inventory in July, disposing of them in December. Swordfish seaplanes were added to the establishment in August again disposing of them in December.

No 203 Squadron disposed of its Singapores in March and re-equipped with Blenheim Is and IVs in May 1940, moving at the same time to Khormaksar with a detachment to Berbera.

No 244 Squadron reformed at Shaibah from "S" Squadron in November 1940, equipped with Vincents.

CHAPTER NINETEEN

1941

Air Chief Marshal Bowhill, the AOC-in-C, was posted in June 1941 and relieved by Air Marshal Joubert, who had been the AOC-in-C in 1936-37. He had stimulated the development of radar for finding ships. He had been posted to India and on his return had held the post of Assistant Chief of Air Staff (Radio), where he oversaw the various aspects of radar. It was because the war at sea was becoming increasingly dependent on radar that Joubert had been re-appointed.

Bowhill handed over a Command with a high morale. He had overseen the fitting of 50 percent of the aircraft with the latest ASV, which had twice the range of the first radar, ASV I, the introduction of the Leigh Light and new camouflage for Maritime aircraft. The Command had about 400 aircraft and the quality had improved. The Anson had been replaced by Hudsons, Whitleys and Wellingtons. While Catalinas and Sunderlands were coming into service increasingly, none of them could reach out into the mid-Atlantic. With two hours on patrol the Hudson, the Whitley and the Wellington had a range of 500 miles, the Sunderland 600 miles and the Catalina 800 miles. Beyond this was the "Atlantic Gap" where the U-Boats did not worry about attack from the air. Closer inshore the convoys were relatively safe

TORPEDO BOMBER/ANTISHIPPING UNITED KINGDOM 1941

No 22 Squadron moved to Thorney Island in June and then to St Eval in October with Beauforts Is.

No 42 Squadron went to Leuchars in March with Beaufort Is. Detachments were at North Coates, Sumburgh, Coltishall, St Eval and Wick.

No 48 Squadron had given up its Beauforts and converted to Hudson IIIs and Vs in September. It went to Stornoway in August with detachments at Aldergrove and Limavady and on conversion to Hudsons went to Skitten.

No 59 Squadron was at Detling in June and Thorney Island a month later. Here the unit converted to Hudson IIIs, but these aircraft were ferried to the Far East for No 62 Squadron in December 1941. The squadron was then re- equipped with Hudson Vs.

No 86 Squadron gave up its Blenheim IVs in June 1941 in favour of Beaufort Is, which in turn were replaced in December by Beaufort IIs. The unit was based at North Coates with a detachment at St Eval.

No 143 Squadron was reformed in June 1941 at Aldergrove from a nucleus provided by No 252 Squadron and equipped with Beaufighter Ics. It had various bases but by December it was back at Aldergrove, having exchanged its Beaufighters for Blenheim IVs in November.

No 217 Squadron was at Thorney Island with Beaufort IIs. Detachments were at St Eval, Manston, North Coates and Skitten.

No 235 Squadron moved to Dyce with a detachment at Sumburgh and received Beaufighter Ics in place of its Blenheim IFs in December.

No 236 Squadron moved to Carew Cheriton in March 1941 with a detachment at St Eval and converted to Beaufighter Ics in October 1941.

No 248 Squadron exchanged its Blenheim IVFs in July 1941 for Beaufighter Ics and was based at Bircham Newton with detachments at St Eval and Portreath.

No 404 Squadron Royal Canadian Air Force was equipped with Blenheim IVFs and based at Sumburgh, having formed at Thorney Island in April.

No 415 Squadron Royal Canadian Air Force formed and remained at Thorney Island in August 1941, and was equipped with Beaufort Is.

No 455 Squadron Royal Australian Air Force formed at Swinderby in June 1941, with the Australian element forming at Williamstown at the end of this month. They set out for the UK in July, arriving in September. The squadron was equipped with Hampdens in July 1941 but was with Bomber Command until April 1942.

No 254 Squadron, still with its Blenheim IVFs, was at Dyce.

No 489 Squadron Royal New Zealand Air Force formed at Leuchars in August 1941 and was equipped with Beaufort Is.

The Germans had intended that the new *Bismarck*, together with *Prinz Eugen*, *Scharnhorst* and *Gneisenau,* would cause havoc in the convoy routes. *Bismarck* was sunk at the end of May.

Between the beginning of March and the end of June,

No 2 Group Bomber Command Blenheims flew over a thousand sorties against enemy merchant shipping at sea, losing some 36 aircraft. During the same period 143 Coastal aircraft delivered attacks losing 52 aircraft.

On 28 March photographic reconnaissance confirmed the presence of the *Scharnhorst* and the *Gneisenau* in Brest harbour. Some 200 bombers attacked over the next few nights in adverse weather but with no result. However, the *Gneisenau* was moved to the outer harbour due to the presence of an unexploded 250lb bomb. Four Beauforts of No 22 Squadron were briefed to attack, but only Flying Officer Kenneth Campbell and crew found the target in the haze. He pressed home his attack through the flak ships at mast height, dropping the torpedo at 500 yards. The aircraft was shot down, none of the crew surviving. However, the torpedo hit the stern of the battle cruiser beneath the waterline. The starboard screw shaft was still being repaired eight months later. Fg. Off. Campbell was awarded the Victoria Cross.

On 13 June Beauforts of No 42 Squadron found and torpedoed the *Lutzow*, which returned to Germany with great difficulty. This battlecruiser was originally named the *Deutschland*.

In June some attempt at co-ordination was achieved when the AOCs-in-C of Fighter, Bomber and Coastal Commands agreed that the Blenheims with Fighter Command should attack the Bethune-Lens industrial area while Coastal should attack all enemy shipping during daylight in the Channel. Thus on 27 June No 16 Group's Nos 22 Beaufort and 59 Blenheim Squadrons began intensive operations in the Channel. However, AOCs in C

Bomber and Coastal disagreed about the responsibility for bombing. It was then agreed that Bomber should be responsible for anti shipping operations between Cherbourg and Texel, later agreed to be Wilhelmshaven, and Coastal to be responsible for the rest of the sea areas around the British Isles. Two squadrons from No 2 Group were to be stationed near the South East coast and Fighter Command would help by providing fighter escort and strafing attacks.

From then to the end of the year No 18 Group aircraft attacked 160 vessels in the north of the North Sea, sinking 16, probably loaded with iron ore. The Group lost 33 aircraft. In the same period No 2 Group, No 16 Group and fighter aircraft attacked 499 ships between Wilhelmshaven and Cherbourg, sinking 23 and losing 55 bombers, 23 coastal aircraft and four fighters. Again in the same period, from Cherbourg to and in, the Bay of Biscay, No 19 Group attacked 36 ships, losing eight aircraft. Bomber aircraft attacked three ships losing no aircraft. The two Groups sank two ships. The Admiralty was reasonably happy with this but the RAF was not. Bomber Command was relieved of this duty in November as the aircraft involved, the Blenheim, was required in the Middle East. Coastal was then responsible for all sea areas with assistance from Fighter Command in the Dover Straits and its approaches. Grand Admiral Raeder reported that RAF air superiority was making life difficult. Throughout 1941 Coastal and Bomber Commands attacked the *Scharnhorst, Prinz Eugen* and *Gneisenau* in their French ports, inflicting some damage.

MARITIME PATROL UK 1941

No 10 Squadron Royal Australian Air Force moved to Pembroke Dock in June 1941 from Mountbatten. It received a Short S-26 Flying Boat, which was a longer range version of the Empire boat and used for flying stores to Gibraltar and the Middle East. The RAF fitted it with gun turrets and bombs under the wings.

No 95 Squadron reformed January 1941 at Pembroke Dock from No 210 Squadron operating Sunderland Is. In March it moved to Freetown.

No 119 Squadron was reformed at Bowmore in March 1941, being "G" Flight redesignated and equipped with Short S-26Ms. The following month Short S-23Ms were added. This was another version of the Empire boat. The squadron took delivery of Catalina Ibs in June 1941, losing them to other units the following month. In August the squadron moved to Pembroke Dock, losing its Short S-23Ms, again to other units. In October it was reduced to a cadre.

No 120 Squadron had reformed in June 1941 at Nutt's Corner, Belfast and were operating Liberator Is. Liberator IIs followed in November in addition.

No 201 Squadron took delivery of some Sunderland IIs in addition to its Mark Is in May 1941. In October 1941 the squadron moved from Sullom Voe to Lough Erne, Northern Ireland.

No 209 Squadron exchanged its Lerwick Is for Catalina Is in April 1941. In January it was in Stranraer and in March in Lough Erne. In May Pilot Officer D. A. Briggs and crew found the *Bismarck* after surface forces had lost her. Briggs' aircraft was hit and he lost contact.

However, an aircraft from No 240 Squadron regained contact shortly after. In July the squadron moved to Reykjavik.

On 25 August 1941, Fg. Off. E. Jewiss and crew were on convoy escort. Some ten hours after arriving on task a surfaced submarine was sighted from a quarter of a mile. Four depth charges were dropped as the boat was submerging, which blew it back to the surface. It then sank stern first. The U-boat was U-452, a type VIIc commanded by Kapitänleutnant Jurgen March. The sinking was shared with a trawler, HMS *Vascama*. Fg. Off. Jewiss was awarded the DFC. The squadron moved to Pembroke Dock in October. On 30 October 1941, Fg. Off. D. Ryan and crew on a crossover patrol sighted U-81, a type VIIc, commanded by Oberleutnant zur See Johan Krieg. The Catalina and the U-Boat exchanged gunfire, the aircraft being hit on the tailplane. Then a Hudson from No 53 Squadron arrived and attacked as the boat began to submerge. The Catalina then attacked with four depth charges, one failing to release. U-81 was en route from Brest to the Mediterranean, had been damaged and had to return to Brest. It successfully reached La Spezia, Italy, and was involved in the sinking of HMS *Ark Royal* in November 1941.

No 210 Squadron exchanged its Sunderland Is in April 1941 for Catalina Is. The squadron was based at Oban, Argyll with detachments at Sullom Voe, Reykjavik and Stranraer.

No 221 Squadron had been based at Limavady with detachments at Reykjavik, St Eval and Bircham Newton. It moved to Reykjavik with a detachment at Limavady in

September and on Christmas Day to Docking, north east of King's Lynn. It had been flying Wellington Ics, but was now about to exchange them for Wellington VIIIs and go to the Mediterranean.

No 228 Squadron left Alexandria in June 1941 for Bathurst by sea. The aircraft arrived there on 1 August 1941, but were detached to Calshot on 28 August, the remainder of the squadron following on 26 September 1941. It was re-established at Stranraer in November 1941 with Sunderland Is and IIs.

No 240 Squadron exchanged its Supermarine Stranraer flying boats for Catalinas in March 1941 while based at Stranraer with a detachment at Lough Erne. In March it moved to Killadeas, one of the three bases on Lough Erne. At the end of May an aircraft relieved a No 209 Squadron Catalina which had located the Bismarck but had been hit.

No 321 Squadron Royal Netherlands Navy was disbanded and absorbed into No 320 Squadron in January 1941.

No 330 Squadron Royal Norwegian Air Force was formed at Reykjavik in April 1941 with Northrop N3P-Bs. It had detachments at Akureyri and Budreyeri.

No 413 Squadron Royal Canadian Air Force was formed at Stranraer in June 1941 with Catalina Is and IVs. It moved to Sullom Voe in October 1941.

No 502 (Ulster) Squadron Auxiliary Air Force was still operating its Whitley Vs but had moved to Limavady with a detachment to St Eval in January 1941. On 10 February 1941, Fg. Off. J. Walker and crew were escorting convoy WS6 when they sighted a surfaced submarine in position

5630N 01438W. The aircraft approached downsun, but at two miles the U-Boat started to submerge. Two depth charges were dropped. The boat resurfaced, emitting white smoke, and opened fire, hitting the front turret. A short while later the boat submerged stern first. This was U-93, a type VIIc, commanded by Kapitänleutnant Klaus Korth. It had been damaged and returned to base.

On 1 December 1941 Fg. Off. W. Cave and crew sighted a periscope from 4500 feet at two miles in position 4700N 01135W. An attack was made from 100 feet with six depth charges, resulting in a good straddle. Five gun attacks were made until the boat submerged. A spout of oil and bubbles were seen and the conning tower was seen again for about half a minute and nothing further. This was U-563, a type VIIc, commanded by Oberleutnant zur See Klaus Bargsten. The boat was damaged and had to return to Lorient. Fg. Off. Cave received the DFC.

No 612 (County of Aberdeen) Squadron, Auxiliary Air Force, was also operating Whitley Vs and had moved to Wick in April 1941 with detachments at Limavady, St Eval and Reykjavik. In September 1941 some Whitley VIIs were taken on strength and by December the squadron was based at Reykjavik.

AIR SEA RESCUE

A meeting chaired by the Deputy Chief of the Air Staff (DCAS) was held on 14 January 1941 in the Air Ministry to discuss methods of improving and expanding the Rescue Service. Also present were representatives of the Royal Navy and the various RAF operational Commands, together with Group Captain L.G. Le B. Croke who was the Station Commander at St Eval and had shown great interest in the matter. This meeting recommended the formation of a Directorate of Sea Rescue Services with Croke as its first Director. This was approved by the Secretary of State on 24 January 1941. The Admiralty appointed Captain C. L. Howe RN as the Deputy Director. The title of the Directorate was changed to the Directorate of Air Sea Rescue Services and it took up its duties at Headquarters Coastal Command (HQCC) on 6 February 1941. Officers of the Directorate were appointed to the Area Combined Headquarters of Nos 15, 16, 18 and 19 Groups. For sea search purposes the British Isles were divided into four areas coinciding with the Coastal Command area boundaries. Close-in search, which was defined as twenty miles from the coast, was the responsibility of Fighter Command's Lysanders.

This aircraft carried an apparatus consisting of four "M" type dinghies, each of which contained water, food and distress signals and each packed in a valise inside a small bomb container. These were carried on the stub wings of the aircraft, just above the undercarriage.

The other type of aircraft used for SAR was the Walrus amphibian, of which Coastal Command had three. The Royal Navy had many more, but could not release them as they were required for cruiser protection. Appeals were made to the USA for Catalina flying boats but with no result, there being none available. A desperate appeal was made by the Director of Air Sea Rescue and the AOC-in-C Fighter Command to the Fifth Sea Lord, with the result that six Walruses were delivered to Fighter Command at the beginning of August.

Between February and August 1941 1200 aircrew had ditched and 444 had been rescued. It was believed that more could be done. Indeed the Treasury had asked in January for a review of the new system after six months. Accordingly, in August 1941 it was decided to place executive control of Search and Rescue (SAR) in the hands of one person, and that was AOC-in-C Coastal. At the same time the Directorate of Air-Sea Rescue at the Air Ministry was merged with the Directorate-General of Aircraft Safety, and Marshal of the RAF Sir John Salmond was asked to preside. The resources used by the rescue services were the Post Office Radio Stations, the Royal Observer Corps, the Coastguard, Trinity House, the Royal National Lifeboat Institution and the Merchant Navy. The RAF had their own High Speed Launches and other craft and of course, the Lysanders and Walruses, dedicated to SAR.

In September 1941 it was agreed that the first squadrons to be dedicated to SAR were to be formed from the Lysanders and Walruses. These squadrons were No 275, formed at Valley in October 1941, No 276, formed in October at Harrowbeer, No 277 in December 1941 at Stapleford Tawney, and No 278, formed at Matlask from No 3 ASR Flight. These squadrons were not part of Coastal but were part of Fighter Command and remained so for the rest of the war. The squadrons were also equipped with the Boulton Paul Defiant, a fighter with no forward firing guns but with a four-gun turret. It was not successful as a fighter and as a consequence some were transferred to the SAR squadrons. In 1942, there being an increase in opposition, it was agreed at Fighter Command Headquarters that the SAR squadrons should not have to rely on other squadrons for fighter cover but should have their own. It was decided to replace the Defiants with Spitfires.

In November 1941 No 279 Squadron was formed at Bircham Newton with Hudson IIIs, Vs and VIs and in the following month No 280 Squadron was formed at Thorney Island but with no aircraft. The formation of No 279 was hampered by the lack of aircrew and C-in-C Coastal stated that he could not let the training of SAR aircrews interfere with operational training. There were no Hudsons available with which to equip No 280 Squadron. These squadrons were part of Coastal Command.

By February 1941, 22 high-speed launches had been produced. The original version was a 64-foot boat, but this had been replaced by a 63-feet model. However, these boats were difficult to maintain and suffered from a high degree of unserviceability.

There were a number of different types of marine craft apart from the high-speed launches, in use in early 1941. There were 14 diesel-engined 60-foot pinnaces used for torpedo recovery and other jobs. They were reasonable sea boats but not good in very rough weather. They were located at Sullom Voe, Invergordon, Gosport and Calshot. The flying boat bases had a number of 40-foot seaplane tenders used as transport between shore and the moored flying boat but they were no good for open sea rescue. The Royal Navy made a number of motor launches available for rescue work when they were not required for coastal patrol duties. These were 110 feet long and had a speed of 20 knots. Some 20 of these were used in the areas of

Portland, Dover, Newhaven, Dartmouth, Milford Haven and Falmouth. In practice, of course, most ships were available to assist in a rescue depending on the circumstances. In short, the situation was not satisfactory.

The requirements for the boats were a capability of a low-speed search for a long period and a capability for a high-speed transit to an operating area in rough seas. However, no increase in production in the UK was possible because of the increasing demands put on the manufacturers for naval boats. The only progress was an agreement by the Ministry of Aircraft Production that an additional forty 60-foot pinnaces could be built by December 1941. In June the Deputy Chief of the Air Staff agreed that they should be built for rescue purposes. The situation was to be reviewed in January 1942.

In May 1941 D.A.S.R. authorized the establishment of 34 high-speed launches for Overseas Commands. This was reconsidered in August by the Air Staff and it was decided that all needs for overseas Commands should be met by High Speed Launches (HSLs) at Gibraltar, Malta, Mersa Matruh, Alexandria, Port Said, Cyprus, Haifa, Aden, Singapore, Kuantan, Khota Bahru, Freetown and Bathurst to a total of 33 boats.

No 279 Squadron was formed in November 1941 at Bircham Newton with Hudson IIIs, Vs and VIs.

No 280 Squadron was formed at Thorney Island to be equipped in the New Year with Anson Is.

THE HUDSON SQUADRONS 1941

No 48 Squadron converted to Hudson IIIs and Vs in September 1941 and moved to Skitten in October 1941.

No 53 Squadron was moved to St Eval in March and to Bircham Newton in July where it converted to Hudson Vs, disposing of its Blenheims. It maintained detachments at St Eval and Limavady and was moved to St Eval in October and to Limavady in December. On 30 October Plt. Off. Henry and crew joined in the attack on U-81 with the No 209 Squadron Catalina captained by Fg. Off. D. Ryan. The Hudson dropped three depth charges. A large patch of white foam was observed. As stated, the U-Boat was damaged and returned to base.

No 206 Squadron exchanged its Hudson IIs in June 1941 for Hudson IIIs and Ivs, which the squadron kept until August 1942. In October 1941, it received Hudson Vs which again it held until August 1942. The squadron moved to Aldergrove in August 1941.

No 220 Squadron started 1941 with Hudson with Hudson Is and IIs. The Mark IIs were exchanged in June 1941 for Hudson IIIs and Vis, which were retained until June 1942. The Hudson Is were retained until December 1941 when Fortress Is were taken on strength. Also in December No 90 Squadron detachment at Shallufa was renumbered No 220 Squadron detachment. This squadron was operating Fortress Is. The UK element of No 220 squadron had moved to Wick in April. During the summer the squadron flew a number of anti-shipping sorties over the North and Norwegian Seas. In September Fg. Off. K. Tarrant attacked a large tanker, scoring two hits. It had a naval escort. In October the squadron attacked shipping in Alesund port and again at the end of the month. Seven ships were sunk or damaged and a fish oil factory was set alight.

No 233 Squadron exchanged its Hudson Is and IIs in June 1941 for Hudson Vs. It had received Hudson IIIs in January 1941. It had moved from Aldergrove to St Eval in August 1941 with detachments at Thorney Island and Gibraltar.

No 269 Squadron exchanged its Hudson IIs in May 1941 for Hudson IIIs when it moved to Kaldadarnes, south west Iceland. On 27 August 1941 Sgt Mitchell and crew located U-570, a type VIIc submarine, and attacked, but the depth charges failed to release. Accordingly the Hudson crew homed in Sqn Ldr J Thompson and crew who attacked with four depth charges and heavy machine gun fire. The boat started to dive and then resurfaced. A white flag was seen. Sqn Ldr Thompson requested assistance and he and his crew were relieved by Fg. Off. Jewiss from No 209 Squadron.

Four hours later Flt Lt B. Lewin and crew from No 209 Squadron arrived. Surface ships arrived in the area and the U-Boat was towed to Iceland. The empty box of an Enigma cipher machine was found, which had been modified to accommodate a fourth rotor. She subsequently became HMS/M *Graph*. Thompson and his second pilot, Fg.Off W. Coleman, were awarded DFCs.

No 500 (County of Kent) Squadron, Auxiliary Air Force, exchanged its Ansons for Blenheim IVs in April 1941. These in turn were exchanged for Hudson Vs in November 1941.

No 608 (North Riding) Squadron, Auxiliary Air Force, had disposed of its Bothas and re-equipped with Blenheim Is in February 1941, followed by Blenheim IVs in March. These were disposed of in August and September, having received Hudson Vs in July and Hudson IIIs in August. The squadron was based at Thornaby.

No 407 Squadron Royal Canadian Air Force had been formed at Thorney Island in May 1941 with Blenheim Ivs, which it disposed of in July 1941 in exchange for Hudson IIIs and Vs. Again in July the squadron moved to North Coates.

No 320 Squadron Royal Netherlands Navy was at Leuchars with Hudson Is and IIs and Anson Is. It had absorbed No 321 Squadron Royal Netherlands Navy in January 1941. It disposed of its Ansons in October 1941 and its Hudson IIs in September 1941, receiving Hudson IIIs in July 1941.

MEDITERRANEAN TORPEDO BOMBER/ANTISHIPPING 1941

No 38 Squadron was at Shallufa with Wellington IIs and detachments throughout the area.

No 39 Squadron had been re-equipped with Maryland Is in January 1941 and with Beaufort Is in August. The squadron was based at LG86, south west of Alexandria, with detachments at Sidi Barani, Luqa BU Amud, Shallufa, Shandur and Bir El Gobbi.

No 252 Squadron had disbanded in June 1941 at Aldergrove. In April the aircrew had detached to Luqa, Heraklion and Abu Sueir, with their Beaufighter Ics. After the disbandment the aircrew continued to operate with No 272 Squadron, also with Beaufighter Ics at Idku. In September 1941 the squadron nameplate was in use again, but the squadron was not reformed until November 1941, when it was based at Idku, again with Beaufighter Ics.

No 272 Squadron had re-equipped with Beaufighter Ics at Chivenor in April 1941 and was moved to Abu Sueir in May. At the end of the year it was Idku with detachments at Luqa and LG10, which was Gerawala south east of Mersa Matruh.

This was one squadron of Wellingtons, one of Marylands and Beauforts and two with Beaufighter Ics.

MEDITERRANEAN MARITIME PATROL 1941

No 202 Squadron was at Gibraltar. It had given up its Swordfish floatplanes in June 1941 and its London IIs in June 1941 and in April it had re-equipped with Catalina Ibs, which it operated until January 1945. On 25 October 1941 Sqn. Ldr. N. Eagleton and crew were escorting convoy HG75 carrying out a creeping line ahead search in front of the convoy. The Italian submarine *Galileo Ferraris,* commanded by Tenente di Vascello Filippo Flores, was sighted on the surface. It was attacked with two depth charges which failed to explode. The aircraft orbited the submarine and requested assistance. HMS *Lamerton* gave chase and opened fire. The submarine crew scuttled their boat and was rescued by HMS *Lamerton.* The sinking was credited to HMS *Lamerton* and the No 202 Squadron Catalina. In December 1941 the squadron received Sunderland Is and IIs, which it operated until September 1942.

On 6 December 1941 Flt. Lt. H. Garnell and crew sighted U-332, a type VIIc commanded by Oberleutnant zur See Eberhard Huttemann in position 3645N 00925W, from six miles. At one and a half miles the U-Boat had completely submerged, but three depth charges were dropped. Two exploded in the swirl. Oil and bubbles were seen but this is not conclusive evidence of a sinking. U-332 was damaged but managed to reach La Pallice.

No 228 Squadron left the area in June 1941 for West Africa, arriving in Bathurst in August. However, in September the squadron returned to the UK to be re-established at Stranraer. The squadron was re-equipped with Sunderland Is and IIs in November 1941.

No 230 Squadron moved to Aboukir in June 1941 and in October 1941 received Sunderland IIs in addition to its Sunderland Is. In June 1941 No 2 Squadron Yugoslav Air Force was attached with Dornier Do 22s. A Sunderland of No 230 Squadron was involved in a hunt on 1 August 1941 for a reported submarine in the Gulf of Sollum. This submarine threatened shipping supplying the Tobruk garrison. The Sunderland, L2166, was captained by Flight Lieutenant Engert Brand. His crew sighted the submarine and attacked in position 3212N 02446E, in the face of heavy gunfire which hit the aircraft. Brand released a stick of six depth charges but did not damage his target. The Sunderland was now on fire and crashed in the sea. The submarine, the Italian *Delfino*, rescued four of the crew, who became prisoners. This was the first recorded action between an aircraft and a submarine which resulted in the loss of the aircraft.

MEDITERRANEAN AIR SEA RESCUE

Six high-speed launches were allotted in June 1941 to the Middle East, one each at Port Said, Aboukir and Mersa Matruh. Three were to be based at Malta. At that time Malta was under heavy air attack and only one launch was available, HSL 107 based at Kalafrana. The first launch of the three was to have been shipped out with the ground personnel of the third fighter squadron. The crew went but due to loading difficulties, the launch was left behind. In July it was decided to fit all three launches with extra fuel tanks, ship them to Gibraltar and let them proceed under their own power to Malta. This involved the use of a tanker along the route, but the Navy considered this to be too dangerous and the idea was cancelled. A convoy in October was successful in taking two launches to Malta. In the meantime HSL 107, three seaplane tenders and twelve various craft rescued 30 British pilots during the course of the summer. HSL 107 rescued 17 of these.

By the summer of 1941 much of the air fighting was taking place over the sea and the provision of rescue facilities became a top priority. In August, an ASR Flight, with three Wellington Ics, was established under the operational control of No 201 Group. It was initially based at Kabrit, but in September it moved to Burg-el-Arab. Shortly after forming, a reconnaissance aircraft reported a ship's lifeboat with ten on board 100 miles north of Ras-el-Kanazis. A Wellington from the Sea Rescue Flight took off and located the lifeboat, dropped supplies and gave them a course to steer. It remained with them until dusk. They were rescued next day and it turned out that they were escapees from Crete. Three further successes were achieved in the next two months.

Further aircraft were added to the inventory in the next months. A Walrus was loaned by the Royal Navy and a Fairchild and a Grumman which had been presented to the RAF by American wellwishers were passed to the

Flight. By the end of the year five of the six additional launches allocated the previous June had arrived at their respective bases. There were three at Malta, three in the Middle East and one in Aden.

After the arrival of the two HSLs at Malta, a combined Marine and High Speed Launch section was formed in November with Headquarters at Kalafrana. The third HSL and a seaplane tender were based at St Paul's Bay. During the last two months of the year 38 attempted rescues were carried out. Twelve RAF aircrew and one Reggia Aeronautica aircrew were rescued.

The siege of Malta meant that only submarines and flying boats were able to bring in supplies. The Unit was vital here, handling the offloading in the hours of night.

Other roles included bringing in injured personnel, transporting medical staff to ships, firefighting and taking out salvage equipment to damaged ships.

The total for 1941 was 34 Allied aircrew and 12 enemy aircrew.

WEST AFRICA MARITIME PATROL 1941

No 95 Squadron, having reformed in the UK in January, arrived in Freetown in March 1941 with Sunderland Is. Detachments were at Apapa, Bathurst, Libreville, Pointe Noire and Gibraltar.

No 200 Squadron had formed in May 1941 at Bircham Newton from a nucleus of No 206 Squadron with Hudson IVs and was sent to Jeswang (Bathurst) with detachments to Takoradi, Accra, Apapa, Hastings, Robertsfield, Port Etienne, Pointe Noire and Waterloo.

No 204 Squadron left Reykjavik in June for Pembroke

Dock, but went to Gibraltar in July only to move on to Bathurst in August. It still retained its Sunderland Is but in addition received Sunderland IIs in June.

WEST AFRICA SEARCH AND RESCUE

While West Africa was not an active combat area, it was nevertheless an important part of the reinforcement route for aircraft from the UK to Egypt and later for the USA to Egypt. It was also an important base for maritime aircraft escorting convoys through the South Atlantic. A Search and Rescue service was therefore very necessary. In August West Africa was allotted four High Speed Launches (HSLs), but due to shortages none arrived until late 1942.

MIDDLE EAST 1941

No 8 Squadron added Blenheim IVs to the inventory in January 1941 and Vincents in May. Detachments were at Perim Island, Assab, Aischa and Riyan.

No 203 Squadron moved to Kabrit, Egyptian Canal Zone in April 1941.

No 244 Squadron was still at Shaibah with Vincents.

FAR EAST

No 36 Squadron added Albacores to its inventory in December.

No 100 Squadron added Beaufort Is to its inventory in December. It had a detachment at Kuantan.

No 205 Squadron added Catalina Is to its inventory in April, disposing of its Singapore IIIs in October.

FAR EAST SEARCH AND RESCUE

In October 1941 the first Air Sea Rescue Officer was appointed to the staff of Air Headquarters Far East. He was given limited resources but managed to obtain one HSL, a pinnace and a marine tender with which to cover the approaches to Singapore. He also obtained the co-operation of the Royal Navy. In December the unit rescued 11 aircrew from the sea.

CHAPTER TWENTY

1942

MARITIME PATROL 1942

In the UK the maritime patrol effort was spreading and the technology was improving. As an aid to the identification of U-Boats the Leigh Light, a searchlight fitted to the aircraft, was developed. Radar, or ASV, Air to Surface Vessel, was coming on stream.

For some time Operation Fuller had existed. This was the Operation Order to counter the dash up the Channel by *Scharnhorst, Prinz Eugen* and *Gneisenau* and it was implemented on 3 February. Submarine patrols off Brest were intensified and Naval light forces at Dover were brought to readiness. Coastal Command aircraft flew extra patrols off Brittany and between Le Havre and Boulogne and the torpedo bombers were at readiness at St Eval, Thorney Island and Manston. Bombers and fighters were made available. C-in-C Coastal had only two squadrons of Hudsons available and it was difficult to maintain continuous patrols particularly in the face of fighter opposition. In addition the weather was bad and the ASV radar was not proving to be reliable. On 11 February, sixteen Wellingtons from Bomber Command attacked the enemy ships but caused no damage. However, Vice Admiral Ciliax, the German commander, decided to delay his sailing by a few hours.

'Stopper' was a patrol which covered the exits from Brest and was backed up by others to the south, west and north, that is, a total of four aircraft on task continuously. That night it was flown by a Hudson from No 224 squadron. ASV at that time had a detection range of 13 miles. The aircraft was moving away as the ships moved out of Brest. This aircraft was relieved by another Hudson and during the last eight minutes of this sortie, when it was at its northern extremity, the ships came within ASV range. The operator saw nothing unusual on his screen, even though the equipment was serviceable. It should be noted that crews estimated that ASV was no more than 50% reliable.

The next obstacle to the enemy was "Line South East", a patrol line from north west of Ushant to Jersey. When the ships crossed it there was no aircraft on task. This was because firstly, the aircraft had been recalled due to ASV failure. Secondly, due to shortage of aircraft and, because the C-in-C believed that, as there was no report from "Stopper", the ships were probably past "Line South East". The third line of detection was "Habo", a line patrol from Cherbourg to Boulogne. An aircraft was on task but due to a forecast of bad weather on the south coast airfields, it was recalled. That ended the reconnaissance effort of Coastal for now. For the torpedo bomber effort, see below. It was noted by radars situated on the coast that German fighters were flying unusual profiles. Spitfires were sent to investigate and eventually the capital ships and their escorts were discovered. After dark on 12th, reconnaissance aircraft gained ASV contact and two visual sightings were gained. As a result of these sightings Hampdens and Manchesters laid mines in the Elbe estuary, but no results were achieved. However, as a result of mines laid earlier, both *Scharnhorst* and *Gneisenau* were damaged, *Scharnhorst* seriously.

No 10 Squadron Royal Australian Air Force was operating Sunderland Mark IIs. In January the squadron moved to Mountbatten from Pembroke Dock. On 5 June 1942 Flt Lt R. C. Wood and crew arrived on task and very soon after obtained a radar contact from 5000 feet, at eight miles off the starboard bow. This was then seen to be a surfaced U-Boat, U-71, commanded by Kapitänleutnant Walter Flachsenberg. The aircraft was flown down to 50 feet and Wood attacked with eight depth charges. The boat surfaced and seemed to be down at the bows and a 15 degree list to port. The aircraft made several machine gun attacks and U-71 replied with the deck gun and cannon fire. The Sunderland was hit several times. The U-boat then dived. In the early evening the Sunderland was attacked by a Focke Wulf FW200 Kondor. Both aircraft were hit and the Kondor left the area. Two Sunderland crew members were injured. U-71 had been damaged and returned to La Pallice. Flt. Lt. Wood was awarded the DFC.

On 7 June 1942, the Italian submarine *Luigi Torelli*, fresh from her damaging experiences with No 172 Squadron and having been forced to sail from Aviles in Spain, had the misfortune to meet Plt. Off. T. A. Egerton and crew, who sighted her from 1500 feet at five miles. The Sunderland attacked with a stick of depth charges and machine gun fire on a flight path from out of the sun. The submarine opened fire at 3000 yards, causing hits and injuring two of the crew. Flt. Lt. E. StC. Yeoman and crew from the same squadron intercepted Egerton's sighting report and went to assist. As they arrived the *Luigi Torelli* opened fire hitting the aircraft in the fin. However, Yeoman attacked with a stick of depth charges, two of which exploded under the boat. It was seen to lift out of the sea, ejecting what looked like a torpedo from the stern tubes.

Yeoman's aircraft had reached its Prudent Limit of Endurance (PLE) and had turned for base when it was attacked by an Arado seaplane. Both aircraft fired on each other, causing hits. The Arado turned away. The *Luigi Torelli* was badly damaged and was beached at Santander Harbour and interned. Repairs were made, the crew escaped, recaptured the boat and reached Bordeaux.

On 11 June Flt. Lt. E. B. Martin and crew sighted U-105, a type IXB, commanded by Oberleutnant zur See Jurgen Nissen, from 2000 feet at five miles off the port bow. A stick of depth charges was dropped from 40 feet, causing the boat to stop. Two further attacks were made, dropping one anti-submarine bomb from 600 feet each time. Smoke was seen coming from the conning tower, but the aircraft had to return to base due to shortage of fuel. The U-Boat was badly damaged and went into Ferrol in Spain for repairs, leaving for Lorient on 28 June.

On 1 September 1942 Flt. Lt. S. R. C. Wood and crew sighted the Italian submarine *Reginaldo Giuliani,* commanded by Capitano di Corvetta Vittore Raccanelli. As the Sunderland attacked, the boat opened fire. A stick of four depth charges was dropped accurately from 400 feet. Two more Sunderlands, one from No 10 Squadron, captained by Flt. Lt. H. G. Pockley, and another from No 461 Squadron, were seen approaching and the three crews agreed to make a joint attack. However, Woods was ordered to continue his patrol. Pockley then started his attack, but he in turn was ordered discontinue his attack. However, the boat opened fire so Pockley dropped two 250lb bombs on it. A further attack was made with one bomb causing casualties among the submarine's crew. A joint attack was agreed by Pockley and the No 461 Squadron aircraft, but then Maritime Headquarters (MHQ) ordered both Sunderlands to continue their patrols. It is possible that MHQ was aware of fighter activity in the area. Pockley's aircraft was slightly damaged and the Italian boat was damaged and its captain killed. The *Reginaldo Giuliani* met a Wellington from No 304 Squadron the next day.

No 51 Squadron was a bomber squadron equipped with Whitley Vs and was detached to RAF Chivenor, Coastal Command from 6 May 1942 to 27 October 1942. On 31 August 1942 Flt. Lt. E. O. Tandy and crew were on patrol, in the rough area of Bishop's Rock, when the WOP/AG intercepted the sighting report of U-256 from the No 502 Squadron Whitley. The crew set heading for the area and sighted U-256 on the surface from three miles. Tandy attacked and at one mile the boat dived. The front gunner opened fire and a stick of depth charges was dropped ahead of the swirl. Nothing further was seen. Several unidentified aircraft were seen in the area and as the aircraft was also suffering from a problem with the port engine, Tandy turned for home. The boat was returning to

Lorient when it was attacked. It was so badly damaged that it was a candidate for the scrapyard, but it became a flak boat instead.

In December 1942 No 58 Squadron was at Holmesley South near Bournemouth, exchanging its Whitley VIIs for Halifax IIs. It had transferred from Bomber Command in April 1942 and moved to St Eval, Cornwall. On 23 June 1942, Flt. Sgt. W. Jones and crew were on patrol over the Bay of Biscay. U-753, a type VIIc boat, commanded by Korvettenkapitän Alfred Manhardt von Mannstein, was sighted on the surface. A stick of depth charges was dropped as the boat dived. Several patches of oil were seen and then U-753 surfaced. The crew manned the guns and opened fire, causing hits on the Whitley. It then dived, leaving a patch of oil. The boat had been on patrol in the Caribbean and had been badly damaged by the Whitley crew. She returned safely to port but major repairs were necessary.

On 15 September 1942 Sgt. B. Snell and crew were flying over a rough sea with about 20 miles visibility. At seven miles a surfaced U-Boat was sighted in position 5949N 00928W. Three depth charges were dropped from 20 feet, one hitting the boat. Snell made a follow-up attack with his remaining war load. Debris and an oil patch were seen and U-261 a type VIIc boat commanded by Kapitänleutnant Hans Lange had gone to the bottom on her first patrol. Snell was awarded the DFM.

No 59 Squadron went to North Coates with its Hudson Vs in January 1942. It added some Hudson VIs in July 1942. It disposed of all its Hudsons in August 1942, re-equipping with Liberator IIIs. It had a detachment at St Eval. By December 1942, it was at Thorney Island exchanging its Liberator IIIs for Fortress IIAs. It had a detachment at Chivenor, North Devon. On 26 November 1942 Flt. Lt. F.G. Tiller and crew found and attacked U-263 in Henday's Bay. This boat had already been damaged by a No 233 Squadron aircraft on 24 November 1942.

No 61 Squadron of Bomber Command was detached to Coastal Command at RAF St Eval with Lancaster Is in May 1942. On 17 July 1942 Flt. Lt. P. R. Casement and crew were on patrol in the vicinity of 45N012W. About an hour after Plt. Off. Hunt and his crew from No 502 Squadron had attacked U-751, Casement found an oil patch and then the U-boat on the surface. The first attack was made with depth charges and the second was from 700 feet using anti-submarine bombs. The boat was sunk. As this was a Bomber Command crew without Coastal experience, a qualified Coastal Navigator, Fg. Off. Wright, went along as a guide.

No 77 Squadron was another Bomber Command squadron of Whitley Vs loaned to Coastal, from May to October 1942, and based at Chivenor. On 3 September 1942 Flt. Sgt. A. A. MacInnes and crew sighted a U-Boat from 2500 feet at five miles. A depth charge attack was made from 50 feet and what appeared to be a perfect straddle was achieved. This was U-705, a type VIIc boat on its first patrol and commanded by Kapitänleutnant Karl-Horst Horn. The boat was sunk in position 4642N 01107W. The Whitley did not carry radar.

No 86 Squadron was at Thorney Island with Liberator IIIAs, having handed over its Beauforts earlier in the year.

No 119 Squadron was re-established after six months as a cadre in April 1942 at Lough Erne with Catalina IIIas, which it received in May. In September the squadron moved to Pembroke Dock and was re-equipped with Sunderland IIIs. The Catalinas were disposed of the following month.

No 120 Squadron moved to Ballykelly, Northern Ireland in July 1942 with Liberator Is and IIs. In the same month it received some Liberator IIIs in addition. It had detachments at Reykjavik, Aldergrove, Northern Ireland, Predannack, South West Cornwall and Fayid on the Suez Canal. On 16 August 1942 Sqn. Ldr. T. Bulloch and crew joined a convoy in position 4650N 02110W. One and a half hours into the on task period, U-89, a type VIIc, commanded by Kapitänleutnant Dietrich Lohmann was sighted. An attack with six depth charges was carried out. U-89 had been damaged and had to return to base. This was Sqn. Ldr. Bulloch's first success, although not a sinking, and he became the most successful U-Boat hunter in the RAF. Two days later, Sqn. Ldr. Bulloch with the same crew were operating out of Predannack escorting convoy SL118. U-653 was sighted on the surface and was attacked with six depth charges. A straddle was achieved but no result was seen. The aircraft attacked again with cannon and machine gun fire and later with two A/S bombs. The boat submerged and the Liberator was recalled because of bad weather at base. The boat had been badly damaged and had to return to Brest where she remained for three months.

On 12 October 1942 Sqn. Ldr. Bulloch and crew took off from Reykjavik briefed to escort convoy ONS 136. A little after midday, a radar contact was gained and a radar homing carried out. A submarine was sighted and an attack carried out. The boat was U-597, a type VIIc, commanded by Kapitänleutnant Eberhard Bopst and had been sunk by this Liberator crew in position 5647N 02800W. Clay Blair's *Hitler's U-Boat War* states that Bulloch reported that the boat blew up, hurling a large chunk of steel skyward. On reaching the convoy the attack was reported to the Escort Commander.

Some 24 minutes after going off task, the crew sighted another boat in position 5722N 02741W and attacked it, but the result is unknown. On 5 November 1942, Sqn. Ldr. Bulloch and crew were en route to convoy SC 107 when they gained a radar contact at five and a half miles. A homing was carried out and the radar contact was converted to a visual contact in position 5830N 03252W. The boat dived and no attack was made. The U-Boat was reported to the SC 107 escort commander. Some four and a half hours later a Huffduff, or more properly, a High Frequency Direction Finding (HFDF) bearing, was reported by one of the escorts and the Liberator flew along it to investigate. The right tactic probably would be to search visually with the radar off in order that the submarine would not detect the radar transmissions on his Metox receiver. On the other hand, being in the vicinity using the radar would cause the boat to submerge, thus preventing it from attacking the convoy. A visual sighting was gained from 3500 feet at five miles, position 5808N 03313W. Six depth charges were dropped and some air bubbles were seen. The crew had to leave the area as the escort commander requested a search for another contact. Two hours later another U-Boat was seen and attacked with two depth charges, but no results were observed. The earlier sighting that had been attacked with six depth charges was an old enemy U-89 and was so badly damaged that she was forced to return to port. Bulloch was awarded a Bar to his DFC in October and the DSO in December.

No 159 Squadron formed at Molesworth with its ground echelon in January 1942 and set off for Fayid, Egypt in February, where it arrived in April 1942. Leaving an element at Fayid, the ground crew set off fourteen days later for Deolali north east of Bombay, to Chakrata, north of Delhi in June and to Salbani, west of Calcutta. Meanwhile the aircrew trained at Polebrook with No 1653 Heavy Conversion Unit. They went to Lyneham in April to collect Liberator Mark IIs, which arrived in May. The squadron arrived in Fayid in June and went to St Jean, near Haifa in July 1942. It moved to Aqir near Tel Aviv in August. The squadron merged with No 160 Squadron in June 1942, carrying out bombing operations in the Middle East. The merged squadron was numbered No 160 Squadron and No 159 Squadron's aircraft were sent to the Far East. No 159 Squadron moved to Salbani in September 1942 and was employed on bombing operations. This squadron is mentioned in this narrative, although it did not carry out maritime operations because it was so closely involved with No 160 Squadron which did carry out such operations.

No 160 Squadron was formed at Thurleigh in January 1942 with its ground echelon and they set off to Drigh Road in February, arriving in June 1942 and moving a few days later to Quetta near the Afghanistan border. Meanwhile, the aircrew trained at Polebrook with No

1653 HCU. In April they moved to Lyneham and collected their Liberator Mark IIs the following month. That month the crews went to Knutts Corner to join No 120 Squadron for anti-submarine experience. In June the squadron went to Fayid where Nos 159 and 160 Squadrons merged, to be then numbered No 160 Squadron and carried out bombing operations in the Middle East. In November 1942 the squadron moved to Shandur on the Great Bitter Lake, Egypt. In January the squadron merged with No 178 Squadron on its formation. This No 160 Squadron was known as No 160 (Middle East Detachment) by way of an Air Ministry Order which also authorised a new No 160 Squadron, which was formed in the UK at Thorney Island and began working up with No 86 Squadron using Liberator IIIs. Those personnel who were not involved with the Nos 159/160/178 squadron merger moved to Salbani.

No 172 Squadron had been formed in April 1942 from No 1417 Flight at Chivenor with Wellington VIIIs and XIIs. This was the first unit equipped with the Leigh Light. The Leigh Light gave maritime aircraft the ability to see the enemy U-Boat, once detected by other means, at night and was a turning point in submarine detection. It was pioneered by this squadron and by Squadron Leader Jeff Gresswell. He and his crew gained two U-Boat contacts on the night of 4 June 1942. He made the first attack, with his second pilot using the light, which was against the Italian *Luigi Torelli*. The commander was Tenente di Vascello Augusto Migliorini. Initially, it was a radar contact converted to a visual sighting, but the attack was aborted as the aircraft was too high. Greswell went round again and dropped four depth charges from 50 feet. Three exploded, causing severe damage. The submarine diverted to St Jean de Luz in France but hit rocks off the Spanish coast. Tugs took her into Aviles. However, she was forced to leave on 6 June and met No 10 Squadron RAAF on 7 June. Creswell and crew found a second submarine 12 miles away which was attacked with machine guns. Sqn Ldr Gresswell later commanded No 179 Squadron.

On 6 July 1942 Plt. Off. W. B. Howell and crew gained a radar contact in the early hours of the morning at seven miles. They homed in and at one mile switched on the Leigh Light, illuminating a surfaced submarine. This was U-502, a type IXc commanded by Kapitänleutnant Jurgen von Rosenstiel. A stick of four depth charges was dropped from 50 feet on the diving boat. Flame floats were dropped to mark the position and the crew remained in the area for around 25 minutes, but nothing further was seen. The boat had sunk in position 4610N 00640W. She was returning from the Caribbean on her fourth cruise. Howell, an American in the RAF, was awarded the DFC.

Six days later, Howell and his crew were on another night patrol in a similar area. At 1000 feet a radar contact was gained at seven miles. The Leigh Light was switched on at 1500 yards, illuminating a surfaced submarine. This was U-159, a type IXc boat, commanded by Kapitänleutnant Helmut Witte, also returning from the Caribbean. The boat opened fire as Howell dropped a stick of four depth charges from 100 feet. The crew remained in the area for two hours but nothing further was seen. The boat was damaged but returned to Lorient.

On 10 November 1942 Fg. Off. D. E. Dixon and crew

gained a radar contact from six miles at 1000 feet. A homing was initiated and at half a mile the Leigh Light was switched on, illuminating a U-Boat. This was U-66, a type IXc commanded by Korvettenkapitän Richard Zapp, in position 4613N 00740W. Four depth charges were dropped across the bows, causing damage sufficient for the boat to put back to Lorient, which it had left the previous day. The aircraft remained in the vicinity of the attack until it had to return to base due to fuel considerations.

No 179 Squadron was formed from a detached flight of No 172 squadron at Skitten, near Wick in September, 1942 with Wellington VIIIs. This was the second unit to be equipped with the Leigh Light. On 22 October 1942 Flight Sergeant A. Martin and crew were flying a creeping line ahead search to the North of the Shetland Islands. A radar contact was gained on the port beam at five miles but was lost immediately. Some time later a further radar contact was gained at five miles. Martin reduced height, turned on to the contact and homed in, turning on the Leigh Light at one and a half miles and illuminating a surfaced submarine. Martin attacked from 150 feet with four depth charges. Oil and bubbles were seen, but nothing else. This was U-412, a type VIIc, commanded by Kapitänleutnant Walther Jahrmarker. She was sunk on her first patrol in position 6355N 00024W.

The squadron was moved to Gibraltar in November 1942. On 27 December 1942 Flt Lt A. Comfort and crew were on task at 2000 feet in the early hours of the morning (it was still dark) using intermittent all-round scan on their "Special Equipment" or, as it is now known, ASV radar.

In other words it was switched on and off so that any U-Boat detection device such as "Metox", while detecting the ASV transmission, would not provide enough information to establish the track of the aircraft. That meant that a U-Boat commander would have to be more alert than usual.

The radar picked up a radar contact at four and a half miles and the pilot turned on towards it, descending to 400 feet. The Leigh Light was switched on and a U-Boat was sighted submerging. Time at the datum, or on top of the swirl left by the now-submerged submarine, was too late to drop any weapon and the captain adopted baiting or gambit tactics by flying away from the area for some while (this would usually about 45 minutes to an hour) to encourage the U-Boat commander to think his boat had not been spotted. The Wellington returned to the datum (the point where contact was lost) and commenced a square search. No contact was established, so the search was abandoned until first light, when the aircraft returned once more to the area with radar on. Contact was gained at four and a half miles, but at on top of the datum and not in full daylight nothing was seen.

The aircraft went into an orbit and contact was regained in the form of a surfaced U-Boat 3729N00120E. They attacked and the U-Boat, which was U-73, returned fire, scoring hits on the port engine which started a fire. Four depth charges were dropped from 100 feet, exploding about 50 yards from the submarine. The aircraft was forced to abandon the patrol and any further attack and went to Tafaroui rather than its base at Gibraltar. This incident was instrumental in the fitting of front guns to maritime patrol aircraft.

The U-Boat was attacked an hour later by a Hudson
from No 500 Squadron, captained by Pilot Officer J.
Pugh. The crew found the boat on the surface about 50
miles from land. Pugh attacked, dropping four depth
charges across the boat's stern and causing some damage.
However the aircraft was mortally hit in the starboard
engine and forward of the cockpit. The Hudson ditched
and the crew boarded the dinghy. A No 608 Squadron
Hudson found them. Later a No 500 Squadron Hudson
arrived and dropped rations. A Royal Navy Walrus from
No 700 Squadron landed and picked up two injured
crewmen, the navigator, Sergeant Broomfield and one of
the wireless operators (WOPs), Flight Sergeant Emberson.
The two Hudsons remained as top cover until the Walrus
returned to pick up Pugh and the other WOP, Flight
Sergeant Wilkins, and took them to safety. Pugh was
awarded the DFC and Wilkins the DFM.

No 201 Squadron was at Lough Erne in Northern
Ireland with Sunderland IIIs, which it received in January
1942 when it disposed of its Mark Is. It still retained its
Mark IIs.

No 206 Squadron moved to Benbecula in the Outer
Hebrides in July 1942 when it re-equipped with Fortress
IIs. It disposed of its Hudsons in August. On 27 October
1942 Plt. Off. R. Cowey and crew were escorting convoy
SC105. U-627, a type VIIc boat commanded by
Kapitänleutnant Robert Kindelbacher, was sighted on the
surface in position 5914N 02249W. The boat dived when
the Germans saw the aircraft but Cowey dropped a stick
of seven depth charges ahead of the swirl and along the
estimated submarine's track. U-627, on her first patrol,
had sunk.

CHAPTER TWENTY

No 210 Squadron moved to Sullom Voe in February 1942 with a detachment at Grasnaya, in North Russia. In July it added Catalina IIs and in August Mark Ibs to its inventory. In October it moved to Pembroke Dock, South West Wales with a detachment at Gibraltar.

No 220 Squadron moved to Nutt's Corner, Belfast in January 1942 with a detachment at Polebrook. The Shallufa detachment transferred to the Far East in May and left No 220 Squadron. By June the squadron was at Ballykelly with Fortress IIs which it received in July, disposing of its Mark Is in August. It had detachments at Benbecula and Reykjavik.

No 224 Squadron moved to Limavady with a detachment at Stornoway in February 1942, when it disposed of its Hudson IIIs. In April it went to Tiree and in July received Liberator IIIs. In September it disposed of its Hudson Vs and moved to Beaulieu, south of Bournemouth. On 20 October 1942 Fg. Off. D. M. Sleep and crew were off task and returning to base when a surfaced U-Boat was sighted and attacked with six depth charges from 30 feet. These exploded on impact, causing the destruction of the boat and considerable damage to the Liberator. The submarine was U-216, a type VIId minelayer, commanded by Kapitänleutnant Karl-Otto Schultz, on its first patrol, having left Kiel on 29 August. It was sunk in position 4841N 01925W. The Liberator had suffered severe damage to its elevators and it took both pilots to control the aircraft. Finally the control column had to be tied in a forward position. The aircraft crash landed at Predannack and was destroyed. A crew member, Sgt. R. Rose, suffered a broken leg, but the rest of the crew escaped with minor injuries. Fg. Off. Sleep received the DFC.

On 24 October 1942 Plt. Off. B. P. Liddington and crew were tasked with convoy escort to convoy KX 2. The convoy was not met. While searching for the convoy a surfaced submarine was sighted and attacked. This was U-599, a type VIIc, commanded by Kapitänleutnant Wolfgang Breithaupt, and it was sunk by this attack in position 4607N 01740W on its first patrol. The aircraft continued its search for the convoy but it was not located. In November it added Liberator IIs to its inventory.

No 228 Squadron moved to Oban in March 1942 and added Sunderland IIIs to its establishment. In December the squadron moved to Castle Archdale on Lough Erne.

No 246 Squadron was reformed at Bowmore in August 1942 with Sunderland IIIs.

No 304 Polish Squadron was equipped with Wellington Ics at Dale, South West Wales. On 2 September 1942 Fg. Off. M. Kucharski and crew sighted the Italian submarine *Reginaldo Giuliani* fresh from its mauling by No 10 Squadron the previous day. It was on the surface about five miles on the port bow in position 4430N 00442W. A stick of six depth charges was dropped accurately and the aircraft gunners opened fire, killing and injuring some crew members. The boat did not open fire but did fire two five-star red Verys. By now the submarine had stopped and Kucharski dropped two 500lb bombs. These undershot slightly, but the boat was now listing. Crew members were seen and the Wellington's gunners continued to fire at them, causing casualties. The aircraft had to leave the area because of fuel considerations. The boat finally got under way and arrived in Santander heavily damaged.

When Italy surrendered, the *Reginaldo Giuliani* was in Singapore. The Germans took her over, numbering her UIT23. She was later sunk in the Malacca Strait by a British submarine.

No 311 Czech Squadron was equipped with Wellington IIcs and was in South West Wales at Talbenny. On 27 July 1942 Sqn. Ldr. J. Stransky and crew were on patrol at 1500 feet when a U-Boat was sighted at two miles. This was U-106, a type IXB, commanded by Kapitänleutnant Hermann Rasch. As the aircraft attacked, the boat remained on the surface and opened fire with its aft guns. A stick of four depth charges was dropped from 50 feet, which apparently caused the boat to list and stop. A second attack was made from 10 feet with two depth charges. The boat submerged in position 4625N 00928W. It had left Lorient on 25 July and the damage was such that it was forced to return there, arriving on 28 July. Sqn. Ldr. Stransky was awarded the DFC. On

10 August 1942 Fg. Off. J. Nyvlt and crew were on patrol in the Bay of Biscay when a U-Boat was sighted on the surface. This was U-578, a type VIIC, commanded by Korvettenkapitän Ernst-August Rehwinkel. Three depth charges were dropped in the face of gunfire from the boat. The Wellington turned for a second attack as the boat dived and three depth charges were dropped on the conning tower. This sank U-578 in position 4559N 00744W.

No 330 Squadron Royal Norwegian Air Force "A" flight was equipped with Northrop N3P-Bs, while "B" Flight had Catalina IIIs. Both flights were based at Reykjavik. On 21 September 1942 Catalina III FP525 flying out of Akureyri was escorting convoy QP14 Russia to UK, somewhere north east of Jan Mayen Island. When astern of the convoy the crew sighted U-606 commanded by Kapitänleutnant Dietrich von der Esch,on the surface. The Catalina attacked, the captain, Lieutenant C. J. A. Stansberg, releasing four depth charges which caused no real damage. The aircraft was hit and the pilot was forced to ditch near the convoy. All of the crew were rescued by the destroyer *Marne*.

No 405 Squadron Royal Canadian Air Force was a bomber unit and had been loaned to Coastal at Beaulieu for a period. On 27 November Flt. Lt. C. W. Palmer and crew were hunting U-263, a type VIIc boat commanded by Kapitänleutnant Kurt Nolke. This boat had been damaged by a Hudson from No 233 Squadron in position 3634N 01200W on 24 November and had been attacked again by a No 59 Squadron Liberator. When Palmer and crew met the boat, she was accompanied by two minesweepers which promptly opened fire in position 4335N 00255W. The Halifax dropped a stick of six depth charges with a follow up attack of four. These lifted the boat, but only slight damage was caused. The minesweepers had suffered casualties from the Halifax gunners. U-263 was on its first patrol and reached La Pallice with a depth charge lodged in its foredeck. She did not sail again until 19 January 1944 and hit a mine on the 20th, causing her to sink.

No 415 Squadron Royal Canadian Air Force flew Hampdens out of Thorney Island.

No 422 Squadron Royal Canadian Air Force had formed at Lough Erne in April 1942 and was equipped with Lerwick Is until September. In August it was re-equipped with Catalina Ib's but it exchanged these in November for Sunderland IIIs and flew from Long Kesh in October, only to move to Oban, Argyll a few days later on 5 November 1942. It had a detachment at Jui Freetown, West Africa.

No 423 Squadron Royal Canadian Air Force had formed at Oban in May 1942, initially with Sunderland IIs but in November was at Castle Archdale, Lough Erne, Northern Ireland flying Sunderland IIIs as well, which it had received in September.

No 461 Squadron Royal Australian Air Force formed at Mountbatten, Plymouth in April 1942 from a nucleus of No 10 Squadron Royal Australian Air Force operating Sunderland IIs. In August it received, in addition, Sunderland IIIs. In September the squadron moved to Hamworthy Junction (Poole Harbour). On 1 September an aircraft joined with Sunderlands from No 10 Squadron RAAF in the attack on the Italian submarine, *Reginaldo Giuliani*, but was ordered back on patrol before the crew could make an attack.

No 502 Squadron Auxiliary Air Force was flying Whitley VIIs from St Eval with a detachment at Holmesley South. On 1 April 1942 Flt. Sgt. V. Pope and crew sighted U-129 from 700 yards in position 4630N 00635W at 2350 hours. Pope attacked with six depth charges. Bubbles were seen and the aircraft loitered in the vicinity but nothing further was seen. U-129, a type IXc, commanded by Kapitänleutnant Nicolai Clausen was damaged and she remained in port for almost six weeks. On 14 April 1942 Fg. Off. E. Cotton and crew were on patrol south west of Ireland and investigated a number of radar contacts which turned out to be Spanish fishing vessels. After almost three hours on task, a radar contact nine miles on the port was gained from 1000 feet. This was U-590, a type VIIc commanded by Kapitänleutnant Heinrich Muller-Edzards, en route from Kiel to St Nazaire, in position 4909N 01201W. As she dived, Cotton attacked with six depth charges from around 40 feet. No results were seen and Cotton adopted a baiting tactic, returning 30 minutes later, but still nothing was seen. The boat arrived at St Nazaire damaged. Cotton was awarded the DFC.

On 17 July 1942, Plt. Off. A. R. A. Hunt and crew gained a visual sighting of U-751, a type VIIc boat, commanded by Korvettenkäpitan Gerhard Bigalk in position 4513N 01222W and attacked with depth charges from 50 feet. The boat circled slowly to port. Two 100lb anti submarine bombs were dropped from 600 feet but missed. Machine gun attacks were made and then the boat dived stern first. Nothing further was seen until a No 61 Squadron Lancaster arrived on the scene. On 31 August 1942, Fg. Off. E. G. Brooks and crew gained a radar contact at 18 miles off the port bow. A homing was commenced and on breaking through the cloud a U-Boat was sighted underneath the aircraft. The submarine was U-256, a type VIIc commanded by Kapitänleutnant Odo Loewe. An attack was made with eight depth charges, but three hung up. The boat dived. Meanwhile Flt. Lt. E. O. Tandy and crew from No 51 Squadron were on task and heard the sighting report (see above). No 502 Squadron was to re-equip with Halifax IIs in February 1943.

No 547 Squadron was formed in October at Holmesley South with Wellington VIIIs and went to Chivenor in December 1942.

AIR SEA RESCUE UK

No 279 Squadron was still at Bircham Newton with its Hudsons. In January AOC-in-C Coastal informed the Director General of Air Safety that he was obliged to withdraw nine Hudsons from the squadron. It was agreed that Ansons could fill the gap, although they did not have the required range, nor could they carry the Lindholme gear.

No 280 Squadron was at Bircham Newton with Anson Is as no Hudsons were available.

No 281 Squadron was formed at Ouston in March with Defiant Is but as part of Fighter Command. As with the other Fighter Command SAR squadrons, executive control rested with AOC-in-C Coastal.

As a result of an allocation of extra high speed launches, in October 1942, No 111 OTU in the Bahamas could expect a Unit of HSLs. No 44 Air Sea Rescue Marine Craft Unit was at Padstow.

THE HUDSON SQUADRONS
No 48 Squadron moved to Wick in January 1942 with detachments at Sumburgh and Kaldadarnes. In September it moved to Sumburgh. On 26 September 1942 Plt. Off. E. Tammes and crew sighted U-262, a type VIIc commanded by Kapitänleutnant Heinz Franke, at four miles in a position north east of the Faeroe Islands. Four depth charges were dropped on the partly-submerged boat from 50 feet. Air bubbles were seen but nothing else. Tammes stayed in the area for 30 minutes and then carried out a baiting gambit (to encourage the boat to surface), returning after 20 minutes. Tammes went

off task some two and a half hours later, being relieved by Plt.Off R. Horney and crew, also from No 48 Squadron. U-262 was relocated on the surface by this crew and was attacked with four depth charges from 50 feet. Similar tactics to those used by Tammes were employed but nothing was found. U-262 was on her first patrol and had to return to Bergen. In November 1942 it disposed of its Mark Vs and in December of its Mark IIIs. It converted to Hudson Mark VIs in November when it moved to Gosport. The squadron moved to Gibraltar to cover the Western Mediterranean and the Eastern Atlantic.

No 53 Squadron had been to the British West Indies during 1942 with its Hudsons and was in the process of returning to the UK. This was when shipping in the area was being badly hit. Hudson V9253, captained by Flight Sergeant R. R. Silcock of the RAAF, on 10 November found U-505 on the surface. An attack was made with four depth charges, one of which made a direct hit and exploded on impact. It was this that caused the aircraft to crash. However, although the submarine was not sunk it was sufficiently damaged to cause it to return to Lorient. By 1 January 1943 the squadron was at Davidstow Moor, Cornwall. By February 1943 it had given up its Hudson Vs and exchanged them for Whitley VIIs at Docking.

No 269 Squadron was at Kaldadarnes, Iceland with Hudson IIIs. On 5 October 1942, Fg. Off. J. Markham and crew were on escort to convoy ONS 136 carrying out a Creeping Line Ahead (CLA) search at 4000 feet and gained a visual sighting of a surfaced U-Boat at five miles. Markham attacked from 20 feet with four 250lb depth charges and with the front guns. Oil and wreckage were seen half an hour later and this was confirmed by another No 269 Squadron aircraft which arrived later. The boat was U-619, a type VIIc, commanded by Oberleutnant zur See Kurt Makowski and had been sunk in this attack in position 5841N 02258W. Markham was awarded the DFC.

No 320 Squadron Royal Netherlands Navy had Hudson VIs and was based at Bircham Newton. This unit was to be re-equipped with Mitchells and transferred to bomber duties in March 1943.

No 407 Squadron Royal Canadian Air Force flew Hudson Vs, disposing of its Mark IIIs in May 1942. In February the squadron moved to Thorney Island and then to Bircham Newton in March. In October 1942 the squadron moved to St Eval and then in November to Docking, King's Lynn.

No 608 Squadron moved to Wick in January 1942 with a detachment at Skitten. In July it moved to Sumburgh and refitted with Hudson IIIAs, disposing of these and its Mark IIIs the following month when it moved to Gosport. In November 1942 it moved to Gibraltar.

Due to a shortage of aircraft, Air Chief Marshal Harris, Air Officer Commanding in Chief Bomber Command, was on occasion asked for help. Despite his view that the war would be won through bombing he often helped out by lending squadrons and No 10 Operational Training Unit (OTU). No 77 Squadron, flying Whitley Vs, was detached to Chivenor in May 1942 for the period ending October 1942. In early September Whitley Z9515, commanded by Pilot Officer Cassie, found and attacked U-256 commanded by Kapitänleutnant Odo Loewe. However, the Whitley was shot down. Again the information comes from the U-Boat's Daily War Diary, where it is stated that the aircraft disappeared out of sight pouring smoke. A faint distress message was picked up by St Eval. A search was carried out, but nothing was found. The following day No 77 squadron had its revenge when it sank U-705 west of Ushant. It also attacked U-660, with no result.

TORPEDO BOMBER/ANTISHIPPING/UK

The torpedo bomber/anti shipping squadrons had increased in strength and aircraft capability.

Coastal Command was trying to make life difficult for German shipping. The successful low-level attacks caused the enemy to improve his anti-aircraft defences, which in turn led the strike aircraft to attack from a higher level. However no suitable bomb sight was available and shipping losses went down. The idea of a Strike Wing was evolved, whereby there was concentration of force, a flak suppression squadron and a torpedo squadron for sinking ships. The rocket projectile gradually became the favoured weapon in lieu of the torpedo. In August, September and November 1942 Nos 143, 236 and 254 squadrons moved to North Coates and formed the first Strike Wing. All three squadrons were flying Beaufighters but No 254's aircraft, the Torbeaus, were armed with torpedoes. Their first operation was not a success, due mainly to bad weather and inexperience. This took place on 20 November when 14 Beaufighter VICs of No 236 Squadron led by Wg. Cdr. H. D. Fraser and 12 Torbeaus of No 254 Squadron led by Wg. Cdr. R. E. X. Mack attacked a convoy. The Schiff 49 and two escorts were damaged and a naval tug was sunk. However, three

Beaufighters were shot down and two crashed on landing. The technique had not been perfected and the squadrons were taken out of the line and given a period of extensive training. We shall see more of them in 1943.

The reconnaissance effort against the *Scharnhorst*, the *Prinz Eugen* and the *Gneisenau* has been described above. Having evaded the Coastal Command patrols, they were discovered by radar and visually identified by Spitfires. In the early afternoon of 12 February six Swordfish of the Fleet Air Arm attacked the enemy ships with torpedoes. They all missed and all six aircraft were shot down. The Dover and Ramsgate MTBs attacked but missed. On 10 February, Air Marshal Sir Philip Joubert de la Ferte, AOC-in-C Coastal, had ordered No 42 Squadron from Leuchars to North Coates but both this airfield and the other Coastal airfield in the area were snowbound. They therefore had to land at Coltishall. Because of snow, the squadron did not arrive until 12 February.

One Flight of No 217 squadron was at St Eval with No 86 Squadron. The remainder of No 217, seven aircraft, was at Thorney Island. All of these aircraft were Beauforts. Because two aircraft were loaded with bombs and a third was unserviceable, only four of No 217's Beauforts took off for the attack. They were 20 minutes late for their rendezvous with their fighter escort and to make up for this delay both units of aircraft were ordered to proceed independently to the enemy and were briefed in the air. Unfortunately No 16 Group failed to appreciate that the Beauforts had changed from W/T to R/T and therefore they did not receive the message.

They set off for Manston and then two of them set

heading for the French coast and found nothing. The other two landed at Manston, received a briefing and set off for the enemy. When they arrived destroyers were making an ineffective attack. The Beauforts made an attack on what they believed to be the *Prinz Eugen* but missed. Several waves of Bomber aircraft made attacks amounting to 242 aircraft in all, of which only 39 bombed. Fifteen aircraft were lost. No 42 Squadron, now at Coltishall, a fighter airfield with no facilities for torpedo bombers, could not get its torpedoes serviced. There was a Mobile Torpedo Servicing Unit at North Coates but it arrived too late to be of any help. Fourteen Beauforts had come from Leuchars but only nine were loaded with torpedoes and these took off to join the fray. They were to rendezvous with fighters and several Hudson bombers at Manston.

Unable to communicate with each other, all aircraft circled the airfield. The Beaufort leader took the initiative and set off for the enemy, followed by six of the Hudsons. The Hudsons gained radar contact and attacked through heavy flak and bad weather. Two were shot down and no hits were achieved. Six Beauforts attacked to but to no avail.

The two No 217 Beauforts which had failed to find the ships earlier now took off and made independent attacks but missed. No 86 Squadron and the remaining flight of No 217 had been ordered from St Eval to Thorney Island. After refuelling and checking the torpedoes they were ordered off to join up with fighters over Coltishall, but on reaching the airfield there was no sign of the escort. The Beauforts headed out to sea to have one last attempt at the enemy. However, it was last light, the visibility was poor and the cloud base very low. They saw four enemy minesweepers and one pilot saw what he thought was a capital ship, but could not drop his weapon as his aircraft was so badly damaged. The Beauforts returned to Coltishall having lost two aircraft and crews.

No 86 Squadron had Beaufort IIs at the beginning of 1942 and in July the air echelon moved to Luqa, Malta and was absorbed by No 39 Squadron in August. The Squadron Headquarters moved to Thorney Island from Skitten, Wick in August and in October 1942 the Squadron was equipped with Liberator IIIas, leaving the torpedo bomber role and becoming a maritime reconnaissance squadron.

No 143 Squadron moved to Limavady in April 1942 with Blenheim IVs, to Thorney Island in June and to Docking in July. In August it exchanged its Blenheims for Beaufighter ICs and a month later it exchanged these for Mark IIFs. It moved to North Coates in August 1942.

No 144 Squadron transferred to Coastal Command from Bomber Command on 22 April 1942 at Leuchars with Hampdens. There were detachments at Skitten, Sumburgh, Wick, Afrikanda on the White Sea and Vaenga near Murmansk, North Russia.

No 235 Squadron was equipped with Beaufighter VIcs at Leuchars, Fife. It had exchanged its Blenheims in December 1941 for Beaufighter Ics at Dyce, Aberdeen and in July 1942 had re-equipped with Beaufighter VIcs.

No 236 Squadron also had Beaufighter VIcs and was at North Coates. It had disposed of its Blenheims in February 1942 but had started to re-equip with Beaufighter Ics in October 1941. In September 1942 it received Beaufighter VIcs and had detachments at Wick, Sumburgh and Predannack.

No 248 Squadron was equipped with Beaufighter VIcs at Talbenny, South West Wales.

No 254 Squadron was at North Coates with Beaufighter VIfs.

No 404 Squadron Royal Canadian Air Force was at Dyce with Beaufighter IIfs.

No 415 Squadron Royal Canadian Air Force was at Thorney Island with Hampdens.

No 455 Squadron Royal Australian Air Force had Hampdens at Leuchars and had been transferred from Bomber Command to Coastal in April. It had detachments at Sumburgh, Benbecula, Tain, Wick and Vaenga in North Russia.

No 489 Squadron Royal New Zealand Air Force was at Wick with Hampdens.

This was a total of eleven squadrons.

MEDITERRANEAN MARITIME PATROL

No 159 Squadron was a Liberator II bomber unit, formed at Molesworth in January 1942. It was sent to the Far East, but a detachment remained at Aqir and St Jean in Palestine for anti-submarine duties. On 15 July 1942 a Liberator AL566 captained by Warrant Officer W. S. Pottie failed to return from such a sortie. The only information comes from the Germans. It is believed that Pottie attacked U-561 commanded by Kapitänleutnant Robert Bartels, and was shot down. Only one member of the crew was found; the body of Sergeant Hilary Eldred Birk from New South Wales was washed ashore and was buried at Benghazi.

No 202 Squadron was at Gibraltar with Catalina IBs and Sunderland Is, IIs and IIIs. On 2 May 1942 Flt. Lt.

R. Y. Powell and crew in a Catalina gained visual contact on a U-boat at seven miles and from 3000 feet. Powell attacked and dropped seven 250lb depth charges just ahead of the swirl left by the diving boat. The boat was U-74, a type VIIb, commanded by Leutnant zur See Karl Friedrich. No confirmation of a kill was made but two destroyers arrived an hour and a half later, made contact with the U-boat and sank it in position 3716N 00100E. On 7 June 1942 Fg. Off. R. M. Corrie RAAF and crew in a Catalina was 13 minutes into a CLA search when they gained a radar contact 16 miles to port while at 1500 feet. A homing was initiated and a surfaced U-Boat was sighted. An attack was made, but the bomb racks failed to roll out. They went round again and this time only the four depth charges on the port released, hitting the boat. As it dived another attack was made on the swirl. Oil patches were seen. The boat, which was the Italian Maecello class *Veniero*, commanded by Tenente di Vascello Elio Zappetta, was sunk. Fg. Off. Corrie flew to Ansiola so that an injured crew member, Sgt. Lee, could receive medical treatment, and then returned to the scene, where more oil was seen. Corrie received the DFC.

On 13 June 1942 Sqn. Ldr. R. B. Burrage RAAF and crew in a Sunderland were in support of a Malta convoy. Off the Sardinian coast they gained a visual sighting of the surfaced *Otaria*, an Italian Glauco class submarine commanded by Tenente di Vascello Alberto Gorini. An attack was made, achieving a straddle with seven depth charges. The boat listed initially but came to an even keel and smoke was seen coming from the conning tower. The crew lost sight of it and it had probably dived. About an hour and a half after the initial contact a radar contact was gained at 12 miles, but nothing was seen at the end of the homing.

On 14 September 1942 Fg. Off. P. Walshe RAAF and crew in a Sunderland were operating near Algiers. *Alabastro*, an Italian Platino class boat commanded by Tenente di Vascello Giovanni Bonadies, was sighted at five miles and Walshe made an attack with six depth charges. One hung up and another had a fusing wire still attached. The boat remained on the surface and opened fire with a machine gun. Nevertheless a good straddle was achieved. The boat was down by the bows and after a feint attack crew members were seen to jump into the sea. The boat then sank in position 3728N 00435E. The squadron disposed of its Sunderlands in September and continued operations with Catalinas.

No 203 Squadron operated Blenheim IVs until November 1942 and Maryland Is until December 1942. On 2 June 1942 it is believed that a Blenheim from this squadron attacked U-565 commanded by Kapitänleutnant Wilhelm Franken, but the boat escaped undamaged. It began conversion to Baltimore Is and IIs in August 1942 and Blenheim Vs in October 1942, but disposed of them a month later. It was based at the end of the year at LG 227 Gianaclis.

No 221 Squadron had disposed of its Wellington 1cs at Docking in December 1941 and in January 1942, it re-equipped with Wellington VIIIs and moved to Landing Ground (LG) 39, Burgh el Arab South, south west of Alexandria, with a detachment at Luqa, Malta. The following month it moved to LG 87 with detachments to Luqa, LG 05 and St Jean. It was attached to No 47

Squadron temporarily. In March 1942 the squadron re-established itself at LG 89 with detachments at LG 05, Luqa and LG 99.In June 1942, the squadron moved to Shandur with detachments at Gianaclis, south of Alexandria, St Jean and Luqa. In August 1942 they moved again, this time to Shallufah Satellite and ten days later to Shallufah itself, just south of the Great Bitter Lake, with detachments at Idku, St Jean, Gianaclis, LG 143 and Berka II. On 4 August 1942 Flt. Sgt. Gay and crew were on a night escort of a convoy. Just after midnight a submarine was seen in position 3236N 03436E. Flares were dropped and the aircraft positioned for an attack, but the boat dived. This was U-372, a type VIIc commanded by Kapitänleutnant H. Neumann. The crew requested support from surfaces forces and HMS *Sikh, Zulu, Croome* and *Tetcott* arrived at the datum. Depth charge attacks were carried by these ships and it was assessed that the boat had been sunk.

No 230 Squadron was at Aboukir, east of Alexandria, Egypt with Sunderland IIIs.

No 233 Squadron moved to Thorney Island in January 1942 with detachments at St Eval and Gibraltar. On 1 May 1942 Sgt Brent and crew, detached to Gibraltar, gained a visual sighting of U-573, a type VIIc boat commanded by Kapitänleutnant Heinrich Heinsohn. Brent attacked from 1700 feet, dropping three 250lb depth charges from 30 feet and gaining a good straddle. The boat went under, but then the bows came up perpendicularly and the boat settled on an even keel. The crew appeared to surrender, but the aircraft was unable to accept and had to go off task. The boat's crew managed to repair the damage sufficiently to allow them to sail the boat to Cartagena. She was later sold to Spain.

In July the squadron moved to Gibraltar and exchanged its Hudson Vs for Hudson IIIAs. It provided a detachment at Lajes in the Azores at the same time. On 1 November just before Operation Torch, the landings in North Africa, one of 233's aircraft sighted U-565 commanded by Kapitänleutnant Wilhelm Franken and attacked in position 3735N 00138E south of the Balearic Islands. The U-Boat had been on the surface and dived, but the first attack of four depth charges forced the boat to resurface. The boat's gunners inflicted hits on the Hudson, V9169, on its second attack when the Captain, Flight Sergeant S. Woodward, dropped an anti-submarine bomb. Hits on the tailplane caused the bomb to fall wide. A third attack was attempted, but the pilot was having trouble with the aircraft so he decided to go home. A second Hudson AE591 captained by Sergeant D.H. Jenkins from 233 had received Woodward's sighting report and joined in the action. This aircraft dropped three bombs which fell wide, but it was hit and crashed about some 500 yards away. There were no survivors.

On 14 November 1942 Plt.Pff. J. W. Barling and crew gained a visual sighting of a wake from a small boat. Following it a surfaced U-Boat was sighted in position 3620N 00101E. Three depth charges were dropped from 40 feet. The crew had sunk U-605, a type VIIc boat commanded by Kapitänleutnant Herbert Victor Schutze.

On 17 November 1942, Sgt. E. H. Smith and crew sighted a wake which they followed, sighting a U-Boat in position 3540N 01118W. This was U-566, a type VIIc, commanded by Oberleutnant zur See Gert Remus. Smith attacked with four depth charges from 100 feet. Oil and bubbles were seen and the crew orbited for half an hour, but nothing further was seen. U-566 was seriously damaged with an irrepairable oil leak and had to return to Brest. Sgt. Smith was awarded the DFM.

On 24 November 1942, Sgt. Smith and crew gained a visual sighting from six miles of U-263. This was a type VIIc boat commanded by Kapitänleutnant Kurt Nolke. Smith attacked U-263 in position 3634N 01200W with four depth charges from 50 feet. The boat dived amid oil and bubbles and was believed damaged. It had already been damaged by escorts which had dropped 119 depth charges on it and it was on its way to France. This boat was attacked again by a No 59 Squadron Liberator on the 26th and then again on the 27th by a No 405 Squadron Halifax. The boat reached La Pallice on 29 November.

No 240 Squadron was en route to the Far East and while in Gibraltar Flt. Lt. D. E. Hawkins and crew flew a sortie. They were at 2000 feet near the Balearics when they gained a visual sighting of a submarine at ten miles in position 3821N 03021E. Under fire from the boat Hawkins attacked and dropped four 450lb depth charges from 100 feet. Gunfire was exchanged until the boat dived. It was the *Zaffiro*, an Italian Sirena class boat commanded by Tenente di Vascello Carlo Mottura. The boat surfaced and the crew abandoned ship. The aircraft opened fire until a white flag was waved. Hawkins attempted a landing but the swell was too heavy, the hull being slightly damaged in the attempt. Hawkins received a bar to his DFC, which had been awarded for a Special Operation in April 1942.

No 500 (County of Kent) Squadron was equipped with Hudson Vs and was operating from Blida and Algiers. Five aircraft, captains Wing Commander D. Spotswood, Flying Officer H. M. S. Green, Flt. Lt. H. G. Holmes, Plt. Off. J. H. Simpson and Flying Officer G. A. B. Lord, took over the attack on U-595 commanded by Kapitänleutnant Jurgen Quaet-Faslem on 14 November 1942 from No 608 Squadron. U-595, being damaged, opened fire as the Hudsons attacked with depth charges. Green's depth charges hung up but two aircraft made two attacks, neither of which hit the boat. One of these aircraft made a further attack with an anti-submarine bomb. Three aircraft were hit. However, all returned to base and no aircrew were injured. The U-Boat was forced to beach and the crew became prisoners.

On the same day Fg. Off. M. A. Ensor and crew were operating out of Oran and sighted U-458, a type VIIc boat commanded by Kapitänleutnant Kurt Diggins. Ensor attacked, dropping four depth charges from 30 feet and achieving a good straddle. Ensor climbed to 500 feet and dropped an anti-submarine bomb. Gunfire was exchanged. The aircraft had to go off task at its Prudent Limit of Endurance (PLE) and the boat was still on the surface and circling. U-458 eventually reached La Spezia in Italy.

On the 15 November Flying Officer Mick Ensor attacked U-259 commanded by Kapitänleutnant Klaus Kopke. One depth charge exploded on impact, causing the aircraft to become uncontrollable, and the crew baled out. Only Fg Off Ensor and one other survived.

On 17 November three crews, captains Sqn. Ldr. I. C.

Patterson, RNZAF, Flt. Lt. A.W. Barwood and Sgt.Young were operating from Tafouri. Patterson and crew gained a visual sighting of U-331, a type VIIc boat commanded by Kapitänleutnant Hans-Friedrich Freiherr von Tiesenhausen, on the surface. He attacked with three depth charges, which caused the bows to lift. Some of the boat's crew dived into the sea. He made a follow-up attack with an anti-submarine bomb from 600 feet. Sgt Young attacked with depth charges and guns. Barwood attacked with four depth charges.Young and Barwood then left the area. A white flag was waved from U-331.

Patterson then had to go off task and proceeded to Maison Blanche, where he reported events to the Navy, who promised that a destroyer would be sent to the boat. Patterson then returned to the area escorted by a Hurricane and found the boat's crew sitting on deck.Two more Hudsons came to the area. Then a Martlet, a Swordfish and an Albacore from HMS *Formidable* arrived and, despite signals from the three Hudsons, the Martlet attacked the U-Boat. The Albacore attacked with a torpedo, destroying U-331. Seventeen survivors were picked by a Walrus and landed at Gibraltar. A very angry Patterson returned to Maison Blanche. He was awarded the DSO and Flt. Lt. Barwood was awarded the DFC.

No 608 (North Riding) Squadron operated from Blida south west of Algiers from December 1942 with a detachment at Bone with Hudson IIIAs. On 14 November 1942, operating from Oran, Fg. Off. G.Williams and Plt. Off. C. A. Livingstone with their respective crews gained contact with U-595, a type VIIc boat commanded by

Kapitänleutnant Jurgen Quaet-Faslem. Williams attacked with four depth charges from below 50 feet, achieving a straddle. The boat went under but shortly after resurfaced, after which Williams and crew attacked it with machine-gun fire. Livingstone then attacked with four depth charges, again achieving a straddle. The boat circled and seemed to be sinking. Both aircraft attacked with guns, the submarine replying with cannon fire. A Junkers 88 briefly appeared but was engaged by one of Williams' gunners and was not seen again. At this point the U-Boat was damaged. The attack was resumed by six Hudsons of No 500 Squadron.

On 19 November Fg. Off. A. F. Wilcox and crew gained a visual sighting from 2200 feet at nine miles of U-413 in a moderate sea, in position 3640N 01158W. This was a type VIIc boat commanded by Kapitänleutnant Gustav Poel. Taking advantage of cloud, Wilcox made an attack with four depth charges straddling the mean line of advance of the boat. A patch of oil was seen, but the Hudson had go off task shortly afterwards at its Prudent Limit of Endurance (PLE). The boat had been severely damaged and had to return to Brest.

MEDITERRANEAN TORPEDO BOMBER/ANTI SHIPPING 1942

In the torpedo bomber/anti-shipping role in the Mediterranean there had been seven squadrons operating during 1942, but by the end of the year only two, Nos 38 and 39, remained. No 22 Squadron was sent to the Far East by air with their Beaufort Is in February 1942, but on arrival at Luqa, Malta it was retained for operations in the region based at Luqa and North Africa. The groundcrew had gone by sea. The Squadron was released in April 1942 and carried on to Ceylon.

Similarly, No 42 Squadron was sent to the Far East by air with their Beaufort IIs in June 1942 but was also retained at Luqa for operations in the region. Again the groundcrew had gone by sea. The Squadron moved on to Ceylon in November, 1942.

No 39 Squadron started to convert to Beaufort IIs in April 1942, retaining its Mark Is until November. It had been operating from Shandur in the Canal Zone with detachments to Gianaclis south of Alexandria and Luqa. In August the squadron moved to Luqa and absorbed Nos 86 and 217 Squadrons. It maintained its detachments in North Africa.

No 47 Squadron was re-established at Shandur from elements of Nos 39 and 42 Squadrons. The squadron had been a Wellesley squadron and elements of this remained at LG 07 until disbanded in March 1943. The new squadron was re-equipped with Beaufort Is and detached to Gianaclis.

No 227 Squadron reformed at Luqa from a detachment of No 248 Squadron in August 1942 and was equipped with Beaufighter ICs and VIcs. In November it moved to Takali.

No 252 Squadron was at Idku east of Alexandria with Beaufighter VIcs.

At Takali, Malta No 272 Squadron was equipped with Beaufighter VIcs.

No 459 Squadron Royal Australian Air Force was equipped with Hudson IIIAs and based at Landing

Ground (LG) 143 Gambut, Libya. It had detachments at Khormaksar in Aden, Berka just outside Benghazi, Gianaclis and LG91 both south of Alexandria, LG07 between Mersa Matruh and Sidi Barrani, Nicosia, Cyprus and Lydda, Palestine.

AIR SEA RESCUE MEDITERRANEAN

The Air Sea Rescue Flight at Burg-el-Arab moved to El Adem near Tobruk in January 1942, but as the Afrika Corps advanced, so the Unit moved back to Gambut and then Fuka in February. The calls on the flight were ever increasing. Up to June there were 67 callouts, of which 16 were successful with 75 persons rescued. As Field Marshal Rommel and his army advanced further so the Flight was pulled back to Abu-Sueir. However, as the Eighth Army advanced, the Unit was moved forward to Burg-el-Arab. There were detachments at Gambut, Benghazi and Sidi Barani.

In July it was decided for operational and administration purposes that HSLs were to be organized in pairs in numbered units. It was intended that the number of units should be increased. There were nine boats at overseas units and 13 were on the way. An additional launch had reached Malta but it served only as a replacement as the original had been destroyed in an air raid.

In October it was decided to allot 135 boats to Overseas Commands, which would allow the formation of a further 34 units in addition to the 13 already authorized in July.

MIDDLE EAST 1942

No 8 Squadron had been based at Khormaksar, Aden since February 1927. Until April 1942 it had Vincents on strength and until August it also had Blenheim IVs. In September it converted to Blenheim Vs. It maintained detachments at Scucuiban and Bandar Kassim, both in British Somaliland, Riyan in the Aden Protectorate, and Salalah in the Sultanate of Oman along the coast of the Arabian Peninsula.

No 244 Squadron moved to Sharjah, Trucial States of Oman in May 1942, flying Blenheim IVs until December. It had been equipped with Blenheim Vs in October 1942.

WEST AFRICA 1942

No 95 Squadron moved to Jui in April 1942 with detachments at Bathurst and Fisherman's Lake. In July it received Sunderland IIIs and disposed of its Mark Is in December.

No 200 Squadron was at Jeswang near Bathurst in the Gambia, where it had been since June 1941 after its formation from a nucleus of No 206 Squadron at Bircham Newton in May 1941. It was equipped with Hudson IIIs, IIIAs and VIs.

No 204 Squadron with its Sunderland IIIs was also at Bathurst.

No 270 Squadron was reformed in November 1942 at Jui, Freetown, Sierra Leone with Catalina Ibs with detachments at Bathurst and Fisherman's Lake in Liberia. This was the first time the squadron had been active since it had disbanded in September 1919 and merged with No 269 Squadron.

This was a total of four squadrons, one of Hudsons, one of CatalinAs and two of Sunderland's to cover a vast sector of the Atlantic Ocean.

AIR SEA RESCUE

In August 1941 West Africa had been allotted four HSLs, but it was not until October 1942 that two arrived.

As a result of a decision in October 1942 to allocate 135 High Speed Launches to Overseas Commands, new Units of HSLs were expected. It was not until mid 1943 that any more arrived in West Africa. An ASR officer was appointed to Air Headquarters West Africa in October 1942. The Sunderlands based at Jui had been carrying out rescue work. Survival kits based on the Thornaby Bag had been locally produced from kitbags and filled with food and pyrotechnics.

On 9 October Sunderlands had been involved in the rescue of the 266 survivors of the 20,000-ton SS *Oronsay* en route Suez to UK and torpedoed by the Italian submarine *Archimede,* commanded by Guido Saccardo. A Sunderland found six lifeboats about 300 miles off the coast of Liberia the following morning. Survival packs were dropped and a naval vessel summoned to their aid. The following day another Sunderland found a further nine lifeboats and the day after that a Sunderland found the remaining three.

In December Lindholme gear arrived for use by the Hudsons of No 200 Squadron.

SOUTH EAST AFRICA

No 209 Squadron was at Kipevu, near Mombasa, Kenya with Catalina IIAs. It had many detachments at Kisumu on Lake Victoria, Kenya, Pamanzi, an island halfway between Tanganyika and Madagascar, Diego Suarez on the northern tip of Madagascar, Congella, just outside Durban, South Africa, Tulear, in the southwest of Madagascar, Port Victoria, in the Seychelles, Aden and Masirah, an island off the south-east tip of the Arabian Peninsula..

No 262 Squadron was formed at Hednesford in September 1942 and sent out to Congella in November. It received its first aircraft, Catalina Ibs, in February 1943.

FAR EAST 1942

In early 1942 No 222 Group, with a joint Naval and Air Operations Room, was established at Colombo under Air Forces in India. The group was to be responsible for operations in the Indian Ocean. Two new airfields were built, at Ratmalana and China Bay near Trincomalee. The first two squadrons were part of No 205 and No 273, the latter equipped with Seals and Vildebeeste IIIs until March 1942, when it re-equipped with Fulmars and became a fighter squadron.

No 36 Squadron moved to Kalidjati, South East of Batavia on Java, in February 1942 in an effort to find a suitable airfield from which to strike at the invading Japanese. It was then forced to move to various airfields, namely Tijkampek, Madioen, Andir, Tijkembar and finally Tasikmalaj all in a matter of 37 days, after which the squadron was captured, on 9 March 1942. The squadron was reformed in October 1942 at Tanjore, South India and in December equipped with Wellington Ics.

No 100 Squadron moved to Kemajoran at Batavia on Java in January 1942 and in December merged with No 36 Squadron.

No 205 Squadron was in a similar position to No 36 Squadron. In January 1942 it was sent to Batavia with a detachment at Seletar in Singapore. At the beginning of February it was at Oesthaven in southern Sumatra and a fortnight later it found itself at Tjilitjap near Batavia. On 1 March the squadron was evacuated to Fremantle, South West Australia, and was disbanded on 31 March. In July it was reformed at Koggala in Ceylon with Catalina Is and maintained various detachments at Red Hills Lake near Madras, Addu Atoll in the Maldives, Diego Garcia, Coconada on the coast of East India, China Bay in East Ceylon, Kelai at the Northern end of the Maldives and Cocos Island.

No 212 Squadron was reformed in October 1942 at Korangi Creek near Karachi, operating Catalina Ibs. It had detachments at Masirah, Jiwani on the Persian Coast, Bahrain, Red Hills Lake near Madras, Trombay, near Bombay, Cochin, South West India, Koggala in Ceylon and Bally near Calcutta.

No 321 Squadron Royal Netherlands Navy officially reformed at China Bay in August 1942, but its number had been in use since May. It was equipped with Catalina IIs and in October Catalina IIIs were added. Detachments were at Addu Atoll (Gan), Red Hills Lake, Cochin, Socotra ,an island off the Aden coast, Langebaan, north west of Cape Town, Congella near Durban and Masirah Island, Sultanate of Oman.

No 354 Squadron was formed at Drigh Road, near Karachi, on 10 May 1943. In August 1943 it moved to Cuttack, south west of Calcutta, and was equipped with Liberator Mark Vs. In December 1943, the squadron received Liberator Mark IIIAs.

FAR EAST AIR SEA RESCUE

In January 1942, the Moths of the Malaya Volunteer Air Force aided in the rescue of 12 pilots. This was the last report received by the Directorate of Air Sea Rescue before the fall of Singapore. After that, all Far East services were maintained by Air Headquarters (AHQ) India. However, that area was considered to be of low priority and no rescue launches were established there.

In February, the Air Ministry asked the Admiralty for 16 Walrus aircraft, but it was not until April that such an arrangement could be made. At the same time AHQ India asked for Lysander rescue aircraft but was advised by the Air Staff that there were higher priorities.

In January 1942 a production order had been given for HSLs for overseas theatres. At this time the overseas establishment was increased from 33 to 66 boats. A month later it was obvious that the requirements would have to be increased and 80 craft were earmarked for Australasia and the Far East. However, a month later the Japanese had captured Singapore and the Dutch East Indies and these boats were no longer needed, although the Air Staff did agree that they might well be needed a little later when the offensive against Japan was resumed.

In the summer the Americans agreed to assume responsibility for rescue operations in their area. Thus it was considered that for operations in the British zone only 30 boats would be required, making a total of 70 boats in the Far East and the Indian Ocean. These were split 30 for India, 30 for future forward operations and 10 for East Africa, although this area was at that time part of Middle East Command. It was expected that 20 out this total would be delivered in 1943.

As a result of a decision in October 1942, to allocate 135 new high speed launches to Overseas Commands, new Units of HSLs were expected.

METEOROLOGICAL CALIBRATION
No 521 Squadron was formed at Bircham Newton in July 1942 from No 1401 Flight with Blenheim IVs, Gladiator IIs, Spitfire Vs, Mosquito IVs and Hudson IIIAs.

PHOTOGRAPHIC RECONNAISANCE
The work of the Photographic Reconnaissance Units (PRUs) was growing in importance. Mosquitoes were added to the inventory of the high-level Spitfires, enabling longer range sorties to be attempted. The number of sorties had grown from four a day to ten. A new camera, the F53, was introduced in January 1942, which was an improvement on the F24. Larger magazines gave more film and better cover. The Central Interpretation Unit at Medmenham employed over 1000 personnel by the end of the year.

No 1 Photographic Reconnaissance Unit split into five squadrons:

No 540 Squadron was formed in October 1942 at Leuchars from "H"and "L" flights flying Spitfire IVs and Mosquito Is, IVs and VIIIs. The Spitfires were disposed of in December 1942. There were detachments at Gibraltar and Benson.

No 541 Squadron was formed at Benson from "B" and "F" Flights in October 1942 with Spitfire D's, IVs, IXs and XIs. There were detachments at St Eval and Gibraltar.

No 542 Squadron was formed in October at Benson from "A" and "E" flights with Spitfire IVs.

No 543 Squadron was formed at Benson in October from other elements of No 1 PRU with Spitfire IVs.

No 544 Squadron was formed at Benson from other elements of No 1 PRU with Anson Is, Maryland Is, Wellington IVs and Spitire IVs. There were detachments at Leuchars, Gibraltar, Marrakesh and Agadir.

There were other PRUs that were not part of Coastal Command. No 2 operated in the Middle East, while No 3 was originally part of Bomber Command but was absorbed into No 1 PRU in June 1941. It was reformed in India. No 4 PRU was formed in October 1942 to operate in French North Africa.

CHAPTER TWENTY ONE

1943

SITUATION AS AT 31 DECEMBER 1943

Coastal Command, after successful British/Portuguese negotiations, set up No 247 Group in the Azores. Operations began in August with two Wellington squadrons, No 172 and No 179, detached from Gibraltar, followed in October by Nos 206 and 220 Squadrons operating Fortress IIs. These aircraft had originally been obtained for use by Bomber Command but were found unsuitable and were transferred to Coastal.

MARITIME PATROL UNITED KINGDOM

The Leigh Light had proved to be very effective in identifying U-Boats after they had been located by radar (or Special Equipment as it was then known for security purposes). Admiral Dönitz therefore ordered that boats should sail by day and that they should stay on the surface and fight unless they could dive well before the aircraft reached them. He also ordered group sailings so that combined flak from all boats would protect all of them. However, this went partway to solving the detection problem. A surfaced submarine is easier to locate both visually and by radar than a submerged boat: a surfaced boat is easier to attack than the swirl left behind as it submerges. It does give a flak problem to the attacking aircraft but another aircraft could be called in thus splitting the defence.

U-Boats were fitted with "Metox" radar detection equipment. It did give off some radiation and Dönitz thought this was helping the antisubmarine aircraft. It was not the case. He did not know that the aircraft were fitted with centrimetric radar, the ASV3, which "Metox" was unable to detect. Thus Coastal Command flooded the Bay of Biscay with antisubmarine aircraft patrols. On 30 July 1943 U-461, U-462, both U-Tankers and U-504 a type IXC/40 were destroyed by No 461 Squadron, No 502 Squadron and Commander Walker's No 2 Escort Group. This was a disaster for the Kriegsmarine, paralyzing all long-range operations. The summer was disastrous for the U-boats and Dönitz rescinded his orders to fight it out on the surface. A number of U-Boat commanders did not agree and continued to stay on the surface and fight.

No 10 Squadron Royal Australian Air Force had a number of engagements.

On 18 April, 1943 Sunderland III DV969 was on patrol over the Bay of Biscay captained by Fg. Off. E. H. Farmer. The aircraft was flying at 3500 feet, the sea was calm, the radar was off and visibility was good. A member of the crew sighted a surfaced submarine about eight miles away. Farmer dived to 500 feet, but at about half a mile from the target he broke off the attack as the U-Boat had not attempted to dive as was normal. After a while Farmer attacked down sun, dropping two 250 lb general purpose bombs. The gunners on the boat and the aircraft exchanged fire but the Sunderland was not hit.

Farmer attacked again and the U-boat flak responded, hitting two crew members. Six depth charges were dropped, no results were seen and the boat dived. The commander of this boat, U-634, was Oberleutnant Eberhard Dahlhaus. The boat was undamaged. This was probably the first time a U-Boat had decided to fight it out on the surface.

On 7 May 1943 Flt. Lt. G. G. Rossiter RAAF and crew gained a visual sighting of a U-boat but it dived before an attack could be initiated. Later a further boat was sighted in position 4706N 01058W and attacked with four depth charges. A follow-up attack was made with another four depth charges and the boat was seen to settle by the stern. This was U-663, a type VIIc commanded by Kapitänleutnant Heinrich Schmidt and had been severely damaged. It was never heard from again and therefore may well have been sunk in this attack.

On 31 May 1943 Flt. Lt. M. S. Mainprize RAAF and crew was ordered to join in the fight against U-563 which had been attacked by two No 58 Squadron Halifaxes. Mainprize attacked U-563 with a stick of four depth charges, which caused the boat to stop. A follow-up attack of four depth charges was made and this caused the boat to start to sink. Then a No 228 Squadron Sunderland arrived on the scene and completed the destruction of the submarine. Mainprize was awarded the DFC.

On 30 June 1943 a Sunderland captained by Flt. Lt. H. W. Skinner located U-518, commanded by Kapitänleutnant Friedrich-Wilhelm Wissmann, in position 4453N00821W and attacked. The aircraft was fired at but not hit. The captain could not lose sufficient height to drop depth charges and went round again, attacking from 150 feet. His depth charges undershot. The flying boat was badly hit, killing the rear gunner. Skinner and crew returned to base. This U-Boat had been severely damaged by a No 201 Squadron Sunderland W6005 captained by Fg. Off. B. E. H. Layne RNZAF on 27 June.

On 1 August Flt Lt K. G. Fry RAAF and crew in Sunderland W4020 joined five ships from an escort group in a submarine hunt. From 1700 feet they gained a visual sighting of the outbound U-454, a type VIIc, commanded by Kapitänleutnant Burkhard Hacklander in position 4536N01023W. Fry attacked immediately. He encountered intense flak, but he dropped his stick of depth charges and the U-Boat broke in two. The aircraft was badly hit and crashed. Six survivors were picked up by HMS *Wren* of the No 2 Escort Group. HMS *Kite* from the same Group picked up 14 survivors from the U-Boat, including Hacklander. The squadron lost seven aircraft in this year.

No 48 Squadron was at Gibraltar with Hudson VIs. There was a detachment at Agadir. On 26 September 1943 Hudson EW924 captained by Fg. Off. E. L. Ashbury was homed in to U-667 by Fg. Off. Frandson of No 233 squadron. He attacked with rockets and guns, causing some damage, but was hit himself and returned to base. This was the last in a series of eight attacks in the area of 37N 009W in two days. Kapitänleutnant Heinrich Schroteler was forced to abandon his attempt to enter the Mediterranean, his batteries practically exhausted.

No 53 Squadron re-equipped with Whitley GRVIIs at Docking in February 1943. It moved to Bircham Newton in March and in April to Thorney Island. In May it converted to Liberator Vs and moved to Beaulieu in September. On 3 July 1943 Warrant Officer L. L. Esler and crew gained a radar contact at 20 miles and homed in, finding a submerging U-Boat. No attack was made. Later a further radar contact was gained at 12 miles. A homing was initiated and a U-Boat was found in position 4450N 00950W and attacked with depth charges. The boat was U-386, a type VIIc commanded by Oberleutnant zur See Fritz Albrecht and had been damaged, forcing her return to St. Nazaire.

On 5 July Flt. Sgt. W. Anderson RNZAF and crew were engaged on a search with four sloops of the 2nd Escort Group investigating a report of a U-Boat from a No 10 Squadron RAAF aircraft. As the aircraft reached PLE it turned for its home airfield. Then three U-Boats were sighted. The first attack missed as the U-Boat evaded and on the second the depth charges hung up, but the third was much more successful and eight depth charges straddled the boat. This sank U-535, a type IXc/40 commanded by Kapitänleutnant Helmut Ellmenreich. U-535 had been damaged by Sgt R. B. Couchman and crew from No 269 Squadron on 8 June 1943. The other boats were U-170 and U-536 and these got away. There had been heavy flak and the Liberator was damaged and the beam gunner wounded. The aircraft returned to base.

The U-Tankers U-461 and U-462 were sailing in company with U-504, a type IXC/40, and were sighted by Fg. Off. W. J. Irving and crew in Liberator (BZ730) on 30 July 1943. Coastal Command Instructions were that if more than one U-Boat were sighted then other aircraft had to be called in. The sighting reports brought in a No 228 Squadron Sunderland (JM679), a No 210 Squadron Catalina, a No 461 Squadron (RAAF) Liberator (W6077), two No 502 Squadron Halifaxes and an American Liberator from the 19th Squadron. Shortly after, Commander Walker's Escort Group of five sloops arrived. A battle followed.

The second pilot of the No 53 Squadron Liberator, Fg. Off. R. E. Dobson, reported that it was not possible to organize a concerted attack as they could not establish radio contact, so his crew attacked the outside boat. Two of their engines were hit and the depth charges undershot. However the No 461 squadron Sunderland followed them in and the No 53 squadron rear gunner reported that the U-Boat had been blown out of the water. U-461 had been destroyed by No 461 Squadron with an aircraft that was identified by the letter "U". The No 53 Squadron Liberator was badly hit and the captain headed off towards Cape Finisterre and then down the coast to Gibraltar. However fuel was low and they were forced to land at Portela, near Lisbon.

Norman Franks states in his book that Fg. Off. Dobson's father worked for a shipbuilder on the Tyne which had built most of the Portuguese Navy's ships. He asked his Director if he could help and it was not long before the crew was back in the UK. A No 502 Squadron Halifax destroyed U-462 and No 2 Escort Group finished off U-504. Sqn Ldr K. A. Aldrich and crew took off from St Eval in the Leigh Light Liberator BZ816 on 20 November 1943 for escort duties to convoy SL139/MKS30. Nothing further was heard from her. U-

618, commanded by Kapitänleutnant Kurt Baberg, shot her down and the event is noted in the boat's operations record book. The Liberator strafed the boat, but apparently no bombs or DCs were dropped.

On the morning of 21 November 1943 Wg. Cdr. H. R. A. Edwards, the squadron commander, and crew were on escort duty around convoy SL139 in Liberator BZ819. Edwards reported that they had gained a radar contact at 14 miles and homed in at 300 feet, switching on the Leigh Light at one mile. The boat opened fire and the aircraft gunners replied, including the midupper. Edwards was blinded by the tracer and lost sight of the target, but dropped his DCs and returned to the convoy. Another contact was gained at 15 miles but this time the light failed.

The second pilot reported seeing a U-Boat and advised the Escort Commander. The Liberator left the convoy at 0800 and some while later three of the engines failed and the aircraft ditched. Edwards, the only survivor, was rescued by HM Trawler *Lincolnshire*. A report was made to the effect that at night the midupper guns should not be used. U-648 reported what is believed was the first incident claiming hits on the aircraft. The second boat may have been U-967 commanded by Oberleutnant zur See Herbert Loeder. He stated that he drove it off with flak. The alternative may have been U-575 commanded by Oberleutnant zur See Wolfgang Boehmer, who also stated he fired on the aircraft.

On 13 December 1943 Sqn. Ldr. G. Crawford and crew were ordered by No 19 Group, the controlling MHQ, to locate a U-Boat in position 4544N 00930W. This had initially been located by Flt. Lt. J. Barton and crew from the same squadron but had to leave the area. Crawford's aircraft had radar and intercom problems and when they started a square search at the datum, the radar was switched off after three minutes of operating. This would now be called an intermittent radar policy, used to confuse the submarine as to the whereabouts of the aircraft. However, in this case it was due to a lack of serviceability and not a matter of tactics.

A radar contact was gained and a homing commenced. The radar failed but on using the Leigh Light a submarine was seen. The U-Boat then opened fire, causing damage to the aircraft. Six depth charges were dropped in an up-moon attack and sank the U-Boat, which was U-391, a type VIIc commanded by Oberleutnant zur See Gert Dultgen. It was on its first patrol and had been damaged by a No 179 Squadron aircraft in position 3904N 01625W in November 1943. Crawford was awarded the DFC.

No 58 Squadron, having converted to Halifax IIs, moved to St Eval in March, Holmesley South in June and to St David's in December 1943. Wing Commander W. E. Oulton, the Officer Commanding, was on task in Halifax HR745 in the early hours of 7 May when his second pilot Plt Off W. H. A. Jones sighted a surfaced submarine and they attacked with six depth charges from 300 feet. This was U-306. About three and a half hours later, flying around above broken cloud, Jones sighted another U-Boat. Manoevering to take advantage of cloud cover, the captain homed in to the target and broke cloud at 3000 feet at four miles from the submarine, which opened fire. The Halifax was hit in the supercharger control, a constant speed control and various other places. The remaining three depth charges were dropped but the boat, U-214, was not sunk although the commander, Kapitänleutnant Gunter Reeder, was seriously wounded.

At about the same time another Halifax HR792, of No 58 Squadron, captained by Sergeant N. F. Robertson of the RAAF, attacked U-228, commanded by Kapitänleutnant Erwin Christopherson. The only information comes from the U-Boat's logbook, in which it is stated that the aircraft attacked with six bombs and machine guns and that the boat returned fire and then submerged, believing the aircraft to have been shot down.

Halifax HR743, captained by Flight Sergeant James Hoather DFM, found U-666, commanded by Oberleutnant zur See Herbert Engel,on 9 May 1943. The U-Boat's defences prevented an attack on the first run in. Hoather went round again but this time the boat's gunners hit his port engine, causing the aircraft to crash. There were no survivors. U-666 was found again by a No 10 OTU Whitley, as stated further on.

On 11 May Plt. Off. J. B. Stark and crew joined convoy OS47. As radio silence was in force the aircraft intended to overfly the convoy in order to communicate visually with the escort commander. It was well known that convoy gunners were, and still are, trigger happy, so the colours of the day were fired from the Very pistol. The crew received its orders by Aldis Lamp to carry out plan Cobra, which was a square search around the convoy. A visual contact was gained but the boat dived before an attack could be carried out. Stark returned to the convoy to report the contact and then returned to the last known position of the contact. There, in position 4655N 01444W, was a surfaced submarine on which Stark made an attack. This was U-528, a type IXc/40 commanded by Oberleutnant zur See Georg von Rabenau. The stern lifted, there was a secondary explosion and the boat disappeared, leaving an oil patch. The boat was damaged and the escorts HMS *Mignonette* and HMS *Fleetwood* finished the job and rescued 15 survivors. The boat had already been damaged by a USN Catalina and was returning to base. Stark, who was on his 52nd patrol, received the DFC.

On 15 May 1943 Wg. Cdr. W. E. Oulton and crew gained a visual sighting of a U-boat and attacked out of the sun with depth charges. The bows rose into the air and then the boat sank. This was U-266, a type VIIc commanded by Kapitänleutnant Ralf von Jesson. On 16 May Fg. Off. J. W. Birch and crew gained a visual sighting of a U-Boat in the late evening. An attack was made out of the sun with depth charges as the boat dived. This was U-463, a type XIV tanker commanded by Korvettenkapitän Leo Wolfbauer. This sinking was in position 4557N 01140W and was the first U-Tanker to be lost.

On 31 May Wg. Cdr. W. E. Oulton and crew gained a visual sighting of a U-Boat which he attacked with depth charges, achieving a straddle. A follow-up attack was made and oil was seen coming from the boat. The engagement was continued with gunfire. The boat was U-563, a type VIIc commanded by Oberleutnant zur See Gustav Borchardt. Another No 58 Squadron Halifax captained by Plt. Off. E. L. Hartley arrived on the scene and attacked but his depth charge attack missed. The fight was continued by a Sunderland from No 10 Squadron RAAF and then by a Sunderland from No 228 Squadron. Oulton was later awarded the DSO and DFC for various engagements against U-Boats.

On 13 July 1943 Fg. Off. A. R. D. Clutterbuck and crew gained a sighting of three U-Boats, U-607, U-445 and U-613. U-607 was commanded by Oberleutnant zur See Wolf Jeschonnek, U-445 by Oberleutnant zur See Rupprecht Graf von Treuberg and U-613 by Kapitänleutnant Helmut Koppe. A Sunderland of No 228 Squadron captained by Fg. Off. R. Hanbury arrived on the scene almost simultaneously and the two crews worked together. As U-607 altered course to present a small target, Hanbury attacked. At the same time Clutterbuck made an attack on U-445 with eight depth charges, but only two were on target and the boat was undamaged. OC No 53 Squadron, Wg. Cdr. H. R. G. Edwards, with his crew came upon the scene shortly afterwards and saw a patch of oil and the dinghy, the occupants of which were picked up by HMS *Wren*. This crew, like that of Hanbury, saw some aircraft which looked like Ju88s, but they made no attack. They could have been the U-boat Group's escort.

On 27 September 1943, Fg. Off. E. L. Hartley and crew, together with their Station Commander, Group Captain Roger Mead, as second pilot, were on patrol south west of Ireland in Halifax HR982. They were investigating a possible contact when a surfaced U-Boat was sighted dead ahead at six miles in position 47N 018W. This was U-221, commanded by Kapitänleutnant Hans Troger. Hartley attacked with eight Mark IX depth charges and sank the boat. Survivors were seen and a dinghy dropped to them. Unfortunately the boat's gunners hit the aircraft and it was ditched. The crew survived, apart from the front gunner, Sergeant M. Griffiths, and the rear gunner, Sergeant R. K. Triggol. The crew were not rescued until by chance on 8 October by HMS *Muhratta*. They had survived on chocolate, condensed milk and Horlicks tablets. Hartley received the DFC and the midupper gunner, Flight Sergeant K. E. Ladds, the DFM.

No 59 Squadron moved to Chivenor in February 1943 and to Thorney Island in March, maintaining a detachment at St Eval. It converted to Liberator Vs in April and went to Aldergrove in May and thence to Ballykelly in September.

On 1 March 1943, Fg. Off. N. Barson and crew were on patrol in Fortress IA FL463 at 2000 feet under 8/10 cloud based 3000 feet with a moderate sea when the starboard waist gunner sighted a U-Boat, U-223 commanded by Oberleutnant Karl-Jurgen Wachter, about two miles away. Manoeuvering the aircraft to approach the boat from the sun, Barson descended and attacked with seven depth charges across the port bow. However they overshot. The U-Boat's gunners meanwhile opened fire on the Fortress, hitting the hydraulic system, the auto pilot and one of the engine controls. Barson held off for about a minute to assess the situation, but when he resumed the attack the submarine had submerged.

On 29 May Fg. Off. H. A. L. Moran, RAAF, and crew were providing escort to a convoy. A visual sighting was gained on U-552, a type VIIc, commanded by Kapitänleutnant Klaus Popp in position 4815N 01405W. An attack was made with four depth charges on the conning tower, causing the boat to surface. A follow-up attack was made with four depth charges. The U-Boat crew came on deck and opened fire on the aircraft. The boat later submerged, but the aircraft had exhausted its weapons and could do nothing further except to report the incident. U-552 eventually became a training boat.

On 14 June Flying Officer E. E. Allen and crew were on task in Liberator V FL973 at 1500 feet, over a moderate sea and with seven miles visibility, when a radar contact was gained at 13 miles. Descending, the crew sighted three U-boats in position 4322N01413W in Vic formation. These were U-600, U-615 and U-257, which had sailed from La Pallice. They had encountered No 220 squadron, No 228 Squadron and No 10 OTU. They were to survive No 59 Squadron. Allen attacked with six depth charges but under a hail of flak suffered damage. He made a second attack but by this time, interestingly, the boats were submerging rather than capitalizing on their ability to inflict damage on the Liberator. Allen dropped his remaining depth charges, but no results were observed.

On 19 July Flt Lt Allen and crew investigated a radar contact gained at eight miles and located U-667, commanded by Kapitänleutnant Heinrich Schroteler in position 4515N01640W. On the initial attack the aircraft met heavy flak and was forced to abort, having been hit in the port wing. The aircraft then circled the boat exchanging fire. Two attacks were carried out, the first from 3300 feet with one depth charge which overshot and did not appear to explode, and the second from 75 feet with two depth charges which also overshot. On the face of it these were unusual bombing tactics, however, Allen had only three depth charges and two 600lb antisubmarine bombs. These last were designed to cause maximum damage under water and Allen was trying to force the U-Boat to dive.

On 16 October Plt. Off. W. J. Thomas and crew in Liberator FL984, escorting convoy ONS 206, followed Flt Lt. Bland's Liberator of No 86 Squadron in the attack on U-844. He attacked the surfaced boat but he was hit in the starboard engine. He then made a follow up attack with four depth charges which sank U-844 in position 5830N 02716W. U-844 was a type IXc/40 boat commanded by Oberleutnant zur See Gunther Moller. However, Thomas had to return to base in Iceland. On the return they saw another U-Boat, U-540, which they strafed as they were out of depth charges. This boat was sunk the following day in a combined action by Liberators of No 59 and No 120 squadrons. Thomas was awarded the DFC.

Again on 16 October, Plt. Off. W. Loney and crew were escorting convoy ON 206 together with Flt. Lt. Kerrigan and Flt. Lt. Peck from No 120 Squadron. In between Peck's attacks on U-470, Loney made two attacks (see under No 120 Squadron for more details of this action). The kill was shared between the three crews. Loney was just on PLE at his last attack and returned to Ballykelly, landing with about 15 minutes' fuel remaining. The Flight Engineer, Sergeant W. Sills, got Loney to climb to Rated Altitude and fly at reduced power at between range and endurance speed. There was an undercarriage problem caused by flak and Sills suggested that the wheels should not be lowered until about to land. Apparently only the wheel on one side had gone, leaving the oleo. Nevertheless they landed safely.

On 17 October Flt. Lt. E. Knowles and crew located U-540, a type IXc/40 commanded by Kapitänleutnant Lorenz Kasch on the surface in position 5838N 03156W. Knowles and crew were returning to Meek's Field in Iceland and fuel would have been marginal, but nevertheless an attack was made with a stick of four depth charges which overshot. A follow-up attack was made with two depth charges which straddled the target. It was now the turn of Warrant Officer Turnbull and crew of No 120 Squadron to attack (see below).

No 86 Squadron moved to Aldergrove in March 1943, receiving some Liberator Vs in April, which it handed back in September when it moved to Ballykelly. On 6 April Flying Officer C. W. Burcher and crew were on patrol escorting convoy HX 231 using radar. A visual sighting was gained, at one mile, of a surfaced submarine, the crew of which appeared to be getting ready to submerge. This was U-632, a type VIIc, commanded by Kapitänleutnant Hans Karpf in position 5802N 02842W. An attack was made from 50 feet but only one of the selected four depth charges dropped. A follow-up attack with four depth charges was made on the diving boat. A patch of oil was seen but no other results. This was insufficient to award a kill.

The attack was reported to the escort commander and the patrol resumed. About two and a half hours later another U-boat was sighted and attacked with the remaining depth charges, but again only a patch of oil was seen. It was later assessed that the first attack was made on U-632, which failed to return from patrol, and the kill was awarded to Burcher and crew.

On 4 May 1943 Pilot Officer J. C. Green and crew

were providing escort to convoy HX 236. A visual sighting of a submarine in position 4710N 02257W was gained and an attack with four depth charges was made. Wreckage was seen and it was assessed that the boat had been sunk. This was U-109, a type IXB, commanded by Oberleutnant zur See Joachim Schramm. On 12 May 1943 Flt Lt J. Wright and crew in a Liberator Mk III was providing escort to convoy HX 237. A visual sighting was gained on U-456, a type VIIc commanded by Kapitänleutnant Max Martin Teichert in position 4640N 02620W. The boat submerged and a Mark 24 homing torpedo was dropped. The boat was hit and surfaced. The escort commander was informed of the attack and a destroyer was sent to the scene. Teichert dived his boat, but because of the damage it sank.

On 12 June Flying Officer C. W. Burcher was captain of Liberator FL932. He and his crew were in support of convoy TA48 when they sighted U-645, commanded by Oberleutnant zur See Otto Ferro, in position 4850N02500W. The Liberator attacked, dropping depth charges, but no results were observed. Heavy flak was experienced. Burcher made a second attack with guns but the turning boat made this difficult. Burcher headed towards the convoy to advise the escort of events and on his return to the area realized that the boat had submerged. About two and a half hours later U-645 was attacked again with five depth charges by another No 86 Squadron aircraft, Liberator FK226, Captained by Flying Officer A. C. I. Samuel, also in support of convoy TA48. The crew sighted the conning tower in position 4815N02510W from two and a half miles at 1500 feet.

The initial attack was met by heavy flak and the pilot turned off to go in from another direction. The boat's manoeuvres stopped him from doing this. After an exchange of gunfire he attacked with depth charges as stated above. The aircraft was badly hit, one of the WOP's being killed, and damage sustained to a fuel tank. Samuel turned off for base.

On 23 June 1943 Flt. Lt. J. Wright and crew were escorting convoys WS 31 and KMF 17. A visual sighting was gained of three U-Boats which dived on being attacked. Almost seven hours later the crew again visually sighted three U-boats. One dived while the others opened fire. They then commenced diving. An attack was made with a 600lb bomb on one of these. No results were observed. This was U-650, a type VIIc commanded by Oberleutnant zur See Ernst von Witzendorff and it was damaged by this attack.

On 19 July Flt. Lt. Willis Roxburgh DFC and crew were on task in Liberator V BZ772 in the outer Bay of Biscay and sighted two U-Boats on the surface, U-43 (type IX) commanded by Oberleutnant zur See Hans-Joachim Schwantke and U-403 (type VIIC) commanded by Kapitänleutnant Karl-Franz Heine. The position was 4710N01410W. U-403 immediately dived with U-43 providing fire. Sergeant Richard Thomas, a waist gunner, reported that U-43 opened fire and that the Liberator returned fire. The first run was a failure. The aircraft was carrying a new weapon, the Mark 24 acoustic homing torpedo, which for security purposes was known as a mine. It was also known as "Fido". To be effective the attack had to be precise.

Roxburgh released two torpedoes on the second attack just as the U-Boat's swirl began to disappear. The torpedoes either hit the sea bed or self detonated; either way they missed the U-Boat. U-43 was sunk by a Fido dropped by an Avenger from the USS Santee on 30 July 1943.

On 8 October 1943 Flt. Lt. J. Wright and crew were escorting convoy SC143. A visual sighting of a U-boat was gained in position 5631N 02656W. The boat, U-419, a type VIIc commanded by Oberleutnant zur See Dietrich Giersberg, immediately dived. A stick of four depth charges was dropped on the swirl. No results were observed and, as per instructions from the escort commander, the aircraft resumed patrol. One hour later Wright returned to the area of the attack and relocated U-419 on the surface. Two depth charges were dropped on the still-surfaced boat, causing a large explosion. The boat sank, leaving some 15 submariners in the sea. The aircraft returned to the convoy and was given further tasking, during which a second U-Boat was sighted and attacked, but there being no depth charges left, machine guns were used.

The crew homed in another aircraft from No 86 squadron captained by Fg. Off. C. Burcher. This boat was U-643, a type VIIc commanded by Kapitänleutnant Hans Harold Speidel. Burcher and crew were also escorting convoy SC143 and at similar times. The crew intercepted Flt. Lt. Wright's sighting report and was homed in and sighted the boat in position 5600N 002710W. It began to submerge, and a stick of four depth charges was dropped which straddled the track. Oil was seen but nothing else substantial. Burcher returned an hour later only to find Fg. Off. D. C. L. Webber and crew from No 120 Squadron attacking a surfaced U-Boat. Burcher attacked with depth charges. Webber attacked again and then both aircraft attacked with machine guns. Burcher had to leave the area due to lack of fuel, having reached his PLE.

Warrant Officer B. Turnbull and crew from No 120 Squadron and Flt. Lt. E.Bland and crew from No 86 Squadron entered the scene. Turnbull attacked another U-Boat (U-762) with a 600lb bomb and then made a follow-up attack with three depth charges on the swirl of the diving submarine. Bland requested support from the escorts, as he could see that the U-Boat was being abandoned. The escort commander ordered a ceasefire and later the boat blew up.

On 15 October U-844, commanded by Oberleutnant zur See Günter Moller, was held underwater by HMS *Duncan,* escorting convoy ONS20. The next day she surfaced only to be found by a No 86 Squadron Liberator captained by Flt Lt E. A. Bland. He attacked immediately but was hit in both port engines and the depth charges hung up. A No 59 Squadron Liberator captained by Plt. Off. W. J. Thomas intercepted the locating report and joined in, dropping a stick of depth charges. A follow-up attack was made on the swirl of the now submerged U-Boat, but no results were observed. Thomas' aircraft had been hit in the starboard inner engine on the first attack and now had to return to Iceland. On the return they found yet another U-Boat, but having no DCs left could only make a strafing run. Meanwhile Bland tried for another attack, but the bomb release system was so badly damaged it could not release the DCs. However, U-844 was finished and went down with no survivors.

Bland was in trouble and knowing that he could not make base he ditched near HMS *Pink*, a Flower-class corvette. Reports are confusing; one or two aircrew were killed, the second pilot, Fg. Off. R. H. Cox, being one. Bland received the DSO and Thomas the DFC.

On 16 October 1943, Fg. Off. G. D. Gamble and crew were escorting convoy ON206. Convoy ONS20 was not far away. The crew gained a visual contact on a U-Boat in position 5727N 02817W. This was U-964, a type VIIc, commanded by Oberleutnant zur See Emmo Hummerjohann. In the face of intense anti-aircraft fire, Gamble attacked with three depth charges, but no results were observed. A follow-up attack was delayed due to the flak and an attempt was made to contact the escort commander to request a Surface Attack Unit, but this was unsuccessful. Then a follow-up attack was made with three depth charges and this proved to be successful, the boat sinking and leaving 35 sailors in the sea. The escort commander of ONS20 was contacted, informing him of the position.

On 17 October 1943 Warrant Officer B. W. Turnbull RNZAF and crew were returning to Meek's Field in Iceland after escorting convoy ON 206 when the radar operator, Flt. Sgt. N. R. Tingey RNZAF, gained a contact and homed in the aircraft. The target was sighted visually, as was the Liberator of Flt. Lt. Knowles and crew of No 59 Squadron which was attacking. Turnbull attacked with the front cannons around the same time as Knowles and then made an attack with a stick of four depth charges with a follow-up attack, also of depth charges. This broke the boat in two. The submarine was U-540, a type IXc/40 commanded by Kapitänleutnant Lorenz Kasch. Survivors were seen. Turnbull credited the success of the attack to the Flight Engineer, Flt. Sgt. A. G. Storey, who he sent to check the setting of the bomb release switches, which he did in sufficient time to allow the release of four depth charges.

On 16 November 1943 Fg. Off. J. H. Bookless RAAF and crew were escorting convoy HX265 in Liberator FL931. They visually located and attacked U-280 commanded by Oberleutnant zur See Walther Hungerhausen. There was a heavy exchange of fire and the first DCs overshot, the aircraft losing one of the outer engines. Bookless made a follow-up attack which was more successful, and the boat was sunk in position 4911N 02732W.

No 119 Squadron disbanded in April 1943.

No 120 Squadron moved to Aldergrove with a detachment to Reykjavik in February 1943. On 6 February 1943 Sqn. Ldr. D. J. Isted and crew joined convoy SC118 and was given a Mamba patrol. A submarine had been seen by a crew member astern of the convoy but they were not able to prosecute it. Due to their distance from base the aircraft could spend only three hours and five minutes on task.

On return to base at 3000 feet a surfaced U-Boat was sighted in position 5433N 02927W and not far from the convoy. Isted took advantage of the cloud, remaining in it until ahead of the boat, and then attacked with six depth charges from 40 feet. The boat went under but was not sunk. As the prudent Limit of Endurance (PLE) had been reached, Isted returned to Ballykelly in Northern Ireland. The boat was U-465, a type VIIc commanded by Kapitänleutnant

Heinz Wolf and was forced to return to St Nazaire. Later, Fg. Off. Fleming-Williams and crew, en route to escort this convoy, attacked a U-Boat with depth charges in position 5430N 02828W. Some wreckage was seen.

On 8 February 1943 Sgt. B. W. Turnbull of the RNZAF and crew, who were en route to join convoy SC118 at 1000 feet in showers, gained a visual sighting of a U-Boat at 15 miles. The aircraft remained in cloud to avoid being seen by the boat and attacked visually with four depth charges, but three of these hung up. The U-Boat was U-135, a type VIIc commanded by Kapitänleutnant Siegfried Strelow. It was damaged by one depth charge and had to return St. Nazaire. No results were seen and the aircraft carried on to the convoy.

On 15 February Fg. Off. R. T. F. Turner and crew escorting convoy SC 119 gained a visual sighting of a surfaced U-Boat at seven miles in position 5545N 03109W. A stick of six depth charges was dropped from 70 feet, giving a good straddle. This was U-225, a type VIIc commanded by Oberleutnant zur See Wolfgang Leimkuhler and was sunk in this attack.

On 21 February, Sqn. Ldr. D. J. Isted and crew took off from Aldergrove to escort convoy ON166. The crew joined the convoy and was tasked by the escort commander. The crew sighted a U-Boat at nine miles in sea state zero to one. Isted took advantage of the cloud and headed towards the boat. Breaking cloud at about five miles from the boat, a second boat was seen about three miles away. Isted attacked the first boat from 50 feet with six depth charges, achieving a straddle. The boat, which was U-623, a type VIIc commanded by Oberleutnant zur See

Hermann Schroder, was seen to go down slowly. Meanwhile the second boat dived. A marine marker was dropped and the engagement reported to the escort commander, who sent a destroyer and a corvette to the area. Two large oil patches were found. U-623 was sunk and her loss was reported by the second boat, which was U-91.

In April 1943 the squadron reversed its February move by returning to Reykjavik with a detachment to Aldergrove. On 5 April Fg. Off. G. L. Hatherly and crew departed Reykjavik to escort convoy HX231. Homing on to the convoy at 3000 feet in and out of cloud a surfacing submarine was sighted. A pilot attack, i.e. one where the navigator did not use the Low Level Bombsight but where the pilot judged the release point and used his bomb release button, was made with six depth charges from 50 feet. Nothing further was seen, but U-635, a type VIIC commanded by Oberleutnant zur See Heinz Eckelmann, had been sunk. This was reported to the Escort Commander, who sent an escort to investigate. The aircraft continued to patrol around the convoy until recalled to base due to bad weather.

On 6 April Fg. Off. J. K. Moffatt and crew were escorting convoy HX231. The escort commander advised the crew that there were several submarines astern of the convoy. Accordingly a search was carried out in this area at 1000 feet just below cloud. A visual sighting was gained of a surfaced U-Boat at two and a half miles. This was U-594, a type VIIc commanded by Kapitänleutnant Friedrich Mumm. Moffatt descended to 60 feet and dropped a stick of four depth charges in position 5811N 02813W. After the water had subsided there was no sign of the boat.

An hour and a half later another boat was sighted in position 5808N 02753WW. Moffatt attacked but the boat dived when the aircraft was a mile away; nevertheless two depth charges were dropped. No results were observed. U-594 had been damaged and was forced to return to St. Nazaire. Moffatt and crew were active on 23 April 1943 when they were en route to escort convoy HX 234. Two boats were visually sighted on the surface, one at four miles and the other at eight miles. Moffatt attacked U-189, a type IXc/40 commanded by Kapitänleutnant Hellmut Kurrer with a stick of four depth charges from 50 feet with a follow-up attack of two more. The boat went down in position 5950N 03443W. The other boat was U-413, which reported the sinking. Moffatt reported the sightings to the escort commander but he had no spare vessels to investigate the other boat.

On 20 May 1943 Sqn. Ldr. J. R. E. Proctor and crew were escorting convoy SC 130. A visual sighting at eight miles was gained of a surfaced U-Boat in position 5518N 02749W. Proctor dropped a stick of four depth charges from 200 feet. The stern was seen to lift and an oil patch was also seen. This was U-258, a type VIIc commanded by Kapitänleutnant Wilhelm von Massenhausen, and it had been sunk by this attack.

This was a busy day for Proctor and crew. They had sighted a U-Boat earlier but no action against it was possible. A third boat was sighted and a machine gun attack was carried out. A follow up attack was made with the cannon and a 600lb bomb was dropped. The boat was seen down by the stern and the escort commander advised, but it was a heavy sea and he could not send an escort. A fourth was gained shortly after going off task and although an attack was initiated, contact was lost.

Flt. Lt. W. J. F. McEwen and crew were also escorting this convoy and gained five sightings, one boat being attacked twice. On 28 May 1943 Fg. Off. D. C. Fleming-Williams and crew were en route to escort convoy HX 240 flying at 7000 feet just under complete cloud cover when a visual sighting was gained of a U-Boat at five miles in position 5450N 03720W. This was U-304, a type VIIc, commanded by Oberleutnant zur See Heinz Koch. An attack was made from 100 feet with a stick of four depth charges. Oil and debris were seen, signifying the sinking of this boat. On 15 June 1943 Flt. Lt. S. E. Esler and crew were flying a Cobra patrol escorting convoy ONS 10 when a visual sighting was gained at 12 miles from 6200 feet of a surfaced U-Boat in position 5713N 03004W. Under heavy flak, Esler dived at the boat, dropping a stick of four depth charges from 100 feet. The boat, U-449, a type VIIC commanded by Kapitänleutnant Hermann Otto, was seen to be down at the stern before it dived. Two destroyers arrived in response to the locating report but nothing further was found. U-449 had been damaged and was forced to return to France, but was sunk by the 2nd Escort Group on 24 June in position 4500N 01159W.

On 24 June Flt. Lt. A. W. Fraser and crew were en route to escort convoy ONS 11 when they gained a visual sighting of a surfaced U-Boat in position 5815N 02525W. This was U-200, a type IXD2, commanded by Kapitänleutnant Heinrich Schonder on its first war patrol. Fraser attacked, the gunners exchanging fire. The aircraft was hit, causing damage to the hydraulics and a petrol leak in the wing. Four depth charges were selected but only two were released, the other hanging up due to the hydraulic damage. A follow-up attack was made and the selected 600lb bomb failed to release, again due to the hydraulic damage. However, the two depth charges had done their work. Oil and wreckage were seen and then a number of survivors. The escort was informed but the aircraft had to return to Reykjavik, not only because of the damage but due to the Flight Engineer being slightly wounded. Fraser suspected that the nose wheel might not be locked down when the landing was made and accordingly he had the crew take up positions in the rear of the aircraft. The aircraft landed safely with minimum damage to the rear.

On 4 October 1943, Wing Commander R. M. Longmore, the Squadron Commander, and crew were on convoy escort to ONS19 when they located and attacked U-539 commanded by Oberleutnant zur See Hans-Jorgen Lauterbach-Emden. The stick of depth charges caused some damage but the boat shot down the Liberator. A garbled message was received by MHQ but the source of information comes from the U-Boat's Operations Record Book. This boat had nearly shot down Flight Sergeant E. L. J. Brame and crew of No 269 Squadron on 21 September.

Again on 4 October 1943, Flt. Lt. W. J. F. McEwen and crew were also escorting convoy ONS 19. The wireless operator heard Longmore's sighting report and on Group instructions went to investigate. Nothing was found. Later a sighting report of a surfaced submarine was heard from a Hudson, and Group authorised the crew to investigate although it was going off task. On arrival at the last known position a square search was initiated. Shortly after, a surfaced submarine was sighted. This was U-389, a type VIIc commanded by Kapitänleutnant Udo Heilmann. An attack with depth charges was made, sinking the U-Boat. Some dinghies and emergency rations were dropped to the survivors.

On 8 October Fg. Off. C. Webber and crew joined in the action with Fg. Off. Burcher and crew from No 86 Squadron against U-643. Webber was flying just under the cloud base when the radar operator gained a contact ahead at 10 miles. Webber entered cloud to avoid being seen and then descended to be at bombing height at on top the target. Unfortunately he was a little too high and he went round again under heavy fire, but the aircraft was not hit. This was a navigator attack using the Low Level Bombsight with a stick of four depth charges. A follow-up attack was made by the navigator (Fg. Off. H. L. Matthews) from 30 feet with another four depth charges, achieving a perfect straddle. The submarine's crew was seen to abandon the boat, which later blew up in position 5614N 02655W. An escort, HMS *Orwell*, was homed in to pick up the survivors. Webber and Matthews were awarded the DFC and the Flight Engineer, Flight Sergeant J. G. Jeans, was awarded the DFM.

On the same day Warrant Officer B. W. Turnbull RNZAF and crew were en route to escort convoy SC 143 and gained a visual sighting of a U-Boat in position 5743N 02538W. This was U-762, a type VIIc commanded by Oberleutnant zur See Walther Pietschmann. An attack was made with a 600lb antisubmarine bomb with a follow-up attack on the now-submerged boat with three 250lb depth charges. The boat had been damaged and had suffered casualties and had to sail to Brest.

On 16 October 1943 Flt. Lt. H. Kerrigan and crew and Flt. Lt. B. Peck and crew were escorting convoy ON206 together with a No 59 Squadron Liberator GR V captained by Plt. Off. W. Loney. Shortly after, on task time, Peck's crew heard on the radio that another Liberator had been hit by gunfire from a U-boat. The escort commander advised the captain to ditch in the middle of the convoy. This turned out to be a Sunderland of No 422 Squadron (see below). Kerrigan's crew sighted a submarine in position 5820N 02920W and attacked it in the face of heavy flak. A follow-up attack was made a quarter of an hour later with four depth charges. Meanwhile, Peck's crew had been directed to the area by the escort commander. They were at 500 feet with a sea state of around zero. A radar contact was gained and a homing was carried out. The U-Boat, which was U-470, a type VIIc, commanded by Oberleutnant zur See Gunter Grave, was attacked, again in the face of heavy fire, with a stick of six depth charges. A follow-up attack was made by the navigator, Fg. Off. J. Pickard RCAF, using the Mk III Low Level Bombsight. Two depth charges straddled the boat, which was blown clear of the water and then sank.

Peck requested an escort to confirm the kill and to pick up the survivors. There was much U-Boat activity in the vicinity of this convoy and HMS *Duncan* had to sail at a moderate speed and only managed to pick up two survivors. In between Peck's attacks, Loney from No 59 Squadron made his attacks. On board Flt. Lt. Peck's aircraft was a Mr Clearwater, a civilian technician from the United States whose company had just produced a sonobuoy which was intended to be tested for underwater submarine activity if the opportunity had presented itself. However there was no point in using it against U-470 for tracking purposes as it did not dive. One was dropped near the site of the sinking and breaking-up noises were heard, including a "violent explosion". In December 1943 the squadron converted to Liberator Vs, disposing of their Mark IIIs the following month.

No 172 Squadron remained at Chivenor and in August 1943 converted to Wellington XIVs. There were detachments to Lajes in the Azores, and Gibraltar. Fg. Off. G. D. Lundon and crew in a Wellington VIII, MP505, found U-268, a type VIIC, on 19 February 1943. The aircraft was flying at 2000 feet under a continuous cloud base and gained a radar contact at four miles ahead in position 4703N 00556W. Having illuminated her with the Leigh Light, a stick of four depth charges was dropped which sank her. On 3 March 1943 Flt. Sgt. J. L. Tweddle and crew were at 500 feet when a radar contact was gained slightly starboard at six miles. This was U-525, a type IXc/40 commanded by Kapitänleutnant Hans-Joachim Drewitz. Tweddle illuminated the target with the Leigh Light, revealing a surfaced boat. He dropped three depth charges from 60 feet. Sgt. D. A. Radburn, a WOP/AG, saw two bright blue flashes and fired at them, but nothing further was seen. The boat had been damaged and was returning to Lorient.

Fg. Off. Lundon and crew, again in MP505 on 4 March, found U-333 commanded by Oberleutnant zur See Werner Schaff in the Bay of Biscay. She was illuminated by Leigh Light and attacked with four depth charges, one of which hit the boat, causing minor damage.

However, the boat's gunners opened fire and shot down the Wellington. There were no survivors. There had been no warning to the U-Boat crew of the proximity of the aircraft by the radar warning device "Metox" as the aircraft was fitted with ASV III, a centimetric radar with wavelength of 9.7 cms.

On 21 March 1943 Fg. Off. I. D. Prebble and crew gained a radar contact and homed in to it, switching on the Leigh Light at one mile. This of course presented a target to the U-Boat and the light was switched off. The aircraft flew over the boat but did not drop anything, although the rear gunner fired a few bursts. A follow-up attack was attempted but the contact was lost. Later another radar contact was gained a few miles away from the original position and a U-Boat was sighted by moonlight. A stick of six depth charges was dropped in position 4520N 00800W. Prebble positioned for a further attack, the conning tower being seen, but it then disappeared. U-332, a type VIIc, commanded by Oberleutnant zur See Eberhard Huttemann, was damaged in this attack.

On 10 April Plt. Off. G. H. Whiteley and crew were at 2500 feet in darkness and gained a radar contact at six miles. It was out to port, and an immediate turn to port would have brought the contact too close before the aircraft could reach attacking height, so a turn to starboard was made. The aircraft homed in and switching on the Leigh Light a U-boat was sighted three quarters of a mile ahead in position 4648N 00900W. A stick of depth charges straddled the boat, but no results were observed either visually or on radar. This was U-376, a type VIIc commanded by Kapitänleutnant Friedrich Marks and she had been sunk in this attack.

On 26 April Sgt. A. Coumbis and crew were flying at night under 10/10 cloud at 1700 feet base with a rough sea and visibility of four miles. A radar contact was gained at four miles and a homing was carried out. The Leigh Light was switched on at three quarters of a mile, illuminating a submarine with decks awash. This was U-566, a type VIIc commanded by Kapitänleutnant Hans Hornkohl in position 4629N 00921W. Coumbis attacked with a stick of six depth charges. The crew turned on to the target and could see the boat in the Leigh Light. It opened fire and evasive action was taken by Coumbis. The radar contact then faded. U-566 had been damaged and had to return to Brest.

On 29 April Fg. Off. P. H. Stembridge and crew, flying at night, gained a radar (ASV III) contact at eight miles in position 4508N 00943W. A wake was sighted at one and a half miles and at three quarters of a mile a surfaced U-Boat was illuminated in the Leigh Light. In the face of heavy gunfire, an attack was made with six depth charges from 100 feet. Flame floats had been dropped to mark the attack and Stembridge flew towards them, again in the face of gunfire. Flame floats only burned for about six minutes so marine markers were dropped as soon as possible, these having a burning time of around one hour. The aircraft remained in the area for over an hour but no results were observed. The Boat was U-437, a type VIIc commanded by Oberleutnant zur See Hermann Lamby. It had been severely damaged and was forced to return to St.Nazaire.

CHAPTER TWENTY ONE

On 1 May 1943 Flight Sergeant P.W. Phillips, captain of a No 172 Squadron Wellington, and his crew gained a radar contact in position 4445N 01157W which they illuminated with the Leigh Light and made a good attack with six depth charges. Nothing further was seen and the crew resumed patrol, discovering a while later that the aircraft had taken hits in the hydraulic system. When they landed at Predannack they also discovered that the port wheel had been hit. The aircraft crashed but no one was hurt. The U-Boat concerned was U-415, a type VIIc commanded by Oberleutnant zur See Kurt Neide. The boat had been damaged by this attack and was attacked two more times on this day, once by a No 461 Squadron Sunderland and finally by a No 612 Squadron Whitley. On 3 July 1943 in the early hours of the morning Flt. Sgt. A. Coumbis and crew gained a radar contact at 13 miles and homed in, illuminating with the Leigh Light at three quarters of a mile. U-126, a type IXc commanded by Oberleutnant zur See Siegfried Kietz, was seen and attacked with depth charges from 50 feet. A follow-up attack was begun but nothing was seen. U-126 had been sunk in position 4602N 01123W.

On 24 July 1943, Fg. Off. W.T. Jennings and crew in a Wellington located and attacked U-459 commanded by Korvettenkapitän Georg von Wilamowitz-Mollendorf. The boat was surprised and the aircraft was already close in before the U-Boat's gunners opened fire. Their flak was accurate, perhaps too accurate, because the aircraft crashed into the U-Boat. Only the rear gunner, Sergeant A. A. Turner, whose turret broke off, survived. Some of the boat's crew found two depth charges on the decking

287

and rolled them off. Unfortunately for them the charges were fused and they exploded under the boat, causing considerable damage. In this chaos a Wellington of No 547 Squadron arrived and dropped seven depth charges on the boat. The U-Boat commander realized that the game was up and scuttled his boat, going down with her.

The Polish destroyer *Orken* arrived on the scene later and picked up the survivors, including Sergeant Turner. U-459 was a "Milch Cow" tanker and had sailed from Bordeaux meeting up with another tanker U-117 in the Gironde estuary. These boats were so important that they were provided with a destroyer escort to 10 west longitude. On 29 July 1943 Wg. Cdr. R. G. Musson and crew were flying at 1200 feet in cloud when a radar contact was gained at six and a half miles. A homing was initiated and at three quarters of a mile the aircraft broke cloud and the crew sighted a surfaced submarine. This was U-614, a type VIIc commanded by Kapitänleutnant Wolfgang Strater. A stick of six depth charges was dropped from 50 feet giving a straddle. The boat was sunk in position 4642N 01103W but there were survivors in the water who were shaking their fists at the aircraft.

On 7 September 1943 a Wellington, MP791, captained by Fg. Off. T. Armstrong located U-402 on radar at six miles in position 4635N 00900W. The boat was commanded by Korvettankapitän Siegfried Freiherr von Forstner. Armstong struck (switched on) the Leigh Light at one mile, sighted the U-Boat on the surface and attacked with a stick of six depth charges from 50 feet. Ten minutes later they attacked again, but only with guns. At this point the crew saw another Leigh Light close to the

U-Boat, an exchange of fire and then the aircraft catch fire and crash. This was Fg. Off. Payne in Wellington MP509, also from No 172 Squadron. Armstrong's aircraft had been hit in the port undercarriage, the tyre bursting on landing. It was a safe landing. U-402 was to meet No 612 Squadron the next day.

On 27 November 1943 Plt. Off. T. B. Wilkin and crew were operating out of Lajes in Wellington HF153 as escort to convoys SL140/MKS31 and reported a U-Boat contact, which was probably U-764 commanded by Oberleutnant zur See Hanskurt von Bremen. Two minutes later a distress call was picked by shore stations and after that nothing was heard. U-764 claimed hitting an aircraft, probably shooting it down. U-262 was nearby and while she did not claim a victory she did report an aircraft crashing. U-764 was sunk later by aircraft from VC19 flying off the carrier USS *Bogue*.

No 179 Squadron was operating Wellington VIIIs from Gibraltar with detachments at Agadir and Blida. On 9 July 1943 Fg. Off. E. J. Fisher and crew were on patrol west of Portugal when they received a message to investigate a possible U-boat in position 3959N 01523W. Nothing was found in this position but half an hour later a wake was seen by Fisher and shortly after, at four miles and 1300 feet, a surfaced U-Boat was sighted. A stick of four depth charges was dropped from 50 feet, giving a good straddle and causing the boat to lose way. There were two explosions and the boat turned over and sank. It was U-435, a type VIIc commanded by Kapitänleutnant Siegfried Strelow.

On 24 August, Fg. Off. D. F. McRae RCAF and crew gained a radar contact at five miles and homed in. On switching on the Leigh Light a surfaced U-Boat was sighted. McRae went round again and dropped a stick of six depth charges in the face of enemy fire. No results were observed except that gunfire ceased. The boat was U-134, a type VIIC commanded by Kapitänleutnant Hans-Gunther Brosin and sank after this attack in position 4707N 00930W. There were no survivors. McRae and his WOP/AG, Fg. Off. R.K. Senior RAAF, were awarded the DFC.

On 6 September 1943, Fg. Off. McRae and crew again gained a radar contact at two miles but the aircraft was too close to make an attack. Turning, the radar operator regained contact at three miles and the Leigh Light illuminated a fully surfaced U-Boat which was attacked with a stick of six depth charges and machine-gun fire. No results were observed. On the return home, the port engine failed, followed shortly after by a failure of the starboard engine. McRae forcelanded the aircraft in a field and no one was hurt. The U-Boat was U-760, a type VIIc commanded by Kapitänleutnant Otto Erich Blum. She was very badly damaged and was forced to go to Vigo, where she was interned.

The squadron re-equipped with Wellington XIVs in August 1943 and sent a detachment to Lajes in the Azores. On 12 September 1943, Sqn. Ldr. D. B. Hodgkinson RCAF and crew located and attacked U-617, a type VIIc commanded by Kapitänleutnant Albrecht Brandi off North Morocco at 3517N 00320W. The stick of depth charges disabled the boat. This left a trail of oil, which after gaining radar contact, was seen in the moonlight by Plt. Off. W. H. Brunini and crew in another Wellington, also from No 179 Squadron. This aircraft had been homed in by Hodgkinson's crew. When the Leigh Light was struck the U-Boat opened fire, hitting the aircraft and killing the rear gunner, Flight Sergeant W. Jones of the Royal Australian Air Force. Bruini dropped his depth charges accurately and flames were seen coming from the conning tower. The boat was eventually beached in Spain and all its crew survived. Hudsons of No 48 and No 233 Squadrons bombed and rocketed the boat and Swordfish aircraft of No 33 and No 886 Squadrons FAA also rocketed it. As their boat had been sunk, by international law the crew was entitled to be repatriated and this is what happened, Brandi being given another boat.

On 24 September 1943 Flight Sergeant A. W. Ellis in a Wellington found and attacked U-667, commanded by Kapitänleutnant Heinrich Schroeteler. There was an exchange of fire but neither side was hit. Later that day another No 179 Squadron Wellington, captained by Fg. Off. A. Chiltern, attacked the boat in position 3652N 00908W, causing some damage. On 25th Flight Sergeant D. J. McMahon and crew attacked with six depth charges, but U-667 survived. Later Flight Sergeant R. W. Dix and crew found her but the aircraft was damaged by flak, causing the depth charges to hang up. The aircraft was also hit in the port engine and elsewhere and Dix wisely returned to base. That night, while on the surface trying to recharge her depleted batteries, Sqn. Ldr. G. H. Riddell and crew attacked her, but were shot down and there were no survivors.

On 26th September Fg. Off. S. H. Nicholson in another 179 Wellington was on Search and Rescue looking for Riddell when they found and attacked U-667. The depth charges exploded astern and they exchanged fire to no effect. Then, Fg. Off. A. G. Frandson, also on Search and Rescue for Riddell, in a No 233 Squadron Hudson AE505, followed by another Hudson EW924, captained by Fg. Off. E. L. Ashbury of No 48 Squadron, attacked with rockets. Both aircraft were hit but returned to base. The damage built up by these engagements caused Schroeteler to abandon his attempt to enter the Mediterranean.

On 21 October 1943 Sgt D. M. Cornish RCAF and crew gained a radar contact at 14 miles off the port bow. A homing was initiated at the end of which was a very large warship which opened fire. At briefing no mention had been made of this ship and it was not supposed to be in that position. One of the rudders was slightly damaged. The ship was not identified except as a destroyer or cruiser. A further radar contact was gained at 11 miles and again a homing was initiated. The Leigh Light was struck at a quarter of a mile to reveal a surfaced submarine, which opened fire, causing some damage. This was U-431, a type VIIc commanded by Oberleutnant zur See Dietrich Schoneboom. The boat was attacked in position 3704N 00035E. No results were observed but it was later (post war) confirmed that U-431 had been sunk.

On 24 October Sgt. D. M. Cornish RCAF and crew gained a radar contact which was converted to a visual sighting in the moonlight. The Leigh Light was not used initially until Cornish had achieved an attack position when the U-Boat opened fire, causing some damage to the tail. The boat was U-566, a type VIIc commanded by Kapitänleutnant Hans Hornkohl. The attack immobilized the boat and Hornkohl ordered its scuttling in position 4112N 00920W. The survivors were picked up by a Spanish fishing boat and taken to Vigo, from whence they took the train to Germany.

On 1 November Fg. Off. A. H. Ellis and crew gained a radar contact at two and a half miles, which was confirmed as a U-Boat as the crew overflew it. Ellis turned back at six miles and attacked at 100 feet with a stick of six depth charges in position 3500N 00600W. No results were observed and as an engine problem had occurred Ellis turned for home. The U-Boat had been damaged and was located by HMS *Active*, HMS *Witherington* and HMS *Fleetwood*. The boat was U-340, a type VIIc commanded by Oberleutnant zur See Hans-Joachim Klaus. It had been so badly damaged that Klaus decided that it was impossible to continue and scuttled the boat. The crew was picked up by a Spanish fishing vessel, but they were seen on its deck by HMS *Fleetwood*. The fishing vessel was stopped and the Germans taken as prisoners.

On 19 November 1943, Fg. Off. D. M. McRae RCAF and crew located what was assumed to be convoys SL 139 and MKS 30 in position 4050N 0200W. It was too dark to be certain and the crew resumed their search. An hour and a half later a radar contact was gained at three miles and an attack was made with a stick of four depth charges and without the use of the Leigh Light. As the moon was up, McRae was hoping to surprise the U-Boat. Gunfire was exchanged and the rear gunner saw blue flashes amidships. Nothing further was seen. The boat was U-211, a type VIIc commanded by Kapitänleutnant Karl Hause and was sunk in this attack in position 4015N 01918W.

On 26 November 1943 Flt. Sgt. D. M. Cornish and crew were flying a creeping line ahead search over a rough sea in low cloud and a high wind velocity. A radar contact was gained and a homing carried out, the Leigh Light being illuminated at a quarter of a mile. A surfaced submarine was seen and an attack was made with a stick of six depth charges in the face of heavy flak. The two gunners returned fire. The boat was U-542, a type IXC/40 commanded by Oberleutnant zur See Christian Brandt Coester. No results were seen, but the boat had been sunk in position 3935N 01951W. (ref Norman Franks' *Search, Find and Kill*).

The internet site www.U-boat.net stated in January 2007 that U-542 was sunk on 28 November 1943 in position 3903N 01625W by a No 179 Squadron Wellington fuselage letter "H" which was the same aircraft that Cornish flew. There had been an attack by a No 179 Squadron aircraft, again on 28 November, in position 3904N 01625W, in which it was believed that U-542 had been sunk. However, U-Boat.net states that it was U-391 which had been damaged. U-391 was sunk by a No 53 Squadron Liberator on 13 December 1943.

No 190 Squadron was formed in February 1943 from a nucleus provided by No 210 Squadron at Sullom Voe and equipped with Catalina Ibs. There was a detachment at Reykjavik. On 26 March 1943 Plt. Off. J. Fish and crew were on an ice reconnaissance patrol flying at 350 feet when a visual sighting was gained of a surfaced U-Boat. This was U-339, a type VIIc commanded by Kapitänleutnant Georg Wilhelm Basse. A stick of four depth charges was dropped from 50 feet in the face of gunfire. A follow-up attack with two depth charges was made and the boat dived. An oil slick was seen and a second swirl, fuelling speculation that there had been a second submarine in the area. U-339 was badly damaged, causing her return to Trondheim and thence Kiel for repairs. She was then relegated to the status of a training boat.

On 17 May 1943 Flt. Lt. F. J. Gosling and crew flying from Castle Archdale gained a radar contact. Descending through cloud, the contact was converted to a visual sighting of a surfaced U-Boat. On his initial approach, Gosling was badly positioned for a depth charge attack, but nevertheless used the machine guns. As the boat was diving a second attack was made with four depth charges, the stick falling alongside the boat. The boat partly surfaced and then went down leaving oil and air bubbles. This was U-229, a type VIIc commanded by Oberleutnant zur See Robert Schetelig and had been badly damaged causing her return to Bordeaux.

On 30 May Squadron Leader J. A. Holmes and crew in Catalina FP183 of 190 Squadron visually sighted U-667 commanded by Kapitänleutnant Heinrich Schroteler, from nine miles. The aircraft was at 1200 feet in the Iceland/Faeroes Gap. The boat opened fire and the Catalina dropped six depth charges, which missed. The aircraft was hit but returned to Sullom Voe safely. Squadron Leader Holmes was a Flight Commander of the Squadron and flew with different crews, and as such he had to be captain. The usual captain, Flying Officer C. B. White, was on the aircraft that day. On 14 June Sqn. Ldr. Holmes and crew rescued Wg. Cdr. R. B. Thomson and crew from No 206 Squadron, who had ditched after their attack on U-417.

On 3 August 1943 U-489, a type XIV, commanded by Oberleutnant Adalbert Schmandt, was south east of Iceland when she was sighted by a No 190 Squadron Catalina FP280 captained by Flt Lt B. Crosland. Schmandt had sailed from Kiel on 22 July and on 28th he had rescued three survivors from a Blohm und Voss 138 floatplane which had been shot down by a Beaufighter. The U-Boat was sighted at five miles at 1150 feet, as was a B-17 Fortress, which attacked. Crosland attacked with guns at the same time but the Fortress apparently did not drop depth charges and flew off and was not seen again. In the meantime the Catalina suffered severe damage including the IFF (Identification Friend or Foe) and the Distant Reading Compass, which were destroyed. Crosland returned to base. While this action was happening Flight Sergeant E. L. J. Brame and crew arrived in a No 269 Squadron Hudson and attacked with anti-submarine bombs and guns. This badly damaged the boat and it submerged. The next day a No 423 Squadron Sunderland DD859 captained by Fg. Off. A. A. Bishop RCAF gained visual contact from four miles on U-489 in position 6111N 01438W. Bishop attacked with depth charges and sank the boat, but the aircraft was badly damaged and ditched. There were only six survivors from the aircraft. Shortly afterwards the destroyers HMS *Castletown* and HMS *Orwell* arrived on the scene and rescued survivors from both the aircraft and the U-Boat.

In October 1943 the squadron received some Catalina IVs. The squadron was disbanded on 1 January 1944 and renumbered No 210 Squadron, this latter unit having been disbanded at Hamworthy near Bournemouth on 31 December 1943.

No 201 Squadron was still at Lough Erne operating Sunderland IIIs. On 31 May 1943 Flt. Lt. D. M. Gall and crew gained a visual sighting of U-440, a type VIIc, commanded by Oberleutnant zur See Werner Schwaff, in position 4538N 01304W. Gall homed in on the target, exchanging gunfire. A pilot attack was made, Gall dropping four depth charges from 50 feet. He would have missed but for the boat turning into the stick. The bows went up and the submarine sank.

On 27 June Fg. Off. B. E. H. Layne and crew gained a visual sighting of U-518 at five miles. This boat, a type Ixc, was commanded by Kapitänleutnant Freidrich-Wilhelm Wissmann. The Sunderland attacked with two depth charges from 75 feet, but the boat had dived. However, after three minutes it surfaced and the aircraft made a follow-up attack in the face of enemy fire. The submarine dived while Layne's W/OP began homing in other aircraft. The U-boat was severely damaged and was forced to return to France. En route it was attacked again by a No 10 Squadron RAAF Sunderland captained by Flt. Lt. H. Skinner. U-518 was sunk on 22 April 1945 by USN destroyers. Her first patrol had been to land an agent on the shores of the Gulf of St Lawrence.

As the year opened, No 206 Squadron was still at Benbecula. On 15 January, 1943, Plt. Off. L. G. Clark and crew, while searching for convoy ON 160, gained a visual sighting of a surfaced U-Boat from 2000 feet over a sea state one at five miles off the port bow. This was U-632, a type VIIc commanded by Kapitänleutnant Hans Karpf in position 5740N 02710W. Clark attacked with seven depth charges but three hung up. The remainder straddled the boat, causing some damage.

On 9 February 1943 Sqn. Ldr. R. C. Patrick and crew were escorting convoy SC118. A destroyer with a corvette in tow in position 5617N 02039W was sighted. The destroyer signalled, requesting an escort while towing. The crew of the Fortress began a square search around the ships. A visual sighting was gained of U-614, a type VIIc boat commanded by Kapitänleutnant Wolfgang Strater, about six miles on the nose. Six depth charges were dropped, achieving a straddle and lifting U-614 out of the sea. The vessel went under in position 5612N 02059W but she did not sink. She was badly damaged and arrived in St. Nazaire 17 days later.

On 19 March Plt. Off. L. G. Clark and crew were escorting convoy HX 229. They were astern of the convoy under a rain squall and gained a visual contact on U-384 a type VIIc, commanded by Oberleutnant zur See Hans-Achim von Rosenberg-Gruszcynski, in position 5418N 02615W. Clark attacked with depth charges and achieved a straddle which sank the boat. Clark was awarded the DFC. On 25 March 1943 Flt. Lt. W. Roxburgh and crew were carrying out a creeping line ahead search for convoy RU 67 above cloud using radar. A radar contact was gained, a homing commenced and the contact was converted to a visual sighting, at approximately five miles, of a surfaced U-Boat. This was U-469, a type VIIc, commanded on her first patrol by Oberleutnant zur See Emil Claussen. Roxburgh attacked with six depth charges from 200 feet, achieving a straddle. The remaining depth charges were used in a follow-up attack and the boat was sunk in position 6212N 01640W. Roxburgh was awarded the DFC.

On 27 March Fg. Off. A. C. I. Samuel and crew were carrying out a creeping line ahead search at 2000 feet. At four hours into the patrol, the second pilot sighted a surfaced U-Boat at three miles. This was U-169, a type IXc/40 boat commanded on her first patrol by Oberleutnant zur See Hermann Bauer. A depth charge attack was made against flak opposition causing the boat to heel over. A follow-up attack was made and the submarine was sunk in position 6054N 01525W.

On 24 April 1943 Flying Officer R. L. Cowey and crew were escorting convoy ONS 5. A surfaced submarine was sighted at ten miles in clear weather in position 6130N 02010W. This was U-710, a type VIIc commanded by Oberleutnant zur See Dietrich von Carlowitz. The aircraft attacked immediately. The boat's gunners opened fire but no hits were achieved and six depth charges were dropped in a straddle across the boat. The boat sank, leaving about two dozen survivors in the water. The aircraft had to divert to Iceland as the weather at its base, Benbecula, was below limits and it was short of fuel.

On 11 June the Officer Commanding the squadron, Wing Commander R. B. Thomson, was captain of Fortress FA704 flying from Benbecula. He and his crew found and attacked U-417 commanded by Oberleutnant zur See Wolfgang Schreiner in position 6320N 01030W. The depth charge drop was accurate and the boat was sunk, but the Fortress was badly hit by flak and forced to ditch. None of the U-Boat crew survived but Thomson's crew of eight managed to board one dinghy albeit, without supplies, and remained there for three days before a No 190 Squadron Catalina and a US Navy Catalina from

VP84 found them. The American Catalina tried to land but crashed, the crew boarding liferafts. The RAF crew was picked up but it took five days to rescue the Americans, only one of whom survived. Thomson became an Air Vice Marshal with a CB and a DSO.

The Squadron moved from Benbecula to Lajes in October 1943 with its Fortress IIs. On 17 June 1943 Fg. Off. L. G. Clark and crew were on offensive operations flying from St Eval. The front observer sighted a surfaced U-Boat at seven miles in position 4342N 00937W. This was U-338, a type VIIc commanded by Kapitänleutnant Manfred Kinzel who began manoeuvring his boat. The Fortress crew attacked with six depth charges and then made a follow-up attack on the stern of the diving submarine. The boat was damaged and had to return to St. Nazaire.

No 210 Squadron disposed of its Catalina IIs in March 1943 and moved to Hamworthy in the following month with its Catalina Ibs. It was disbanded 31 December 1943, only to come into existence again on 1 January 1944 when No 190 Squadron was renumbered.

On 10 April 1943 Flt. Lt. F. Squire and crew gained a radar contact at four miles and turned to investigate. A U-boat was sighted but then lost. The aircraft remained in the vicinity and regained contact with the boat, which was attacked from 60 feet with four depth charges. The Boat was U-465, a type VIIc commanded by Kapitänleutnant Heinz Wolf and was damaged in this attack, forcing her return to Lorient.

On 30 May Catalina FP264, captained by Flight Lieutenant D. W. Eadie was on task in the Bay of Biscay.

The crew sighted what was probably U-418 commanded by Oberleutnant zur See Gerhard Lange. The Catalina started its attack but the U-boat opened fire, killing the front gunner and wounding two others. Depth charges were dropped but no results were observed. Due to the injured, the captain went straight back to Pembroke Dock. The aircraft was badly holed and began to sink on landing. This action was not reported by the U-Boat, whichever it was, and there is no record book entry to confirm this event or otherwise. U-418 was sunk two days later by a Beaufighter of No 236 Squadron.

On 7 July 1943 Fg. Off.J.A.Cruickshank and crew were on patrol from Gibraltar and gained a sighting of a U-Boat. This was U-267, a type VIIc commanded by Kapitänleutnant Otto Tinschert. Although no results were observed, the boat was damaged and was forced to return to St. Nazaire. On 8 July 1943 Fg. Off. D. H. Clarke and crew from the Squadron's Gibraltar detachment sighted a wake from a U-Boat and then the boat itself at seven miles in position 4202N 01410W. The radar was not in use. This was U-641 commanded by Kapitänleutnant Horst Rendtel. Clarke descended and attacked with six depth charges on the swirl of the diving boat. No results were observed. About two hours later Clarke and crew were at 3000 feet when they saw U-228 commanded by Erwin Christophersen fully surfaced at five miles. Clarke, having no remaining depth charges, attacked with guns. The boat replied with guns to no effect and then dived.

On 9 July Flt Lt D. Ryan and crew, based at Gibraltar, were on task at 5000 feet west of Lisbon when they sighted what was probably U-642 commanded by Kapitänleutnant

Herbert Brunning in position 3830N 01402W about 14 miles away. The pilot descended breaking cloud at 2500 feet four miles from the target. The U-Boat's gunners opened fire at 1500 yards, hitting the wings, a fuel tank and the hull. The flying boat opened fire at 300 yards and dropped depth charges, those on the port side hanging up being damaged by flak. The Catalina was now on fire and the pilot decided to ditch, all of the crew getting out apart from Sergeant L. Yarnell, a WOP/AG, and Fg. Off. R. L. Hunter RCAF, the navigator. Petrol was pouring out on to the sea on the port side and burning. There was a danger that the fire would spread to the hung-up depth charges, which were then likely to explode. They had two dinghies with four crew members in each. After about ten minutes the Catalina blew up, leaving a small patch of burning petrol. They were rescued after six days by the frigate HMS *Swale* and taken to Casablanca. They had drifted about 100 miles in their dinghies. A Catalina, co-operating with the Second Escort Group, responded to the request for help from the No 53 Squadron Liberator on 30 July 1943 concerning U-461, U-462 and U-504. The aircraft arrived on the scene but was not required, the U-Boats having been sunk.

No 220 Squadron, still with its Fortress IIs, moved to Aldergrove in February. On 3 February 1943 Plt. Off. K. Ramsden and crew were escorting convoy HZ 224 at 3000 feet in and out of cloud. Through a gap a visual sighting was gained of a surfaced U-boat at four miles in position 5635N 02249W. With the sun behind him Ramsden dropped seven depth charges from 80 feet. No results were seen, neither then nor one hour later when the crew came back to the area. The submarine, U-265 commanded by

Oberleutnant zur See Bernhard Auffhammer, had been sunk. On 7 February 1943 Plt. Off. G. Roberson and crew were escorting convoy SC 118 in frequent showers with good visibility in between. A visual sighting of U-624, commanded by Kapitänleutnant Ulrich Graf von Soden-Fraunhofen, was gained at nine miles. To avoid visual detection by the U-boat Robertson climbed into cloud and then descended towards the target, breaking cloud at around 1500 yards. He dropped seven depth charges from 50 feet, achieving a good straddle. Debris and oil were seen. U-624 had been sunk in position 5542N 02617W.

On 7 March 1943, Fg. Off. W. Knowles and crew, escorting convoy SC121 and flying at 2500 feet, gained a visual sighting of the wake of a U-Boat and then the boat itself. Knowles attacked with seven depth charges from 80 feet. The boat had submerged by now but a good straddle was achieved. The stern of the boat rose from the sea and then went down, leaving oil on the surface. This was believed to be U-633, a type VIIc, commanded by Oberleutnant zur See Bernhard Muller. It was sunk in position 5714N 02630W. On 19 March Fg. Off. Knowles and crew again were again in action. They were escorting convoy SC 122. Shortly into the patrol at 5000 feet visual contact was gained on U-666, a type VIIc boat commanded by Oberleutnant zur See Herbert Engel. Knowles attacked with four depth charges, which hit the sea just in front of the swirl left by the diving boat. Oil rose to the surface, followed by the boat. A follow-up attack with three depth charges was made, but by then the boat had submerged. U-666 had been damaged and she returned to St. Nazaire on 10 April 1943.

On 6 June 1943 Sqn. Ldr. H. Warren and crew were searching for a missing Sunderland. A fully-surfaced submarine was sighted in position 6212N 01528W. This was U-450, a type VIIc commanded by Oberleutnant zur See Kurt Bohme. An attack with three depth charges was made and the boat was damaged. A follow-up attack was attempted but the remaining depth charge hung up. The boat went down by the stern but was able to reach Brest.

On 14 June Fortress FK212 was shot down by JU88s. The squadron moved to Benbecula in March and Lajes in the Azores in October 1943. From there it maintained detachments at Gibraltar and Thorney Island. On 9 November 1943 Flt. Lt. R. Drummond and crew were en route to convoy MKS 29A which they were to join for escort purposes. At 40 miles from the convoy, the Flight Engineer, Flt. Sgt. J. Fitzpatrick, saw a U-Boat immediately below the aircraft. This was U-707, a type VIIc commanded by Oberleutnant zur See Gunter Gretschel. Fire was exchanged as the Fortress moved into an attacking position. A stick of four depth charges was dropped from 40 feet and the boat went down by the stern. A follow-up attack was made with a stick of three depth charges. There appeared to be an underwater explosion and the boat sank in position 4031N 02017W. One survivor was seen and a dinghy was dropped to him together with some rations. Drummond was awarded the DFC.

No 224 Squadron was re-equipped with Liberator Vs in January 1943, disposing of its Mark IIIs in April when the squadron moved to St Eval. On 26 February 1943 Sqn. Ldr. P. Cundy and crew were flying over a sea state zero with visibility in the region of 14 miles when a radar contact was gained on the ASV range 30 miles in position 4133N 02149W. This was U-508, a type IXc, commanded by Kapitänleutnant Georg Staats. A radar homing was carried out and an attack was made with a stick of four depth charges. No results were observed. It subsequently transpired that it had been damaged. Cundy's navigator, Fg. Off. R. R. Fabel DFC, became a navigator Captain.

On 29 April Flt. Lt. A. R. Laughland and crew gained a radar contact at eight miles in position 4554N 01022W. A homing was initiated and the contact was converted to visual at four miles. An attack was made with six depth charges as the boat submerged. This was U-332, a type VIIc commanded by Oberleutnant zur See Eberhard Huttemann. No results were observed from this attack. Consequently, Laughland resolved to carry out a gambit where the aircraft departed the area for around an hour to mislead the submarine crew that they were safe from attack. On return to the area a radar contact was gained at 18 miles and at two miles the U-Boat was sighted. A stick of six depth charges was dropped from 50 feet, lifting the boat out of the water. The U-Boat was sunk.

On 16 May Flight Sergeant J. S. Powell was captain of Liberator FL948 on patrol in the Bay of Biscay when he sighted U-648 commanded by Oberleutnant zur See Peter-Arthur Stahl on the surface at around five miles. He attacked under cannon, machine gun and deck gun fire. The deck gun scored a hit just as Powell was releasing the depth charges, causing them to undershoot. U-648 dived and Powell made an attack on the wake, but no results were observed. The captain had suffered a minor injury in that he was feeling dizzy, but recovered and continued with the patrol. Shortly after, another surfaced U-Boat was sighted. It remained on the surface while the aircraft circled it, both sides shooting at each other. The captain decided to make a dummy attack, there being no weapons left, and this caused the U-Boat to dive. This meant that the boat had now to use its batteries, making it vulnerable in the long term. Flight Sergeant Powell was awarded the Conspicuous Gallantry Medal (CGM). Flight Sergeant J. S. Edwards and crew in a 224 Squadron Liberator were on close escort to convoy SL129 (West Africa to UK) and located U-594 under Kapitänleutnant Friedrich Mumm on 27 May. Edwards attacked with six depth charges which failed to release. The aircraft was damaged in this attack but Edwards went round again and this time the depth charges released. The stick overshot. The next day U-594 was to meet No 502 Squadron.

On 31 May 1943 Plt. Off. R. V. Sweeney and crew gained a radar contact at eight miles. A homing was initiated through cloud but unfortunately they broke through the cloud at on top the target. Sweeney was forced to go round again under fire from the U-Boat. This was U-621, a type VIIc commanded by Oberleutnant zur See Max Kruschka. The first attack was made from 50 feet with six depth charges, but this was an overshoot. A follow-up attack was made with six more depth charges as the boat dived. The boat was en route to Brest at the end of its patrol and was damaged.

Sweeney was an American whose brother was a member of one of the Eagle Squadrons. Sweeney and four others had been part of Sqn. Ldr. Cundy's crew. On 2 July 1943 Warrant Officer E. J. Spiller and crew gained a radar contact at 189 miles and initiated a homing. The contact disappeared at three miles and on reaching the datum nothing was seen and thus no attack was carried out. A little later another radar contact was gained. Two U-boats were sighted at two miles in position 4337N 01005W. The leading boat was attacked first in the face of flak. The second boat was seen to dive and this was attacked next. U-462, a type XIV tanker commanded by Oberleutnant zur See Bruno Vowe, was damaged in this attack. The other boat was U-160, which escorted U-462 back to Bordeaux.

On 3 July 1943 Squadron Leader P. J. Cundy and crew in Liberator FL963 found and attacked U-628 commanded by Kapitänleutnant Heinrich Hasenschar in position 4411N 00845W. Two attacks were made, the first dropping for the first time the new 35lb anti-submarine bombs in a stick of eighteen. Four depth charges were dropped in the second attack and the U-Boat was destroyed, there being no survivors. However flak damaged the starboard wing, a fin and rudder and a fuel tank. Peter Cundy received a DSO to add to his DFC and Flight Sergeant E. S. Cheek, a WOP/AG, received a DFM. The aircraft returned safely to St Eval.

The same day Sqn. Ldr. T. M. Bulloch and crew were on patrol in excellent weather conditions in a Liberator GR V equipped with a new weapon. These were rockets and this crew was charged with an operational trial. An armament officer, Flt. Lt. C. Campbell, was on board and it was he who sighted a U-Boat amongst a number of Spanish vessels. Bulloch attacked immediately with a pair at a range of 800 feet, another pair at a range of 600 feet and the remaining four at a range of 500 feet. This was U-

514, a type IXC commanded by Kapitänleutnant Jurgen Auffermann. The boat was seen to go down and then surface. It finally sank in position 4337N 00859W. This aircraft was carrying a Mk 24 Torpedo and a half load of depth charges. Bulloch decide to drop the torpedo and within a few moments an object was seen moving fast through the water. It was uncertain as to whether or not this was the U-Boat or the torpedo. Bulloch dropped depth charges on it and it exploded with a large flash. Bulloch had destroyed the torpedo. This was a good decision as the weapon was Top Secret and if it had been picked up by one of the fishing vessels great damage could have been done to the war effort.

On 17 July 1943 Wing Commander A. E. Clouston DFC AFC and crew gained a radar contact at 18 miles and homed in, dropping 24 x 35lb antisubmarine bombs from 300 feet. The navigator, using the nose guns, exchanged fire with the U-Boat, which was U-558 commanded by Kapitänleutnant Günter Krech, in position 4251N 01107W. The aircraft was hit in the wings, an engine and fuselage by flak and bomb fragments. The boat dived and got away but on 20 July she was attacked by an American B-24 (a Liberator) with seven depth charges. Both submarine and aircraft were damaged and the B-24 broke off the action. At that moment a No 58 Squadron Halifax (DT642) captained by Flt Lt G. A. Sawtell attacked with depth charges and sank U-558. On 28 July 1943 U-404 commanded by Oberleutnant zur See Adolf Schonberg was sighted by Major S. D. McElroy of the 4th US Squadron, 479th Group in a Liberator, or B-24 as the Americans preferred to call it. Radar contact had been gained and converted to a visual sighting. He attacked, but the depth charges hung up. The U-Boat dived. The Liberator stayed in the area and sighted the boat as it resurfaced. McElroy attacked again but the aircraft was hit in the cockpit by flak. The aircraft returned fire, hitting several sailors. The boat started to dive. McElroy dropped eight depth charges which exploded in the swirl. At this point McElroy was forced to return to base as the oil pressure on his damaged engine was falling. He had sent sighting reports and in response to these another Liberator captained by First Lieutenant Arthur J. Hammar arrived on the scene. U-404 resurfaced and was attacked twice by Hammar. Heavy flak caused damage to the tail, the fuselage and the port outer, whose propeller had to be feathered. Hammer headed home.

A third Liberator arrived, this time from No 224 Squadron captained by Fg. Off. R. V. Sweeny, who was an American! He seems to have taken over Sqn. Ldr. Cundy's crew from 3 July. The crew had seen the exploding depth charges and headed towards them. At 1000 yards the RAF gunners opened fire. The U-Boat returned fire, hitting the starboard outer. Depth charges were dropped and this time U-404 was finished and sank in position 4553N 00925W. It had taken 27 depth charges. None of the crew survived.

The 224 crew sent a SOS to No 19 Group at Plymouth and had to jettison the guns and all loose equipment in order to maintain height. They made it back to St Mawgan rather than St Eval as it had a longer runway and this was necessary for a three-engined landing. The two airfields are three miles apart as the crow flies.

On 23 October 1943 Sqn. Ldr. E. J. Wicht and crew were briefed to escort convoy ON 207 but en route they were to drop a radar transformer to Escort Group B7. A radar contact was gained at 10 miles and Wicht climbed into cloud to avoid visual detection. On descent the radar contact was converted to a visual sighting of a surfaced U-boat at two miles. This was U-274, a type VIIc, commanded by Kapitänleutnant Gunther J. Jordan. Wicht attacked with rockets, two at 1000 feet and 1000 yards range, two at 800 feet and 800 yards range and the last four at 400 yards. No damage was observed although it was thought that the stern might have been hit. The Escort Group was only 18 miles away and a sighting report was made to them.

The U-boat now began to fire at the aircraft whenever it seemed to be in range. Then it headed in a westerly direction and began to dive, at which point Wicht attacked with two depth charges from 50 feet. The Group arrived and took over the prosecution of U-274 and finally sank her. Wicht dropped the transformer and set off for the convoy.

No 228 Squadron moved to Pembroke Dock in May 1943 from Lough Erne with its Sunderland IIIs. On 24 May Flying Officer H. J. Debden and crew of this squadron in EJ139 found and attacked U-441, a type VIIc flak boat, commanded by Kapitänleutnant Klaus Gotz von Hartmann. Clay Blair states that there was confusion over the name of the U-Boat commander. At this time he was Gotz von Hartmann. The earlier commander was Klaus Hartmann. This boat had additional armament for the very purpose of attracting aircraft and shooting them down. The Sunderland dropped depth charges but was badly hit and crashed, leaving no survivors. (Per U-441's operations record book). However the U-Boat was seriously damaged and returned to her base. She was repaired and went to sea, only to meet No 248 Squadron.

On 31 May Fg. Off. W. M. French and crew arrived on the scene of the attacks on U-563 by Nos 58 and 10 Squadrons in position 4700N 00940W. French made two attacks and saw 30 to 40 survivors in the water. The U-Boat had been sunk. French received the DFC and a member of his crew, Flt. Sgt. J. de Bois, received the DFM.

Flying Officer L.B. Lee in a Sunderland on 13 June 1943 sighted a group sailing of U-564 and U-185 from Bordeaux, U-134 and U-653 from La Pallice and U-358 from St Nazaire. These boats had sailed on 11 June and were seen on the 12th, but night fell before more aircraft could be brought to the scene. Due to the risk of sighting by Leigh Light aircraft, the group submerged for the night. By the time Fg. Off. Lee and crew saw them they had reached 4430N01500W. Lee attacked immediately but was shot down. There were no survivors. However, Lee managed to drop depth charges on U-564, a type VIIc commanded by Hans Fiedler, and caused serious damage, enough to make her abort her patrol. U-185, commanded by Kapitänleutnant August Maus, was detached to act as escort. These boats were to meet No 10 OTU and No 415 Squadron later.

On 13 July 1943 Fg. Off. R. D. Hanbury and crew were on patrol in the Bay of Biscay when they gained a sighting of three U-Boats. The Sunderland orbited, transmitting a radio message and requesting assistance from other aircraft in adjacent areas. One boat, U-607, a type VIIc commanded by Oberleutnant zur See Wolf Jeschonneck, detached from the other boats and Hanbury took the opportunity to attack with seven depth charges. The bows of the boat were blown off at the conning tower and the boat was sunk. Twenty five men were seen in the water. A dinghy was dropped and some of them climbed into it. A Ju88 was in the area but made no attack. The other two boats were U-445 and U-613. A Halifax, captained by Fg. Off. A. R. Clutterbuck of No 58 Squadron had sighted the three boats earlier and was co-operating with Hanbury.

On 30 July 1943, a No 53 Squadron Liberator located the Group of U-461, U-462 and U-504. This locating report was 80 miles in error but Fg. Off. S. White and crew sighted the Group visually and sent a correct locating report. This was interpreted by No 19 Group MHQ as being a second Group. White then had to leave the area as he was being pursued by a Ju88. A Catalina of No 210 Squadron then sighted the boats and reported the sighting to Captain Walker's Second Escort Group. A Liberator of the 19th Squadron USAAF arrived on the scene having picked up White's report. White returned at about the same time. Fg. Off. W. S. Biggar and crew in a No 502 Squadron Halifax arrived in the area.

On 1 August 1943 Flt Lt S. White and crew in Sunderland JM678 located U-383 commanded by Kapitänleutnant Horst Kremser in position 4724N 01210W. The captain attacked, aircraft and U-Boat exchanging fire. The Sunderland lost the starboard float and aileron and suffered other damage and the boat took violent evading action. Thus the first attack was aborted.

White attacked again, dropping a stick of seven depth charges. The boat was seen to be in trouble with sailors jumping overboard but White could not stay due to the damage to his aircraft. A signal was sent by U-383 to Befehlshaber der U-Boote (BdU) but she sank during the night. There were no survivors.

On 2 August a squadron aircraft gained a visual of three torpedo boats reporting them as destroyers. These had been sent to escort U-106, which had been damaged by Wg. Cdr. J. C. Archer and crew earlier. This was a type IXB commanded by Oberleutnant zur See Wolfdietrich Damerow. The locating report on the torpedo boats brought a No 461 Squadron Sunderland, captained by Flt. Lt. I. A. F. Clark RAAF, and a No 228 Squadron Sunderland, captained by Fg. Off. R. Hanbury, to the scene. A Halifax and a Liberator also joined in the shadowing operation. Then U-106 was sighted and Hanbury and Clark began a gun duel with the boat. Depth charges were dropped and the boat was abandoned. Then U-106 blew up. The 40th Escort Group picked up 37 survivors.

No 246 Squadron was disbanded at Bowmore at the end of April 1943 after some nine months.

No 304 (Czech) Squadron moved to Docking in April 1943, exchanging its Wellington Ics for Wellington Xs. It moved to Davidstow Moor, Cornwall, in June 1943 and exchanged its Mark Xs for Mark XIIIs. There was a further exchange in September 1943 when the Mark XIIIs were exchanged for Wellington XIVs. The Squadron moved to Predannack in December 1943.

No 311 (Czech) Squadron moved from Talbenny, South West Wales to Beaulieu between Bournemouth and

Southampton in May 1943 and in June exchanged its Wellington Ics for Liberator IIIAs and Vs. On 10 November 1943 Flt. Sgt. O. Zanta and crew gained a radar contact and located U-966, which had been under continuous attack during the day from No 612 Squadron, VP 103 and VP 110 USN. Zanta attacked with rockets in two pairs, which failed. He then fired four from 600 feet which were seen to enter the sea and not emerge. The boat reached the Spanish coast, where the crew blew it up.

No 320 Squadron Royal Netherlands Navy left Coastal Command and joined the light bomber force, exchanging its Hudson VIs for North American Mitchells (B25s) at Methwold in March 1943.

No 330 Squadron Royal Norwegian Air Force left Iceland in January 1943, although it maintained detachments at Reykjavik and Budareyri and went to Oban, Argyll. In February it converted to Sunderland IIs and IIIs, giving up its Northrop N3Ps in June. In July the squadron moved to Sullom Voe.

No 333 Squadron Royal Norwegian Air Force was formed by renumbering No 1477 Flight, "A" Flight being at Woodhaven, Dundee and "B" Flight at Leuchars. "A" Flight was equipped with Catalina Ibs and "B" Flight with Mosquito IIs until September when the Flight re-equipped with Mosquito VIs. The Catalinas were detached to Sullom Voe.

No 407 Squadron Royal Canadian Air Force started to exchange its Hudson Vs for Wellington XIs in January 1943. In February it moved to Skitten, April to Chivenor and in June it added Wellington XIVs to its inventory. On 2 August 1943 Wg. Cdr. J. C. Archer and crew attacked

U-106 with depth charges, but no damage was evident. Nevertheless slight damage had occurred and the boat began a return to base. Then it met No 228 and No 461 squadrons and others and was sunk.

On 7 September 1943 Plt. Off. E. M. O'Donnell RCAF and crew were on patrol at 1500 feet in two miles visibility. A radar contact was gained at eight miles, and descending, the aircraft homed in. At three quarters of a mile the Leigh Light was switched on, revealing a submarine. which was U-669, a type VIIc commanded by Oberleutnant zur See Kurt Kohl. The homing was not good and O'Donnell was not in the right position for an attack and was forced to go round agin. He sighted the wake and attacked with six depth charges on the submerging boat, which sank in position 4536N 01013W. At the beginning of November the squadron moved to St Eval but by early December it was back at Chivenor.

No 415 Squadron Royal Canadian Air Force at Thorney Island converted to Wellington XIIIs in September, disposing of its Hampdens in the same month. A Hampden was lost on 14 June 1943 (for the circumstances see the entry under No 10 OTU). On 2 August 1943 Sqn. Ldr. C. G. Ruttan RCAF and crew gained a visual sighting of U-706, a type VIIc commanded by Kapitänleutnant Alexander von Zitzewitz. A stick of six depth charges was dropped, but the results could not be confirmed. The Hampden front gummer had opened fire but the gun jammed after ten rounds. Then a B-24 Liberator from No 4 Squadron USAAF flown by 1st Lieutenant J. L. Hamilton and crew arrived on the scene. They had gained a radar contact at 20 miles and had then seen the Hampden at 10 miles. Hamilton dropped 12 depth charges from 50 feet in the face of heavy flak which hit the aircraft. U-706 sank in position 4516N 01025W. Hamilton dropped a dinghy to the survivors and a Catalina and a Sunderland homed HMS *Waveney* to the scene and survivors were picked up.

In October 1943 the squadron received some Albacores in addition to the Wellingtons. In November the squadron moved to Bircham Newton with Wellington detachments at North Coates and Docking and Albacore detachments at Manston in Kent, Thorney Island and Winkleigh.

No 422 Squadron Royal Canadian Air Force with its Sunderland IIIs moved to Bowmore in May 1943.

On 16 October 1943 Flt. Lt. P. T. Sargent RCAF and crew were escorting convoy ONS20 in JM712. A radar contact was gained in position 5950N 03000W. They homed in to find two U-Boats, which were believed to be U-448, commanded by Oberleutnant zur See Helmut Dauter and U-281, commanded by Oberleutnant zur See Heinrich von Davidson. Sargent attacked one of them, but his DCs undershot. During the follow up attack the aircraft was badly hit by gunfire from both U-Boats but he was able to drop two DCs, a third failing to release. The autopilot and radio were destroyed, the radar and engine controls damaged and the aircraft generally riddled with holes. Fg. Off. C. B. Steeves RCAF, the navigator, and Flt. Lt. P. A. S. Woodwork RAF, the Group Gunnery Officer, were dead. Sargent ditched the Sunderland near the convoy in heavy weather but he failed to survive. Flight Sergeant J. Y. Rutherford, a WOM, was wounded and

Flight Sergeant L. T. Needham, Flight Engineer, also RAF, failed to survive. Fg. Off. A. R. B. Bellis RCAF, the second pilot, and Warrant Officer W. F. Beals RAF, the squadron gunnery leader, received the DFC. U-448 was forced to abandon her patrol and return to base. The other boat may have been U-470. There were seven survivors from this crew. See Norman Franks' *Search, Find and Kill*.

The squadron moved in November to St Angelo, Lough Erne. On 20 November Fg. Off. J. D. B. Ulrichson RCAF and crew in W6031 were on escort to convoys SL139 and MKS30 and were due to land at Gibraltar. U-648, commanded by Oberleutnant zur See Peter-Arthur Stahl, was in the vicinity. This boat was fitted with the successor to Metox, the Naxos search receiver or Electronic Counter Measures (ECM), which could detect centimetric radar. The Sunderland crew sent a message to the effect that they had found and were about to attack a U-Boat. Unfortunately the boat had been alerted by her Naxos and opened fire, badly damaging the flying boat. Gibraltar received a distress message stating that the aircraft was about to ditch in position 4240N 01910W. Nothing more was heard and there were no survivors. U-648 was found by RN escorts to convoy KMS30/OG5, and sunk by HMS *Blackwood*, in position 4240N 02037W north east of the Azores on 23 November.

No 423 Squadron Royal Canadian Air Force remained at Castle Archdale, Lough Erne, with its Sunderland IIIs. It disposed of its Mark IIs in April 1943. Flight Lieutenant J. Musgrave and crew were on convoy escort to convoy HX237 on 12/13 May 1943. Having joined the convoy north north east of the Azores and been given a task, they located a surfaced submarine about ten miles from the convoy in position 4845N02215W. Then Musgrave dived the aircraft from 10,000 feet and at one mile the boat opened fire. The boat, U-753, a type VIIc commanded by Korvettenkapitän Alfred Manhardt von Mannstein, seemed to make no attempt to dive, so Musgrave broke off the attack and called the Escort Commander. A Surface Attack Unit (SAU) in the form of one corvette (HMCS Drumheller) was sent. The Sunderland kept the U-Boat under observation, both exchanging fire. The aircraft was hit but not seriously. When the corvette came within range she opened fire, at which the boat dived. Musgrave made an attack with two depth charges. A Swordfish from the convoy's escort carrier joined in and the corvette depth charged the area. The Sunderland returned to base, leaving the corvette and the U-Boat to fight it out, a battle which U-753 lost.

It is of interest to note that Musgrave's Commanding Officer made a report that Musgrave had complied with Coastal Command Instructions by calling on the convoy escort ten miles away. HQCC was obviously not encouraging aircraft to fight surfaced U-Boats if there was an alternative. On 4 August 1943, Fg. Off. A. A. Bishop and crew in Sunderland DD859 gained a visual sighting from four miles of U-489 in position 6111N 01438W after its encounters with the No 190 Squadron Catalina and the No 269 Squadron Hudson. The boat was in a bad state with its batteries drained, which prevented her from diving. However her guns were operational. Bishop attacked with depth charges but was hit, causing fires in the galley and in the bomb bay. He had to ditch, but he had killed the submarine. On hitting the sea the left wing dropped, catching the float, and the aircraft cartwheeled. There were six survivors, including Bishop, who together with survivors from the U-Boat were picked up by HMS *Castletown* and HMS *Orwell*. Bishop was awarded the DFC.

The 8 October 1943 was a day of continuing battles around convoy SC143. Fg. Off. A. H. Russell and crew were on patrol astern of the convoy. They came out of cloud to find a surfaced submarine 100 yards ahead. This was too late for an attack, although the rear gunner fired. The boat replied with its deck gun and machine guns. Russell attacked with four depth charges, but only three dropped. That was sufficient and the boat was lifted out of the water and then sank in position 5545N 02433W. This was U-610, a type VIIc commanded by Kapitänleutnant Walter Freiherr von Freyberg-Eisenberg-Allmendirgen. Russell was awarded the DFC.

No 461 Squadron Royal Australian Air Force moved to Pembroke Dock from Hamworthy Junction (Poole Harbour) in April 1943 with its Sunderland IIs, which it exchanged the following month for Sunderland IIIs. On 1 May 1943 Flt. Lt. E. C. Smith RAAF and crew gained a visual sighting at six miles of U-415, which earlier in the day had been attacked by a No 172 Squadron Wellington. Smith attacked with a stick of depth charges, causing further damage to U-415, which dived. The following day Flt. Lt. Smith and crew, coming out of cloud, sighted a U-Boat at four miles. Smith attacked and at one mile the boat opened fire. A stick of four depth charges was dropped, with a follow-up attack of a further four. The boat sank stern first in position 4448N 00858W, leaving 15 men in the water. This had been U-465, a type VIIc, commanded by Kapitänleutnant Heinz Wolf. On 30 July 1943 Flt Lt D. Marrows RAAF in Sunderland W6077 lettered "U" intercepted the locating report from the No 53 Squadron Liberator concerning U-461, U-462 and U-504. He followed the Liberator in the attack on U-461. Seeing that his depth charges had missed he dropped a stick of his own, which blew the boat out of the water. Thus aircraft "U" of No 461 Squadron had sunk U-461. U-461 was a type XIV supply boat commanded by Korvettenkapitän Wolf-Harro Stiebler and sank in position 4542N 01100W.

No 502 Squadron gave up its Whitleys in February 1943 and converted to Halifax IIs. It moved to Holmesley South near Bournemouth in March but within the month it returned to St Eval. Plt. Off. L. J. McCulloch and crew on 22 March were en route for a convoy escort when they found and attacked U-338, a type VIIC, commanded by Kapitänleutnant Manfred Kinzel. The boat's gunners opened fire and shot down the Halifax. U-338 rescued the sole survivor, Flight Sergeant Taylor.

The squadron returned to Holmesley South in June and then to St Davids in December 1943. On 28 May 1943 Flying Officer A. J. Davey and crew in a Halifax of No 502 Squadron located and attacked U-94 with a 600lb antisubmarine bomb. The boat had submerged and the aircraft was late on the swirl, meaning that the U-Boat was probably out of range of the bomb. Gunfire had been exchanged, but the aircraft was not hit. Two aircraft from the squadron were involved in the action on 30 July 1943 with U-461, U-462 and U-504, one of them captained by Fg. Off. August van Rossum, sinking U-462 in position

4508N 01057W. This was a type XIV supply boat commanded by Oberleutnant zur See Bruno Vowe. As the boat began to sink shells from the 2nd Escort Group fell close by. The other No 502 Squadron aircraft was captained by Fg. Off. W. S. Biggar and he endeavoured to establish communications with the other aircraft, orbiting the U-Boat Group, but to no avail. Thus he made an attack with a stick of three 600lb depth bombs from 1000 feet but overshot. The Sunderland from No 461 Squadron sank U-461.

On 16 November Fg. Off. F. T. Culling-Mannix RNZAF and crew located U-256 commanded by Oberleutnant zur See Wilhelm Brauel in position 4717N 00820W visually at one mile, conning tower awash. The boat opened fire and the aircraft took avoiding action and lost height to make an attack. When he came back over the position the boat had dived. The U-Boat commander thought he had shot down the aircraft, which he believed to be a flying boat! The Halifax landed at base after a 13 hour and 20 minute sortie, which at that time was a record for No 502 Squadron.

No 524 Squadron was formed at Oban in October 1943 with Mariner Is but was disbanded in December.

No 547 Squadron moved to Tain, Ross-shire in January 1943 and then to Chivenor in April with a detachment at Tain. In May 1943 it exchanged its Wellington VIIIs for Wellington XIs and moved to Davidstow Moor, Cornwall. On 14 June Pilot Officer J. W. Hermiston and crew were driven off by the gunfire from U-600, U-615 and U-257, sailing together as a group. On 24 July Fg. Off. J. Whyte and crew arrived on the chaotic scene of a No 172 Squadron Wellington which had crashed on top of U-459. Whyte dropped seven depth charges on the boat, causing enough further damage to make the U-Boat commander scuttle his boat. On 2 August 1943 Plt. Off. J. W. Hermiston and crew were on patrol at 3000 feet when the co-pilot, Flt. Sgt. F. G. Duff, gained a visual sighting of the wakes of three U-Boats. A bomb was dropped from 2000 feet, to no effect except that the U-Boats returned defensive fire. A depth charge attack on one of the boats was made from 50 feet in position 4712N 01054W, but it missed. Machine gun attacks were made from 50 feet. While no damage was caused to the boat, it had to return to Brest to give medical aid to several casualties. The boat was U-218, a type VIID minelayer commanded by Kapitänleutnant Richard Becker. In October 1943 the squadron received some Wellington XIIIs and moved to Thorney Island with a detachment at Aldergrove. In November the squadron said goodbye to its Wellingtons and converted to Liberator Vs.

No 612 Squadron exchanged its Wellington VIIIs in March 1943 for Wellington XIIIs. In April it went to Davidstow Moor and in May to Chivenor. In June, Wellington XIVs were added to its inventory. Some Whitley VIIs were still retained until June 1943. On 1 May 1943 Flt. Sgt. N. Earnshaw and crew were flying in good weather at 3000 feet with visibility at least 10 miles. They gained a visual sighting at five miles of U-415, which had been attacked twice that day by No 172 Squadron and No 461 Squadron aircraft. The Whitley dived to attack in the face of gunfire and dropped six depth charges as the boat was diving. This stick was wide by 200 yards and a follow-up attack was made with two depth charges on the swirl. A patch of oil was seen. The U-boat had been damaged again but made port.

On 8 September 1943 Fg. Off. J. M. Bezer and crew in Wellington HF126 gained a radar contact at four miles. They homed in and at 600 feet saw a wake. The captain carried on for three miles, dropping to 100 feet, and turned back on to the contact. At 1500 yards the Leigh Light was struck and the U-Boat immediately opened fire, hitting the aircraft in the nose, port engine, starboard fuel tank and radar. The front gunner tried to return fire, but the guns jammed. Bezer dropped six depth charges and turned for home due to the condition of his aircraft. A crash landing was made at Portreath with no injuries incurred.

U-402 was sunk on 13 October 1943 by aircraft of VC9 from the escort carrier USS *Card*. The squadron spent the month of November at St Eval and then returned to Chivenor. On 8 October, 1943 Pilot Officer M. H. Paynter RAAF and crew were on a Search and Rescue sortie when, with the aid of the Leigh Light, they found U-256, commanded by Oberleutnant zur See Wilhelm Brauel in position 4728N 00936W. They attacked with six depth charges and while it was an excellent straddle the U-Boat was undamaged. The same could not be said of the Wellington and indeed the U-Boat thought it had shot down the aircraft. Damage to the starboard elevator and the rear turret had been incurred. However the aircraft was still flying. The crew tried for a follow-up attack, but nothing could be seen apart from the flame floats that went down with the DCs. The crew later found the dinghy they were looking for.

Fg. Off. R. S. Yeadon and crew were on patrol north of Cape Ortega on 30 October 1943 when they located U-415, which they attacked with four depth charges and guns. The boat was badly damaged and was forced to return to base. However, the aircraft was shot down, crashing 50 metres from U-415. On 10 November 1943 Warrant Officer I. D. Gunn and crew gained a radar contact, which was then visually sighted in the moonlight. Six depth charges were dropped from 100 feet which missed and after an exchange of gunfire, the boat submerged. This was U-966, a type VIIc commanded by Oberleutnant zur See Ekkehard Wolf in position 4439N 00908W. First Lieutenant K. L. Wright and crew in a Liberator of VP 103, USN were informed of the incident and headed for the scene. Because of Ju88 activity they took a devious route. Radar contact was gained and then a visual sighting. A stick of five depth charges was dropped, the sixth hanging up, and then a 600lb depth bomb. The boat was seen to be damaged and down by the stern. First Lieutenant J. A. Parrish and crew in a Liberator of VP 110 USN located the crippled boat and dropped a stick of six depth charges, but still the boat carried on, apparently trying to reach Spain. Flt. Sgt. O. Zanta and the crew of No 311 Squadron attacked it with rockets, slowing down the boat further. It eventually reached De Sanatafata Bay, where the crew blew up the boat.

No 10 Operational Training Unit (OTU) was on loan from Bomber Command.   It was not a squadron but, as its name shows, was a training unit equipped with Whitleys, responsible for training crews before they went to Bomber Command squadrons. The OTU had been loaned to Coastal Command. Nevertheless, when the unit's aircraft went on sorties over the sea they carried weapons. On 22 March 1943 one such aircraft, a Whitley captained by Sergeant J. A. Marsden, was on patrol in what can be described as typical Atlantic weather, that is total cloud cover at around 3500 feet, pouring rain and visibility of half a mile. The rear gunner sighted a periscope wake from 1500 feet at 200 yards range. It disappeared and no attack was made but later when flying at 100 feet the crew gained a visual sighting of the conning tower of a U-boat with decks awash. This was U-665, a type VIIc commanded by Oberleutnant zur See Hans-Jurgen Haupt. Marsden attacked with six depth charges, but due to the weather no results were seen. However, the boat had been sunk in position 4804N 01026W.

On 6 May 1943 Sgt. S. J. Barnett and crew gained a visual sighting of a U-boat at three miles. Barnett attacked from 300 feet with a stick of depth charges, causing slight damage. This was U-214, a type VIId mine layer commanded by Kapitänleutnant Rupprecht Stock. However, the front gunner had caused so many casualties before his guns jammed that U-214 was forced to return to Brest. As the attack was taking place another aircraft had been seen but was never identified.

On 9 May 1943, a Whitley, captained by Sergeant A. J. Savage from this unit, found and attacked U-666 a few hours after the boat had been found by the No 58 Squadron Halifax, which it later shot down. Again the gunners made their mark and hit the Whitley in the tail. The aircraft returned to base safely. U-666 was commanded by Oberleutnant zur See Herbert Engels. On

15 May Flt. Sgt. G. W. Brookes and crew gained a visual contact on a U-Boat in position 4649N 01156W and attacked with five depth charges, the sixth being a hang up. The boat lifted and then went under. This was U-591, a type VIIc commanded by Kapitänleutnant Hans-Jurgen Zetzsche, which had been damaged in this attack. An hour later a further boat was sighted in position 4615N 01150W and the remaining depth charge was dropped, falling wide. Gunfire had been exchanged and the Whitley was hit, but only slightly damaged. The boat submerged.

Whitley Z9438 and Whitley BD260 left St Eval on 17 May and failed to return. Whitley Z9438 found and attacked U-648, which had been attacked the previous day by Flight Sergeant Powell and the crew of No 224 squadron. Four depth charges were released but caused no damage, and the aircraft was shot down by U-648. This boat was commanded by Oberleutnant zur See Peter-Arthur Stahl. The Whitley was captained by Sgt. J. H. Casstles. Whitley BD 260 was shot down by Ju88s of Kampfgeschwader (KG) 40. The crew was rescued and landed at Vigo, Spain.

On 22 May Whitley Z9440, commanded by Flight Sergeant D. W. Brookes, on task at 4500 feet, found and attacked U-103 commanded by Kapitänleutnant Gustav-Adolf Janssen. The boat opened fire on the aircraft, causing the bomb aimer to lose his bomb release switch, thus failing to release the depth charges. The U-Boat submerged and the Whitley resumed patrol. On 24 May 1943 Sgt. S. C. Chatton and crew, flying at 6000 feet, gained a visual sighting of a wake, which they followed to find a U-Boat in position 4626N 01053W. Chatton dived to attack and reached 2000 feet at one mile from the target. The front gunner opened fire, Chatton dropped a stick of depth charges and the rear gunner opened fire as they overflew the target. The boat was U-523, a type IXc commanded by Kapitänleutnant Werner Pietzsch. It was forced to return to Lorient after suffering damage in this attack. On 30 May Whitley Z9440 commanded by Sergeant L. O. Slade located and attacked U-459, commanded by Korvettenkapitän Georg von Wilamowitz-Mollendorf. The boat's logbook records that there were two attacks and four bombs were dropped on each run, but no hits were achieved. The aircraft was badly damaged and crashed in position 4648N 00900W. The crew survived to be rescued by a Spanish Boat and were eventually taken prisoner. A No 224 Squadron Liberator attacked this U-Boat just after the Whitley, again with no result.

On 14 June a Whitley V BD220 captained by Sergeant A. J. Benson was on the lookout for the group of U-Boats that Fg. Off. Lee of No 228 Squadron had attacked. Lee and his crew had been shot down. Benson and his crew were part of a group of nine Whitleys from No 10 OTU that took off at about the same time from St Eval and were carrying out a parallel track search for these U-Boats. Benson and his crew found U-564 and U-185 in position 4417N 01025W. He shadowed them and initiated a homing procedure to bring in other aircraft as ordered. However nobody turned up, because the other Whitleys had found the other U-Boats. By now, Benson's aircraft was approaching its Prudence Limit of Endurance (PLE). He requested permission to attack from his Maritime Headquarters (MHQ). This was approved just as a No 415 Squadron Hampden arrived.

Benson targeted U-564. Depth charges went down and proved fatal for the U-boat. Only 18 of her crew were rescued by U-185. However, the Whitley had been hit and eventually the starboard engine failed. Benson was forced to ditch and he and his crew were rescued by French fishermen, who had no alternative but to take them to France, where they were taken prisoner. Benson was awarded the DFM, the announcement being made in the prison camp! U-185 rendezvoused with Kriegsmarine destroyers Z24 and Z25 and handed over the survivors. A schwarm (roughly equivalent to an RAF flight) of Junkers JU88s was sent out as escort and shot down the Hampden.

On 14 June Pilot Officer Orr and later Sergeant Manson were seen off by U-600, U-615 and U-257. These boats had sailed from La Pallice as a group. On 20 June 1943 two Whitleys captained by Pilot Officer Orr and Sergeant H. Martin located what was probably the Italian boat *Barbarigo*, commanded by Tenente di Vascello Umberto De Julio, in position 4528N 00931W. Orr attacked first, dropping depth charges, but missed. Martin attacked next, also releasing depth charges, but he was hit and crashed. There were no survivors. *Barbarigo* had sailed from Bordeaux on 16 June bound for the Far East but was lost due to unknown causes. Whether or not this attack had anything to do with it is unknown. It should be remembered that the No 10 OTU crews were trainees and that their Whitleys were twin engined and did not perform well on one. The flights were of the order of ten hours' duration.

No 10 Squadron RCAF was not under Coastal Command control but Flt. Lt. R. F. Fisher and crew of this squadron had been part of the escort to Winston

Churchill, who had been to the Quebec Conference. On 19 September 1943 on their way back to Canada they spent some time with convoy ONS 18. Flying at 3000 feet they gained a visual sighting of a surfaced U-Boat at a mile and a half in position 5840N 02530W. An attack was made, but initially the aircraft was too high to drop weapons and it overflew the boat at 500 feet under heavy flak. The boat was U-341, a type VIIc commanded by Oberleutnant zur See Dietrich Epp. The aircraft attacked again and this time dropped a stick of six depth charges. This caused an explosion in the bows of the boat and it went under. A follow up attack was made with a stick of four depth charges. The boat was assessed as probably destroyed, but it was in fact sunk. This same Liberator, while under the captaincy of Flt. Lt. R. M. Aldwinkle RCAF, attacked what was thought initially to be U-420 on 26 October 1943. Later evidence on the internet in 1996 shows this to have been U-91. This aircraft was under Canadian control.

AIR SEA RESCUE UK

The Command operated ASR squadrons in addition to those operated by Fighter Command. In March 1943 it was stated in the provisional Expansion Programme that the long-range squadrons were to be equipped with Warwicks, four in Coastal Command and one in Fighter Command. The amphibian squadrons and flights were to be equipped with Walruses until replaced by its successor, the Sea Otter. This aircraft looked very similar to the Walrus except that its engine was in the tractor mode as opposed to a pusher mode in the Walrus. The high-speed squadrons were to be equipped with Spitfires or Mosquitoes if available. There were delays in the production of the Warwick as well as problems to its clearance as a rescue aircraft, which is not unknown for a new aircraft. There was therefore no chance of the squadrons being equipped with these aircraft until the late summer.

No 280 Squadron was still operating Ansons and had no experience of modern aircraft. There was no chance of the unit receiving Hudsons as they were scarce, so it was agreed that three Wellingtons would be issued to it for training purposes. No 279 Squadron was down to 12 Hudsons from its establishment of twenty. However, a number of what were called Intermediate Stage Warwicks had been produced, which fulfilled some of the requirements of a rescue aircraft. To prevent further delay, the Director of the Directorate of Air Sea Rescue (DDASR) agreed to accept these aircraft. Ten were available in July and a further twenty in August.

On 1 June the re-equipment of No 280 Squadron was authorized, to commence on 9 July. The aircraft were to be equipped with the airborne lifeboat and the Lindholme gear. Similar authority was given for No 279 Squadron on 16 September. There was a transport version of the Warwick and this suffered from similar production problems. The Ministry of Aircraft Production tried to transfer ASR Warwicks to transport but ACAS (Ops) managed to prevent this, recommending to the Secretary of State that ASR Units should not suffer from a cut in production as the programme was already late and AOCs in C of the various commands laid great emphasis on the importance of ASR. No 280 Squadron did not receive its full quota of aircraft until October and was then withdrawn for training.

In the meantime, Coastal Command made representations to DDASR that rather than re-equip No 279 Squadron with Warwicks, they would prefer to retain the Hudsons and form a new squadron with Warwicks. As three squadrons were within the Command's target, this was agreed. However, the total number of ASR squadrons in the Metropolitan Air Force was at the expansion number, so no new fresh squadron number could be issued. In November the merger of Nos 281 and 282 Squadrons in Fighter Command was authorized. The new unit was given the number plate of No 282 Squadron. The number plate of No 281 Squadron was now available and was reformed in Coastal Command with Warwicks on the same day as the merger.

Up to September 1943 Fighter Command was responsible for rescue within forty miles of the coast and Coastal for rescue elsewhere. At this point, both Commands recommended to the Air Staff that Fighter should be responsible for rescues adjacent to enemy-held coasts and Coastal for the remaining areas. This was approved in February 1944.

No 279 Squadron remained at Bircham Newton with its Hudsons.

No 280 Squadron moved to Thorney Island in September 1943 and thence to Thornaby in October. In October it converted to Warwick Is.

No 281 Squadron, a Fighter Command unit, added Walrus amphibians to its inventory in January and Anson Is in March. In June it moved to Woolsington with a detachment at Drem and then moved to Drem in October with a detachment at Ayr. In November it disbanded, being absorbed by No 282 Squadron. The squadron reformed on the same day at Thornaby as part of Coastal Command and in December it was equipped with Warwick Is and sent a detachment to Davidstow Moor. This aircraft was a great advance on the Ansons, Walruses and Defiants. It could carry an airborne lifeboat and had a much longer range.

No 282 Squadron was formed on 1 January 1943 at Castletown with detachments at Peterhead, Drem and Ayr. It was equipped with five Walrus amphibians and in March seven Anson Is were added. It was a Fighter Command squadron, but as with Nos 275, 276, 277, 278 and 281 Squadrons, executive control rested with AOC-in-C Coastal.

THE HUDSON SQUADRONS

No 233 Squadron remained in Lajes, Azores. On 28 March 1943 Plt. Off. E. F. Castell and crew responded to a sighting report from another aircraft to the effect that a damaged submarine had been sighted. The Hudson went to the position given and located the submarine on the surface. An attack was made with a stick of four depth charges and machine-gun fire. A follow-up attack was made with an anti-submarine bomb. This sank the U-Boat, which was U-77, a type VIIc commanded by Oberleutnant zur See Otto Hartmann, in position 3742N 00010E. There were nine survivors. On 5 April 1943 Flt. Sgt. K. R. Dalton and crew operating out of Agadir and escorting convoy RS 3, sighted at three miles, U-167, a type IXc/40 commanded by Fregattenkapitän Kurt Sturm in position 2748N 01458W. A stick of four depth charges was dropped. Oil and bubbles were seen. A little over seven hours later, Flt. Lt. W. E. Willets and crew located this U-Boat in position 2734N 01518W. A stick of four depth charges was dropped from 50 feet while the boat was still on the surface and a follow-up attack was made with an anti-submarine bomb after the boat had dived. The boat was very badly damaged and was scuttled just east of Grand Canary Island. The crew escaped, being interned on a German freighter which had been itself interned in the Canaries. They were then transferred to U-455, and later to U-159 and U-518. The U-167 crew returned to Germany and some, including Sturm, were given another Type IX boat (Clay Blair, *Hitler's U-Boat War*).

On 7 May 1943 Sgt. J. V. Holland and crew and Sgt. J. W. McQueen and crew were operating out of Gibraltar. Both crews sighted U-447, a type VIIc commanded by Oberleutnant zur See Friedrich-Wilhelm Bothe in position 3530N 01155W. Holland attacked with four depth charges, gaining a good straddle and lifting the boat. McQueen then attacked with four depth charges which missed by 60 yards. Both aircraft then attacked with machine-gun fire, the U-Boat firing back. The boat was then seen to settle and then to sink by the stern. There were no survivors.

On 26 September, Fg. Off. A. G. Frandson in Hudson AE505, while on Search and Rescue with a Wellington captained by Fg. Off. Nicholson of No 179 Squadron, joined in the attack on U-667 with rocket projectiles. The aircraft was hit but returned to base. The U-Boat already attacked by Nicholson was hit. Frandson then homed in a No 48 Squadron Hudson.

No 269 Squadron moved to Reykjavik with its Hudson IIIs in March 1943. On 17 May 1943 Sgt. F. H. W. James and crew were on patrol at 3500 feet with a calm sea state. At 10 miles a visual sighting was gained of a U-Boat fully surfaced. A descent was made to just above sea level, climbing to 50 feet to drop a stick of four depth charges. Wreckage and oil patches were seen, signifying the sinking of U-646, a type VIIc commanded by Oberleutnant zur See Heinrich Wulff in position 6210N 01430W.

On 19 May Fg. Off. J. N. F. Bell and crew gained a visual sighting of U-273, a type VIIc commanded by Oberleutnant zur See Hermann Rossmann. The contact was lost and Bell carried out a gambit or baiting tactic, the object of which was to make the submarine commander believe that the aircraft had lost him. Returning to the area Bell descended and gained a visual sighting of the boat in position 5925N 02433W. He attacked with a stick of four depth charges and then with machine-gun fire. The boat sank shortly afterwards.

On 8 June Sergeant R. B. Couchman and crew were on task near convoy SC132 in a Hudson when they located and attacked U-535, a type IXC/40, commanded by Kapitänleutnant Helmut Ellmenreich. Depth charges were dropped, causing some damage. The boat fired back but missed the aircraft. The U-Boat submerged, and although the Hudson returned a short while later there was no sign of her. The boat was forced to return to France, being refueled by other U-Boats en route. However she did not make it. She was sunk by a No 53 Squadron aircraft on 5 July. Flying Officer J. A. Turnbull and crew arrived just as U-535 surfaced and the Hudson attacked. The depth charges hung up. The aircraft had not been hit and Turnbull made a second attack with guns, hoping to release the depth charges. This time the aircraft was hit in the wings, the radar, the starboard propeller and the tailplane. Again the depth charges failed to release and Turnbull headed for base. An American Catalina arrived at this moment and Turnbull warned him that the U-Boat was a fighter. The American decided to shadow the boat, which set off for the Azores. She was sunk on 5 July by a Liberator from No 53 Squadron.

On 3 August 1943 Flight Sergeant E. L. J. Brame and crew joined in the action between a No 190 Squadron Catalina and U-489 in position 6203N 01252W, and attacked with guns and depth charges. This attack badly damaged the boat but she dived and Brame left the area. The next day, Fg. Off. A. A. Bishop RCAF and the crew of No 423 Squadron found U-489 and sank her. On 21 September, Flt. Sgt. Brame and his crew were on patrol south east of Iceland in Hudson V9161 at 1500 feet below 3/10 cloud with a calm sea and visibility 15 miles when they sighted a surfaced U-Boat six miles away in position 6222N 01434W. This was U-539, commanded by Oberleutnant zur See Hans-Jurgen Lauterbach-Emden. As the aircraft homed in, the boat opened fire, hitting the port wing. Brame decided to try to bluff the U-Boat into diving in order to make a low level attack. He climbed to 3000 feet, from which height he dropped a 100lb anti-submarine bomb. This missed, and he dropped another one which also missed. Brame then decided to make a low-level attack anyway and dropped his depth charges, but a last minute alteration of course by the boat caused them to miss. The boat dived and was not seen again.

On 4 October 1943 Flt. Sgt. G. C. Allsop RAAF and crew were escorting convoy ONS 19 when they gained a visual sighting of a surfaced U-Boat from one mile in position 6243N 02717W. Allsop attacked with rockets in the face of enemy fire, the first pair from 800 feet and 800 yards, the second from 600 feet and 600 yards and then four from 400 feet and 400 yards. Hits were scored from each firing and the boat sank with its gunners still firing. This was U-336, a type VIIc commanded by Kapitänleutnant Hans Hunger. Allsop received the DFM. Again on 4 October 1943 Plt. Off. H. M. Smith and crew were escorting convoys ONS 19 and ON 204. A visual sighting from six miles was gained on a surfaced submarine in position 6202N 02827W. This was U-731, a type VIIc commanded by Oberleutnant zur See Alexander Graf Keller. An attack with guns and depth charges was made, followed by two gun attacks. The boat submerged but had been damaged and was forced to return to Brest. She was attacked again while en route by American carrier-based aircraft, but reached Brest safely.

TORPEDO BOMBER/ANTISHIPPING/UK

NORTH COATES STRIKE WING

The Commander in Chief, Slessor, wanted three Strike Wings but the shortage of Beaufighters precluded that for the time being. However, after their intensive training in the winter and spring, the North Coates Strike Wing went into action again on 18 April 1943. Led by Wg. Cdr. H.

N. G. Wheeler, OC No 236 Squadron, 21 Beaufighters from Nos 143, 236 and 254 Squadrons with an escort of 22 Spitfires from Nos 118 and 167 Squadrons and eight Mustangs from No 613 Squadron attacked a convoy of eight merchant ships, eight minesweepers and a flak ship off Texel. It was an unqualified success. The main target, the *Heogh Carrier* of 4900 tons, was sunk and four escorts were badly damaged. On 29 April 1943 Wg. Cdr. Wheeler led 27 Beaufighters from Nos 143, 236 and 254 Squadrons with an escort of 24 Spitfires from Nos 118 and 267 Squadrons and six Mustangs from No 613 Squadron in a strike. The *Alundra*, 4930 tons, the *Narvik*, 4251 tons, and a flak ship, *Auguste Kampf*, were sunk. One aircraft and crew from No 143 Squadron was lost. On 17 May Wg. Cdr. Wheeler led 27 Beaufighters with an escort of 59 Spitfires from Nos 118, 167, 302, 308 and 402 Squadrons in an attack on six merchant ships escorted by seven minesweepers and flak ships. One merchant ship was sunk and one minesweeper and a flak ship were damaged. On 24 May Wg. Cdr. Wheeler led an attack against a convoy, but the position was unknown. However a convoy was found and attacked. No ships were sunk and no aircraft were lost. On 13 June the Wing attacked a convoy of three merchant ships and seven escorts. A 5000 ton merchant ship, a flak ship and an escort were sunk. A Beaufighter from No 143 Squadron was shot down. On 22 June Wg. Cdr. Wheeler led the Wing in the first rocket attack. Thirtysix Beaufighters, together with three Spitfire squadrons and two Typhoon squadrons, took part in an attack against five merchant ships and 15 minesweepers or flak ships. The defences consisted of parachute and cable rockets and flamethrowers. Three flak ships were damaged. The Torbeaus of No 254 Squadron had to attack slightly later than normal in order to avoid the rockets from the aircraft. This allowed the convoy time to alter course and avoid the torpedoes. Two Beaufighters were shot down and three crashed on landing.

On 27 June Wg. Cdr. W. A. L. Davis, OC Flying Wing, led 36 Beaufighters from Nos 143 and 236 Squadrons against four merchant ships and eleven escorts. There were no sinkings and no aircraft were lost. Rocketry had not yet been mastered. On 2 August Wg. Cdr. Wheeler led 36 Beaufighters from Nos 143, 236 and 254 Squadrons. The escorts consisted of 51 Spitfires from Nos 118, 402, 416 and 611 Squadrons. The target was a convoy of six merchant ships escorted by four minesweepers and 10 flak ships. Rocket-firing Beaufighters severely damaged seven flak ships and the Torbeaus sank the merchant vessel *Fortuna* of 2700 tons and the flak ship, Vp1108. The Spitfires shot down four Bf109s. All Allied aircraft returned safely.

On 16 September Wg. Cdr. Davis led 12 Beaufighters from No 236 Squadron and 11 Beaufighters from No 254 Squadron in an attack on six minesweepers and two trawlers. Two squadrons of Spitfires were in attendance. There were no sinkings and two Beaufighters failed to return. On 25 September, escorted by Spitfires, Wg. Cdr. Davis led 11 Beaufighters from No 236 Squadron and 13 from No 254 in an attack on four merchant vessels and 14 escorts. The flak ship Vp316 was sunk and two Beaufighters were shot down, including OC No 254 squadron. On 19 October Sqn. Ldr. W. D. L. Filson-

Young, OC 254 Squadron led 12 Beaufighters from No 236 Squadron and 15 from 254 on a Rover patrol. The liner *Strasburg* was found with escorts and attacked. The liner and a tug were set on fire. On 22 November Sub. Lt. Eriksud and his navigator Erling Johannsen from No 333 Squadron shot down a Ju88.

SECOND TACTICAL AIR FORCE

On 27 November 3 Mosquitoes Mark VI from No 487 Squadron RNZAF, escorted by 12 Typhoons attacked the merchant ship *Pietro Orseolo*, causing slight damage.

LEUCHARS STRIKE WING

No 455 Squadron was joined by No 235 Squadron in January and by No 489 Squadron in October.

PREDANNACK STRIKE WING

On 18 December six Torbeaus from No 254 Squadron and six anti-flak Beaufighters from No 248 attacked the *Pietro Orseolo*, which was escorted by six minesweepers. She was hit by two torpedoes and finally blew up the following day. Some of the minesweepers were damaged. All aircraft returned to base.

PORTREATH STRIKE WING

The Wing started operations in August with No 235 Squadron and was supplemented with No 143 Squadron in September.

WICK STRIKE WING

The Wick Strike Wing was formed in October 1943 with

No 144 and No 404 Squadrons. No 404 had arrived in April. No 489 Squadron moved to Leuchars from Wick during October.

SQUADRON MOVEMENTS

No 143 Squadron at North Coates exchanged its Beaufighter IIFs for Mark XIs in March and in August moved to St Eval. In September it went to Portreath and Beaufighter Xs were added to its inventory.

No 144 Squadron started to exchange its Hampdens for Beaufighter VIcs in January 1943. In April it moved to Tain. The following month the Beaufighter VIcs were exchanged for Beaufighter Xs. There were detachments at Wick, Blida near Algiers and Protville II/Mabtouha 2, North West of Tunis. In July the squadron moved to Benson, Oxfordshire, maintaining its detachment at Protville. In August it went back to Tain and then to Wick in October. On 22 December 1943 in conjunction with three aircraft of No 404 Squadron, four Torbeaus and two flak suppressors attacked a minesweeper (M-403) and a U-Boat. The boat was U-1062, a type VIIf, a torpedo transporter, commanded by Oberleutnant zur See Karl Albrecht, in position 5759N 00652E just south of Egersund. The U-Boat suffered slight damage and reached Bergen. Two No 404 Squadron Beaufighters were shot down. Four of the Beaufighters were fitted with torpedoes (Torbeaus) and the remainder were flak suppressors. All the torpedoes missed but U-1062 was badly damaged. The No 144 squadron crews were:

Flt. Lt. R. A. Johnson and Plt. Off. M. C. Potts.

Flight Sergeant P. G. Smith and Sergeant F. S. Holly

Fg. Off. S. R. Cooke and Sergeant J. E. Beaman

Fg. Off. N. T. Lawrence and Sergeant D. H. Hogg

Fg. Off. R. S. Cheshire and Fg. Off. W. B. Naples

WO W. A. Baughman and Fg. Off. K. E. B. Wilks.

No 235 Squadron moved to Leuchars in January 1943 with detachments at Sumburgh, Tain and St Eval, then in August it went to Portreath. In October the squadron exchanged its Beaufighter VIcs for Mark Xs and sent a detachment to St Angelo on the shores of Lough Erne.

No 236 Squadron, still based at North Coates, exchanged its Beaufighter VIc's for Mark Xs in July 1943. On 1 June, Flying Officer M.C.Bateman sank U-418, a type VIIc commanded by Oberleutnant zur See Gerhard Lange, in position 4705N00855W. This was the boat that probably damaged the No 210 Squadron Catalina on 30 May.

No 248 Squadron moved to Predannack in January 1943 with a detachment to Gibraltar. In June it began to exchange its Beaufighter VIcs for Mark Xs. This was only for a six month period for in December it received Mosquito VIs.

On 12 July, three Beaufighters found U-441, which had been damaged by a No 228 Squadron Sunderland in May. The crews were Flt C. R. Schofield and Sgt. J. A. Mallinson, Lt. G. C. Newman FFAF and Fg. Off. O. C. Cochrane and Fg. Off. P. A. S. Payne and Fg. Off. A. M. McNichol. Each aircraft made five runs over the boat. This time she was very badly damaged and some ten of her crew were killed and 13 wounded. The boat was forced to return to Brest. During this patrol the Beaufighters shot down two Ju88c fighters.

No 254 Squadron, also still at North Coates, swapped its Beaufighter VIFs for Mark Xs in August 1943. No 236 and No 254 Squadrons formed the first Strike Wing, the North Coates Strike Wing, with responsibility for attacking enemy shipping along the Dutch, German, Belgian and French coasts.

No 333 Squadron Royal Norwegian Air Force "B" Flight, as mentioned above, was at Leuchars with Mosquito VIs.

No 404 Squadron Royal Canadian Air Force went to Chivenor in January 1943 and swapped its Beaufighter IIfs for Mark XIs in March. The squadron went to Tain at the beginning of April, only to move on to Wick 18 days later. In September it converted to Mark Xs. As reported above, three flak suppressor aircraft from the squadron joined with No 144 Squadron in an attack on a minesweeper (M-403) and U-1062 on 22 December 1943. The crews were:

Plt. Off. K. S. Miller RCAF and Plt. Off. J. Young

Flt. Lt. R. Munro RCAF and Fg. Off. W. B. Conn RCAF

Fg. Off. J. Gillespie RCAF and Plt. Off. J. E.
Glendinning RCAF.

The aircraft flown by Munro and Gillespie were shot down. The U-Boat was badly damaged.

No 407 Squadron exchanged its Hudsons for Wellington XIs in January 1943.

No 455 Squadron Royal Australian Air Force was at Leuchars. On 30 April 1943 Flight Sergeant J. S. Freeth and crew, in Hampden AN149, gained a visual contact with a U-Boat at a mile and a half in position 6405N

00640W in a heavy sea. The U-Boat immediately opened fire. Freeth attacked with a stick of six depth charges from 50 feet, straddling the boat. A follow-up attack was made with two depth charges and the boat sank, leaving some 30 sailors in the sea. This had been U-227, a type VIIc, commanded by Kapitänleutnant Jurgen Kuntze. The squadron at last exchanged its Hampdens for Beaufighter Xs in December 1943. These carried torpedoes and were known as Torbeaus. It remained at Leuchars.

No 489 Squadron Royal New Zealand Air Force moved to Leuchars in October 1943 and exchanged its Hampdens for Beaufighter Xs or Torbeaus at the same time. These two squadrons formed a second Strike Wing.

No 618 Squadron was formed at Skitten in March 1943. This was intended to be another bouncing bomb squadron like No 617, but this time to try to sink ships such as the *Tirpitz*. It was operating Mosquito IVs and Beaufighter IIs with detachments at Manston, Turnberry in Ayrshire, Dyce, Benson and Wick. The Beaufighters stayed with the squadron until June and in October it converted to Mosquito XVIIIs with a detachment at Predannack. This was known as the No 618 Squadron Special Detachment and was attached to No 248 Squadron, then operating Beaufighter Xs until December, when it re-equipped with Mosquito VIs. The bouncing bomb idea against shipping having been scrapped, the 618 aircraft were now being equipped with the Molins gun, a 57mm weapon known colloquially as the Tsetse gun as its bite was more severe than that of the Mosquito! The unit was ready by October and began to carry out patrols either singly or in pairs over the Bay escorted by No 248

Squadron. On 7 November 1943 Fg. Off. A. J. L. Bonnett
and his navigator, Fg. Off. A. M. McNicol, were on patrol
and located U-123, a type IXB commanded by
Oberleutnant zur See Horst von Schroeter, in position
4715N 00438W. Bonnett fired eight rounds of Tsetse
scoring several hits. A further attack was made but the gun
jammed. The boat was damaged.

MEDITERRANEAN 1943

No 13 Squadron was based at Protville II, North West of
Tunis, operating Blenheim Vs, usually known as the Bisley.
The squadron was under the command of North West
Africa Coastal Air Force. On 12 September 1943, Fg. Off.
G. H. Finch and crew gained a visual sighting of a surfaced
submarine in position 3839N 00922E. This was the
Topazio, an Italian Sirena class, commanded by Tenente di
Vascello Pier Vittorio Casarini. An attack with machine
guns and a stick of four depth charges was made. The boat
disappeared and survivors were seen in the sea.

No 36 Squadron added some Wellington VIIIs to its
inventory in January 1943. It moved to Dhubalia, north
of Calcutta, in April. In June it left the Far East and went
to the Mediterranean, Blida near Algiers. In the same
month it acquired some Wellington XIs and XIIIs and the
following month some Mark Xs and XIIs. Detachments
were at Bone, Montecorvino, La Senia, Gibraltar,
Tafaroui, Grottaglie, Bo Rizzo and Ghisonaccia. Having
received Wellington XIVs in September the squadron
disposed of the Mark Ics, VIIIs and Xs in September, the
Mark XIs in November and the Mark XIIs and XIIIs in
December 1943.

On 13 December Fg. Off. C. F. Parker and crew in Wellington MP816 was engaged in a "Swamp" operation for the U-Boat which had sunk the escorts HMS *Tynedale* and HMS *Holcombe*. A Swamp operation was an intense search by air and surface assets for a U-Boat that was known to be in a specific area. In the early hours the aircraft gained a radar contact in position 3730N 00600E north east of Bone. The Leigh Light jammed and the aircraft suffered flak damage and became uncontrollable. A sighting report and a distress call were transmitted and the pilot managed to bring the aircraft under control, landing at Bone. The contact was U-593, commanded by Kapitänleutnant Gerd Kelbling. It was sunk as a result of the sighting report which brought ships to the area.

No 38 Squadron disposed of its Wellington Ics in March 1943. It had received Mark VIIIs in February. Again in February it moved to Berka III, near Benghazi, with detachments at Misurata, in Cyrenaica, LG91, south west of Alexandria and St Jean, north of Haifa.

On 19 February 1943 Fg. Off. I. B. Butler and crew were escorting convoy Roman. Sgt. J. I. Brown, the rear gunner, gained a visual sighting of a U-Boat directly below the aircraft. It was at periscope depth in an attack position. An unsuccessful attack was made but the destroyers HMS *Isis* and HMS *Hursley* were homed in and they sank the boat in position 3257N 02054E. This was U-562, a type VIIc commanded by Kapitänleutnant Horst Hamm. In June Wellington XIs arrived on the Squadron and in October the Mark VIIIs were exchanged for Mark XIIIs.

No 39 Squadron was at Luqa with its Beauforts IIs in January with detachments at Shallufa and Gianaclis. On

14 January 1943, Fg. Off. J. N. Cartwright and crew were operating South of Luqa escorting a convoy. A visual sighting was gained of a submarine which was attacked with a stick of four depth charges. The crew was seen on deck with a white flag, but the aircraft was fired on. Cartwright sent a locating report and requested assistance from the convoy escort. The Destroyers HMS *Pakenham* and *Hurley* arrived, shelled the boat and sank it. The boat was the *Narvalo*, an Italian Squalo class commanded by Tenente di Vascello Ludovico Grion, and she sank in position 3408N 01604E. Allied prisoners of war were on board and some were rescued. In June it was at Protville II, north west of Tunis, and two days later it was at LG224, Cairo West. A few days after that, it was back again at Protville II. Again in June it exchanged its Beauforts for Beaufighter Xs and had a detachment at Shallufa, north of Suez. In October it moved to Protville I, also north west of Tunis, for a couple of days when it went to Sidi Amor with a detachment at Grottaglie, near Taranto. In November the squadron went to Reghaia, with detachments at Grottaglie and Marrakesh.

No 47 Squadron was moved to Gianaclis with its Beaufort Is and then detached to Berka in January 1943. On 28 March 1943 Fg. Off. J. B. Harrop and crew gained a visual sighting of a wake from 1700 feet and two miles. The submarine, U-77, a type VIIc commanded by Oberleutnant zur See Otto Hartmann, was then seen. The boat dived as Harrop dropped a stick of depth charges. Oil and bubbles were seen but nothing else. U-77 was later found by Plt. Off. E. F. Castell and crew of No 233 Squadron and destroyed. In March the squadron was moved to Misurata West and in June re-equipped with Beaufighter Xs. That month it was moved to Protville II and in October to Sidi Amor and detached to El Adem. In November it was moved to El Adem and then in November to Gambut 3. Strike and escort operations were carried out in the Aegean Sea.

No 48 Squadron was at Gibraltar with Hudson VIs. On 4 June 1943 Fg. Off. H. C. Bailey and crew gained a visual sighting of a wake from 4000 feet. A U-Boat was then sighted and an attack was made with rockets as the boat began to dive. The boat resurfaced and then sank in position 3555N 00925W. It was a type VIIc commanded by Kapitänleutnant Friedrich Mumm and had been en route from St. Nazaire to the Mediterranean.

On 12 February 1943 Fg. Off. G. R. Mayhew and crew gained a visual sighting of a surfaced U-Boat in position 3732N 01156W from 3500 feet. This was U-442, a type VIIc commanded by Korvettenkapitän Hans Joachim Hesse returning to St Nazaire. Mayhew dropped a stick of four depth charges from 40 feet and firing all guns. It was a perfect straddle, which sank the boat. On 26 September 1943, Fg. Off. E. L. Ashbury and crew intercepted the sighting report about U-667 which was being attacked by aircraft from No 179 and No 233 squadrons and joined in. Rockets were fired, but no results were observed. The Hudson was hit and was forced to return to base. The squadron added Beaufighter IIFs to its inventory in July 1943.

No 202 Squadron remained at Gibraltar. On 10 February 1943 Sqn. Ldr. W. E. Ogle-Skan and crew gained a visual sighting from 10 miles of a surfaced U-Boat in position 3234N 01608W. The boat, U-108, a type IXB commanded by Korvettenkapitän Klaus Scholtz, dived at four miles and a stick of four depth charges was dropped. No results were seen, but the boat had been damaged and had to return to Lorient. The U-Boat web site states that the CO was Korvettenkapitän Ralf-Reimar Wolfram. On 13 February 1943 Flt. Lt. H. R. Sheardown RCAF and crew were on a 21-hour patrol escorting convoy KMS 9. The crew gained a contact at 16 miles in the afternoon, but nothing further was seen. Late at night a visual contact in the moonlight was gained, in position 3911N 01107W but it submerged well before an attack could be made. Shortly afterwards, a radar contact was gained, illuminated with the landing lights, and the vessel was attacked with a stick of six depth charges. The target was missed and the boat submerged.

In the early hours of the morning another U-Boat was seen on the surface and an attack was made with depth charges. No results were observed and the crew resumed patrol around the convoy. In fact the first attack had sunk U-620, a type VIIc commanded by Oberleutnant zur See Heinz Stein. The second attack damaged U-381, a type VIIc commanded by Kapitänleutnant Wilhelm Heinrich Graf von Puckler und Limpurg. The Catalina crew reported that on previous sorties a number of radar contacts had been gained which disappeared once the aircraft got into an attack position. On this night a different tactic was adopted, in that once a contact had been gained and plotted, the radar was switched off until close to the contact. This seemed to work. The crew believed that this was the birth of Electronic Counter Measures (ECM). On 8 July 1943 Flt. Lt. G. Powell and crew gained a visual sighting of a surfaced U-Boat and attacked with depth charges and machine gun fire. The boat dived and oil and bubbles were seen but nothing else. It was U-603, a type VIIc commanded by Oberleutnant zur See Rudolf Baltz and it was badly damaged in this attack. It was en route to Brest and remained out of service for some time.

No 203 Squadron moved to Berka III in March 1943. In June it received Baltimore IIIAs and the following month Mark IVs in addition to its Mark Is, IIs and IIIs. In November 1943 the squadron went to Santa Cruz near Bombay disposing, of all its Baltimores and receiving Wellington XIIIs.

No 221 Squadron moved to Luqa in February 1943. In June it received some Wellington XIs and had a detachment at Grottaglie. On 18 July 1943 Fg. Off. E. Austin, RCAF and crew gained a visual sighting of a submarine in position 3720N 01618E and attacked with a stick of six depth charges. One failed to release. The stick straddled the boat, which lost way. This was the Italian boat *Romolo* of the Romolo class commanded by Capitano di Corvette Alberto Crepas; she was on her first cruise, having been completed in June. Fg. Off. W. Lewis RNZAF and crew from the same squadron then arrived on the scene and attacked. The boat was circling, probably out of control. Ships were called in to help. The boat later sank. In September the squadron disposed of its Wellington VIIIs and received some Mark XIIs which it held for one month when it received Mark XIIIs.

No 227 Squadron disposed of its Beaufighter ICs in February and moved to Idku in March 1943 with a detachment at Gambut. In May it moved to Derna, in

June to El Magrun, in July to Gardabia West, eleven days later to Derna, in August to Limassol, Cyprus and in September to Lakatamia, also in Cyprus. In September it added Beaufighter XIs to the inventory and in October Mark Xs. In November the squadron moved to Berka III with a detachment at Reghaia. Strike and escort operations were carried out in the Dodecanese and in the Aegean Sea in support of the invasion of, and withdrawal from, the islands.

No 230 Squadron moved to Dar-Es-Salaam in January 1943 with detachments at Aboukir, Bizerta, Jui near Freetown, Tulear in Madagascar and Pamanzi on the islands between Madagascar and Mozambique.

No 252 Squadron was at Berka III in January 1943. The following month it went to El Magrun with detachments at Berka III, Misurata, Gambut and Bersis. In June Beaufighter XIs were added to the inventory. In August the squadron was moved to Berka III with detachments at El Magrun, Gambut and LG91. In September it went firstly to Limassol and then to Lakatamia, both in Cyprus. In December the squadron was back at LG91 with a detachment at Shallufa.

No 272 Squadron moved to Luqa in June 1943 and a day later to Gardabia, south west of Misurata. Twelve days later it was back in Luqa. In September Beaufighter XIs were added to the inventory and the squadron moved to Bo Rizzo at the western end of Sicily. The following month the squadron went to Catania and in December Beaufighter Xs were added to the squadron.

No 459 Squadron Royal Australian Air Force was still based at LG143, with detachments at Khormaksar, Berka

III, LG227, Nicosia, LG91, LG07 and Lydda. On 16 June
1943 Flt. Sgt. D. T. Barnard RAAF and crew were briefed
to fly to Lydda, refuel and then take off in pursuit of a U-
Boat which had earlier torpedoed a tender off the Palestine
coast. The crew was to co-operate with some Navy ships.
These were not found, so Barnard climbed to 3000 feet
and carried out a patrol. A visual sighting at four miles was
gained of a U-Boat in position 3256N 03400E. An attack
was made with a stick of four depth charges which gave a
good straddle. One charge scored a direct hit and also
damaged the aircraft badly. The boat was U-97, a type VIIc
commanded by Kapitänleutnant Hans-Georg Trox. The
U-Boat sank with 21 survivors, who were rescued by ships.
Barnard was awarded the DFM. The squadron received
some Hudson VIs in August 1943 followed by some
Hudson Vs in September but these were given up in
November in favour of Ventura Vs. Detachments were now
at Berka III, LG07, Gianaclis, Nicosia, El Adem, St Jean,
Lydda and Ramat David.

No 500 Squadron moved to Tafaraoui with
detachments to Blida, Bone, Ghisonaccia, Montecorvino
and Grottaglie. On 4 March 1943 Sgt G. Jackimov and
crew were on an antisubmarine patrol about 80 miles
north east of Oran. Although the visibility was bad, the
aircraft was at 3500 feet but the crew sighted from five
miles the wake of a surfaced submarine. An attack was
made with a stick of three 100lb antisubmarine bombs
from 1500 feet. The Hudson came under machine-gun fire
but was not hit. Fire was returned. A follow-up attack was
made with a stick of three depth charges and these sank
the boat. This was U-83, a type VIIb commanded by

Kapitänleutnant Ulrich Worishoffer. Survivors were seen and two dinghies were dropped to them. A relief aircraft arrived and Jackimov and crew returned to Blida.

On 23/24 April Warrant Officer R. Obee was captain of Hudson AM781 on patrol off Oran. A radar contact was gained and the aircraft descended from 3000 feet to 200 feet and attacked. It was probably U-453, commanded by Kapitänleutnant Egon-Reiner Freiherr von Schlippenbach. The boat opened fire and Obee was hit in the abdomen, probably killing him instantly. Flight Sergeant Kempster, a WOP/AG, took over the aircraft until Sergeant A. F. Blackwell, the RAAF navigator, took over flying it back to Tafaraoui. Blackwell was awarded the Conspicuous Gallantry Medal (CGM) and Kempster the Distinguished Flying Medal (DFM).

In May a Hudson captained by Squadron Leader H. G. Holmes DFC located U-755 by radar at eight miles and from a height of 1500 feet. This boat was commanded by Kapitänleutnant Walter Going and was north of Alboran Island. Holmes attacked with three depth charges, but missed. He attacked twice more with anti-submarine bombs, causing the death of one of the sailors and the wounding of two. The boat and the aircraft had exchanged fire and the Hudson was badly hit. U-755 was forced to abort the mission. However she failed to return, as she was located and sunk by a No 608 Squadron Hudson a few days later. In December the squadron added Ventura Vs to its inventory.

No 603 Squadron (AAF) changed into the anti-shipping role in January 1943 when it moved to Idku. This meant that navigators were posted in, some of these coming from No 227 Squadron. The following month it received Beaufighter Ics and VIcs. It had a detachment at Berka III. In February, a number of convoy escort sorties were carried out and this continued for the next few months. In March it moved to Misurata West with detachments at Berka III and El Magrun. In August it added Beaufighter XIs to its inventory and started armed rover sorties along the southern Peloponnese. In September it moved to BoRizzo and supported operations in Sicily and Italy.

Meanwhile, despite American protests, the British had occupied islands in the Dodecanese and the squadron carried out escort and strike operations in support. However, British forces were withdrawn from these islands after ten weeks, the operation having been a failure. Nevertheless the squadron continued operations in the Aegean Sea. In October the squadron moved to LG91. The Beaufighter VIcs and XIs were disposed of in October in exchange for Beaufighter Xs. The Mark Ics went in November. The squadron moved to Gambut 3 in October with detachments at El Adem.

No 608 Squadron received Hudson VIs in March 1943. On 28 May 1943 Fg. Off. G. A. K. Ogilvie and crew gained a visual sighting of a U-boat which they attacked with rockets and sank in position 3958N 00141E. This was U-755, a type VIIc commanded by Kapitänleutnant Walter Going. Forty survivors were rescued by the Spanish Navy. This boat had been attacked previously by a Hudson from No 500 Squadron. In August the squadron moved to Protville and in September to Augusta for two days. Then it moved to Bo Rizzo with detachments at Grottaglie and Montecorvino. The squadron moved to Montecorvino in November with detachments at Grottaglie and Gaudo. In December Hudson IIIAs were added to its inventory.

MEDITERRANEAN AIR SEA RESCUE

No 283 Squadron was formed at Algiers in February 1943 with six Supermarine Walruses and spent the year moving bases. This was the first Overseas Air Sea Rescue Squadron to be formed. The Walruses came from No 700 Squadron of the Fleet Air Arm at Algiers. No 283 went to Maison Blanche at the beginning of May 1943, Tingley, south west of Bone a week later, La Sebala I at the end of May and a detachment was at Pantellaria during Operation Husky.

On 5 August a Walrus from Pantellaria was sent to look for a dinghy with three enemy aircrew aboard. The dinghy was located and the aircraft was landed to rescue them. However, the sea was too rough for a take off and the pilot opted to taxi to Salina Island, which was reached that night. The problem was - had the island been taken by the Allies? Their luck was in and they were welcomed by the British garrison. There was no radio on the island and the crew was posted missing until an HSL arrived on 10th with supplies for the garrison and their safety was reported. The squadron moved to Palermo in August, Ajaccio on Christmas Day and Borgo, north east Corsica, at the end of the month.

No 284 Squadron was formed at Gravesend in May 1943 and was sent to Martlesham Heath a few days later. It was sent to Hal Far in Malta in July and equipped with Walruses from the Naval Pool at Gibraltar, which the crews picked up en route. It moved to Cassibile later in July, where the unit had a successful record picking up eight Allied and one German aircrew. Once Sicily had been taken, the Squadron moved to Lentini East in August with a detachment at Milazzo, to Scanzano in September, to Gioia del Colle in October and to Brindisi in November.

On 30 August 1943 the establishment of four Air Sea Rescue Squadrons for Mediterranean Air Command (MAC) was authorized by the splitting of Nos 283 and 284 Squadrons to form No 293 and 294 Squadrons. The reason for this was the forthcoming invasion of Italy. The Air Ministry had suggested that two large squadrons would be more efficient than four smaller ones, but Mediterranean Air Command countered by stating that it would not be possible to administer half units, elements being detached, outside their Command area. This argument was successful. MAC now had on paper its target of 60 ASR aircraft but on 20 August they were informed that due to technical faults which had just arisen the Warwicks would not arrive until late September.

No 293 Squadron was formed at Blida in November 1943, equipped with Warwick Is. In December it moved to Bone and sent detachments to Pomigliano.

No 294 Squadron was formed in September at Berka and was equipped with Walruses and Wellington Ics. Detachments were sent to LG07, Lakatamia, Mellaha, Limassol, Derna and Gambut. In October it was all change again with a move to LG91 and detachments at Derna, Lakatamia, Berka III, LG07, Mellaha, St Jean, Gambut and Castel Benito just outside Tripoli, which was later called Idris.

No 614 Squadron was called into the SAR role as no Warwicks were supplied to the Mediterranean in time for the invasion of Italy. Their Blenheim Vs or Bisleys were fitted with Lindholme gear and they operated from Borizzo.

The Middle East Air Sea Rescue Flight, now responsible for a long stretch of coastline, was equipped with additional aircraft. In January, Blenheims were added and in February a Walrus was received. However, Middle East Command had few HSLs and could not expect to cover the rescue commitments which were their responsibility. Headquarters Middle East requested 32 twin-engined land-based aircraft and 16 amphibian versions of the Catalina to cover their area of the Eastern Mediterranean, which included Tripoli, Malta, Iraq, Persia, Aden and Central and East Africa. Light aircraft for communications and land rescue were also requested. This may seem a lot to ask for, but the Air Staff requirement to cover the whole of the Mediterranean and the Middle East was for 40 long-range and 20 high-speed aircraft. Even so, the request was impossible to supply. The supply of Hudsons (a twin-engined aircraft) was insufficient for the Coastal search squadrons in the UK and there were no amphibian Catalinas available. Instead, to cover the whole of the Mediterranean, Middle East was offered 20 Warwicks and 10 Walruses. However, none of these aircraft would be available until August.

The Warwick was a problem. Originally designed as a replacement for the Wellington, it was not found to be suitable as a bomber. Some had come off the production line in this role and were diverted to ASR squadrons but could not carry the Airborne Lifeboat, unlike the redesigned ASR Warwicks which would not be available until later in the year. It was the bomber version which DDASR agreed to supply to the newly-formed Mediterranean Air Command until the ASR Warwicks came off the line. It was expected that the re-equipment of Nos 283 and 284 Squadrons with Warwicks was to take place between the invasions of Sicily and mainland Italy. On 1 July 1943 the organization of the Air Sea Rescue was changed. Since the formation of the Mediterranean Air Command it had been the responsibility of North West African Coastal Air Force. An Air Sea Rescue Service was formed for the Central Mediterranean which was at the disposal of Malta, Middle East and North West African Coastal Air Force. Each Command was delegated its own area of responsibility.

There were difficulties in the production of HSLs back in the UK and there was a shortage of shipping space. Thus, the equipping of the Mediterranean and Middle East had fallen short of the programme agreed in October 1942, which was for 47 Air Sea Rescue Units for Overseas Commands with a total of 135 boats. In the period October 1942 to March 1943 only eight boats had been delivered. Middle East requested 55 boats and this was agreed by the Air Ministry. There were only 17 HSLs operating in the Middle East including Malta. By 20 May the total stood at thirty one. At the same time as the formation of No 284 Squadron was agreed, authority was given for the formation of No 253 ASR Unit with six HSLs. Mediterranean Air Command requested, as a matter of urgency, a further unit and in May the formation of No 254 ASR Unit with eight HSLs and two pinnaces was approved.

In July 1943 a revised programme to suit the Mediterranean needs was set out. By now 16 ASR Units had been formed in the Mediterranean Air Command. There were seven in North African Air Forces, eight in Middle East and one in Aden. This gave a total strength of 43 HSLs and 12 pinnaces. It was expected that 24 boats would arrive in the area before 31 August and this would help to form another Unit in the Middle East, four in East Africa and three in Iraq and Persia.

German resistance in Tunisia came to an end on 13th May, 1943. The invasion of Sicily, Operation Husky, began on 10th July and that of mainland Italy on 3rd September, the same day as the Armistice between Italy and the Allies was signed. By 17th August the island was in Allied hands. For Operation Husky, three special zones were set up for which North West African Coastal Air Force, Malta and Middle East were respectively responsible. Wellingtons and Catalinas were moved to Bizerta for long-range searches and rescues and No 230 Squadron's Sunderlands were made available for the first two weeks of July. As stated above, some crews of No 284 Squadron were based at Hal Far Malta. The Air Sea Rescue Unit at Malta was reinforced to a total of eight HSLs, four pinnaces and six seaplane tenders. The ASR Units in North West Africa, although having had considerable difficulties in receiving spares, were operating by the time Husky started.

Land rescues were undertaken. An American Liberator returning from a raid on 10th July on Sicily became lost over the Libyan Desert. When the fuel ran out the ten crew members baled out, 300 miles south of Benghazi into an area of coal-like black volcanic lava. An SOS had been transmitted by the crew and this was heard by a High Frequency Direction Finding (HFDF) station. An ASR Wellington and two US Liberators were sent on a search the next morning. There being no result, a further search was planned using US Liberators and Wellingtons and Blenheims from the Sea Rescue Flight.

The Liberators sighted a group of five survivors and then a further group of two. A Light Car Patrol from the Sudan Defence Force was asked to help but in this area of lava the difficulties of both a land and an air rescue were immense. Surveillance of the survivors was continued in daylight hours using Wellingtons and Liberators. The group of five was confirmed by a Wellington crew as a group of four on 13th July. This aircraft dropped supplies. Another land patrol was requested from Derna the following day. On 15th another Wellington took off with the crew who had previously found the survivors and who now obviously knew the area. The two groups were relocated, eight miles apart. Meanwhile the land rescue parties battled on through the lava, manhandling large blocks of it out of their way and managing to reach a rendezvous established by a Wellington crew. There, they prepared a landing strip for an aircraft.

On the 18th a Wellington landed on the strip, followed two and a half hours later by a Miles Magister, a two-seat trainer. On 19th a patrol reached the survivors, two of whom were injured. They were taken back to Berka and then a search was mounted for the remaining four. No trace was found and the search was abandoned. The ASR aircraft of Middle East Rescue Flight had flown 120 hours and searched an area of 15,500 square miles. The land party covered 1350 miles.

From the start of Operation Husky search aircraft and HSLs were continuously searching for missing aircrew, with Sunderlands and US Catalinas assisting. Between 3rd and 10th July 45 lives were saved. On 17th seven dinghies were reported in the sea south west of Naples and a Sunderland with an escort of US P-38 Lightnings were dispatched to search for them. Enemy aircraft drove off the Sunderland but the following morning a second Sunderland found and rescued six aircrew and a third searched for the remainder. On the return the escort intercepted 15 Ju-52s and shot down all of them.

On 2nd August a Catalina landed on the sea four miles south of Cagliari and picked up the two-man crew of a Beaufighter. The sea state was rough and in trying to take off the starboard float was damaged. Shore batteries opened fire and then enemy fighters attacked. The Catalina's escort shot down three of these. However, the Catalina was set alight and the crew and the Beaufighter crew had to take to the dinghies. They were rescued by an HSL, despite being under fire from the shore.

Over the period of Husky, from 8 July to 17 August 427 rescue sorties were made. In the first 14 days 45 lives were saved.

The Middle East Rescue Flight operated from Benghazi during 1943, covering from the Turkish coast to Tunis. From July 1941 to June 1943 it had assisted in the rescue of 222 Allied and 12 enemy aircrew. Of these 92 were desert rescues. Its Blenheims had been replaced by Wellingtons and the number of Walruses had been increased to nine. In June a detachment had been sent to Misurata with four Wellingtons and a Walrus to cover

Operation Husky, but it turned out that the detachment had little to do. The Wellingtons and the Walruses of the Flight were passed to No 294 Squadron when it was formed in September.

At the beginning of October MAC's ASR Service was re-organised. Air Headquarters (AHQ) Malta took responsibility for ASR in Sicily and the Toe of Italy. By now most of the Allied Air Forces had moved to the mainland and rescues were not so numerous. Apart from the Walruses the ASR squadrons were non-operational as they were slowly re-equipping with Warwicks. These aircraft, it will be recalled, were the machines that were unsuitable as bombers and were not modified as rescue aircraft. All General Reconnaissance (GR) squadrons were ordered to keep one aircraft, fitted with a Lindholme gear, on standby for rescue duties. The Fighter Sectors had fighters available for close-in search. The Walruses were detached to Palermo, Ajaccio, Monte Corvino, Brindisi, Catania and Malta. Italian Air Force (now on the Allied side) Cant aircraft were available from Brindisi and Taranto. The HSLs were at Naples, Salerno, Termoli, Bari, Corsica, Sicily, Sardinia, Malta and Tunisia.

In November, MAC appealed for more rescue aircraft as the rescue resources were inadequate. For example only 13 Warwicks had been delivered. There was little chance that more than 20 further aircraft could be delivered before January 1944.

In December the Air Staff agreed that further rescue facilities could neither be provided for transit routes nor to cover GR activities in non-operational areas such as parts of the Indian Ocean. It was agreed that MAC should retain its four squadrons, that Middle East should be relieved of rescue responsibilities outwith the Mediterranean and that these should be taken by Air Command South East Asia.

MIDDLE EAST

No 8 Squadron was still at Khormaksar operating Blenheim Vs and with the usual detachments. In February Hudson VIs were added to the inventory. On 14 July 1943 Flt. Sgt. N. Miller and crew, operating from Scuscuiban, in British Somaliland, gained a visual sighting at six miles on the starboard beam of a surfaced submarine in position 1213N 05113E. This was the Japanese submarine I-29 commanded by Lt. Cdr. Juichi Uizu. An attack was made. It was intended to be a stick of four depth charges, but one DC hung up. It was a good straddle, causing the boat to submerge, then resurface and then submerge again. A large oil trail was seen and it was believed that the boat had been damaged. It was eventually sunk by an American submarine a year later. The squadron exchanged its Hudson VIs in December for Wellington XIIIs.

No 244 Squadron was still at Sharjah with its Blenheim Vs. In May Wing Commander Rotheram was appointed as Commanding Officer. These Blenheim Vs or Bisleys were prone to engine failure due to sand getting into them. Rotheram ordered more frequent engine changes and arranged for the removal of the armour and the gun turrets which, when done, improved the aircraft's performance. U-533, a type IXc, was sunk in position 2528N 05650E on 16 August 1943 by a Sergeant pilot and his crew using Depth Charges.

FAR EAST 1943

No 22 Squadron moved to Vavuniya, North East Ceylon, with its Beaufort Is in February 1943.

No 36 Squadron moved to Dhubalia, North of Calcutta, in April 1943 and then to Blida near Algiers in June.

No 42 Squadron exchanged its Beaufort Is for Blenheim Vs in February 1943 and sent a detachment to Rajyeswarpur, North East India, close to Imphal. In October it exchanged its Blenheim Vs for Hurricane IVs and ceased engagement in the maritime role.

No 160 Squadron was a Liberator bomber squadron that had been formed in January 1942 and had flown anti-submarine training sorties with No 120 Squadron from Nutts Corner near Belfast in May 1942. In June 1942 the squadron began to move to Egypt and was absorbed into No 159 Squadron. This unit was absorbed into No 178 Squadron, a bomber unit, in January 1943. No 160's aircraft, Liberator IIs, gradually moved from November 1942 to Salbani situated to the West of Calcutta. In February 1943 the squadron moved to Ratmalana, near Colombo. In March the squadron received Liberator Mark IIIs and in June, Mark Vs. In August 1943 the Squadron moved to Sigiriya with detachments at Cuttack and Addu Atoll in the Maldives. The delay in getting to the Far East was due to the need to keep heavy bombers for the Battle of El Alamein. From India, the squadron carried out shipping protection sorties, photographic reconnaissance and then special duties, with its "C" Flight, dropping agents and supplies to the resistance in Sumatra and Malaya.

No 191 Squadron formed at Korangi Creek in May 1943, equipped with Catalina Ibs. There were detachments at Red Hills Lake, Jiwani, Trombay and Cochin.

No 203 Squadron moved to Santa Cruz near Bombay in November 1943, disposing of its Baltimores in exchange for Wellington XIIIs.

No 205 Squadron was still at Koggala flying Catalina Is.

No 212 Squadron was still operating Catalina Ibs from Korangi Creek and its usual detachments.

No 217 Squadron received some Hudson VIs in January 1943 and moved to Vavuniya the following month. In April it converted to Beaufort Is again and disposed of its Hudsons in May and June. In April it had detachments at Addu Atoll (Gan), Santa Cruz, Cochin and Ratmalana near Colombo, Ceylon.

No 240 Squadron remained at Red Hills Lake with its many detachments and was operating Catalina IIAs.

No 321 Squadron still operated its Catalina IIs and IIIs from China Bay and its detachment bases.

FAR EAST AND INDIA AIR SEARCH AND RESCUE

An Air Sea Rescue officer was appointed to the India area in March 1943 but he had few facilities with which to work. Luckily, demands for help were few and there were General Reconnaissance (GR) Squadrons upon which he could rely.

The establishment of India's first Air Sea Rescue (ASR) Unit was authorized in July 1943. It was given the number 203 and had two HSLs. A further unit was formed in October. There were many alterations to the original allocations to India due to the priority given to the

Mediterranean theatre. Five HSLs had arrived in India by July and another four arrived that month, but that was the last until the following year.

In February the Air Staff had proposed that India should have a long-range search squadron. The aircraft would be Warwicks but as discussed elsewhere, the production of these was slow. These aircaft would not arrive until 1944. In November the first supplies of Lindholme gear and the Bircham Barrel arrived. By now the ASR organization had been formed and the responsibility for rescues would pass from the Royal Navy and the Fleet Air Arm to the Royal Air Force. The organization was expected to be operational by March 1944, when the long-range squadron was to be formed.

WEST AFRICA

No 95 Squadron moved to Bathurst/Half Die in March 1943 with detachments at Jui, Dakar and Port Etienne. In the same month some Sunderland Is were added to the inventory.

No 200 Squadron moved to Yundum/Bathurst in March 1943 with detachments at Jeswang, Port Etienne, Hastings, Robertsfield, Rufisque and Waterloo. In July 1943 it began to exchange its Hudsons for Liberator Vs. On 11 August 1943 Fg. Off. L. A. Trigg and crew in Liberator BZ832 on an anti-submarine patrol south west of Dakar sighted U-468, commanded by Oberleutnant zur See Klemens Schamong on the surface. She was returning from patrol early as she was unable to refuel from U-462, which had been sunk by a No 502 Squadron Halifax. Trigg attacked immediately with six depth charges but came under heavy fire, crashed and blew up. There were no survivors. However, the attack had severely damaged the U-Boat. Fuel tanks were split, engines were torn from their mountings and worst of all sea water had penetrated the batteries, releasing chlorine gas. She sank in position 1220N 02007W. Of those who had survived the depth charges, many did not survive the gas or the sharks. Seven sailors were rescued by HMS *Clarkia*, which had been guided to the area by a No 204 Squadron Sunderland which had located the dinghy. Trigg was awarded the Victoria Cross on the basis of the U-Boat's survivors' testimony.

On 17 August 1943, Fg. Off. P. R. Horbat and crew in a Hudson, escorting convoy SL 135, gained a sighting of an object which disappeared. Two hours later, it was seen again and confirmed as a U-Boat. It was U-403, a type VIIc commanded by Kapitänleutnant Karl-Franz Heine. An attack with a stick of four depth charges was made from 50 feet in position 1411N 01740W. Horbat closed with the convoy to advise the Escort Commander of the incident. On returning to the scene an oil streak was seen. The Hudson was relieved by a Sunderland. U-403 had been sunk in this attack and the kill was shared with a French Wellington from No 344 Squadron. There were no survivors.

No 204 Squadron was still at Bathurst operating Sunderland IIIs.

No 270 Squadron moved to Apapa near Lagos in July 1943 with detachments at Jui, Abidjan and Libreville. In December Sunderland IIIs were added to the inventory.

No 490 Squadron Royal New Zealand Air Force was formed at Jui, Freetown in March 1943, with a detachment to Stranraer. In June it was equipped with Catalina Ibs and had detachments at Fisherman's Lake in Liberia, Apapa at Lagos, Half Die at Bathurst and Abidjan in the Ivory Coast.

WEST AFRICA SEARCH AND RESCUE

The Air Ministry increased the establishment of Air Sea Rescue Units to five with two HSLs each and in the same month four pinnaces arrived, which were added to the two HSLs already in the Command. Thus was formed another Unit based at Takoradi. There were units at Freetown and Bathurst. The third, fourth and fifth units were to be based at Port Etienne and Pointe Noire.

On 11 August 1943 Sunderlands and Liberators were sent to search for Flying Officer Trigg's aircraft (see No 200 Squadron above). One of them located an empty dinghy and nearby a dinghy with seven men on board. Survival equipment was dropped and HMS *Clarkia* homed to the position, where it was found that they were survivors from U-468 which had been sunk by Trigg's crew. The search for Trigg and his crew was immediately resumed, but with no success.

SOUTH AND EAST AFRICA

No 209 Squadron remained at Kipevu with its Catalina IIAs. No 259 Squadron reformed at Kipevu in February 1943 with Catalina Ib's. There were detachments at Congella, Langebaan and Tulear in Madagascar. In August 1943 Flt. Lt. L. O. Barnett and crew operating from St. Lucia in Natal commenced a Creeping Line Ahead search. The visibility was five miles. The copilot gained a visual sighting of a submarine in position 2840N 04215E. An attack was made with a stick of six depth charges and machine guns. The boat remained surfaced and returned fire. The boat was U-197, a type IX/D2 commanded by Kapitänleutnant Robert Bartels. The boat had been damaged, but the Catalina had no more DCs and could only shadow and send locating reports. The boat submerged and then resurfaced and continued firing at the aircraft. A relief aircraft, a Catalina from No 265 Squadron, captained by Fg. Off. C. E. Robin RCAF, arrived. Robin decided to try to silence the guns of the U-Boat and the two aircraft made machine-gun attacks. When this had been achieved, Robin made to attack, but Bartels took avoiding action. Finally he took the wrong course and Robin hit the boat with a stick of DCs and sank the boat. Barnett and his WOP/AG, Sgt K. V. S. Caligari, were awarded the DFC and DFM respectively; Robin was awarded the DFC, while his WOP/AG, Sgt S. Oxley, was awarded a Mention in Despatches.

In September the squadron moved to Dar-Es-Salaam with detachments at Diego Suarez, Khormaksar, Masirah, Port Victoria, Tulear and Mauritius. Khormaksar was an airfield and the Catalina Ib was a flying boat. Presumably the aircraft were moored in the bay off Steamer Point, the crews being accommodated at the airfield.

No 262 Squadron was still at Congella with the Catalina Ibs which it had received in February, 1943.

No 265 Squadron was reformed at Kipevu in March

1943 with Catalina Ibs. In April 1943 it moved to Diego
Suarez with detachments at Jui, Pamanzi, Kipevu,
Mauritius, Tulear, Masirah, Port Victoria, Khormaksar,
St Lucia and Congella.

No 621 Squadron was formed at Port Reitz,
Mombasa, Kenya on 12 September 1943 with Wellington
XIIIs. It was probably the only squadron to have been
stationed there. It had a detachment at Mogadishu, Italian
Somaliland and moved there in November with
detachments at Scuscuiban, Bandar Kassim both in
Italian Somaliland, and Riyan on the South Arabian
coast. A month later the squadron moved to Khormaksar
in Aden with additional detachments at Socotra Island off
Aden, and Mogadishu, Italian Somaliland.

AIR SEA RESCUE SOUTH AND EAST AFRICA
As stated in the Air Sea Rescue Section for the
Mediterranean above, four Rescue Units were expected
to be formed by the end of August 1943.

METEOROLOGICAL CALIBRATION
No 517 Squadron was formed in August 1943 from 1404
Flight at St Eval with Hudson IIIs and Hampdens. In
September it gave up its Hudsons for Fortress B-17s,
which were USAAF aircraft attached. This was a
temporary measure when in November they were
exchanged for Halifax Vs. In the same month the
squadron moved to St David's, South West Wales.

No 518 Squadron was formed at Stornoway in July
1943 from 1405 Flight with Halifax Vs. In September it
moved to Tiree in the Western Isles of Scotland.

No 519 Squadron was formed at Wick in August 1943 from Nos 1406 and 1408 Flights with Hampdens and Spitfire VIs. The following month it received Hudson IIIAs and Ventura Vs. In October the Hudsons and the Hampdens were disposed of. In December the squadron moved to Skitten.

No 520 Squadron was formed at Gibraltar in September 1943 from No 1403 Flight with Hudson IIIs and Gladiator IIs.

No 521 Squadron was disbanded in March 1943 and split into Nos 1401 and 1409 Flights. However, in September it all changed when the squadron was reformed at Docking with Hudson IIIs, Hampdens, Gladiator IIs, Spitfire IXs and Ventura Vs.

PHOTOGRAPHIC RECCONNAISSANCE

No 540 Squadron disposed of its Mosquito Is in May 1943 and its Mark IVs and VIIIs in August but received Mark IXs in July. It remained at Leuchars.

No 541 Squadron remained at Benson and retained its various Marks of Spitfire.

No 542 Squadron remained at Benson giving up its Spitfire IVs in July but having received Spitfire XIs in March 1943.

No 543 Squadron received Spitfire XIs n April 1943 but was disbanded in October.

No 544 Squadron remained at Benson but gave up its Anson Is, Maryland Is and Wellington IVs in March 1943 and its Spitfire IVs in October. It received Mosquito IVs in March and Spitfire XIs in August but both types were given up in October. The squadron received Mosquito IXs in August.

CHAPTER TWENTY TWO

1944

◉

This was to be the year of the invasion of Europe, Operations Overlord and Neptune. In June Admiral Dönitz needed to bring his U-Boats into the English Channel to challenge the invasion force. These were inshore waters, where a maritime patrol could keep its radar on all the time and not necessarily give itself away as there would be many other radars transmitting. This would be a nightmare for the U-Boats. Such an area tends to favour the aircraft, and the nearer to the Straits of Dover the invasion beaches were, the greater the advantage.

Coastal Command saturated the area with aircraft. Three Liberators and a Wellington were lost on the night of 6/7 June, probably shot down by U-Boat flak. The details are impossible to confirm as the only message came from one of the aircraft and several of the U-Boats failed to return. U-981, commanded by Oberleutnant zur See Walter Sitek, believed that it had shot down a Halifax. This was a No 502 Squadron aircraft captained by Flt. Lt. W. G. Powell, and it was undamaged. Fifteen boats which had sailed from Brest on 6 June were ordered to make a high-speed run on the surface. This is not the sort of tactic that would make a submariner happy. The non-schnorkel boats sailed as an escorted group. It was a little after midnight that attacks started on these boats. U-621 reported at 0135Z that an aircraft passed just behind her and she opened fire. This was ignored and the aircraft flew towards the group. According to her records there was flak everywhere. The crew saw an aircraft go down but it remains unidentified. A short while later another aircraft was seen to go down; this may have been a Liberator shot down by U-256. This night saw the largest single battle between aircraft and U-Boats of the whole war. There were few survivors on either side.

MARITIME PATROL UK

No 10 Squadron Royal Australian Air Force was at Mountbatten with its Sunderlands. On 8 January 1944. Fg. Off. J. P. Roberts RAAF and crew were flying a Percussion patrol. A U-Boat was sighted, decks awash, from 12 miles in position 4647N 01042W. An attack was commenced and the boat opened fire. The aircraft returned fire and the flak stopped at 600 yards. The depth charges failed to run out in time and the aircraft went round again and dropped a stick of six DCs from 50 feet. Six bodies were seen lying in the conning tower. The boat sank and there were no survivors. It was U-426, a type VIIc commanded by Kapitänleutnant Christian Reich.

An aircraft from this squadron, captain Flt. Lt. H. A. McGregor RAAF, damaged U-333 commanded by Kapitänleutnant Peter Cremer on 11 June 1944. The boat's 37mm gun and radar were put out of action and there were leaks in the hull. This, combined with a further attack a few hours later by a No 228 Squadron Sunderland, forced him to return to La Pallice. On 8 July 1944, Fg. Off. W. B. Tilley RAAF and crew gained a visual sighting of a surfaced U-Boat at six miles. An attack was initiated and at two miles the boat and the aircraft began to exchange fire. A stick of six depth charges was dropped, giving a good straddle. This was U-243, a type VIIC commanded by Kapitänleutnant Hans Martens, and she began to sink, but still kept firing. Soon dinghies were launched by the German crew. Another No 10 Squadron Sunderland arrived followed by a B-24 (Liberator) from VP 105, US Navy. Both of these aircraft dropped DCs. The boat sank stern first in position 4706N 00640W. Tilley dropped a dinghy to the survivors, who were rescued by HMCS *Restigouche*. Martens however, was fatally wounded.

No 53 Squadron moved to St Eval in January 1944. On 6 January 1944 Flt. Lt. E. B. A. LeMaistre RCAF and crew were on a Percussion sortie when they gained a radar contact at 37 miles. At 18 miles in the moonlight they saw a U-Boat in position 4708N 00642W. This was U-107, commanded by Kapitänleutnant Volker Simmermacher. LeMaistre attacked with six DCs and his WOP sent a locating report. On the follow-up attack a second radar contact was gained two miles to starboard, followed immediately by a visual sighting. This was probably U-621 commanded by Oberleutnant zur See Max Kruschka. A second stick, this time of four DCs, was dropped on U-107. No damage was incurred by either boat. U-107 had been detected twice before that night, once by Fg. Off. J. H. Spurgeon and crew of No 502 Squadron and once by

Fg. Off. Jordan and crew of No 407 Squadron. Both boats fired on the Halifax, which was forced to return to base which it reached safely.

On 3 February 1944 Sergeant T. A. Patey and crew in Liberator BZ795 were on a Percussion patrol when they found U-763, commanded by Kapitänleutnant Ernst Cordes, in position 4530N 00700W. The crew reported contact at 0811 hours and nothing further was heard. According to the U-Boat's operations record book the aircraft was shot down, having dropped its DCs. They caused no damage and there were no survivors from the Liberator. The next night Liberator BZ815 from No 53 squadron captained by Plt. Off. L. L. Esler RCAF, found U-763 in position 4527N 00654W while on a ASR sortie. The aircraft homed in and released DCs, but to no effect. The Liberator was hit several times, also to no effect. The aircraft later picked two more radar contacts, but these were Aphrodite decoy buoys released by U-763 which gave a similar return to a real U-Boat. Shortly after, U-763 was located by a No 172 Squadron Wellington.

In the early morning of 10 February 1944 Sqn. Ldr. A. Spooner and crew were on escort to convoy HX277. The crew gained a radar contact and attacked with six DCs in position 4953N 01720W. A follow-up attack of two DCs was made. Apart from some wooden planks, no results were observed. U-608, commanded by Oberleutnant zur See Wolfgang Reisener, reported being attacked by a four-engined aircraft at a similar time and place. They reported firing on the aircraft and smoke coming from one of the engines.

On the night of 6 April Fg. Off. C. Allison RCAF and

crew in Liberator BZ769 gained a radar contact in position 4413N 00341W. What were believed to be two surfaced U-Boats, about 50 yards apart, were seen. One may have been a trawler or an escort. The navigator, Fg. Off. A. W. Goldstone RCAF, saw only the lead boat and directed a turn towards it. The boat was U-618, commanded by Kapitänleutnant Kurt Baberg. Heavy flak was experienced by the Liberator and extensive damage was caused. Allison turned off and when it was found that the bomb doors would not move they headed home.

In the early hours of 10 April Fg. Off. W. J. Irving RCAF and crew were on a Percussion sortie in BZ781. The radar operator gained a contact at 17 miles, holding it to one mile, when it was illuminated by Leigh Light. This was U-821, commanded by Oberleutnant zur See Ulrich Knackfuss. The boat and the aircraft exchanged fire and on the first run the DCs failed to release. Irving went round again, and again the DCs failed to release. This time however, the boat's gunners hit the bomb bay and the rear turret. Irving tried a third time, to no avail. The crew went home finding en route that the nose wheel had been punctured and the hydraulics were damaged. However, Irving made a good landing without flaps or brakes. He received the DFC. This was the same Irving who had been forced to land in Portugal in July 1943.

On 17 April 1944, Flt. Lt. F. M. Burton and crew in BZ945 made a sighting report at 0127Z but cancelled it at 0230Z, presumably declaring the contact to be non sub. At 0304Z ACHQ (19 Group) instructed the crew to look for a U-Boat. A position was given. At 0349Z a flash report was made giving a position 4700N 00930W. This was probably U-993 commanded by Oberleutnant zur See Kurt Hilbig. The boat reported in its operations record book that they opened fire on the aircraft, setting an engine on fire and causing it to crash. Two bombs were dropped but missed. Flt. Lt. C. Roberts and crew were on patrol when they were instructed by ACHQ at 0032Z again on 17 April to look for a U-Boat in position 4626N 01041W. At 0457Z a flash report was received which implied that the crew had sighted something. Nothing further was heard. The probability was that they had found and attacked U-546, commanded by Kapitänleutnant Paul Just. His operations record book showed that the boat had been attacked by an aircraft which had dropped six bombs, that it had been hit by flak and had crashed. The boat dived.

On 25/26 April 1944, Flt. Lt. C. McC. Forbes and crew were on a Rover patrol along the French and Spanish coasts at 500 feet. At 0150Z the radar operator reported several contacts in position 4600N 00146W. They homed in, finding fishing boats and then two U-Boats, which opened fire, hitting the Liberator. Forbes could not see the targets but made a second attack and this time he could see one of them. This time the No 3 engine was hit and set alight and the DCs hung up. A third attack was attempted and again the DCs hung up. Forbes headed for home, gaining more radar contacts en route which turned out to be aircraft. These they avoided successfully. Forbes received the DFC for this and other actions. Subsequent analysis revealed that there were no U-Boats present at that time and that the targets were probably surface warships.

In May the squadron took delivery of Liberator VIs. On 2 May 1944 Flt. Lt. Le Maistre saw an action which may have been the demise of the No 58 Squadron Halifax flown by Flt. Lt. Burton and crew. On 7 June Sqn. Ldr. G. Crawford and crew were shot down, probably by either U-441 or U-629 or U-740 while patrolling off Brest. Flt. Lt. J. W. Carmichael and crew found and attacked U-963 with guns and a stick of six DCs in position 4836N 00521W. An attempt at a follow-up attack was frustrated by flak from three different boats. U-963, although not damaged by this aircraft, was forced to return to base due to other damage. A second attack was made 38 minutes later against what was probably U-629 in position 4834N 00523W. This boat was commanded by Oberleutnant zur See Hans-Helmuth Bugs and was probably sunk in this attack. The aircraft was damaged.

Carmichael was awarded the DFC, which was gazetted in August 1944, but sadly he did not survive the month. On 13th June he and his crew departed St Eval for a Cork patrol. A message was received from them at 2355 hours stating that they were attacking a U-boat south west of Ushant. This was U-270 commanded by Kapitänleutnant Paul-Friedrich Otto. Initially this boat was found and attacked by Wellington MP789 of No 172 Squadron, whose crew saw the demise of Carmichael and crew. The U-Boat's operations record book records two attacks and that return fire set the No 3 engine on fire, causing the Liberator to crash. Although the U-boat commander records both attacks as being carried out by a Liberator, the first was probably that made by the No 172 Squadron Wellington.

On 9 August 1944 Wg. Cdr. R. T. F. Gates AFC and crew gained a visual sighting of an oil slick. On investigation a U-boat was seen under the surface in position 4630N 00308W. A marker was dropped and Gates attacked with a stick of six depth charges from the rear end of the slick, the bombaimer using the bombsight. Air bubbles and oil were seen. The aircraft left the area to contact the 2nd Escort Group and as the Group approached two Sunderlands arrived. Gates resumed patrol, but returned a while later to find more oil and some orange grease on the surface. The ships reported that they had picked some planking. Later HMS *Wren* and HMS *Killin* rescued 51 survivors, who reported that the U-Boat had been damaged by the DC attack and the boat had lain on the bottom until damaged further by the ships. The U-Boat crew surfaced and surrendered. This was a U-608, a type VIIc commanded by Oberleutnant zur See Wolfgang Reisener, which had departed Lorient two days previously. Gates had been on his last flight as Commanding Officer. He was awarded the DFC and promoted to Group Captain.

On 14 August 1944 Flt. Lt. G. G. Potier DFC and crew gained a radar contact at seven and a half miles. Potier manoeuvred the aircraft so that he was upwind at 300 feet and at a distance of eleven and a half miles and then commenced his attack run. On illumination a surfaced U-Boat was seen in position 4722N 00439W. Aircraft and U-Boat exchanged fire and a stick of six depth charges was dropped. The radar contact slowly disappeared, but nothing was seen at the datum. A Wellington was homed in but the crew of this aircraft could see nothing except oil streaks. The Boat was U-618, a type VIIc commanded by Oberleutnant zur See Erich Faust. It was en route Brest to La Pallice and had been damaged. Potier called in the 3rd Escort Group, which later gained an ASDIC contact and depth-charged it. Nothing was seen except for massive amounts of oil, which continued rising to the surface for hours. The squadron moved to Reykjavik with a detachment at Ballykelly in September.

No 58 Squadron was still at St David's with Halifax IIs. On 2 January 1944 Fg. Off. T. A. Griffiths and crew gained a radar contact at nine miles and homed in. Flares were dropped at one and a half miles, illuminating a surfaced U-Boat in position 4531N 00719W. A stick of six depth charges was dropped, although the sixth hung up from 300 feet. The navigator, Fg. Off. H. E. Quinn, opened fire with the nose gun and the boat replied. The submarine looked as though it was diving, radar contact was lost and no results were observed. However, the boat, which was U-445, a type VIIc commanded by Oberleutnant zur See Rupprecht Fischler Graf von Treuberg, had been damaged and was forced to return to St. Nazaire. Griffiths, who had flown 34 sorties and Quinn, who had flown 39 sorties, received the DFC.

On 5 January 1944, Flt. Lt. I. J. M. Christie and crew gained a radar contact at 22 miles. This was an area of many fishing vessels and the crew had already found some this night. However, a homing was initiated and a wake and then a submarine was sighted in position 4644N 00516W. Three flares were dropped, which were fired at by the submarine. A stick of six depth charges was dropped from 150 feet. The Halifax gunners opened fire. The boat dived and nothing further was seen. This was U-415, a type VIIC commanded by Kapitänleutnant Kurt Neide, and it had been damaged. The boat was already on its way back to Brest, where it arrived the next day.

Halifax HX225, flown by Fg. Off. L. A. Hayward and crew, was on a Percussion sortie on 12 March 1944. They failed to return. A message in Brevity Code was received by ACHQ, stating that the crew was in contact with a U-Boat. There was no position, but the time corresponded with a report sent to Befehlshaber der U-Boote (BdU) by U-311 commanded by Kapitänleutnant Joachim Zander, stating that she had been attacked by a Fortress with bombs and guns. Presumably the aircraft was misidentified. The U-Boat did not return from her patrol, so no further information is available.

On 28 April 1944 Flt. Lt. W. D. C. Erskine-Crum and crew in Halifax HX152 gained a radar contact which was lost and then regained. Flares dropped from 600 feet revealed a surfaced U-Boat. This was U-473, commanded by Kapitänleutnant Heinz Sternberg. The boat's guns opened fire and the aircraft navigator replied with the nose gun. Seven DCs were dropped from 100 feet and at the same time the aircraft was hit and became unmanageable. The captain ordered "ditching stations" but almost immediately regained control and cancelled his order. Four DCs were seen to explode alongside the U-Boat and as they headed for home the crew saw blue flames and a red glow along the boat. U-473 was attacked again the next night by a Wellington from No 304 Squadron, but no damage was incurred by either side. U-473 was sunk on 4/5 May 1944 by No 2 Escort Group.

On 2 May 1944 Fg. Off. D. E. Taylor and crew in HR741 were probably shot down by the gunners of U-846 commanded by Oberleutnant zur See Berthold Hashagen.

In any event it failed to return. Flt. Lt. LeMaistre and crew in a No 53 Squadron Liberator saw an action where three flares were dropped and tracer was seen coming up from sea level. Taylor's aircraft had flares but no Leigh Light. Hashagen had reported to BdU an attack on 2 May at 0407Z.

On 7 June 1944 Flt. Lt. J.W. Carmichael and crew gained three radar contacts in the early hours of the morning and a radar homing initiated. The second pilot, Flt. Sgt. E. E. Stevens, sighted a U-Boat at two miles at 100 feet and an attack was carried out with a stick of six depth charges. Heavy flak was encountered from U-415, U-989 and U-963 and Carmichael held off, transmitting a situation report. Then he made a follow-up attack with a further six DCs from 50 feet, which made an excellent straddle. The rear gunner saw a large explosion, but no further results were seen. It is now believed by U-Boat.net that Carmichael sank U-629, commanded by Oberleutnant zur See Helmut Bugs. The heavy flak had achieved results. The No 3 engine had been hit and a shell had exploded in the bomb bay. Carmichael headed for home, the No 3 propeller having been feathered. Carmichael was awarded the DFC and his navigator, Flt. Sgt. J. T. McKeown, the DFM. Carmichael was promoted to Sqn. Ldr. to replace Sqn. Ldr. Crawford, who had been shot down with his crew on 6 June 1944. Unfortunately, on the night of 13/14 June 1944, Carmichael and crew failed to return. They were attacking a U-Boat, probably U-270. On 8 June Sqn. Ldr. A. T. Brock and crew in Halifax HR744 saw U-413 commanded by Oberleutnant zur See Dietrich Sachse in the moonlight in position 4743N 00526W. Brock attacked, receiving flak from possibly two boats. A stick of seven DCs was dropped from 600 feet. No results were observed. About half an hour later the crew saw another aircraft attacking a vessel on the surface and this was probably Fg. Off. Spurgeon and crew in a No 502 Squadron Halifax. On 13th August Flt. Lt. J. M. MacFadyen and crew were on a ranger patrol in the Gironde estuary in JP301. In the area were Fg. Off. W. E. Umpherson RCAF and crew from No 502 Squadron. MacFadyen's crew sighted U-534, U-437, U-857 and four escort vessels in position 4538N 00112W. He dropped four 600lb bombs from 2000 feet but during the run in his aim was spoiled by a shell burst beneath the aircraft. The aircraft was under fire from all seven vessels and shore batteries. MacFadyen and crew returned to base safely after a nine hour ten minute sortie. The squadron moved to Stornoway on 1 September 1944 with its Halifax IIs.

No 59 Squadron remained at Ballykelly with its Liberator Vs. On 13 January 1944, Fg. Off. W. G. Loney RAAF and crew were escorting convoys SL144 and MKS 35. A visual sighting of a surfaced U-Boat was gained at eight miles. Despite an approach from the sun the boat sighted the Liberator at four miles and opened fire. A stick of six depth charges was dropped from 50 feet, giving a good straddle. A follow-up attack was carried out with two DCs and then three machine gun attacks. The boat then dived. This was U-621, a type VIIc commanded by Kapitänleutnant Max Kruschka and was badly damaged, causing a return to Brest.

On 25 May 1944 Sqn. Ldr. B. A. Sisson and crew were carrying out a creeping line-ahead search. A radar contact was gained which proved to be an armed auxiliary vessel.

The vessel opened fire and the Liberator returned fire from the turrets and the port beam. The patrol was resumed and a visual sighting was gained of a surfaced U-Boat escorted by a patrol boat VP5901 in position 6505N 00728W. Taking advantage of a rain shower to avoid flak from both ships, Sisson attacked with a stick of six depth charges. Both ships opened fire and the Liberator responded with nose and tail turrets. The boat was U-990, a type VIIc commanded by Kapitänleutnant Hubert Nordheimer and was en route to Narvik. The boat was seen to sink. Fifty-one survivors were rescued. These included 21 from U-476, which had been sunk by a No 210 Squadron aircraft the previous day.

On 27 May Flt. Lt. V. E. Camacho RCAF and crew gained a radar contact at 15 miles and commenced a homing. Contact was lost at three miles, but a surfaced submarine was found at the end of the homing in position 6237N 00057E. The boat was U-292, a type VIIc/41 commanded by Oberleutnant zur See Werner Schmidt. It was attacked with a stick of six depth charges. A yellow explosion was seen and the boat submerged. It was classified as sunk. Having sustained some flak damage, the aircraft landed at Tain.

On 19 July 1944 Fg. Off. R. C. Fleming and crew were at 1400 feet when the starboard gunner gained a visual sighting of a surfaced U-Boat at six miles in position 7019N 00602E. Radar contact was gained at the same time. The boat was U-716, a type VIIc commanded by Oberleutnant zur See Johannes Dunkelberg. A homing was initiated and the submarine opened fire which was returned by nose gunner. A navigator attack using the

Mark III Low Level Bombsight was made with a stick of six depth charges from 100 feet, giving a straddle. A follow-up attack was made with two DCs. The boat submerged, but it had been damaged and had to return to Hammerfest.

No 86 Squadron moved to Reykjavik in March 1944 with its Liberator IIIAs. There was a detachment at Tain in Easter Ross. A crew from this unit found the survivors of the No 162 Squadron RCAF Canso on 13th June. On 20 June 1944, Fg. Off. E. D. Moffit RAAF and crew gained a visual sighting of a wake which later was seen to be that of a surfaced U-Boat in position 6100N 00025E. It was U-743, a type VIIc commanded by Oberleutnant zur See Helmut Kandzior. An attack with a stick of six depth charges was carried out, but at the last minute the boat took avoiding action and the DCs missed. A follow-up attack was attempted and the boat again took avoiding action, but this time no DCs were dropped. A second follow-up attack was made and two DCs straddled the boat. It was damaged and had to return to Bergen for repairs. Throughout these attacks gun duels were fought between the boat's gunners and those of the Liberator. The aircraft was hit but landed safely.

On 26th June Fg. Of. Moffit and crew were patrolling off the Norwegian coast on a Blue Peter and found and attacked U-771, commanded by Oberleutnant zur See Helmut Block. The aircraft failed to return but the details are given in the U-boat's operations record book. The aircraft apparently flew over the boat strafing, but no DCs were released. The boat opened fire with 37mm and 20mm guns and the Liberator was seen to crash in the sea.

Moffitt was an experienced Coastal pilot. Again on 26th June Flt Lt G. W. T. Parker and crew were on a Blue Peter patrol in Liberator FL916 when they found and attacked U-317, commanded by Oberleutnant zur See Peter Rallff in position 6203N 00145E. The U-Boat was sighted by the second navigator Flt Sgt D. Carter of the RNZAF and the second pilot, Flt Sgt S. Norris. Carter and the U-Boat opened fire almost simultaneously. The DCs undershot and Parker turned for a follow up attack. The No 3 engine was hit and the propeller was feathered. The second stick was released and members of the crew saw a large explosion and large pieces flying into the air. U-317 rolled over and sank.

As the weather was below landing limits at Tain, the crew's detachment base, they were diverted to Stornoway and the aircraft was flown back to Tain when the weather improved. There it was discovered by the ground crew that there was a large hole in the main spar caused by a flak shell. The aircraft should not have been flown out of Stornoway. Parker received the DFC. U-317 was on its first patrol and none of the crew survived.

On 30th June, Fg. Off. N. E. M. Smith and crew in Liberator FL924 were homed in by a Canso from 162 Squadron RCAF flown by Flt Lt R. E. McBride RCAF and crew. They were engaged in an attack on U-478 and the DCs had hung up. A stick of DCs from the Liberator sank the boat with all hands. The Liberator had been hit in No 4 engine but it returned to base. Smith was awarded a bar to his DFC. In July the squadron moved to Tain and exchanged its aircraft for Liberator Vs. On 17 July 1944, Plt. Off. M. G. Moseley and crew gained a visual sighting of a surfaced submarine from 400 feet at 12 miles, sea state calm. Taking advantage of the cloud layer, Moseley turned on, periodically descending below the cloud base for a look, but was greeted each time by flak. The aircraft finally came out of cloud at 800 yards, the front gunner opened fire and a stick of six depth charges was dropped from 125 feet which straddled the boat. It was believed to be U-361, a type VIIc commanded by Kapitänleutnant Hans Seidel. However, there was some discrepancy as to whether the boat was U-361 or U-347. It was eventually resolved that this boat was U-347 and it was sunk by this attack, as observed by the rear gunner in position 6836N 00833E. U-361 was sunk by Fg. Off. Cruickshank's crew from No 210 Squadron on the same day.

On 18th July Sqn. Ldr R. P. Nelms and crew in Liberator FL907 left Tain in the early afternoon for a patrol in the North Norwegian Sea. At 2231 a listening post at Inverness intercepted an SOS from the aircraft giving a position as 6815N 00846E. Again on 18th July, Flt. Lt. J. F. Pettifer RAAF and crew were in Liberator FK225 in area 6700N to 6800N, 00600E to 00900E. At 1002 they found what was believed to be U-307, commanded by Kapitänleutnant Rudolf Buchler, on the surface in position 6838N 00859E some 100 miles west of the Lofoten Islands. Pettifer attacked with six DCs, straddling the stern, and turned for a follow-up attack. Unfortunately the remaining two DCs were dropped prematurely in the run up. Fire from U-307 hit the nose wounding both navigators and the No 3 engine (starboard inner) was hit. The aircraft was diverted to Scatsa, where it landed safely, almost sixteen hours after take off.

Norman Franks in *U-Boat versus Aircraft* states that

this was U-307. However in his *Search, Find and Kill* he states that U-387 was commanded by Rudolf Buchler when he describes an attack by No 330 Squadron on this boat a day later in a similar area. U-Boat.net states that U-307 was commanded by Oberleutnant zur See Friedrich-Georg Herrle at this time. U-307 was sunk on 29 April 1945 under the command of Oberleutnant zur See Erich Kruger in the Barents Sea. U-387 was sunk on 9 December 1944 under the command of Buchler, again in the Barents Sea. Probably it was U-387 that was attacked by Pettifer and under the command of Buchler.

Sqn. Ldr. T. M. Bulloch DSO, DFC, AFC and crew took off at 1755 on 19th July, reaching their patrol area at 0114 on 20th. The area was partly shrouded in fog but as the aircraft reached a clear patch they found U-636, commanded by Oberleutnant zur See Eberhard Schendel. The U-Boat crew had heard the aircraft approaching and had their guns trained on the sound. As the Liberator became visible the U-Boat opened fire, damaging the Nos 3 and 4 engines, starboard rudder, fuselage, bomb bay and rear turret. Bulloch had no choice but to return to base immediately. The crew jettisoned all guns, ammunition, depth charges and any other "not required on voyage" equipment. They returned safely to Tain. Again on the 19 July 1944, Flt. Lt. W. F. J. Harwood and crew gained a visual sighting of a U-Boat in position 6939N 00901E and attacked with a stick of six depth charges but undershot. A follow-up attack was made with two DCs, but again it was an undershoot. The aircraft was under fire during both attacks until the nose gunner silenced the U-boat gunners. The boat was U-968, a type VIIc commanded by Oberleutnant zur See Otto Westphalen, and was forced to return to Narvik with damage.

On 27 July 1944 Fg. Off. G. G. Gates and crew gained a visual sighting of a surfaced U-Boat in position 6440N 2020W. This was U-865, a type IXc/40 commanded by Oberleutnant zur See Dietrich Stellmacher. A stick of six depth charges was dropped but it overshot. Gunfire was exchanged and the aircraft's No 1 and No 2 engines were set alight. Gates was forced to return to base. The fires were extinguished and the aircraft returned safely. U-865 had been damaged and had to return to Trondheim.

No 119 Squadron reformed at Manston from the Albacore Flight of No 415 Squadron Royal Canadian Air Force in July 1944, retaining its Albacores. It moved to Swingfield in August and to Bircham Newton in October with detachments at St Croix, Maldeghem and Knocke le Zout.

No 120 Squadron disposed of its Liberator IIIs in January 1944, having received Liberator Vs the previous month. On 6 March 1944, Flt. Lt. H. F. Kerrigan RCAF and crew in Liberator BZ764 investigated a radar contact and found U-737 on the surface, in position 6857N 00316E. During the approach, the boat, commanded by Oberleutnant zur See Paul Brasack, opened fire and hit the No 4 Engine. Kerrigan dropped a stick of six DCs and the boat dived. The aircraft orbited and then the boat surfaced. Kerrigan attacked again, but gunfire from U-737 damaged the bomb release system and wounded both navigators. Kerrigan turned for home assisted by the first navigator, Fg. Off. P. R. Rackham RCAF, who was wounded in the head, body and legs. The remaining DCs were jettisoned and the fire was put out. Another engine failed and the aircraft was diverted to Skitten near Wick. Kerrigan received the DSO and Rackham the DFC. U-

737 was forced to return to Hammerfest. On 24 March 1944 the squadron moved to Ballykelly.

On 9 June 1944, three days after the invasion of Europe, Flt. Lt. A. K. Sherwood and crew were patrolling the Western Approaches. A visual sighting of a wake was gained and then a submerging submarine. The U-Boat was U-740, a type VIIc commanded by Kapitänleutnant Gunther Stark. An attack with a stick of six depth charges from 60 feet was made on the swirl left by the disappeared boat. Oil was seen in position 4909N 00837W. To confirm the sinking a non-directional sonobuoy was dropped. Motor and clanging noises were heard which stopped shortly after. The U-Boat had indeed been sunk. The Liberator landed at St. Eval. Sherwood was awarded the DFC. In December the squadron started to exchange its Mark Vs for Mark VIIIs.

No 162 Squadron Royal Canadian Air Force was based in Reykjavik, Iceland and did not come into action until February 1944, having been lent to Coastal Command on 1st January 1944. The squadron had been based at Yarmouth, Nova Scotia. On 17 April 1944, Fg. Off. T. C. Cooke RCAF and crew were on a meteorological patrol. The co-pilot gained a visual sighting of a wake at six miles. Homing in, a U-Boat was sighted at four miles in position 6023N 02920W. At 3000 yards the U-Boat opened fire and the nose gunner opened fire at 1200 yards. At 300 yards the flak ceased and an attack was made from 50 feet with three depth charges. The Canso orbited the target. the port blister gunner firing at it. Then there was an explosion forward of the conning tower and the boat sank. It was U-342, a type VIIc commanded by

Oberleutnant zur See Albert Hossenfelder and on her first patrol. Cooke and Flt. Lt. E. W. Wisken RCAF were awarded Immediate DFC's.

A detachment operated from Wick from 25 May until 5 August 1944. The unit operated Cansos, the amphibian version of the Catalina. On 3 June 1944 Flt. Lt. R. E. McBride RCAF and crew were operating out of Wick. A visual sighting of a surfaced U-boat was gained in position 6359N 00137E. It was attacked with a stick of six depth charges which straddled the boat. This was U-477, a type VIIc commanded by Oberleutnant zur See Karl Joachim Jensen. It was seen to lift out of the sea and then sink, leaving five men in the water and an oil slick one mile long. McBride was awarded the DFC in August 1944.

On 11 June 1944, Fg. Off. L. Sherman RCAF and crew gained a visual sighting of a surfaced U-Boat and attacked with a stick of four depth charges from 50 feet. Gunfire was exchanged during and after the attack until the boat sank in position 6307N 00026E. This was U-980, a type VIIc commanded by Kapitän Leutnant Hermann Dahms. Sherman was awarded the DFC. On 13th June Wg. Cdr. C. StG. W. Chapman RCAF and crew were on patrol in Canso 9816. At 2000 feet and from three miles, two feathers were seen (a feather is the wake caused by a submerged submarine's periscope). This was U-715, commanded by Kapitänleutnant Helmut Rottger. The two feathers were caused by the periscope and the schnorkel.

Chapman attacked from 50 feet. The U-Boat seemed to surface but was down at the stern and men were seen in the water. Chapman made a photographic run and one of the boat's guns opened fire. Shots hit the port engine, which was shut down, but the propeller could not be feathered. This would have caused some vibration and increased the drag. The aircraft hit the sea and sank in 20 minutes. The WOP, Warrant Officer J. J. C. Bercevin, transmitted SOS signals until the last possible moment. The crew got into their dinghies, but one burst and two others had holes in them. A Liberator from No 86 Squadron found them and shortly after a Warwick from No 281 Squadron dropped an airborne lifeboat. The navigator, Fg. Off. D. Waterbury, swam to it and he and six others got into it. Flt. Sgt. H. C. Leatherdale, the Flight Engineer, was lost. The lifeboat had been damaged and began to sink. Another Warwick dropped a Lindholme dinghy, but a hole was torn in it when one of the crew was hauled into it. The lifeboat's sail was hoisted and they tried to reach the second dinghy, but that drifted away.

Finally, the ASR launch 2723 arrived collecting the survivors but two WOP/AG's, Flt. Sgt. G. F. Staples and Warrant Officer F. K. Reed, died. Chapman received the DSO and the others received DFCs and DFMs. U-715 sank with all hands in position 6245N 00259W.

Flt. Lt. L. Sherman and crew in Canso 9842 flew out of Wick in the late evening of the 12th June for a patrol in the North West transit zone. In the early hours of the 13th the crew found and attacked U-480 in position 6410N 00011W. A flash report to that effect was sent and nothing further was heard. Sherman managed to ditch the Canso, which had been badly damaged. Five of the crew got out of the aircraft, but the badly burned Sherman was swept away before his crew could get him into the dinghy. Two other members of the crew were lost. Search and Rescue

(SAR) aircraft were ordered out, but nothing was found as the actual position of the ditching was south west of the position in the SOS message.

Conditions in the dinghy were terrible. There was no food, no water and no survival gear. After a week all except Flight Sergeant J. E. Roberts drank sea water and they began to die of exposure. A Norwegian fishing vessel chanced upon the dinghy and Roberts was rescued and taken to Alesund, seriously ill. However, he survived and was made a POW.

U-480 was a type VIIC commanded by Oberleutnant zur See Hans-Joachim Forster and was not sunk until 1945. On 24th June Flt Lt D. E. Hornell RCAF and crew in Canso 9754 were operating out of Wick. North East of the Faeroes, in position 6300N 00050E, they sighted U-1225 commanded by Oberleutnant zur See Ernst Sauerberg. They attacked immediately and met heavy flak, hitting the starboard wing and engine and setting the aircraft on fire. Hornell pressed home the attack, releasing four DCs in a straddle across the bow of the U-boat. At the same time the starboard engine fell off. Hornell, aided by his co-pilot, Fg. Off. B. C. Denomy, landed on the water and all the eight-man crew got into the four-man dinghy. A No 333 squadron Catalina flew over the scene later and saw wreckage from U-1225. Hornell's crew were in the sea for 21 hours before they were rescued. He and his Flight Engineers, Sergeant D. Scott and Sergeant F. St. Laurent, did not survive. David Hornell was awarded the Victoria Cross, his co-pilot Fg. Off. Denomy the DSO, his navigator, Fg. Off. Matheson and WOP, Fg. Off. Campbell the DFC, and the other two WOPs, F/Sgt I. J. Bodconoff and F/Sgt S. R. Cole, the DFM.

On 30th June Flt Lt R. E. McBride and crew in Canso 9841 found and attacked U-478 commanded by Oberleutnant zur See Rudolf Rademacher in position 6327N 00050W. McBride attacked and attracted return fire, hitting the port wing. The DCs failed to release. McBride remained in the vicinity of U-478 while his wireless operator homed in a No 86 Squadron Liberator, captained by Fg. Off. N. E. M. Smith. The Liberator finished the boat with a stick of DCs.

On 4 August Fg. Off. W. O. Marshall RCAF and crew, in the vicinity of convoy UR 130, gained a visual sighting of a wake at three miles and then identified it as a U-Boat. An attack was made with three depth charges from 50 feet, with a follow-up attack of a 600lb anti-submarine bomb. No results were observed, but the boat, which was U-300, a type VIIc/41 commanded by Oberleutnant zur See Fritz Hein, was damaged and had to return to Trondheim.

No 172 Squadron's Wellington HF168, flown by Plt. Off. W. N. Armstrong RCAF and crew, was co-operating with No 6 Escort Group on 13 January 1944. On the basis of a sighting report from an aircraft from the escort carrier USS *Block Island*, they investigated and found a surfaced U-Boat in position 4415N 02038W. This was U-231, commanded by Kapitänleutnant Wolfgang Wenzel. Armstrong dropped three DCs on his first run, but the aircraft was hit and the rear gunner, Fg. Off. B. W. Heard, was badly wounded. The pilot made further attacks, but had return to base to seek help for his gunner. U-231 was abandoned and the crew rescued by USS *Block Island*. Armstrong and Heard were awarded DFCs.

On 30 January 1944, Wellington MP813, captained by

Flight Sergeant L. Richards, departed Chivenor for an overnight Percussion sortie. It was never heard of again and may have been shot down by U-364, commanded by Oberleutnant zur See Paul-Heinrich Sass in position 4525N 00515W. A No 304 squadron crew may have witnessed the end of this crew. While homing on a radar contact they saw a Leigh Light and explosions, which may have been DCs or the aircraft hitting the sea. The operations record book of U-608, commanded by Oberleutnant zur See Wolfgang Reisener, reports firing on an aircraft, but this may have been the No 304 squadron aircraft, which was fired upon. Recent research indicates that U-364 may have been sunk by a No 502 squadron Halifax on 29 January 1944. The situation is confused.

On 4 February 1944 Fg. Off. C. S. Rowland and crew in Wellington HF282 located U-763 in position 4539N 00640W. This was after No 53 Squadron had attacked her. Rowland attacked with DCs but missed, receiving some flak damage which caused him to return to base. U-763 was located again by a Halifax from No 502 Squadron.

On 13 March 1944 Fg. Off. J. P. Finnessey and crew were escorting convoy ON 227 when they gained a radar contact on to which they homed. They sighted a surfaced U-Boat in position 4613N 02728W, which they attacked with depth charges. No results were observed, so marine markers were dropped and a locating report was sent. This contact, which was U-575, a type VIIc commanded by Oberleutnant zur See Wolfgang Boehmer, was prosecuted to destruction by a No 206 Squadron Fortress, a No 220 Squadron Fortress, three ships from TG21.11 and three aircraft from the escort carrier USS *Brogue*.

On 13th June Plt. Off. L. G. Harris and crew were on patrol in Wellington MP789. They found and, with the aid of the Leigh Light, attacked U-270 in position 4759N 00528W with six DCs. A short while later the crew saw an explosion and a fire on the sea near the boat. This was the end of Flt Lt Carmichael and crew in a No 53 Squadron Liberator. U-270, a type VIIc commanded by Kapitänleutnant Paul-Friedrich Otto, was damaged in the attacks and was forced to return to base. Harris was given the credit for this and he received the DFC.

Flt. Lt. L. H. Such and crew set off on anti-submarine patrol in the Bay in the evening of 29th July. A wireless message was received from them a little after midnight on the 30th, indicating that they were about to make an attack on a U-boat. Nothing further was heard. U-618, commanded by Oberleutnant zur See Erich Faust, reported an attack and the gunners shot the aircraft down.

On 12th August Plt. Off. D. S. Bielby and crew in NB833 on a Rover 11 patrol gained a radar contact at 10 miles. Homing in, the crew saw U-766 commanded by Oberleutnant zur See Hans-Dietrich Wilke at three miles, at which point the U-boat opened fire in position 4706N 00409W. Bielby dropped six DCs from 30 feet. The U-Boat was observed turning in circles and an oil patch was seen. Bielby's WOP homed in three Liberators, a Halifax and a Wellington, but U-766 had dived and disappeared. On 14th August Fg. Off. D. A. Adams RCAF and crew apparently made contact with U-445 en route Brest to La Pallice, as was U-766. Adams and crew failed to return. On 27th August Fg. Off. G. E. Whiteley and crew were on patrol in the Bay. Just after midnight a weak message was received in Brevity Code and this caused concern such that other Coastal Command aircraft were sent to search for them. The crew had found U-534, commanded by Kapitänleutnant Herbert Nollau, just out of Bordeaux in position 4528N 00228W. This boat had entered the Gironde on 13th August under attack from Halifaxes from Nos 58 and 502 Squadrons. Whiteley had attacked with four DCs, which had missed but his aircraft had received flak damage, causing it to crash. Warrant Officer G. H. Bulley, WOP/WG of the RCAF, went down with the aircraft but managed to break out through the astrodome. He then found other survivors and helped Whiteley and Sgt. J. W. C. Ford, both of whom had been injured, into the dinghy. Fg. Off. R. B. Gray RCAF, the navigator and Bulley remained in the water, holding on to the dinghy. Gray had a severe leg wound; possibly he had lost part of his leg - and he eventually succumbed to his injuries and the cold. They were rescued by a No 461 Squadron Sunderland some 15 hours after they had been shot down. Whiteley was awarded the DSO, Ford the DFM and Gray the GC. The squadron moved to Limavady in Northern Ireland in September 1944 with its Wellington XIVs.

No 179 Squadron was part of the attack on U-343 on 8 January, 1944. The OC Wg. Cdr. J. H. Greswell DFC and crew, made an attack, followed by Fg. Off. W. F. M. Davidson and crew, who found the boat in position 3654N 00145W south west of Cartagena. He attacked with DCs but was hit in the port wing. It was on fire and he had no alternative but to ditch. Only Davidson survived and he was rescued by HMS *Active* the following day. He was awarded the DFC.

On the night of 1st/2nd March 1944, Sqn. Ldr. K. G. Knott and crew took off from Gibraltar and were near Cape St Vincent at 500 feet over a calm sea and no cloud when the radar operator gained two contacts, one at eleven miles and the other at twelve miles. The nearest was a fishing boat but the other, illuminated by Leigh Light, was a surfaced U-Boat. This was U-421, commanded by Oberleutnant zur See Hans Kolbus. The front gunner opened fire but his guns jammed. The U-Boat returned fire, hitting the starboard engine and blowing up the radar. Knott attacked with six DCs, which according to the boat's operations record book, missed. The book also states that three DCs were dropped and that the aircraft was a Sunderland! Knott and crew set off for Gibraltar, which they reached after a nervous three hours on one engine. The squadron moved to Predannack in April 1944. On 7 June 1944 Flt/Lt W. J. Hill and crew sighted a periscope followed by its owner, U-989, but they were too close for an attack in position 4827N 00512W. Turning for an attack Hill was beaten to it by a Liberator from No 224 Squadron! Turning again, Hill and crew lost sight of U-989 but found U-963.

When homing on to this boat a third was sighted, and this was U-415. This was closer and Hill changed targets, attacking with six DCs and achieving a good straddle. The Liberator was still about and drew the flak away from the Wellington, which strafed the U-Boat. At this point U-963 opened fire on Hill, who then left the area, being out of DCs. Shortly after, a bright flash was seen and this was probably the Liberator being shot down.

This was a very confusing night. U-989, a type VIIc

commanded by Kapitänleutnant Hardo Rodler von Roithberg, U-963, a type VIIc commanded by Oberleutnant zur See Boddenburg, U-256, a type VIIc commanded by Oberleutnant zur See Brauel and U-415 a type VIIc commanded by Oberleutnant zur See Herbert Werner were all damaged in the vicinity of 4827N 00512W. Amongst all this confusion, U-Boat.net now believes that U-629 was sunk by a No 53 Squadron Liberator flown by Flt. Lt. Carmichael and crew. All U-Boats, except U-415, were forced to return to Brest. A No 407 Squadron Wellington, two No 224 Squadron Liberators and one No 53 Squadron Liberator, captain Sqn. Ldr. G. Crawford, were shot down, while one No 502 Squadron Halifax was damaged. Who shot down who and who sank who is still not known for sure.

The squadron moved to Chivenor in early September, Benbecula in late September and St Eval in November. In this last month it exchanged its Wellingtons for Warwick Vs.

No 190 Squadron was disbanded on 1 January 1944 and renumbered as No 210 Squadron.

No 201 Squadron moved to Pembroke Dock in April.

On 7 June 1944 Flt. Lt. L. H. Baveystock DFC DFM and crew were engaged on a creeping line ahead (CLA) search for a U-Boat that had been attacked by a No 201 Squadron aircraft on 5 June. About half an hour after arriving on task a radar contact was gained at nine miles. A homing was initiated, a locating report sent and the depth charges run out. At half a mile flares were dropped. No U-Boat was sighted, but a swirl was seen. Meanwhile a No 461 Squadron Sunderland was homing on to the same contact and in the light of the flares that it had dropped the aircraft was seen to pass under the No 201 Squadron aircraft. Baveystock commenced baiting or gambit tactics, holding off at around four to eight miles and then 12 miles from the datum. Then, after about two hours, a radar contact was gained at 11 miles and a homing commenced. The intention to drop flares was cancelled as the U-boat opened fire. As the aircraft began its attack the front gunner opened fire, followed by the pilot with his four fixed guns and then the midupper. A stick of six depth charges was dropped, one of them exploding under the centre of the hull. The contact disappeared from the radar and no results were observed. The boat was U-955, a type VIIc commanded by Oberleutnant zur See Hans Baden, and it had been sunk in this attack in position 4513N 00830W. Baveystock was awarded a Bar to his DFC and Flight Sergeants D. E. South and D. J. McCurrie were awarded DFMs.

Before take off, Baveystock had been informed that his father had died (not unexpectedly). On return he went on compassionate leave. While he was away, Sqn. Ldr. W. D. B. Ruth took over the crew. On 11th June 1944 Sqn Ldr W. D. B. Ruth DFC and Baveystock's crew were shot down, possibly by U-333 commanded by Kapitänleutnant Peter Cremer in the course of an attack. Another possibility is that the crew might have been shot down by U-993, commanded by Oberleutnant Kurt Hilbig in position 4750N 00600W, also in the course of an attack. There is a loss list which indicates that this aircraft was shot down by U-437, but Norman Franks states that this was incorrect. Some confusion exists as to whether or not it was this aircraft or a No 228 squadron aircraft.

On 11 July 1944 Flt. Lt. W. Walters DFC was supervising a new crew. They were tasked for an area between 4500N and 4700N and 005W and 006W. Further aircraft were to join in this area. The second pilot gained a visual sighting of a Schnorkel and then the U-Boat. Radar contact was gained at the same time at eight and a half miles. A stick of six depth charges (one hung up) was dropped and gave a good straddle. Wreckage was seen which Walters thought could have been decoy material, but it turned out that they had sunk U-1222, a type IXc/40 commanded by Kapitänleutnant Heinz Bielfeld returning to La Rochelle from the Nova Scotia coast.

On 11th August, Fg. Off. A. H. W. Mold and crew in ML768 were on a Rover 11 patrol 50 miles west of Lisbon. At 1800 feet, in haze with no moon, two radar contacts were gained at seven miles together with an aircraft contact. Mold commenced a homing and at half a mile he ordered the dropping of flares. Heavy flak came up which wounded two of the crew. The boat was U-766, commanded by Oberleutnant zur See Hans-Dietrich Wilke en route Brest to La Pallice. There was a second unidentified, U-boat which opened fire. The aircraft contact turned out to be a Sunderland from No 461 Squadron, the crew of which saw the attack but on flying over the scene saw nothing, the two boats having submerged. Wold's aircraft had reached its Prudent Limit of Endurance and he headed for home.

On 18 August 1944 Flt. Lt. L. H. Baveystock DFC DFM and crew were on a patrol in the Bay of Biscay to locate U-Boats that were evacuating high-ranking officers and technicians from Brest and La Pallice to Bordeaux. A visual contact on a periscope was gained at four miles when Baveystock was sitting on the Elsan. The Klaxon was sounded and Baveystock rushed to the cockpit. The first pilot, Fg. Off. B. W. Landers, remained in the left hand seat and ran out the depth charges. The second pilot, Fg. Off. D. D. MacGregor RCAF, got out of the right hand seat and Baveystock got into it. Landers positioned the aircraft and then Baveystock took over and shortened the stick spacing from 60 feet to 50 feet. The spacing is the distance between each charge in the stick. He then dropped a stick of six depth charges and obtained a good straddle. Flying back over the area it was seen that "the sea was a frothing mass of escaping air, oil, debris and German Navy Plotting charts", said Baveystock. The boat was U-107, a type IXb commanded by Leutnant zur See Fritz. Baveystock was awarded an Immediate DSO. The squadron moved to Castle Archdale in November 1944 with its Sunderland IIIs. It disposed of its Mark IIs in March.

No 202 Squadron was involved with the attack on U-343, together with No 36 and 179 squadrons on 8 January 1944. Flt. Lt. J. Finch and crew were attracted by a No 179 Squadron Wellington attacking a U-boat. Finch made an attack, but his flight engineer, Flight Sergeant V. Sheridan, was hit and the aircraft damaged. Finch headed for home. Despite damage, U-343 arrived in Toulon. On 24 February 1944 Flt. Lt. J. Finch and crew intercepted a message reporting a radar contact, probable U-Boat, in position 3551N 00645W. Arriving in the area, depth charge attacks were seen, two destroyers, HMS *Wishart* and HMS *Anthony*, two PBYs (US Navy Catalinas) from VP 63, and a US Navy Ventura from VB 127. Finch made an attack without result. The boat was U-761, a type VIIc commanded by Oberleutnant zur See Horst Geider and en route Brest to the Mediterranean. The boat surfaced and then exploded. There were some survivors, including the commanding officer. The kill was shared between the two PBYs, the Venture and the two destroyers. The boat went down in position 3555N 00545W. This was the first of three U-Boats sunk by VP 63 while under Coastal Command control. The squadron moved to Castle Archdale from Gibraltar in September 1944 with its Catalina Ibs.

No 206 Squadron was in the Azores at the turn of the year. Flt. Lt. A. D. Beaty and crew were sent off to assist a No 172 Squadron Wellington which had reported a U-Boat in position 4613N 02728W. This was U-575, a type VIIc commanded by Oberleutnant zur See Wolfgang Boehmer. Flt. Sgt. J. J. V. Glazebrook recalls that navigation was the problem as it was all dead reckoning in those days. They regularly flew 12½ hour sorties in Mid Atlantic with no navigation aids and returned to an island ten miles long with no alternative airfield within 1000 miles.

The navigator was accurate and they found the Wellington's Marine Markers. Then a surfacing U-Boat was sighted, but the aircraft was too high for an attack. Having lost the element of surprise, they tried to send a sighting report, but the Wireless Operator could not make contact. The problem was, should they attack and risk being shot down without sending the report or should they hold off and risk the boat diving?

They attacked with a stick of four depth charges from 50 feet and gained a good straddle which damaged the boat. They then climbed and were able to send a sighting and attack report. A Fortress from No 220 Squadron was homed in and Task Group 21.11, consisting of HMCS *Prince Rupert*, USS *Haverfield* and USS *Hobson* arrived. The No 220 Squadron Fortress attacked, causing damage, three aircraft from the escort carrier USS *Brogue* also attacked and the boat was finally sunk after she had surfaced and was shelled by the ships. The kill was shared between all participants.

The squadron came back from Lajes to Davidstow Moor, Cornwall in March 1944, where it exchanged its Fortress IIs for Liberator VIs. On 6 January 1944 Flt. Lt. A. J. Pinhorn and crew located U-270, commanded by Oberleutnant zur See Paul-Freidrich Otto, in position 4353N 02332W. A locating report was sent and nothing further was heard. The boat's operations record book notes that the Fortress made two strafing attacks, but no bombs or DCs were dropped. On the third attack flak set the starboard inner engine on fire. Four DCs were dropped and the aircraft then crashed. The boat was forced to return to St. Nazaire. In April, the squadron moved to St Eval. In July it moved to Leuchars.

On 5th July U-319, commanded by Oberleutnant zur See Johann Clemens, departed Stavanger on anti-invasion duty, being stationed off south west Norway. The deception practiced by the Allies as to where the real invasion would land was apparently still working. Nothing further was heard from this boat. It is believed that Fg. Off. D. W. Thynne and crew in Liberator EV947 located and sank her in the vicinity of 5740N 00500E. The aircraft had taken off at 0550 on 15th July and nothing further was heard. On 16th the body of Liberator crew member Sgt N. Hilton was recovered in the area of the believed sinking.

No 210 Squadron was reformed at Sullom Voe on 1 January 1944 by renumbering No 190 Squadron, taking over their Catalina Ibs and IVs. There was a detachment to Pembroke Dock. The Mark Ibs were disposed of in March 1944. On 25 February 1944 Sqn. Ldr. F. J. French and crew had been tasked to escort convoy JW 57 but they did not make contact. However, a radar contact was gained at 24 miles and on homing in a visual sighting was gained of a decks-awash U-boat in position 7026N 01240E. This was U-601, a type VIIc commanded by Oberleutnant zur See Otto Hansen. The boat opened fire on the Catalina but failed to score a hit. French attacked with two depth charges. Wreckage was seen, together with some survivors. Contact was then lost in a snowstorm. French was awarded the DFC.

On 18 May 1944 Fg. Off. B. Bastable and crew gained a visual sighting of a surfaced U-Boat from 200 feet at around six miles in position 6333N 0146E. An attack was made with a stick of six depth charges, which gave a good straddle. The front gunner and the port blister gunner opened fire on the run in. The boat was seen to sink stern first. This was U-241, a type VIIc commanded by Oberleutnant zur See Arno Werr. Bastable and the front gunner, Warrant Officer R. Henderson, were awarded immediate DFCs.

On 24 May 1944 Captain F. W. L. Maxwell SAAF and crew gained a visual sighting of a U-Boat at five miles in position 6503N 00459E. The boat was U-476, a type VIIc commanded by Oberleutnant zur See Otto Niethmann.

As the Catalina homed in for an attack, U-476 opened fire. Maxwell dropped a stick of six depth charges, the last of which landed alongside. The boat was seen to spin around almost full circle and then sink. It resurfaced, then appeared to sink once again. A snow shower prevented any further observations. U-476 was so badly damaged that it later foundered and 21 survivors were rescued by U-990, which was sunk the following day by a Liberator of No 59 Squadron. On 28 June 1944, Fg. Off. J. C. Campbell and crew sighted a ship's balloon in position 6234N OOO46E and shot it down. Some two and a half hours later a radar contact was gained at four and a half miles and was resolved into a visual sighting of a U-Boat. This was U-396, a type VIIc commanded by Kapitänleutnant Hilmar Siemon. The boat opened fire without success and a stick of depth charges was dropped, which missed. A follow-up attack was made with guns and then U-396 dived. Another wake was seen in the vicinity. U-396 had been damaged and had to return to Bergen.

On 17th July Flt Lt J. A. Cruickshank and crew were on patrol in Catalina JV928 over the North Norwegian Sea, west of the Lofoten Islands, when a radar contact was gained in position 6835N 00600E. The crew homed in and sighted a surfaced U-Boat. Cruickshank attacked immediately, facing heavy flak which killed the navigator, Fg. Off. J. C. Dickson, and wounded four others including the captain. The attack continued and the boat was destroyed. The second pilot turned the aircraft for home and Cruickshank was taken to the rest bunk and first aid was administered. On reaching Sullom Voe, Cruickshank, because the second pilot was inexperienced, insisted on landing the Catalina, which he did safely, running it onto the beach. He was given a blood transfusion while still in his seat and then he and the other wounded were taken to hospital. He was awarded the Victoria Cross and the second pilot the DFM. Dickson's son had been born a month previously, but he never saw him.

There has been some confusion over which boat was sunk in this engagement. Initially it was believed that it was U-347, commanded by Oberleutnant zur See Johann de Buhr. At the same time U-361, commanded by Kapitänleutnant Hans Seidel, was believed to have been sunk by Plt. Off M. G. Moseley and crew in a No 86 Squadron Liberator in position 6936N 00833E. Further investigation reveals that the situation is reversed. The following day, 18th July, Fg. Off. R. W. G. Vaughan and crew in Catalina JV929 were on patrol again in the area west of the Lofoten Islands in a 30 x 40 mile area when a surfaced U-Boat was sighted from 15 miles in position 6825N 00951E. This was U-742, commanded by Kapitänleutnant Heinz Schwassman. Vaughan attacked immediately and the U-Boat opened fire. The aircraft was hit and two crewmen wounded, one of them Fg. Off. K. S. Freeman, a WOP/AG, seriously. The starboard engine was hit and the port fuel tank holed, causing a large fuel leak. DCs were dropped accurately. The U-Boat was seen to be sinking and around 40 survivors and bodies were in the water. The Catalina returned to the Shetlands Islands despite the fuel leak. Unnecessary equipment, including the guns, was jettisoned. The aircraft could not quite make Sullom Voe but a successful landing was made on a beach nearby. The navigator reported that there was a long intelligence de-briefing when the crew were in no state to appreciate the necessity for it. Vaughan was awarded the DFC.

No 220 Squadron remained at Lajes. On 13 March 1944 Fg. Off. W. R. Travell and crew were briefed to assist a No 206 Squadron Fortress that was searching for a U-Boat (U-575) which had been reported by a No 172 Wellington. Arriving on the scene they found an oil slick in the form of an arrow head, which they attacked with two depth charges. The Fortress could only carry four DCs when it was flying long range. The boat was finally finished off by warships and carrier aircraft. It added Fortress IIIs to its inventory in July 1944.

On 26 September Flt. Lt. A. F. Wallace and crew were escorting convoy CU 40 North West of the Azores. They located the SS *Irish Rose*, which had broken down. Then a locating report was intercepted from Flt. Lt. M. L. H. Carter's crew, also from No 220 squadron, which gave a U-Boat position at 4255N 03605W. Wallace and crew joined Carter and Flt. Lt. A. R. Chisholm and crew, again from No 220 Squadron. Then Fg. Off. A. Paruk RCAF, Wallace's second pilot, gained a sighting of a periscope wake in position 4318N 03629W. Wallace attacked with a stick of three depth charges from 50 feet and this gave a good straddle on the boat, which was now surfacing. Oil, debris and bodies were seen, signalling the end of U-871, a type IXD2 commanded by Kapitänleutnant Erwin Ganzer. Liberator VIs were added to the inventory in December 1944.

No 224 Squadron was still at St Eval at the beginning of the year. On 2 January 1944 Plt. Off J. E. Edwards and crew on a Percussion patrol gained a radar contact at 20 miles from 1000 feet. They homed in and, striking the Leigh Light, they saw U-625 commanded by Kapitänleutnant Hans Benker. They were fired at immediately and hits were scored, wounding one of the W/Ops. The aircraft orbited and homed in another aircraft. However, the injuries to the W/Op were so serious that Edwards decided to return to base. He left a marine marker on the last known position (LKP) of the boat. Fg. Off. E. Allen and crew arrived. They found the marker and then located a U-Boat, which they attacked with eight DCs. This was not U-625 but probably U-421 commanded by Oberleutnant zur See Hans Kolbus. Neither boat was sunk.

On 3 January 1944 Fg. Off. H. R. Facey RCAF and crew were homed in by a No 612 Squadron Wellington to their datum, that of U-373 which the crew had attacked. Fg. Off. F. H. Hackman, the navigator in the nose, sighted the U-boat. Facey positioned for an attack and was fired on by the boat. The aircraft gunners replied. Without using the Leigh Light, an attack with a stick of eight depth charges was made. Returning to the datum, the Liberator was fired on. Three radar contacts were gained but nothing was sighted. The boat had been damaged and returned to La Pallice. She sailed again on 7 June 1944 and was sunk by a No 224 Squadron Liberator the following day.

On 19 March 1944 a Liberator flown by Flt. Lt. R. Dunn and crew on a Percussion sortie failed to return. They may have been shot down by U-256, commanded by Oberleutnant zur See Wilhelm Brauel, who reported an attack by such an aircraft with six bombs. The boat's flak shot it down.

On 24 May Flt. Lt. E. W. Lindsay and crew gained a radar contact from 300 feet at 12 miles. Homing in, the contact was illuminated by Leigh Light in position 4907N

00441W and attacked with a stick of eight depth charges. No results were observed, although the navigator thought he saw some debris. Later a conning tower was sighted in position 4903N 00411W and attacked with a stick of six depth charges, but again no results were seen. The boat was U-736, a type VIIc commanded by Oberleutnant zur See Reinhard Reff and had been attacked earlier by a No 612 Squadron Wellington. It returned badly damaged to Brest.

On 7 June Fg. Off. R. H. Buchan-Hepburn RAAF and crew joined in the action against U-415, U-963 and U-989 with the No 179 Squadron Wellington flown by Flt. Lt. Hill and crew. After several attacks this crew was shot down by U-415, commanded by Oberleutnant zur See Herbert Werner. For further reading on this see Norman Franks *U-Boat versus Aircraft*. Fg. Off. E. E. Allen DFC RCAF and crew were probably shot down by U-256 commanded by Oberleutnant zur See Wilhelm Brauel.

On 8 June 1944 Flt. Lt. K. O. Moore RCAF and crew were told by their Commanding Officer that there were a number of U-Boats in his area and that they should get at least two. This, of course, was a joke and Moore joked back, replying that they would get them in half an hour. In the early hours they were at 500 feet when a radar contact was gained at 12 miles. Placing the target up-moon, Moore and his radar operator carried a homing and at three miles a surfaced submarine was sighted. The radar was switched off at two and a half miles to avoid detection by the U-Boat's detection equipment. An attack was made with a stick of six depth charges from 50 feet in position 4827N 00547W, which gave a perfect straddle. The boat was lifted out of the water and then wreckage and oil was seen. This was thought to be U-629, a type VIIc commanded by Oberleutnant zur See Hans-Helmet Bugs; it had been sunk and there were no survivors. U-Boat.net now believes that this boat was U-441, commanded by Kapitänleutnant Klaus Hartmann. U-629 was sunk the previous day in position 4834N 00523W, probably by a No 53 Squadron Liberator, flown by Flt. Lt. Carmichael and crew.

Twenty-five minutes later, a further radar contact was gained at six miles at 700 feet. A homing was carried out and at two and a half miles a U-Boat was sighted by the navigator, Warrant Officer T. J. Mcdowell, in the bombaimer's position. Moore manoeuvred the aircraft to put the target in the moonpath and then an attack from 50 feet with a stick of six depth charges was made. The boat was seen to sink and three dinghies and survivors were seen. The boat was U-373, a type VIIc commanded by Oberleutnant zur See Detlev von Lehsten and had been sunk in position 4810N 00531W. The survivors were rescued later.

This was the first time an aircrew had sunk two U-Boats in a single sortie. Moore received the DSO and the American Silver Star, while McDowell and Warrant Officer W. P. Foster, WOP/AG, received DFCs. The Flight Engineer, Sgt. Hamer, received the DFM.

On 11 June Flt Lt J. W. A. Posnett and crew took off for a patrol in the South West approaches. They were buzzed by some Spitfires shortly after take off and then located an empty dinghy. This they attempted to sink by gunfire. In the early hours of the morning of the 12th the radar operator gained a contact at six miles. Homing in, a surfaced U-Boat was sighted with the aid of the Leigh Light in position 4919N 00415W. The boat opened fire, hitting the No 4 engine and damaging the bomb release system. An attack was made with depth charges, but only one fell due to the damage to the system. The ailerons, flaps and bomb doors were badly damaged, so Flt. Lt. Posnett turned for base. The Flight Engineer, Sergeant K. B. Bettany stood on the narrow catwalk in the bomb bay and jettisoned the remaining depth charges manually. This enabled the aircraft to gain more height and Bettany was finally able to close the bomb doors. The boat was probably U-269, commanded by Oberleutnant zur See Georg Uhl. This cannot be confirmed as this boat was sunk by HMS *Bickerton* on 25 June 1944.

In the early hours of 12th June 1944 Flt. Lt. J. E. Jenkinson RNZAF and crew took off for a patrol in the West Channel. The last that was heard was a report at 0305 giving position as 4837N 00526W and mentioning U-Boats. It was at first thought that the aircraft was shot down by U-441, commanded by Kapitänleutnant Klaus Hartmann, but that boat was probably sunk by Flt. Lt. K. O. Moore RCAF and crew of No 224 Squadron on 8th June 1944. There is no evidence from the Kriegsmarine that they shot down Jenkinson and crew.

On 18 September 1944 Fg. Off. P. M. Hill and crew gained a radar contact at 15 miles. A homing was initiated and the Leigh Light switched on at one mile to reveal a surfaced submarine. This was U-1228, a type IXc/40 commanded by Oberleutnant zur See Friedrich-Wilhelm Marienfeld. A stick of depth charges was dropped from 200 feet, but no result was observed. The navigator/bombaimer was also the Leigh Light operator and did not have time to use the bomb sight. The drop was therefore a calculated guess. To an experienced operator that was as good as a sight. A follow-up gun attack was started, but the radar contact was lost at two miles. The U-Boat had been damaged and was compelled to return to Bergen. On 19 September 1944 Flt. Lt. H. J. Rayner and crew gained a radar contact at 15 miles and commenced a homing. The boat was sighted on the surface and a stick of six depth charges was dropped. Gun fire was exchanged.

This was U-867, a type IXc/40 commanded by Kapitän zur See Arved Muhlendahl and it had been attacked by an aircraft from No 248 Squadron the previous day. The boat was damaged and the captain was forced to scuttle the boat in position 6215N 00150E. Photos show crewmen launching dinghies over the side and some 50 men were seen in the water. However, none survived.

On 24 September Sqn. Ldr. J. C. T. Downey and crew were flying a box patrol and gained a radar contact at seven miles in position 6100N 00407E. A homing was initiated, modified to keep the Aurora Borealis behind them, and a surfaced submarine was sighted. A stick of depth charges was dropped across the stern, but no results were observed. The boat was U-763, a type VIIc commanded by Leutnant zur See Kurt Braun and was en route from La Rochelle to Bergen. The boat reached Bergen, but the damage from this attack kept her there for two weeks. On 30 October 1944 Flt. Lt. W. S. Blackden and crew gained a radar contact at 15 miles. A homing was commenced, during which a Wellington (from No 407

Squadron) was seen together with its Leigh Light and two Marine Markers. At three quarters of a mile the Liberator switched on its Leigh Light and saw a surfaced submarine, which opened fire. The boat was diving as a stick of depth charges was released. No results were observed. The boat was U-1061, a type VIIf, torpedo transporter, commanded by Oberleutnant zur See Otto Hinrichs and it had been damaged. The squadron took its Liberator Vs to Milltown, Moray in September 1944, exchanging them for Liberator VIs in December.

No 228 Squadron remained at Pembroke Dock with its Sunderland IIIs. On 7 June 1944 Flt. Lt. C. G. D. Lancaster DFC and crew gained a radar contact at 15 miles. A homing was commenced, flares were dropped near the datum and a surfaced U-Boat was sighted. An attack was carried from 100 feet with a stick of depth charges. No results were observed but the boat had been sunk in position 4515N 00410W. It was U-970, a type VIIc commanded by Oberleutnant zur See Hans-Heinrich Ketels. There were 13 survivors. Lancaster was awarded a Bar to his DFC. On 10 June 1944, Flt. Lt. D. Hewitt DFC and crew located and attacked what was probably U-228 commanded by Kapitänleutnant Erwin Christopherson. The boat's operations record book states that the aircraft dropped six bombs but was shot down. It also states that the aircraft was a Stirling, but the only thing common between a Stirling and a Sunderland is the maker -Short Brothers! U-Boat crew aircraft recognition was never good. This was 228 v 228, another of those rare coincidences of squadron number matching U-Boat number.

On 11th June Flt. Lt. M. E. Slaughter RCAF and crew left Pembroke Dock at 1810 hours and did not return. It is possible that the crew may have been shot down by U-333 during an attack. This boat was commanded by Kapitänleutnant Peter Cremer and was returning to La Pallice having been damaged the day before by a No 10 Squadron Sunderland. On the other hand it may have been a No 201 Squadron aircraft that was shot down. Again the situation was confused.

No 233 Squadron returned to the UK from Lajes in the Azores in March 1944, going to Blakehill Farm, north west of Swindon. It gave up its Hudsons in exchange for Dakotas and became a transport squadron.

No 251 Squadron was reformed at Reykjavik in August 1944 from No 1407 Flight. It was equipped with Hudson IIIs, Ventura Is and Anson Is.

No 304 Squadron was at Preddanack. On 4 January 1944 Fg. Off. H. Czyzun and crew gained a radar contact at seven miles and homed in, sighting a surfaced U-Boat which was U-629, a type VIIc commanded by Oberleutnant zur See Hans-Helmut Bugs. An attack was made with a stick of six depth charges and 1200 rounds from the guns. The boat dived and nothing further was seen. The boat was damaged and forced to return to Brest. This crew was attacked on 26 March 1944 by two enemy aircraft. Sgt. K. Baranski, the rear gunner, shot down one of them and was awarded the DFM.

Flight Sergeant S. Czekaski and crew, on patrol just after midnight on 31 January, were homing on to a radar contact when they saw a Leigh Light and some explosions. They may have witnessed the demise of No 172 squadron's MP813. Czekaski was fired upon. The squadron moved to Chivenor in February 1944 with its Wellington XIVs.

On 12 March a Wellington attacked U-629, still

commanded by Oberleutnant zur See Hans-Helmut Bugs, and forced her to return to Brest. On 29 April 1944 a Wellington, HF386, attacked U-473 in position 4530N 01100W. No damage was incurred by either side. On 18 June 1944 Flt. Lt. L. Antoniewicz and crew gained a visual sighting of a wake and then a U-Boat and dropped a stick of six depth charges from 100 feet, straddling the boat. At the same time a second U-Boat was seen. Oil and wreckage from the attack was seen. The target was believed to have been U-988, a type VIIc commanded by Oberleutnant zur See Erich Dobberstein. The squadron moved to Benbecula in September with a detachment to Limavady, Northern Ireland.

No 311 Squadron moved to Predannack in February 1944 with its Liberator Vs. On 24 June 1944 Fg. Off. J. Vella and crew gained a visual sighting of a U-Boat in position 4900N 00540W and attacked with depth charges and rockets. The boat was U-971, a type VIIc commanded by Oberleutnant zur See Walter Zeplien and it had already been damaged by several air attacks. The last was by No 407 Squadron four days previously. Zeplien decided to scuttle the boat and 52 out of 53 of his crew were picked up by the destroyers HMS *Eskimo* and HMCS *Haida*. The squadron moved to Tain in August.

On 4 November 1944, Fg. Off. F. Pavelka and crew and Sgt. V. Novak and crew located a run-aground U-Boat, U-1060, on Fleina Island. This boat had originally been attacked by a Firefly Mark 1 of No 1771 Squadron, Fleet Air Arm, on board HMS *Implacable*, on 27 October 1944. It was a type VIIf torpedo transporter, commanded by Oberleutnant zur See Herbert Brammer. Pavelka attacked and then two Halifaxes from No 502 Squadron joined in the attack and the boat was seen to keel over. Flak from shore batteries and ships was experienced but none of the aircraft was hit. The sinking is recorded in position 6524N 01200E.

No 330 Squadron disposed of its Sunderland IIs in March 1944 but retained its Mark IIIs and stayed at Sullom Voe. On 16 May 1944 S/Lt. C. T. Johnsen and crew in JM667 were operating west North West of Alesund. The front gunner gained a visual sighting of a U-boat at eight miles. This was believed to be U-668 in position 6305N 00310E, and commanded by Kapitänleutnant Wolfgang von Eickstedt. Heavy flak was met by the Sunderland but it returned fire, killing some of the U-Boat crew.

On the first attack only one DC fell. A second attack was made and flak killed the front gunner and wounded two crewmen, causing fires in the cockpit and in the front turret. Nevertheless the attack was pressed home and four DCs were dropped, apparently sinking the boat. However, the boat continued with its mission, having received minor damage. Both starboard engines of the Sunderland had been hit but fuel was jettisoned and the aircraft made it back to Sullom Voe despite severe damage. This attack was later believed to have been on U-240, but this was later shown to be wrong. U-Boat.net shows that this attack was on U-668 and that it was undamaged. U-668 surrendered in May 1945 at Narvik. U-240 was later believed to have been attacked by S/Lt Hartmann and crew from No 333 Squadron on 17 May 1944. Some sources state that this attack was on U-668. U-Boat.net states that U-240 was listed as missing on 17 May 1944 and that no explanation exists for its disappearance.

On 19 July 1944 Lt. B. Thurmann-Nielsen and crew gained a radar contact at 18 miles in position 6833N 00720E and commenced homing, remaining in cloud. At three and a half miles a surfaced U-Boat was sighted (it is daylight for 24 hours in these latitudes in July) and was attacked with a stick of six depth charges. It was a good straddle but did not sink the boat, which opened fire, causing Thurmann-Nielsen to take evasive action. The boat was U-387, a type VIIc commanded by Kapitänleutnant Rudolf Buchler. The weather was low cloud and rain. U-387 submerged shortly after the attack and had been damaged, forcing her return to Trondheim.

No 333 Squadron "A" Flight added Catalina IVs to its anti-submarine inventory in May 1944. On 17 May 1944 S/Lt. H. E. Hartmann and crew were on patrol in FP121, 125 miles west of Alesund, when they sighted a water disturbance which turned out to be a U-Boat, at first thought to be U-668 but later believed to be U-240 commanded by Oberleutnant zur See Günter Link. The Catalina was met by flak on its attack run, but fire was returned and DCs were dropped from 50 feet. A large hole was blown in the bottom of the hull and one airgunner was killed. However, the U-Boat was assessed initially to have been sunk. The Catalina returned to the River Tay and was beached, a total loss, it never flew again.

On 17 June 1944 Lt. C. F. Krafft and crew gained a visual sighting of a surfaced U-Boat in position 6306N 00202E and attacked with a stick of six depth charges. The boat was U423, a type VIIc commanded by Oberleutnant zur See Klaus Hacklander. It opened fire on the Catalina without success. On the other hand, the straddle was next to perfect and the boat sank, leaving 40 seamen in the water. None survived. In September "B" Flight moved to Banff with its Mosquitoes.

No 407 Squadron Royal Canadian Air Force with its Wellington XIVs moved to Limavady on 1 January 1944. On 6 January 1944 Fg. Off. Jordan and crew detected U-107, commanded by Kapitänleutnant Volker Simmermacher, but no action ensued. On 11 February 1944 Fg. Off. P. W. Heron RCAF and crew gained a radar contact ahead at six miles in position 6045N 01250W. A homing was initiated and at one mile the U-Boat was seen in the moonlight. This was U-283, a type VIIc, commanded by Oberleutnant zur See Gunter Ney. Heron attacked with a stick of six depth charges from 60 feet. A red glow was seen by the rear gunner, but nothing further. U-283 had been sunk. On 11 March 1944 Plt. Off. E. M. O'Donnell and crew were operating in Wellington HF311 to the West of Ireland. They were never heard of again.

U-256 may have witnessed the Wellington crash. It did not open fire on the aircraft and it is believed that it may have crashed, as it was turning in for an attack and was too low. However, it is possible that O'Donnell and crew were shot down by U-625, which was sunk a few hours later by a No 422 Squadron crew. The squadron moved to Chivenor in April.

On 4 May 1944 Flt. Lt. L. G. Bateman RCAF and crew gained a radar contact at seven miles at 500 feet in moonlight. Thus the Leigh Light was not required. A homing was carried and a surfaced U-boat was sighted in position 4604N 00920W. In the face of flak Bateman dropped a stick of six depth charges from 40 feet. Fire was not returned as the nose turret guns had jammed. Returning to the datum, nothing was sighted except for an oil slick. The boat was U-846, a type IXc/40 commanded by Oberleutnant zur See Berthold Hashagen and it had been sunk in this attack.

On 7 June 1944 Sqn. Ldr. D. W. Farrell RCAF and crew were shot down, possibly by a combination of U413, U-441, U-629, U-740 and maybe U-621. On 29 June 1944 Fg. Off. F. H. Foster and crew gained a radar contact at three miles and a homing was initiated. A descent to 200 feet was made and a surfaced U-boat was sighted in the haze. An attack was carried out with a stick of six depth charges from 100 feet, giving a good straddle. Turning for a follow-up attack, the boat was seen on the surface and it then opened fire. Shortly after, it submerged. It was U-971, a type VIIc commanded by Oberleutnant zur See Walter Zeplien, and it had been damaged. On 14th August, Fg. Off. F. A. J. Kemper and crew attacked U-766, commanded by Oberleutnant zur See Hans-Dietrich Wilke en route Brest to La Pallice. The gunners opened fire and shot the Wellington down. There was another action in this area and at a similar time involving a No 172 Squadron aircraft and U-445. This aircraft also failed to return. The squadron moved to Wick in August.

On 30 October 1944, Fg. Off. J. E. Neelin and crew gained a radar contact at five miles in position 6143N 00342E. Homing in, the crew illuminated a partly-surfaced U-Boat and attacked with a stick of six depth charges. Neelin orbited while a Liberator from No 224 Squadron attacked. Maintaining radar contact, another

Wellington from No 407 Squadron was homed in. When daylight broke oil slicks could be seen. Opinion was that there may have been two U-Boats. That which had been attacked was U-1061, a type VIIf torpedo transporter, commanded by Oberleutnant zur See Otto Hinrichs. It had been damaged such that she could not dive. She went to Maaloy Sound. The squadron went back to Chivenor in November.

On 30 December 1944 Sqn. Ldr. C. W. Taylor DFC RCAF and crew gained a visual sighting in the moonlight of a periscope and a schnorkel mast in position 5005N 00231W. The Wellington homed, illuminated the target with the Leigh Light and attacked with a stick of six depth charges. The aircraft remained until PLE but nothing was seen. However, the boat had been sunk. It was U-772, a type VIIc commanded by Kapitänleutnant Ewald Rademacher and had been withdrawing from its attack on convoy TBC 1 when it was attacked by this aircraft.

No 415 Squadron, Royal Canadian Air Force, moved to East Moor in July 1944 and left Coastal Command for Bomber Command. The Albacore Flight became No 119 Squadron.

No 422 Squadron Royal Canadian Air Force was still at St. Angelo at the turn of the year. On 10 March 1944 Warrant Officer W. F. Morton RCAF and crew were on their first operational sortie. The screen pilot and captain was Flt. Lt. S. W. Butler and the screen navigator was Flt. Lt. A. Ormorod. While en route to escort convoy SC 154 a visual sighting was gained of a U-Boat at six miles from 1000 feet. Butler, who was flying the aircraft, took it down to 50 feet in the face of flak and dropped a stick of six depth charges, straddling the boat. The Sunderland was hit in the hull below the waterline. The boat was U-625, a type VIIc commanded by Oberleutnant zur See Siegfried Straub. It submerged and then resurfaced, moving slowly and to the starboard. The Sunderland orbited for 90 minutes and then the boat signalled by light "Fine Bombish". The crew abandoned ship. U-625 sank in position 5235N02019W and there were no survivors. Butler was awarded the DFC.

A few hours earlier this boat had been attacked by Plt. Off. E. M. O'Donnell and crew from No 407 Squadron but the Wellington was shot down. The Squadron moved to Castle Archdale, Northern Ireland in April 1944 with its Sunderland IIIs. On 24 May 1944 Sunderland DV990 under the captaincy of Fg. Off. G. E. Holley found and attacked U-921 commanded by Oberleutnant zur See Wolfgang Leu. U-921's operations record book shows that she was attacked by a Catalina, which strafed the boat and dropped three DCs. U-921 was not damaged and claimed the aircraft shot down. The U-boat got the identification of the aircraft wrong. This was not unusual. U-921 was in this area trying to rescue the survivors of U-476 heavily damaged that morning by a Catalina from No 210 Squadron. Two U-Boats went to her aid, rescuing 21 of her crew. One boat sank her with a torpedo. A Sunderland from No 423 Squadron, captained by Flt. Lt. R. H. Nesbitt, was in a similar area and intercepted a SOS message giving a position of 6358N 00357W. On investigation U-921 was located. The squadron moved to Pembroke Dock in November.

No 423 Squadron Royal Canadian Air Force remained

at Castle Archdale with its Sunderland IIIs. On 24 April 1944 Flt. Lt. F. G. Fellows and crew had intercepted a sighting report of a U-boat from Flt. Lt. Taylor and crew of No 120 Squadron and headed for the position. Taylor had seen the U-Boat with the aid of the Leigh Light in position 5144N 01953W. He attacked with six depth charges from 150 feet, but no results were observed. The boat was U-672, a type VIIc commanded by Oberleutnant zur See Ulf Lawaetz. Fellows came upon the scene some twelve and a half hours later and sighted the boat at 16 miles now in position 5040N 01840W. The Sunderland homed in and at five miles U-672 opened fire. Fellows dropped a stick of six depth charges from 50 feet and one exploded prematurely causing damage to the aircraft electrics and the airframe. The rear gunner was knocked out and the turret damaged. Fellows decided to return to base and the aircraft landed safely. The U-Boat had been seen to rise out of the sea and was badly damaged. On 24 May 1944 Flt. Lt. R. H. Nesbitt and crew in Sunderland DW111 were instructed to home on to the Catalina of No 210 Squadron, which was attacking U-476. On arriving in the area the Catalina was sighted, it having badly damaged the U-boat. An SOS message was intercepted from position 6358N 00357W, probably from Fg. Off. Holley's crew of No 422 Squadron. On investigation they found U-921 on the surface. They attacked, strafing and dropping five DCs. These were avoided, but on diving, the captain, Oberleutnant Leu, shut the hatch from the outside saving his boat. He did not survive. Leutnant Hans Neumann assumed command and took the boat to Trondheim. During the attack Nesbitt's crew had seen some wreckage which they ignored for the time being. They now investigated and realized that it must have come from the No 422 Squadron Sunderland.

No 461 Squadron Royal Australian Air Force remained at Pembroke Dock with its Sunderland IIIs. On 28 January 1944 Flt. Lt. R. D. Lucas RAAF and crew gained a radar contact and then sighted a U-Boat which opened fire. This was U-571, a type VIIC commanded by Oberleutnant zur See Gustav Lussow in position 5241N 01427W. A stick of depth charges was dropped and this was unsuccessful. A follow-up attack was made and the U-Boat blew up. On 11 August 1944 an aircraft from the squadron operating 50 miles west of Lisbon homed onto U-766 just after Fg. Off. Mold in a No 201 Squadron Sunderland. The crew saw the attack but nothing else. On the same day Plt. Off. I. F. Southall RAAF and crew gained a radar contact, which, on homing, they discovered was a decoy balloon, probably from a U-Boat. This, no doubt alerted them. Then radar contact was gained on a U-boat and a stick of six depth charges was dropped, giving a good straddle. The boat stopped and kept firing at the aircraft but Southall remained out of range. An Escort Group was called in and together they prosecuted the contact, which had now dived.

After the Sunderland had departed the scene the U-Boat surfaced where it was sunk by the Group in position 4616N 00245W. This was U-385, a type VIIC commanded by Kapitänleutnant Hans Guido Valentiner. The survivors, rescued by HMS *Starling*, revealed that the boat had been severely damaged by the aircraft. Southall was awarded the DFC. On 12 August 1944 Fg. Off. D. A.

Little RAAF and crew gained a radar contact at six and a half miles and homed in, illuminating the contact at three quarters of a mile. Using the Low Level Bomb Sight, Flt. Lt. L. F. McInnes RAAF, the navigator, dropped a stick of six depth charges from 300 feet and achieved a straddle. On the follow-up attack nothing was sighted. An attempt was made to contact a nearby Escort Group but nothing was heard, although it arrived later.

The Senior Naval Officer called up to say that the boat had been sunk by the Sunderland and survivors were being picked up. It was U-270, a type VIIC commanded by Oberleutnant zur See Heinrich Schreiber, and it had been en route from Lorient to La Pallice, taking important members of the U-Boat flotillas to safety from the invasion forces. She had been under constant air threat for the entire route. The Escort Group rescued 71 out of 81 on board. She went down in position 4619N 00256W.

On 27th August Flt. Lt. W. B. Tilley and crew found the remaining crew of the crashed No 172 Squadron Wellington captained by Fg. Off. Whiteley, in position 4528N 00228W, seeing three men in the dinghy and one in the water. Tilley jettisoned his DCs and made a successful landing on the sea, picked the survivors and returned to Mountbatten.

No 502 Squadron was at St. David's. A Halifax captained by Fg. Off. J.H.Spurgeon detected U-107, a type IXb, on the night of 6/7 January 1944, but she escaped. On 4 February 1944, Fg. Off. F. T. Culling-Mannix RNZAF and crew located U-763 west of Bordeaux. This was after she had been attacked by a No 172 Squadron Wellington. This time the U-Boat's gunners claimed a victim. The Halifax crashed into the sea, there being no survivors. U-763 arrived in port on 7 February.

On 7 June 1944, Flt. Lt. W. G. Powell and crew found and attacked U-981 commanded by Oberleutnant zur See Walter Sitek in position 4655N 00326W. Three 600lb anti-submarine bombs were dropped in the face of intense flak but they missed. Sitek thought that he had probably shot down the Halifax but in the event it was not hit. The U-boat dived.

In the early hours of 8 June Fg. Off. J. H. Spurgeon and crew located a target at five miles, but this turned out to be three surface vessels, which opened fire. Spurgeon turned away and about an hour later saw a U-boat at three miles on the surface. This was U-413, commanded by Oberleutnant zur See Dietrich Sachse, who had already been attacked about 20 minutes earlier by Sqn. Ldr. Brock and crew from No 58 Squadron. As he started an attack, flak opened up. He was not in a good attacking position so he started again. The bombs hung up. Spurgeon went round again and released four 600lb anti-submarine bombs which exploded close to the boat. The aircraft was hit in No 2 engine and the tailplane, so he turned for home, landing safely at Predannack. He received a DFC at the end of the war. U-413 was sunk on 20 August 1944 by RN surface vessels.

On 12 August 1944, Flt. Lt. J. Capey and crew gained a radar contact at eleven miles which turned out to be five contacts. They homed on to the rear contact, which was near Point de la Courbre by the River Gironde. Three flares were dropped when abeam of the contact and two U-boats were sighted in position 4541N 00125W. A second flare drop failed and the third attempt was dropped two miles from the boats. An attack was then made with five 600lb anti submarine depth bombs from 7300 feet in the face of flak from both boats. The boat attacked was U-981, a type VIIc commanded by Oberleutnant zur See Gunther Keller. This boat had previously hit a mine laid by the RAF and was heading for La Pallice. This attack caused her to sink and was the second and last success with this type of bomb. The second U-Boat was U-309, which rescued the 40 survivors. Capey was awarded the DFC in December.

On 13 August 1944, Fg. Off. W. E. Umpherson RCAF and crew flying at 1200 feet sighted U-534, U0437, U-857 and four escort vessels shortly after Flt. Lt. J. M. MacFadyen and crew from No 58 Squadron in position 4535N 00241W. An unidentified twin-engined aircraft was seen to be making a low-level attack and all guns from the group were firing at it. The bombs were seen to fall but no hits were observed. Umpherson then made an attack from 5000 feet with anti-submarine bombs, but again no results were observed. The aircraft was damaged on the starboard elevator, rear fuselage and rear turret, wounding the gunner, Fg. Off. C. W. Davies. The Constant Speed Unit (CSU) on the starboard outer engine was made unserviceable. The Halifax was landed at Predannack and Fg. Off. Davies died the following day. The squadron moved to Stornoway in September 1944 with its Halifax IIs. On 4 November 1944, Flt. Lt. W. G. Powell and crew and Sqn. Ldr. H. H. C. Holderness, DFC, AFC and crew joined in the attack with two Liberators from No 311 Squadron on U-1060, causing the grounded boat to keel over. The sinking is recorded in position 6524N 01200E.

No 524 Squadron reformed, after a four months disbandment, at Davidstow Moor in April 1944 with Wellington XIIIs. In July it went to Docking and later in the month to Bircham Newton. In October the squadron moved to Langham and in December began to exchange its Wellington XIIIs for Mark XIVs.

No 547 Squadron moved to St Eval in January 1944. In August it converted to Liberator VIs, disposing of its Mark Vs in October when it moved to Leuchars.

No 612 Squadron with its Wellingon XIIIs and XIVs moved to Limavady in January, 1944. On 3 January 1944 Wg. Cdr. J. B. Russell DSO and crew were flying a Percussion patrol. A radar contact was gained in position 4602N 00819W and a homing initiated. The Leigh Light was switched on and a surfaced submarine sighted. This was U-373, a type VIIC commanded by Oberleutnant zur See Detlev von Lehsten. The boat dived as a stick of depth charges was released. No results were observed but shortly after, another radar contact was gained at eight miles which proved to be the same submarine. Russell had no more DCs remaining but a Liberator from No 224 Squadron was homed in. Having watched the Liberator attack, the Wellington turned for its base. The boat had been damaged and returned to La Pallice. She did not put to sea again until 7 June 1944, to be sunk by a No 224 Squadron Liberator thye following day.

Fg. Off. R. E. Durnford and crew were operating in the Iceland/Faeroes Gap on the night of 10 February on a Moorings patrol. Another No 612 Squadron crew in an adjacent area intercepted a message from Durnford stating that he was having engine trouble. No indication of the cause was given. This incident was in the area of U-283 commanded by Oberleutnant zur See Günter Ney, who reported an attack by an aircraft and said gunfire had been exchanged. There is little information on this incident. Durnford and crew were lost at about this time in the area of 6032N 01402W. This U-Boat was sunk a few hours later by a No 407 Squadron crew captained by Fg. Off. P. W. Heron, RCAF.

On 10 February 1944, Plt. Off. M. H. Paynter RAAF and crew were escorting a convoy and carrying out a creeping line ahead search when a radar contact was gained at eight miles. Concern was expressed by the captain that this might have been Rockall, which looked like a submarine contact on the radar (and still does to current crews!). The operator, Sgt. D. Smith, was able to reassure him as he had already seen it on the screen. The weather was bad and because of it the aircraft was a little off track. Flame floats had been dropped to provide a datum from which to measure drift, but few had been seen after leaving the aircraft. The U-Boat was sighted at one mile in the moonlight, the weather having improved. A stick of depth charges was dropped and this sank the boat. This was U-545, a type IVC/40, commanded by Kapitänleutnant Gert Mannesmann. Small objects with orange lights were seen by the Wellington crew which was indicative of men in the sea. U-545 was sunk in position 5817N 01322W. The U-Boat crew was rescued by U-714.

On 12 March 1944, Flight Sergeant D. Bretherton and crew gained an intermittent radar contact. The cloud base was low and the weather hazy. Bretherton decided to go lower than the 500 feet shown on the altimeter, switched on the Leigh Light at three quarters of a mile and saw a U-Boat, but was still too high. He went round again and the aircraft was hit by flak in the tail and the rear turret. A stick of depth charges was dropped in the face of further heavy flak, in position 4657N 00905W. The boat was U-629, a type VIIc commanded by Oberleutnant zur See Hans-Helmut Bugs, and was heavily damaged and forced to return to Brest. This was the second time in around a week that the boat had been damaged and compelled to return to base. She had been attacked on 5 March by a Wellington from No 304 squadron. In March the squadron moved to Chivenor and disposed of its Wellington Mark XIIIs.

On 28 April 1944 Fg. Off. C. G. Punter and crew gained a radar contact at thirteen and a half miles which, during the homing, was lost at one mile. Baiting or Gambit tactics were tried in an effort to encourage the U-Boat to believe that the threat had gone, but without success. Later a further radar contact was gained at eleven and a half miles in position 4544N 00945W and a homing was carried out. It was then realized that the Leigh Light was unserviceable. The navigator, Fg. Off. R. Hothersall, went to the nose turret and at one mile he saw a wake and opened fire. The tracer gave Punter sufficient light to see the boat and he attacked with depth charges from 50 feet. It was U-193, a type IXc/40 commanded by Oberleutnant zur See Ulrich Abel. The rear gunner saw the boat roll over and sink. The lights of ten men were seen in the water.

According to *U-Boats Destroyed*, Abel made up in Nazi fervour what he lacked in competency. As First Watch of

U-154 he had denounced Oberleutnant zur See Oskar Kusch for "undermining military strength". Despite a lack of evidence and the retraction of statements by U-154's officers, which Abel had persuaded them to make, Kusch was found guilty. There were appeals to Dönitz and Raeder, but Kusch was shot on 12 May 1944.

On 24 May Fg. Off. K. H. Davies and crew took off for their first operation since arriving on the squadron from No 6 OTU. Nothing further was heard from them. U-736, commanded by Oberleutnant zur See Reinhardt Relf, records that she was located and attacked by a Wellington, which she shot down. This U-Boat was attacked by a No 224 Squadron Liberator on the following day. U-736 reached Brest but was sunk on her next patrol in August. The squadron moved to Limavady in September and to Langham, Norfolk, in December 1944.

No 4 (C) OTU was now at Alness with Sunderlands. On 21 May 1944 Plt. Off. E. T. King and crew were flying at 2000 feet over a rough sea. From two miles a surfacing submarine was sighted in position 6335N 00224E. An immediate attack was made with a stick of six depth charges from 50 feet. The U-Boat appeared to sink on an even keel, leaving an oil patch. This was U-995, a type VIIc/41 commanded by Kapitänleutnant Walter Kohntopp; it had just sailed from Bergen, where it had to return for repairs. It did not sail again until 4 July.

On 24 May Fg. Off. T. F. P. Frizell RNZAF and a trainee crew gained a visual sighting of a surfaced U-Boat at five miles in position 6227N 00304E. An immediate attack was not made as the starboard bomb carrier had to be wound out by hand. The attack was initiated against heavy flak from the boat, but by taking avoiding action the aircraft was not hit. A stick of six depth charges was dropped, although one hung up. It was a good straddle and the boat's bows lifted into the vertical and then it sank. Wreckage, oil drums and bodies were seen. This was U-675, a type VIIc commanded by Oberleutnant zur See Karl-Heinz Sammler. For most of the war this area was a Totally Restricted Bombing Area, as British submarines were operating there. This ban had just been lifted and the area flooded with Allied aircraft, and this caught the Germans unawares. There was a shortage of squadron aircraft as they were engaged in pre-D-Day activities and this was the reason OTU aircraft were being used. The OTU moved to Evanton in September 1944.

ANTI SHIPPING UK/STRIKE WINGS

LEUCHARS STRIKE WING

On 6 February 1944 Lt. Engebrigsten and his navigator from No 333 Squadron in a Mosquito FBIV shot down a Heinkel 115B floatplane. The Wing was formed officially on 1 March 1944, although the squadrons had been operating for some time before that. Five days later four Torbeaus of No 489 Squadron RNZAF and eight from No 455 Squadron RAAF attacked 16 ships off Stavangar. The merchant ship Rabe was sunk. Despite flak from shore batteries and ships and opposition from enemy fighters, all Beaufighters returned safely. Nos 455 and 489 Squadrons departed Leuchars for Langham in April.

LANGHAM STRIKE WING

The Wing started operations with the arrival of Nos 455 and 489 Squadrons from Leuchars. On 14 May 24 Beaufighters from Nos 455 and 489 Squadrons led by Wg. Cdr. J. N. Davenport complete with a fighter escort attacked four merchant ships and 16 escorts. The Merchant ship *Vesta* and one minesweeper were sunk. One aircraft from No 489 Squadron was shot down. On 15 June the Wing consisting of 23 Beaufighters from Nos 455 and 489 Squadrons joined the North Coates Wing in an attack on two large merchant ships and seven escorts. (see below). On 15 July 34 Beaufighters from Nos 144, 455 and 489 Squadrons, led by Wg. Cdr. J. Davenport, attacked a tanker, four merchant ships and five escorts. The tanker was badly damaged and other vessels were left on fire.

PREDANNACK STRIKE WING

No 248 Squadron moved to Portreath in February.

DAVIDSTOW MOOR STRIKE WING

The Wing had been formed in May 1944 with Nos 144 and 404 Squadrons. On 6 June 1944 (D-Day), 16 Beaufighters from No 144 Squadron and 14 from No 404 Squadron (RCAF) led by Wg. Cdr. D. O. F. Lumsden, OC 144 and an escort of eight Mosquitoes from No 248 Squadron attacked three German destroyers. Z-24 and Z-32 were seriously damaged and put into Brest. One Beaufighter ditched but the crew was rescued. The destroyers were repaired and put to sea on 8 June. The 10th Destroyer Flotilla sank ZH-1 and caused Z-32 to be

beached on fire. The Wing sank Z-32 on 9 June. The
mission of these ships was to harry the invasion force. On
8 August 24 Beaufighters from Nos 236 and 404
Squadrons led by Wg. Cdr. K. Gatward, OC 404, on a
sweep found and attacked four minesweepers. All were
sunk but one Beaufighter was lost. On 13 August 10
Beaufighters from No 236 Squadron and eight
Beaufighters from No 404 Squadron led by Wg. Cdr. A.
Gadd attacked and sank two Sperrbrechers. One
Beaufighter from No 236 Squadron was lost.

PORTREATH STRIKE WING

The Wing was formed in June 1944. Nos 235 Squadron
moved out in February to go to St. Angelo but returned
the following month. No 248 Squadron arrived in
February. No 143 Squadron left for Manston in February.
Nos 235 and 248 Squadrons left in September. On 10
June four Mosquitoes from No 248 Squadron led by Flt.
Lt. S. G. Nunn and his navigator Fg. Off. J. M. Carlin
attacked the type VIIc U-Boat U-821 commanded by
Oberleutnant zur See Ulrich Knackfuss. A No 206
Squadron Liberator captained by Flt. Lt. A. D. S. Dundas
then arrived on the scene. This crew attacked with a stick
of five 250lb depth charges and a follow-up attack of six
causing the U-boat to sink in position 4831N 00511W.
The survivors were rescued by a VP boat which was
sighted by six No 248 Squadron Mosquitoes led by Cdt.
Max Guedj later that day. One overflew the boat and was
fired at, causing it to crash. Two of these aircraft were fitted
with the Tsetse gun and they and the others sank the boat.
There was one German survivor.

STRUBBY STRIKE WING
In July Nos 144 and 404 Squadrons arrived to form the Wing. On 8 July the Wing joined with NCSW in an attack on six merchant ships and 10 escorts. (see below). The Wing had been formed on 1 July with Nos 144 and 404 Squadrons.

NORTH COATES STRIKE WING
On 1 March Wg. Cdr. R. E. Burns, OC 254 Squadron, with a Spitfire escort, led nine Beaufighters from No 143 Squadron, three from 236 and nine from 254 in a strike against a large merchant vessel under tow escorted by six flak ships. There were no sinkings and no aircraft were lost. The Wing returned in the afternoon with 21 Beaufighters and a Spitfire escort. The merchant ship the *Maasburg* was left on fire and later sank. All aircraft returned safely. On 7 March, 29 Beaufighters from Nos 143, 236 and 254 Squadrons attacked seven ships plus escorts. Several ships were set on fire but there were no sinkings. Two Beaufighters failed to return. On 29 March six Torbeaus and 23 anti flak Beaufighters from Nos 143, 236 and 254 Squadrons with an escort of two Mustang squadrons, attacked 16 merchant ships, three minesweepers and a Sperrbrecher. Two merchant vessels were sunk and one Beaufighter was lost. On 15 June the Wing joined with the Langham Wing in an attack on two large merchant ships. NCSW consisted of 19 Beaufighters from Nos 236 and 254 Squadrons. A squadron of Mustangs provided the escort and Wg. Cdr. A. Gadd, Wg. Cdr. Flying Wing at North Coates, commanded the force. The operation was successful. The *Schiff 49*, 7900 tons, the *Gustav Nächtigall*,

3500 tons and a minesweeper were sunk. All aircraft returned safely. On 8 July Wg. Cdr. A. Gadd led Strubby and North Coates Strike Wings, consisting of 39 Beaufighters from Nos 144, 236, 254 and 404 Squadrons, in an attack on six merchant ships and 10 escorts. Three merchant ships and one escort were sunk. No 143 Squadron left for Manston in May, only to return in September.

DALLACHY STRIKE WING

In October the Wing was formed with the arrival of Nos 144, 404, 455 and 489 Squadrons. On 15 October 21 Beaufighters from Nos 144 and 404 Squadrons joined the Banff Strike Wing in an attack on the tanker *Inge Johanne* and the flak ship Vp1605 and sank both (see below). On 8 November 22 Beaufighters led by Wg. Cdr. A. Gadd and with a Mosquito outrider or guide from No 333 Squadron attacked ships anchored in Mitgulenfjord. The Aquila and Helga Ferdinand were sunk. The civilian Norwegian ship *Framnes* was badly damaged in error. All aircraft returned to base.

BANFF STRIKE WING

The Wing was formed with the arrival in September of Nos 333, 248, and 235 Squadrons and in October, No 143 Squadron. On 15 October, 17 Mosquitoes from Nos 235 and 248 Squadrons led by Sqn. Ldr. W. R. Christison joined the *Dallachy* in the attack on and sinking of, the tanker *Inge Johanne* and the flak ship *Vp 1605*. Both Wings returned safely. On 23 October 21 Mosquitoes from Nos 235 and 248 Squadrons led by Wg. Cdr. R. A. Atkinson,

OC 235, sank the flak ship V5506 and damaged a merchant vessel. All aircraft returned safely. On 4 November, 16 Mosquitoes from Nos 235 and 248 Squadrons led by Wg. Cdr. G. D. Sise attacked Floro harbour. One flak ship and one merchant ship were left burning. No 235 squadron lost one aircraft. On 5 December Wg. Cdr. G. D. Sise led 33 Mosquitoes from Nos 143, 235 and 248 Squadrons against two convoys at anchor near Svelgen. The merchant ships Ostland, Tucuman, Magdalena and Helene Russ were severely damaged. One Mosquito was lost. On 16 December, Wg. Cdr. J. M. Maurice (real name Max Guedj) led 22 Mosquitoes from Nos 143, 235 and 248 Squadrons with an outrider or guide, from No 333 Squadron. They were looking for merchant ships in Krakhellesund and found the *Ferndale* stuck on rocks, with a salvage vessel, a flak ship and a tug in attendance. The *Ferndale* and the salvage vessel were set on fire but one Mosquito was forced to ditch. Shortly after, Wg. Cdr. Sise arrived, leading six Mosquitoes from the Wing and destroying both vessels. Another aircraft was lost, crashing into the cliffs.

No 143 Squadron moved to North Coates in February 1944 with a detachment at Manston. The squadron moved to Manston in May and back to North Coates in September, where it converted to Mosquito IIs. In October it moved to Banff, exchanging its Mark IIs for Mark VIs.

No 144 Squadron moved with its Beaufighter Xs to Davidstow Moor in May, Strubby in July, Banff in September and Dallachy in October.

No 235 Squadron moved to St Angelo, Northern

Ireland in February 1944 and back to Portreath in March. In April it converted to Beaufighter XIs but in June exchanged these for Mosquito VIs. In September it moved to Banff.

No 236 Squadron remained at North Coates with its Beaufighter Xs.

No 248 Squadron added the Mosquito XVIIIs of No 618 Squadron that were detached to Predannack, to its inventory in January 1944. In February the squadron moved to Portreath. On 25 March 1944 Flt. Lt. L.S.Dobson led a formation of No 248 Squadron, escorting No 618 Squadron against U-976. On 27 March 1944, Flt. Lt. J. H. B. Rollett led six aircraft from No 248 squadron, escorting No 618 Squadron against U-960. On 7 June 1944, Fg. Off. D. J. Turner DFC and his navigator, Fg. Off. D. Curtis DFC in one Mosquito and Fg. Off. A. J. L. Bonnett RCAF and his navigator Fg. Off. A. McD. McNicol in another were on an anti-submarine patrol. Turner gained a visual sighting of a wake and then a submarine with decks awash. The aircraft attacked with their Molins guns and then made a follow-up attack. Bonnett's gun had jammed, but he made a dummy attack to draw flak from Turner. The boat was U-212, a type VIIc commanded by Kapitänleutnant Helmuth Vogler and was damaged, causing a return to La Pallice. On 10 June 1944 four Mosquitoes were on a patrol line at 30 feet between Ushant and Isle de Seine in order to intercept any U-boats trying to enter or leave Brest. The crews were Flt. Lt. S. G. Nunn and Fg. Off. J. M. Carlin, Fg. Off. G. N. E. Yeates and Fg. Off. T. C. Scott, Fg. Off. K. Norrie and Flt. Sgt. B. J. Palmer, Flt. Sgt. W. W. Scott and Flt. Sgt. J. Blackburn.

A conning tower was seen to be breaking the sea surface. The section climbed to 500 feet and attacked the by now fully-surfaced submarine. This was U-821, a type VIIc commanded by Oberleutnant zur See Ulrich Knackfuss, in position 4831N 00511W. There was a large explosion aft of the conning tower, possibly deck gun ammunition exploding. The boat appeared to be out of control and most of the crew had abandoned it.

Flt. Lt. Nunn sighted a Liberator about six miles away and sent one of his crews to lead it in. The Liberator, which was crewed by Flt. Lt. A. D. S. Dundas and crew from No 206 Squadron, dropped a stick of six depth charges which missed, but the follow-up attack straddled the boat and sank it. Those that survived were picked up by a German motor launch. This was sighted by a flight of six No 248 Squadron Mosquitoes led by Commandant Max Guedj DSC DFC CdG, Free French Air Force, later that day. The aircraft, piloted by Flt. Lt. E. H. Jeffreys DFC, was hit by flak but the remaining five attacked, the two Tsetse aircraft blowing the launch out of the water. There was only one survivor.

On 23 June 1944 a flight of six Mosquitoes were on patrol between Ile de Groix and Lorient. The aircraft, piloted by Flt. Sgt. L. C. Doughty and navigated by Flt. Sgt. R. Grime, became separated from the others in bad light. They sighted an enemy convoy and then three escorts and a U-boat. Despite land and ship-based flak they attacked the U-boat with guns and two depth charges. This was U-155, a type IXc commanded by Oberleutnant zur See Johannes Rudolph Altmeier, and it had been damaged in this attack. It did not sail again until

September 1944. Doughty was awarded the DFM and promoted to Warrant Officer. In September the squadron moved to Banff. On 18 September 1944 Warrant Officer H. A. Corbin and his navigator found and attacked U-867, a type IXc/40, but no results were observed.

No 254 Squadron remained at North Coates with its Beaufighter Xs.

No 333 Squadron "B" Flight was at Leuchars with its Mosquitoes. On 26 May 1944, two Mosquitoes were on a sortie from Leuchars. Lt J. M. Jacobsen, pilot and S/Lt L. Humlen, navigator, crewed one of them and Lt H. Engebrigsten, pilot and Lt O. G. Jonassen, navigator, crewed the other. They gained a visual sighting of a U-Boat in position 6135N 00328E and attacked from 500 feet with cannons. The boat, which was U-958, a type VIIc commanded by Kapitänleutnant Gerhard Groth, was seen to have been hit. The aircraft turned for a follow-up attack but the boat dived. U-958 was badly damaged and had to return to Bergen.

On 14 June 1944, Lt. E. U. Johansen and his navigator 2/Lt. L. Humlen gained a visual sighting of a U-Boat in position 6106N 00325E and attacked with guns and one depth charge. It was U-290, a type VIIc commanded by Oberleutnant zur See Helmut Herglotz. The boat was damaged and dived, returning to Egersund for repairs. She did not sail again until August. Two days later, the same crew gained a visual sighting of a surfaced submarine in position 6101N 00300E at eight miles distance. This aircraft was one of three Mosquitoes sent off at two-hour intervals on antisubmarine patrol. Johansen took advantage of cloud cover and attacked with guns and two depth charges from 100 feet. The boat was U-998, a type VIIc/41 commanded by Leutnant zur See Gerhard Fiedler. The boat zigzagged and then dived, only to partially resurface again, bows up. Johansen made a follow-up attack. U-998 then disappeared and was thought to have been sunk. It was badly damaged but unrepairable and was written off. In effect it was a kill. The aircraft was slightly damaged.

Mosquito HP 860, captained by Lieutenant J. M. Jacobsen, with navigator 2/Lt P. C. Hansen, was on patrol on 16th June 1944 when it found U-804 commanded by Oberleutnant zur See Herbert Meyer. Jacobsen attacked, but the aircraft was hit in the port engine and the wing was split open. He ditched successfully and he and his navigator were adrift in their dinghy for some 30 hours. A corrupt message was received at 2259 indicating possible trouble. Ironically they were rescued by U-1000, commanded by Oberleutnant Willi Muller and taken to Bergen and thence to a POW camp. U-804 had been damaged.

On 20 July 1944 two Mosquitoes were on an anti U-Boat patrol off Fedje Island Norway. They located a flak ship which was attacked by one of these aircraft. Lt. R. Leithe and his navigator in the other aircraft gained a visual sighting of a U-Boat astern of the flak ship. They attacked with guns from 100 feet and two depth charges. The boat was U-863, a type IX/D2 commanded by Kapitänleutnant Dietrich von der Esch and had been damaged causing her return to Bergen. On 25 July 1944, two Mosquitoes were on an anti U-Boat Rover patrol off the Norwegian coast. The crews were 2/Lt S. Breck, pilot and 2/Lt P.Hjorten, navigator in one and Plt. Off. J. A.

Stiff, pilot and Flt. Sgt. H. E. Bussey, navigator, in the other. They gained a visual sighting of a surfaced U-Boat with its escort vessel at eight miles. Breck attacked with guns, scoring hits on the U-Boat and the surface vessel and dropping two depth charges as he passed over the submarine. Stiff followed with guns and DCs, causing a big explosion on the escort. The U-Boat was U-244, a type VIIc commanded by Kapitänleutnant Ruprecht Fischer and was damaged and forced to return to Kristiansund.

Two Mosquitoes operating from RAF Leuchars on 2 August 1944 were looking for U-Boats near the Norwegian coast. Early in the afternoon two U-Boats, U-771 commanded by Oberleutnant zur See Helmut Block and U-1163 commanded by Oberleutnant zur See Ernst-Ludwig Balduhn, escorted by two armed trawlers, UJ-1113 and UJ-1163, were sighted in position 5827N 00545E. The first aircraft, flown by Lt. Commander H.Jorgensen and Sub-Lieutenant G. Helgedagsrud, attacked first, U-771 being the target, firing cannon and dropping two DCs which exploded close to the submarine. The second aircraft, flown by Sub-Lieutenant A. R. Eikemo and Petty Officer C. Harr attacked U-1163. They dropped DCs but the aircraft was hit by flak. It hit the mast of one of the trawlers and crashed into the sea. The other Mosquito, having expended all of its ammunition, had no choice but to return to base. The U-boats were en route Stavangar to Egersund, which they reached safely. However, U-771 had to go to Bergen for repairs, which took about two months. The squadron's "B" Flight moved to Banff with its Mosquito VIs in September 1944.

No 404 Squadron Royal Canadian Air Force moved

to Davidstow Moor in May 1944 with its Beaufighter Xs. The squadron kept a detachment there when it moved to Strubby in July. In September it moved to Banff and then to Dallachy in October.

No 455 Squadron Royal Australian Air Force, moved to Langham in April 1944, with detachments at Thorney Island and Manston. In October 1944 the squadron moved to Dallachy.

No 489 Squadron Royal New Zealand Air Force moved to Langham with its Beaufighter Xs in April 1944. Then in October it too moved to Dallachy.

No 618 Squadron had been earmarked for the Far East and handed over most of its Mosquito Mark XVIIIs to No 248 Squadron but retained some for its Special Detachment at Predannack. The squadron had been training with a "bouncing bomb" for anti shipping operations. On 25 March 1944 Fg. Off. D. J. Turner and his navigator, Fg. Off. D. Curtis, and Fg. Off. A. H. Hilliard and his navigator, Warrant Officer J. B. Hoyle, escorted by No 248 Squadron, found and attacked U-976 with Tsetse. Tsetse was the name for the 57mm Molins gun. This boat, commanded by Oberleutnant zur See Raimond Tiesler, was meeting its three escorts outside St Nazaire. Turner attacked four times and Hilliard once. Hilliard was engaged by an enemy destroyer and returned fire before turning away. The U-boat went down, forty-eight survivors being rescued. On 27 March 1944 the same two crews, Fg. Off. D. J. Turner and Fg. Off. A. H. Hilliard, escorted by No 248 Squadron, found and attacked U-960, commanded by Oberleutnant zur See Günter Heinrich. The boat was in company with another

U-Boat, four minesweepers and two Sperrbrechers. U-960 was damaged and suffered casualties including the captain, and was forced to return to La Pallice. The squadron moved to Wick in July 1944 and added Mosquito VIs to its inventory. However, it exchanged these in September/October when it received Mark IVs and XVIs. In October 1944 the squadron set off for Australia on board HMS *Fencer* and HMS *Striker*.

METEOROLOGICAL CALIBRATION

No 517 Squadron went to Brawdy, South Wales in February with its Halifax Vs.

No 518 Squadron remained at Tiree with its Halifax Vs.

No 519 Squadron received Hudson IIIs in August, Fortress Is in October and Spitfire VIIs in November 1944. It disposed of its Ventura Vs in October and of its Spitfire VIs in November. In this last month the squadron moved to Wick.

No 520 Squadron disposed of its Hudson IIIs in March 1944 and its Gladiator IIs in August. In February it received Halifax Vs and Spitfire Vs. In June it received Hurricane IIc's and Martinets in September 1944. The Spitfires only stayed for two months and went in April.

No 521 squadron received Hurricane IIcs in August 1944, Hudson VIs in September and Fortress IIs in December. It disposed of its Ventura Vs in December. The squadron moved to Langham in November with a detachment to Brawdy in December.

PHOTOGRAPHIC RECONNAISSANCE

No 540 Squadron moved to Benson in February 1944 with detachments at Gibraltar, Dyce and Yagodnik near Archangel. In May it added Mosquito XVIs to its inventory

No 541 Squadron added in May 1944, Spitfire IXs, in June Spitfire XIXs and in July, Mustang IIIs to its inventory. In September the Spitfire IVs were disposed of.

No 542 Squadron added Spitfire Xs in May 1944 and Spitfire XIXs in June.

No 544 Squadron added Mosquito XVIs in March 1944, Mark XXXIIs in October, to its inventory. On 9 July 1944 a squadron aircraft located and photographed the German Battleship *Tirpitz*. The crew, pilot Frank Dodd and navigator Eric Hill, landed at Wick after a sortie lasting almost eight hours. Dodd was awarded the DSO and Hill the DFM.

AIR SEA RESCUE 1944

No 269 Squadron returned to the UK from Reykjavik, going to Davidstow Moor, Cornwall in January 1944. It gave up its Hudson IIIs for IIIAs, Martinets, Spitfire VBs and Walruses in February and went to Lajes in March. The Spitfires, Martinets and Walruses were taken to Lajes by escort carrier. The Martinets were disposed of in July. In September it received Warwick Is. A single flight remained under Coastal control for Air Sea Rescue.

No 279 Squadron moved to Thornaby in October 1944 and exchanged its Hudsons for Warwick Is in November.

No 280 Squadron moved to Strubby in May 1944 with a detachment at Thornaby and to Langham in September maintaining its detachment at Thornaby. In October it moved to Beccles with detachments at Langham, Thorney Island and St Eval.

No 281 Squadron moved to Tiree in February 1944 with detachments at Wick, Davidstow Moor, Great Orton, west of Carlisle, Leuchars, Dallachy, Banff and Mullaghmore, south east of Limavady. This squadron was the only one to be based at Mullaghmore. A Warwick from this unit dropped an Airborne Lifeboat to the survivors of the No 162 Squadron Canso, shot down after a successful attack on U-715 on 13 June 1944.

No 282 Squadron disbanded in January 1944 and was absorbed by No 278 Squadron, a Fighter Command unit. It reformed the following month at Davidstow Moor from a nucleus of No 269 Squadron and was equipped with Warwick Is. It then transferred from Fighter Command control to Coastal Command control. Fighter Command was then known as Air Defence of Great Britain. In September the squadron moved to St Eval with detachments at St Mawgan, Great Orton and Exeter.

MEDITERRANEAN MARITIME PATROL

No 36 Squadron moved to Reghaia with its Wellington XIVs in April 1944 with detachments at La Senia, Grottaglie, Bone and Alghero. No 36 Squadron was involved with "Swamp" operations on 7 January 1944. U-343 commanded by Oberleutnant zur See had passed through the Straits of Gibraltar on 5 January and had been located by the Polish destroyer *Slazak*. Fg. Off. R. D.

Bamford RNZAF and crew in Wellington HF245 found her in position 3654N 00156W. Bamford not being in his seat at that moment, the second pilot, Fg. Off. T. J. Masters RCAF, attacked. A stick of depth charges was dropped and the aircraft was hit in the port wing by flak, causing it to catch fire. The aircraft was ditched and the survivors were rescued by *Slazak* the next morning. The captain and the navigator, Fg. Off. L. A. Colquohoun RNZAF, did not survive. Next on the scene was another Wellington from No 36, HF221 captained by Fg. Off. J. T. Hutton. The second pilot, Flight Sergeant R. N. Holton was in control at the time and attacked. Again the U-Boat's gunners scored hits, this time in the port engine. DCs were dropped but the aircraft was in trouble. The remaining DCs were jettisoned and the aircraft managed to reach Bone and landed safely. Masters was awarded the DFC.

Further aircraft attacked, one from No 36, two from No 179 Squadron, the OC Wg. Cdr J. H. Greswell and Fg. Off. W. F. Davidson. Finally, a Catalina from No 202 Squadron captained by Flt. Lt. J. Finch made a run but was hit and was forced to return to base. U-343 survived, staggering into Toulon, but she was sunk a couple of months later, 10 March by the armed trawler HMS *Mull*, north west of Bizerta. On 16 May 1944 Warrant Officer J. M. Cooke and crew gained a radar contact at three miles at 1500 feet in position 3719N 00059E. Cooke turned the aircraft so that the U-Boat was silhouetted against the setting sun. The surfaced U-Boat was seen at one mile and attacked with a stick of six depth charges from 20 feet. This was a good straddle, one DC exploding on the boat's deck. This boat was U-616, a type VIIc commanded by

Oberleutnant zur See Siegfried Koitschka and had been detected by a No 36 Squadron Wellington on 14 May 1944 when she had attacked a convoy, GUS 39. She had been pursued by aircraft from Nos 36, 458 and 500 Squadrons and US Navy destroyers *Nields, Gleaves, Ellyson, Macomb, Hilary P. Jones, Hambleton, Rodman* and *Emmons*. Cooke climbed to 1500 feet, as an oil pressure warning light for his port engine had illuminated. U-616 was still on the surface. Cooke now decided to make a follow-up attack but the boat dived. The crew was relieved by another No 36 Squadron crew, Plt. Off. H. R. Swain RAAF and crew. They gained a radar contact but a radar homing was difficult as the radar was partly unserviceable. However, a wake had been sighted and Marine Markers dropped. Surface ships and more aircraft were homed in and finally the boat surfaced and then sank in position 3747N 00016E. All the crew survived. Interestingly, the pennant number (side number) of the USS *Nields* was DD-616. On 19 May 1944 Plt. Off. K. H. N. Bulmer, RCAF and crew were flying an anti-submarine hunt. The previous day a spread of three torpedoes had been fired at the USS *Ellyson*, which was carrying the survivors from U-616. They missed and five destroyers were sent to the area, together with aircraft. Bulmer gained three contacts but was unable to prosecute them but finally he gained a fourth at eight miles and on reaching the datum dropped Marine Markers. He then homed in two US Navy destroyers. Meanwhile a Ventura from No 500 Squadron had joined and sighted a periscope. This was reported to USS *Niblack* and *Ludlow*, which opened fire . The boat surfaced and Bulmer attacked with a stick of three depth charges from 50 feet which sank the boat in position 3720N 00135E. This was U-960, a type VIIc commanded by Oberleutnant zur See. In September the squadron moved to Tarquinia and eight days later returned to the UK and Chivenor.

No 38 Squadron moved to Kalamaki with Wellington XIIIs in November 1944 and a month later went to Grottaglie.

No 47 Squadron moved to LG91 in March 1944 and was then sent to India a few days later.

No 48 Squadron gave up its Beaufighter IIFs in August 1943 and its Hudsons in February, when it returned to the UK and became a transport squadron.

No 221 Squadron, with its Wellington XIIIs, moved to Grottaglie, near Taranto, with a detachment at Foggia in March 1944 and to Kalamaki/Hassani near Athens in October.

No 459 Squadron Royal Australian Air Force moved to Ramat David near Haifa in April 1944 in which month it disposed of its Hudsons. In May it moved to St Jean and in July it disposed of its Venturas and received Baltimore IVs and Vs. It then became a bomber squadron.

No 500 Squadron moved to La Senia in January 1944 with detachments at Blida, Bone, Ghisonaccia and Bo Rizzo. In April it started to exchange its Hudson Vs for Hudson VIs. On 19 May 1944 Warrant Officer E. A. K. Munday RCAF and crew joined in the prosecution of U-960 sighting its periscope and working with several US Navy ships. (See above under No 36 Squadron). The squadron disbanded in July and the aircraft were handed over to No 27 Squadron SAAF.

No 608 Squadron moved to Grottaglie with its Hudson IIIAs and VIs in January 1944 with detachments at Montecorvino and Gaudo. In February it moved to Montecorvino with a detachment at Bo Rizzo. In June it went to Pomigliano and in July the squadron disbanded.

No 624 Squadron, originally a bomber squadron, was disbanded in September but was reformed at Grottaglie in December 1944 with Walrus aircraft for mine spotting duties.

MEDITERRANEAN AIR SEA RESCUE

In January 1944 Mediterranean Air Command (MAC), which had now become Mediterranean Allied Air Forces (MAAF), was desperate for rescue aircraft. Only 16 Warwicks had been received and these were originally bombers and not ASR aircraft. They could not carry the airborne lifeboat. Further, a multitude of modifications were necessary, although some were downgraded to speed up the delivery of the aircraft. By June, MAAF had received most of the Warwicks required for their four squadrons. Airborne Lifeboats began to arrive in February and later ASR Warwicks.

In January 1944 MAAF had an establishment of 33 HSLs. That was the RAF view of what MAAF needed. The strength, that is the number held, was 45. Middle East had an establishment and a strength of 21 HSLs. The new longer-range 68 feet HSL began to arrive in the spring of 1944. In late February one of these HSLs at Mersa Matruh was called out to look for a dinghy at the far end of its range. After 37 hours with no sightings it returned to base, refuelled and set off once more. An aircraft made contact with the launch and signalled it to follow him. The

HSL reached the dinghy 20 miles off the coast of Crete and picked up the survivors just before a destroyer arrived on the scene. The two survivors had been in the water for seven days. A total of 229 hours were flown by Wellingtons of No 294 Squadron and Baltimores and Beaufighters of other units in this search.

Middle East's No 294 Squadron still had no Warwicks in May. While operational flying in the Eastern Mediterranean was now much reduced, there was still some intensive flying against German shipping in the Aegean Sea. In September MAAF transferred four Warwicks to Middle East for No 294 Squadron.

No 283 Squadron moved to Hal Far, Malta in April 1944 and converted to Warwick Is, disposing of its Walruses. It had detachments at Castel Benito (Tripoli/Idris), Blida, Kalamaki/Hassani and Saki near Sevastopol on the Black Sea. On 27 December, a Yugoslav ship, the SS *Kumonva,* carrying service leave personnel between Malta and Sicily, had engine trouble. This was magnified by the worst storm in years. Naval vessels responded to the distress calls but could not come alongside due to the weather. No 283 Squadron was called in. The aircraft crews passed situation reports (Sitreps) to AHQ Malta and surface vessels. It became obvious that *Kumanova* was going to sink. Lindholme gear and extra dinghies were dropped to the passengers aboard. They were then picked up by the Naval ships. There were 290 passengers and two did not survive. Coincidentally, seven of the survivors were personnel from No 283 Squadron.

No 284 Squadron moved to Alghero in March 1944 and added Warwick Is to its inventory. There were

detachments at Ghisonaccia, Corsica, Ramatuelle, east of
Marseille, Calvi and Bone. In September it disposed of its
Walruses and received Hurricane IIcs with detachments
to Calvi, Bone and Alouina. The squadron moved to Bone
in November with detachments at Elmas, Sardinia, Istres,
southern France and Pomigliano.

No 293 Squadron moved to Pomigliano in March
1944 and in April added Walrus aircraft to its inventory of
Warwicks. It had detachments at Pisa, Rosignano south of
Pisa, Foggia, Rivolto north east of Venice, Cesenatico
south east of Bologna and Udine, also north east of Venice.
In October this squadron rescued or assisted in the rescue
of some 32 aircrew using both Warwicks and Walruses. On
21 October three brilliant rescues were carried out near
Venice in the face of enemy fire.

No 294 Squadron moved to Idku in March 1944 with
detachments at Berka III, Gambut 3, LG07, St Jean,
Ramat David, Lalkatamia, Luxor, Benina, El Adem,
Abukir, Nicosia, Aqir, Hassani and Lydda. In March it
received Wellington XIs in exchange for its Mark Ics. In
June Mark XIIIs were added. The squadron had little
rescue work but in September the squadron rescued seven
aircrew from the sea. For the next three months no rescues
were made, although a few sorties were carried out. On
14th October a search was made for three night-fighter
Beaufighters missing on a flight to Araxos. The Wellington
returned to base having found nothing. At the same time
a Baltimore, after a raid on Maleme, was forced to land at
Kalami in Southern Greece. The same Wellington was
briefed to carry a fitter to Kalami and to combine this with
a search for the Beaufighters. These aircraft were then

reported safe at Ataxos, so the Wellington carried on to Kalami. When it arrived there was a party of Greeks together with some officers of the Allied Military Mission waiting for a supply aircraft which was a month overdue. It appeared that the Mission was desperately short of food and medical supplies. It was found that a few spares could make the Baltimore serviceable and these the Wellington agreed to collect from Gambut. The Mission officers then asked if the Wellington could bring the necessary supplies from Tobruk on its return. This the captain agreed to do and returned to Kalami on 18th October. The Baltimore was made serviceable and was escorted to Araxos, where it remained due to a lack of fuel. The crew was taken back to North Africa by the Wellington. Later in the month the squadron received Warwick Is.

By mid 1944 there was little rescue work to be done and the squadrons provided cover for non-operational areas and ferry routes. In addition convoy work was carried out. Much of the ASR at this juncture was to cover the operations of the US 15th Air Force which was involved in operations in Europe. No 323 Wing of the Mediterranean Coastal Air Force based at Foggia controlled much of the rescue work and the above squadrons . They were assisted by a flight of Catalina amphibians from the 1st United States Emergency Rescue Squadron, the Cants of the Italian Seaplane Wing and Fortresses and Liberators of the 15th United States Air Force.

MEDITERRANEAN ANTI SHIPPING
No 39 Squadron moved to Alghero with a detachment to Grottaglie in February 1944 with its Beaufighter Xs. In

July it went to Biferno with detachments at Reghaia and Hassani. In December it began to change to Marauder IIIs, which had no provision for the carriage of a torpedo. The squadron ceased its maritime connection.

No 227 Squadron moved to Biferno in August and then disbanded, being renumbered No 19 Squadron SAAF.

No 252 Squadron changed its Beaufighter XIs for Mark Xs in January 1944. It moved to Mersah Matruh later in the month, to Gambut in June and back to Mersah Matruh in November.

No 272 Squadron moved to Alghero wih its Beaufighter Xs in February 1944 with detachments to Bo Rizzo, Borgo and Reghaia. In September it moved to Foggia with a detachment to Falconara.

No 603 Squadron (AAF) continued with convoy escorts, intruder and strike operations in the Mediterranean and the Aegean Seas causing havoc amongst enemy shipping until there were virtually no targets left. The squadron was still at Gambut with a USAAF Squadron of B-25 Mitchells, with whom they closely operated. For a detailed history see *The Greatest Squadron of Them All* by David Ross, Bruce Blanche and William Simpson. By the end of October 1944 most of Southern Greece was in British hands, although some of the islands were still occupied by the Germans. The squadron went back to the UK in December 1944 and disbanded.

MIDDLE EAST

No 8 Squadron remained at Khormaksar with Wellington XIIIs. On 3 May 1944 Fg. Off. J. R. Forrester RCAF and crew operating from Scuiscuiban joined in the attack on U-852 (see No 621 Squadron). His first attack was foiled by the U-Boat commander, but his follow-up stick straddled the boat. The aircraft had been hit,but despite this Forrester continued to shadow the boat until darkness fell. The boat was beached by its crew and then scuttled by blowing off the bow and the stern.

No 244 Squadron was still at Sharjah and received Wellington XIIIs in February. It moved to Masirah Island in March with detachments at Khormaksar, Mogadishu and Santa Cruz near Bombay. It disposed of its Blenheim Vs in April 1944.

No 621 Squadron remained at Khormaksar with Wellingon XIIIs. The squadron was very active on the first three days of May 1944. They had been warned that a U-Boat was approaching the Somaliland coast. It was U-852, a type IXD2 commanded by Kapitänleutnant Heinz Eck. He had sailed from Kiel on 8 January 1944 and on the 13 March he had sunk the Greek ship *Peleus*. In order to keep his presence a secret, he had machine-gunned the survivors. However, three men had survived and Eck, two officers, Leutnant zur See August Hoffmann and the medical officer Stabsarzt Walter Weisspfennig and two crewmen were tried for a war crime and were found guilty. The officers were sentenced to death by firing squad, but the others were given long terms of imprisonment which were commuted. Fg. Off. H. R. Mitchell and crew had located U-852 and attacked with a stick of depth charges. The boat had dived but resurfaced and the Wellington maintained surveillance. The following crews attacked U-852:

Fg. Off. E. W. Read and crew on 2 May 1944.

Warrant Officer J. P. Ryall RCAF and crew on 2 May 1944.

Wg. Cdr. P. Green and crew on 2 May 1944.

Flt. Lt. J. Y. Wade and crew on 2 May 1944.

A No 8 Squadron Wellington attacked U-852 on 3 May damaging the boat causing her to be beached in position 0932S 05059E. HMS *Falmouth* and other aircraft joined in the hunt. The survivors of the U-Boat were taken to Aden

WEST AFRICA

No 95 Squadron was still at Bathurst with Sunderland Is and IIIs.

No 200 Squadron still at Yundum, received Liberator VIs in February 1944 and in May set off for India and Ceylon.

No 204 Squadron, with its Sunderland IIIs, moved to Jui in January 1944, with detachments to Half Die near Bathurst and Port Etienne. At the beginning of April the squadron moved to Half Die, but seven days later it moved back to Jui with detachments at Half Die, Port Etienne, Fisherman's Lake, Liberia and Abidjan.

No 270 Squadron remained at Apapa with its Sunderland IIIs.

No 343 Squadron (Free French) remained at Dakar with its Sunderland IIIs.

No 344 Squadron (Free French) also remained at Dakar with Wellington XIs and XIIIs.

No 490 Squadron Royal New Zealand Air Force was still at Jui but in May 1944 started to exchange its Catalina Ibs for Sunderland IIIs.

WEST AFRICA SEARCH AND RESCUE
By January 1944 two HSLs were based at Port Etienne, two pinnaces at Bathurst, two HSLs at Freetown, one HSL and one pinnace each at Takoradi and Banana. The Banana Unit was moved in August to Lagos. In this area the U-Boat war dwindled and operational flying was reduced to a minimum by December.

SOUTH AND EAST AFRICA
No 209 Squadron was still at Kipevu, Mombasa with its Catalina IIAs.

No 259 Squadron remained at Kipevu with its Catalina Ibs.

No 262 Squadron was still at Congella near Durban with its Catalina Ibs. On 11 March 1944 three Catalinas, Flt. Lt. E. S. S. Nash DFC and crew, Flt. Lt. F. J. Roddick RCAF and crew and Flt. Lt. A. H. Surridge and crew were searching for two U-Boats known to be South of Cape Town. One of these had been sighted by a SAAF aircraft three days earlier. Roddick's crew sighted one of them and he attacked with a stick of depth charges. The boat was seen to be listing. One of the DCs had hung up, so Roddick made a follow-up attack with it. He then returned to base as the Catalina had sustained hits from flak.

Nash and Surridge then arrived over the oil patch and the U-Boat surfaced in front of Nash, who attacked with a stick of six DCs, upon which the boat dived. Surridge's gunners opened fire on the boat. The boat was UIT22, the former Italian Console Generale Liozzi class *Alpino Bagnolini* commanded by Oberleutnant zur See Karl Wunderlich, and it had been sunk in position 4128S

01740E. There were no survivors. Roddick was awarded the DFC.

On 5th July 1944 two Catalinas were hunting U-859, a type IXD2, commanded by Kapitänleutnant Johann Jebsen. Shore-based radio stations had gained a D/F fix and the aircraft had been sent to investigate. Flt Lt A. M. Fletcher and crew, flying in good weather with cloud 5/10s at 2500 feet, located the boat in position 3222S 03458E. Fletcher attacked immediately with a stick of six DCs, the last of which hung up. The boat opened fire, hitting the Catalina several times, opening holes in the hull and the port wing. The DCs fell close to the boat and when she submerged a trail of oil was seen. Fletcher made four further attempts to drop the remaining DC but no avail. The schnorkel gear had been damaged, one crewman was killed by machine-gun fire and three others wounded.

In September 1944 the squadron added Catalina IVbs to its inventory. It had detachments at St Lucia, north east of Durban, Tulear, South West Madagascar and Langebaan, South Africa.

No 265 Squadron remained at Diego Suarez, North Madagascar with its Catalina Ibs. On 20th August Flt Lt W. S. Lough and crew in Catalina FP104 were on a transport flight from Mombasa to Durban with instructions to carry out an anti-submarine search en route. A sighting report was received from the aircraft and nothing further. They had sighted U-862 commanded by Korvettenkapitän Heinrich Timm in the North Mozambique Channel. The boat was on the surface and on the bridge was a photographer who courageously captured the events on film. The aircraft attacked, firing its nose gun, and the boat replied with 37mm and 20mm cannon. Hits were scored on the cockpit and the Catalina crashed a few metres ahead of the boat. U-862 looked for survivors but there were none.

FAR EAST

No 22 Squadron moved to Ratmalana near Colombo, Ceylon in April 1944. In May it started to exchange its Beauforts for Beaufighter Xs. In July it moved to Vavuniya north east Ceylon and in December it went to Kumbhirgram, west of Imphal.

No 160 Squadron added Liberator VIs to its inventory in January 1944. In July the squadron moved to Kankesanturai with detachments at Addu Atoll and Kandi.

No 191 Squadron began re-equipping with Catalina IVs in August 1944, disposing of its Mark Ibs in November. It moved to Red Hills Lake in November and had detachments at Cocanada, Trombay, Korangi Creek and Koggala.

No 200 Squadron received Liberator VIs in February 1944 and in May moved to St Thomas Mount, Madras, with detachments at Cuttack, south west of Calcutta and Sigiriya , central Ceylon. In September it disposed of its Liberator Vs.

No 203 Squadron moved to Madura, southern India, in October 1944, exchanging its Wellington XIIIs for Liberator VIs. It had detachments at Cochin, on the south west tip of India, St Thomas Mount, Ratmalana, Sigiriya and Vizagapatam north east of Madras.

No 205 Squadron, still at Koggala received Catalina IVbs in May 1944 in addition to its Mark Is.

No 212 Squadron was still at Korangi Creek, Karachi with Catalina Ibs, which it exchanged for Mark IVs in September/October 1944.

No 217 Squadron moved to Ratamalana in April 1944 with its Beaufort Is. In July it exchanged these for Beaufighter Xs and in September it moved to Vavuniya.

No 230 Squadron moved to Koggala in February 1944 with its Sunderland IIIs from East Africa. There were detachments at Diego Garcia, Addu Atoll, southern Maldives, Kelai, northern Maldives, and Lake Indawgyi, north east Burma.

No 240 Squadron was still at Red Hills Lake with Catalina IIAs. In July 1944 it received Mark IVs and in November it disposed of its Mark IIAs.

No 321 Squadron Royal Netherlands Navy was still at China Bay with its Catalina IIs and IIIs. In May 1944 No 205 Squadron loaned it its Catalina IVs. In December 1944 it received Liberator VIs.

No 354 Squadron added Liberator Mark VIs to its inventory in February 1944 and sent detachments to St Thomas Mount and Sigiriya in the same month. In April 1944 the Mark IIIAs were disposed of, as were the Mark Vs in August 1944. In October 1944 the Squadron moved to Minneriya with detachments to Cuttack and Kankesanturai (known as KKS) on the northern tip of Ceylon.

No 357 Squadron was formed at Digri, near Calcutta in February 1944 from No 1576 Flight, with Hudson IIIs, Liberator IIIs and Catalina IVs which last it disposed of in the following month. In September it moved to Jessore and received Liberator VIs. It had detachments at Dum Dum, Red Hills Lake, China Bay and Minneriya.. In

October it received Dakotas and added Toungoo and Mingaladon to its detachment list.

No 358 Squadron was formed at Kolar, east of Bangalore from No 1673 Heavy Conversion Unit in November 1944 with Liberator VIs.

No 618 Squadron arrived in Melbourne, Australia from the UK.

No 628 Squadron was formed at Red Hills Lake from "B" Flight No 357 Squadron in March 1944 with Catalina Ib's. Its duties were primarily Met Reconnaissance and Search and Rescue. In July it received Catalina IVs and in October it was disbanded.

FAR EAST AIR SEA RESCUE

No 292 Squadron was formed at Jessore in February 1944 with Walrus aircraft. In January, Air Command South East Asia (ACSEA) was informed that the teething troubles suffered by the Warwick would cause a delay in delivery. The establishment was to be 20 Warwicks and 10 Walrus, these last to be replaced by Sea Otters when they were available. In April the Warwick Is began to arrive and there was a detachment at Ratmalana, near Colombo. The intention was to have a detached flight of Warwicks at Bombay and Ceylon with the Walruses also in Ceylon. In November it received Sea Otters and in December, Liberator VIs.

While No 292 was converting to Warwicks, most of the ASR in the Indian area was carried out by aircraft from No 231 Group, mainly Wellingtons, assisted by Catalina amphibians from the US Eastern Air Command.

In May 1944 DDASR had stated an operational

requirement for a new type of HSL for the Indian Ocean which was to be known as the Long Range Rescue Craft (LRRC). The specification was for a range of between 1500 and 2500 miles at cruising speed and a maximum speed of 35 knots. Living accommodation was required for the crew as it was anticipated that such a boat would be away from home for up to fourteen days. The Admiralty agreed to make production facilities available. To fill the gap in time the Admiralty agreed to provide some "D" type Fairmile launches but these had a maximum speed of only 24 knots and a range of 1500 miles. Some 40 of these were to be dispatched in March 1945. However, maintenance problems arose, particularly with the wooden hull, which was prone to damage from the Toledo Worm. Two solutions were possible, namely covering the hull in copper or frequent inspections. The disadvantages were that a copper covering would reduce speed to 18 knots and there were limited docking facilities available in India. However, as there was no alternative, despatch of these vessels would proceed.

By June a marked improvement in the rescue organization had been achieved. A further allocation of HSLs allowed the basing of these craft from Karachi to Chittagong. There was now a total of 45 HSL's in the area. Two ASR Units, one each at Jiwani on the Persian/Pakistan border and at Jask in Persia on the Gulf of Oman became operational in August. ASR Liaison Officers were appointed to the staffs of Third Tactical Air Force, Eastern Air Command and the Group Headquarters.

On 5 June Chittagong Operations received a series of distress calls from a Super Fortress indicating that it was going to ditch. Spitfires and a HSL were dispatched to the area and within 20 minutes the Spitfires located the B29 on a mudbank. One remained as top cover while the other led the HSL to the position. The HSL picked up six survivors and sent a dinghy to collect a man sitting on top of the fuselage. This crewman reported that four more crew members were still inside the pressurized rear part near the tail. Another HSL and a minesweeper endeavoured to rescue these men, but to no avail, although efforts were continued all of the next day. It was known that the men were dead.

The Warwicks were not proving to be successful. There were maintenance problems which existed in all areas where the aircraft operated, but in India the climate caused the fabric covering to rot. A solution was the introduction of the metal-covered Lancaster Mark III, but that aircraft was required for bombing purposes in Europe. The American General Commanding XX Bomber Command complained about the lack of rescue facilities in the area and the low number of successful rescues of American aircrew. He had no complaint about the organization itself. This complaint had already been recognised by the RAF in May 1944 as stated above and action was in hand.

To compensate for the unserviceable Warwicks, ACSEA used their Catalinas and GR Liberators. In December it was agreed that No 212 Squadron operating Catalinas should be earmarked for ASR duties and would be stationed at Karachi and No 292 Squadron would be moved to Ratmalana.

CHAPTER TWENTY THREE

1945

◉

DISPOSITION OF SQUADRONS
30 SEPTEMBER 1945

The European war ceased 8 May 1945 and the Far East war in August 1945, after the atomic bombs were dropped on Hiroshima and Nagasaki. His Majesty's Government began to take steps to disband the squadrons.

MARITIME PATROL ATLANTIC 1945

No 10 Squadron disbanded in October 1945 in the UK. It was to reform in Australia in 1949.

No 36 Squadron moved to Benbecula in March 1945 with its Wellington XIVs and was disbanded on 4 June.

No 53 Squadron received Liberator VIIIs in January 1945 in addition to its Mark VIs which it disposed of in April. In June the squadron moved to St David's, South West Wales, where, in August, it received more Mark VIs. In September it moved to Merryfield, Somerset and to Gransden Lodge, West of Cambridge in December.

No 58 Squadron received Halifax IIIs in March 1945 and was disbanded at the end of May 1945.

No 59 Squadron received Liberator VIIIs in March

1945 and moved to Waterbeach, Cambridge in September, where it added Liberator VIs to its inventory.

No 86 Squadron added Liberator VIIIs to its inventory in January 1945, disposing of its Mark Vs in March. On 20 March 1945, Flt. Lt. N. E. M. Smith and crew gained a radar contact but the contact was lost in the course of the homing, regained at one and a half miles and lost again. Three runs were carried out but on each occasion the contact was lost. A basic sonobuoy pattern was laid in position 5944N 00516W. Contact was gained and two homing torpedoes were dropped. No results were observed. Initially it was believed that the boat was U-905, a type VIIc commanded by Oberleutnant zur See Bernhard Schwarting, but it is not now believed to have been that boat although it is believed that an unidentified boat was sunk.

On 23 April 1945, Flt. Lt. J. T. Lawrence and crew gained a radar contact just as they arrived on task. The contact was at four miles but was lost at half a mile. Homing torpedoes and a basic sonobuoy pattern were laid but no results were observed. The boat was U-396, a type VIIc commanded by Kapitänleutnant Hilmar Siemon and failed to return. It cannot be confirmed that this Liberator crew sank her. It may have been an accident, or a case of diving too deeply to avoid attack. The position of this attack was 5929N 00522W.

On 5 May 1945, Warrant Officer J. D. Nicol and crew were on patrol in the Kattegat and gained a radar contact at four and a half miles in position 5635N 01158E. On homing to the datum, three surfaced U-Boats were sighted, one of them under attack by a No 547 Squadron

Liberator. This was Flt. Lt. Hill and crew and having been hit by flak, they crashed into the sea. There was one survivor and he was picked up by a rescue ship from a lighthouse. The middle U-boat had dived. Nicol attacked the third boat, which was U-534, a type IXC/40 commanded by Kapitänleutnant Herbert Nollau. The stick of six depth charges overshot, but the follow-up attack of four DCs caused the boat to sink stern first. Nicol then guided the rescue boat to the survivor of Hill's crew. Of the other two boats, nothing further was seen. U-534 sank in position 5645N 01152E and was raised in August 1993 and subsequently put on show in Liverpool.

On 6 May 1945 Flt. Lt.M.C.Kay and crew gained a radar contact but it was not seen by the Leigh Light. Then, some 15 minutes later, a wake was seen in the Leigh Light but as they were not in an attacking position they went around and this time saw a periscope and a schnorkel. They attacked from 270 feet with a stick of six depth charges. Flying back over the datum, an oil slick was seen. This was U-3503, a type XXI commanded by Oberleutnant zur See Hugo Deiring and it was so badly damaged that the commander scuttled her on 8 May in position 5739N 01140E.

Again on 6 May Flt. Lt. T. H. E. Goldie DFC and crew gained two radar contacts and a periscope and a schnorkel were sighted in position 5755N 01053E. An attack was made with six depth charges. The U-boat broke through the surface and then went down. Bubbles, oil and wreckage were seen. This was U-3523, a type XXI commanded by Oberleutnant zur See Willy Muller, and it had been sunk, leaving eight survivors. In August the squadron moved to Oakington, adding Liberator VIs to its establishment.

No 120 Squadron was at Ballykelly on 1 January 1945. On 22 March 1945 Sqn. Ldr. L. J. White and crew had been diverted to the position given in a locating report from a No 172 Squadron Wellington. On arrival a basic sonobuoy pattern was dropped. Contact was gained and tracked and then two homing torpedoes were dropped. Explosions were heard. This was initially thought to be U-296, a type VIIc/41 commanded by Kapitänleutnant Karl Heinz Rasch. The sinking was originally credited to No 120 Squadron, but in 1985 the Naval Historical Branch of the Ministry of Defence considered that the two explosions were of the torpedoes hitting the sea bottom, which was only 50 fathoms down. U-296 was sunk from unknown causes. The boat No 172 Squadron had located was probably U-1003, which was scuttled the next day after being rammed by HMCS *New Glasgow*.

On 29 April 1945 Fg. Off. H. J. Oliver and crew gained a visual sighting of a wake at three miles in position 5604N 01106W. At two miles schnorkel exhaust was seen and an attack with a stick of four depth charges and one sonobuoy was made. On passing over this datum another schnorkel and wake was seen about a mile away but it disappeared before an attack could be mounted. Explosions could be heard from the sonobuoy in the water and a pattern of buoys was laid. An explosion and other noises were heard. This was believed to be U-1017, a type VIIc/41 commanded by Oberleutnant zur See Werner Riecken, which failed to return from this cruise. Another possibility was that this was U-398, which also disappeared without trace. The squadron disbanded at Ballykelly in June 1945.

No 172 Squadron was still at Limavady. On 22 March 1945 Plt. Off. Chambers and crew gained contact on a U-Boat twice off Malin Head and attacked with a stick of six depth charges with no result. As stated above a locating report was sent and a No 120 Squadron Liberator, captain Sqn. Ldr. White, was sent to further prosecute the contact. It was probably U-1003, a type VIIc/41 commanded by Oberleutnant zur See Werner Struebing, which was sunk the next day by HMCS *New Glasgow*. The squadron disbanded at Limavady in June 1945.

No 179 Squadron was still at St Eval with its Warwick Vs. On 24 February 1945 Flt. Lt. A. G. Brownshill and crew gained a radar contact at two miles from 600 feet. A wake was sighted in position 4956N 00444W, then a schnorkel. Brownshill flew along the wake and dropped six depth charges from 70 feet, which gave a good straddle. The boat was U-927, a type VIIc commanded by Kapitänleutnant Jurgen Ebert and had been sunk in the only success by this type of aircraft. There were no survivors.

No 201 Squadron took delivery of Sunderland Vs in February 1945. It was to operate these aircraft until 1957. On 30 April 1945 Flt. Lt. K. H. Foster and crew gained a visual sighting of what turned out to be schnorkel exhaust in position 5342N 00455W. An attack was made which was unsuccessful, as the port bomb rack would not run out. A follow-up attack was made but again the same problem was experienced. A basic sonobuoy pattern was laid but only environmental noises were heard. A square search was initiated and then exhaust smoke was seen. A stick of six depth charges was dropped from 70 feet but no results were seen. Then submarine noises were heard on the buoys. Royal Navy vessels arrived and the contact was handed over to them. They gained contact on a bottomed submarine and it was depth charged. Initially it was thought that this was U-246, a type VII commanded by Kapitänleutnant Ernst Raabe, but post war it was reassessed as possibly U-242, a type VII commanded by Oberleutnant zur See Heinrich Riedel.

More recently, it is believed the first assessment was correct, that it was U-246. However, U-Boat.net still shows that U-246 was sunk around 5 April 1945 in position 5340N 00453W. This is the almost the same position as the attack on 29 April 1945. Paul Kemp, in his *U-Boats Destroyed*, states that U-246 may have been lost through an accident, again in almost the same position. The wreckage brought up by the above attack was that of U-246. U-242 is believed to have been sunk by a mine per Paul Kemp's book in position 5203N 00553W on 5 April 1945. The squadron disposed of its Mark IIIs in June and moved to Pembroke Dock in August.

No 202 Squadron disbanded in June 1945 at Castle Archdale.

No 206 Squadron took delivery of Liberator VIIIs in March 1945, disposing of its Mark VIs the following month. At the end of July the squadron moved to Oakington.

No 210 Squadron was still Pembroke Dock. On 7 May 1945 Flt. Lt. K. M. Murray and crew gained a visual sighting of a periscope and attacked with a stick of four depth charges and a sonobuoy pattern in position 6132N 00132E. Mechanical noises were heard and two oil streaks were seen. This continued until the Catalina had to go off task. The boat concerned was U-320, a type VIIc/41, commanded by Oberleutnant zur See Heinz Emmerich and it had been badly damaged. The commander took the boat to the Norwegian coast and scuttled her. All U-Boats had been ordered to surrender by Dönitz but she had been dived, when this order had been transmitted and therefore had not heard it. The Squadron was disbanded at Pembroke Dock in June 1945.

No 220 Squadron moved to St David's in June 1945 and exchanged its Liberator VIs for Mark VIIIs in July. In September the squadron moved to Waterbeach in Cambridge and added some Mark VIs to its inventory again.

No 224 Squadron received Liberator VIIIs in February, disposing of its Mark VIs in March. On 29 March 1945 Flt. Lt. M. A. Graham and crew gained a visual sighting of a wake from three miles at 1000 feet in position 6144N 00223W. At one mile a schnorkel was seen and a stick of depth charges was dropped. The stern of the boat rose and the she went down. A sonobuoy pattern was laid and machinery noises were heard. This was U-1106, a type VIIc/41 commanded by Oberleutnant zur See Erwin Bartke, and it was sunk in this attack. On 5 May 1945 Sqn. Ldr. J. C. T. Downey DFC and crew were one of the crews on patrol in the Kattegat. They saw No 547 Squadron's Liberator submerged in the sea with its wheels protruding from the surface and two other Liberators orbiting. They saw the survivor of the crashed Liberator swimming to the lighthouse. Then they gained a visual sighting of a surfaced U-Boat in position 5650N 01120E, travelling very fast. This was U-2365, a type XXIII commanded by

Oberleutnant zur See Fritz-Otto Korfmann. A depth charge attack was carried out but by the crew's own admission it was badly executed. The subsequent steep turn for a follow up attack caused the gyros in the Mark XIV bombsight to topple. It would have been better if the aircraft had been equipped with a Mark III Low Level sight. Again it was not a good attack and on the third attack the DCs failed to release. Nevertheless the boat was damaged and Korfmann decided to scuttle her. In July the squadron moved to St Eval.

No 228 Squadron received Sunderland Vs in February 1945 and then disbanded in June.

No 251 Squadron remained at Reykjavik, receiving Fortress IIs in March 1945 and Warwick Is in August. It disposed of its Hudson IIIs in August and was disbanded in October.

No 269 Squadron remained at Lajes and disposed of its Hudson IIIs in August.

No 304 Squadron moved to St Eval in March 1945. On 2 April 1945 Warrant Officer R. Marczak and crew gained two radar contacts, one at eight miles in position 4957N 01306W and the other at six miles. A homing was commenced to the nearest contact but it disappeared at three miles. The navigator then saw a schnorkel at one mile and a stick of six depth charges was dropped. This was U-321, a type VIIc/41 commanded by Oberleutnant zur See Fritz Behrends and was sunk in this attack in position 5000N 01257W. The Squadron moved to North Weald in July where it received Warwick Is and IIIs. In September it moved to Chedburgh, near Cambridge. The squadron disposed of its Warwick Is in November and its Wellington XIVs in December.

No 311 Squadron disposed of its Liberator Vs in March 1945 in exchange for Mark VIs. In August the squadron moved to Manston and then to Prague.

No 330 Squadron exchanged its Sunderland IIIs for Mark Vs in April 1945 and moved to Stavangar/Sola in June. The squadron transferred to Norwegian control in November.

No 333 Squadron "A" Flight moved to Fornebu, Norway from Woodhaven with its Catalinas in June 1945 and transferred to Norwegian control in November.

No 407 Squadron Royal Canadian Air Force disbanded in June 1945.

No 415 Squadron Royal Canadian Air Force received Halifax VIIs in March 1945 and disbanded in May.

No 422 Squadron Royal Canadian Air Force disposed of its Sunderland IIIs in June 1945, moved to Basingbourn in July where it received Liberator VIs and VIIIs in August and disbanded in September.

No 423 Squadron Royal Canadian Air Force disposed of its Sunderland IIIs in May 1945 and moved to Bassingbourn in August, where it too received Liberator VIs and VIIIs. It disbanded in September.

No 459 Squadron Royal Australian Air Force returned from the Mediterranean in March to Chivenor and was equipped with Wellington XIIIs, but was disbanded in April 1945.

No 461 Squadron Royal Australian Air Force at Pembroke Dock received Sunderland GR5s in February and disbanded in June.

No 502 Squadron received Halifax IIIs at Stornoway in February 1945, disposing of its Mark IIs in March. It disbanded in May.

No 524 Squadron remained at Langham, disposing of its Wellington XIIIs in January 1945. It disbanded 25 May 1945.

No 547 Squadron received Liberator VIIIs at Leuchars in March 1945, disposing of its Mark VIs in May. On 5 May 1945 Flt. Lt. G. W. Hill and crew in KK299 attacked one of three U-Boats in the Kattegat. The aircraft was hit, setting one of the engines on fire. The entire crew was listed as lost, although one of them was apparently rescued by a boat from the nearby lighthouse. Two of the three boats concerned were U-534 commanded by Kapitänleutnant Herbert Nollau, who had shot down Fg. Off. Whiteley and crew from No 172 squadron and U-3503 commanded by Oberleutnant zur See Hugo Deiring. The third boat had submerged and was unidentified. U-534 was sunk by Warrant Officer J. D. Nicol and crew from No 86 squadron. The boat was raised in 1993 and in 1996 was put on display in Liverpool.

Again on 5 May, Fg. Off. A. A. Bruneau RCAF and crew were one of a number of crews briefed to search for U-Boats trying to reach the Norwegian Fjords from the Baltic. They overflew Denmark and on reaching the Kattegat they gained radar contact on two U-boats at 14 miles. The boats opened fire as an attack was made on the leading boat. This split into two pieces and sank in position 5611N O1108E. The boat was U-579, a type VIIc commanded by Oberleutnant zur See Hans-Dietrich Schwarzenberg. Bruneau turned to attack the second boat, only to find that it was being attacked by another aircraft. Bruneau was awarded the DFC. The squadron disbanded in June.

No 612 Squadron at Langham disbanded in July 1945.

UK AIR SEA RESCUE 1945

The responsibility for Air Sea Rescue belonged to both Fighter and Coastal Commands up to 15 February 1945, when No 278 Squadron was transferred to Coastal and Nos 275 and 277 Squadrons were disbanded. Fighter Command then ceased to have any ASR squadrons, although control of ASR units for quick scrambling remained with the Fighter Command Sector Control Stations.

No 278 Squadron transferred to Coastal with Walrus amphibians, having disposed of its Warwicks in January 1945 and of its Spitfires on transfer. As there was little risk of enemy action in the Channel area, it had been decided to dispose of fighters in the SAR role. In May, Sea Otters were added to its inventory and in October the Squadron disbanded.

No 279 Squadron added Hurricane IIcs to its inventory in February 1945 and had detachments at Banff, Wick, Fraserburgh, Tain and Reykjavik. The UK detachments were mainly in support of the Banff, Dallachy and North Coates Strike Wings. In July it received an updated version of the Walrus, the Sea Otter, but all these aircraft were disposed of when the squadron moved to Beccles and received Lancaster ASR IIIs in September. There was a detachment at Pegu starting in September.

No 280 Squadron remained at Beccles with its Warwick Is until 3 November when it moved to Langham with detachments at Thorney Island, St Eval, Aldergrove and Lajes in the Azores. Later in the month it moved to Thornaby, changing its detachments to Thorney Island,

Aldergrove, Tain, Reykjavik in Iceland and Lossiemouth.

No 281 Squadron moved to Mullaghmore with a detachment at Tiree in February 1945. In March it added Sea Otters to its inventory and moved to Limavady with detachments at Tiree and Valley in Anglesey. In April Warwick VIs came on to the establishment but were removed the following month. In August the Squadron moved to Ballykelly and added Wellington XIIIs to the strength. There were detachments at Tiree and Tain. The squadron was disbanded in October 1945.

No 282 Squadron at St Eval received Walrus and Sea Otter amphibians in March 1945 only to be disbanded in July.

UK ANTI SHIPPING SQUADRONS TO SEPTEMBER 1945

BANFF STRIKE WING

On 25 January, 18 Mosquitoes from Nos 143, 235 and 248 led by Sqn. Ldr. H. H. K. Gunnis attacked shipping in Eidsfjord. The merchant vessels *Ilse Fritzen* and *Bjergfin* were sunk. All aircraft returned to Banff, but one collided with another and crashed, killing the crew. On 17 March, 33 Mosquitoes from Nos 143, 235, 248 and 333 Squadrons attacked merchant ships in Alesund. The *Iris*, the *Remage* and the *Log* were sunk. The *Erna* was severely damaged. Two aircraft were shot down but the Captain, Wg. Cdr. R. K. Orrock, OC 248, survived. On 23 March, 38 Mosquitoes from Nos 143, 235, 248 and 333 Squadrons escorted by Mustangs set off for the Norwegian coast. On arrival the squadrons split into three parts, each accompanied by a No 333 Squadron outrider. No 235 Squadron led by Sqn. Ldr. R. Reid attacked the Rotenfels and set it on fire. Reid's aircraft was hit and crashed into the sea. His body was never found but that of his navigator, Fg.Off A. Turner was washed ashore and he was buried in Stavne Cemetery. On 2 April, 41 Mosquitoes from Nos 143, 235 and 248 Squadrons with two outriders from No 333 Squadron and led by Wg. Cdr. H. N. Jackson-Smith, OC 248, attacked and sank the *Concordia* and the *William Blumer* in Sandefjord. The *Espana* and the tanker *Kattegat* were severely damaged. Two aircraft were hit but landed safely in Sweden.

On 9 April, 35 Mosquitoes from Nos 143, 235 and 248 Squadrons, together with two guides from No 333 Squadron and one from the RAF Film Unit and escorts of Mustangs from Peterhead, ranged over the Kattegat. They were led by Sqn. Ldr. H. H. K. Gunnis. The wakes of the type IX U-Boat U-804 commanded by Oberleutnant zur See Herbert Meyer and the type VII U-1065 commanded by Oberleutnant zur See Johann Panitz were seen and then the boats. They were attacked with cannon and rockets and exploded and sank in position 5805N 01110E. U-804 exploded with such force that it caught the film unit aircraft, which crashed into the sea. Two other aircraft from No 248 Squadron and one from No 235 Squadron were damaged but they landed safely in Sweden.

Fg. Off. A. J. Randell and his navigator, Fg. Off. R. R. Rawlins of No 235 Squadron, had been escorting a Mosquito with engine trouble back to Banff. Confirming that the aircraft could get back safely, they then returned to the scene and located another type IX/40, U-843 commanded by Kapitänleutnant Oscar Herwatz. Randell sank the boat with three rocket attacks. On 11 April, 35 Mosquitoes from Nos 143, 235, 248 and 333 Squadrons led by Wg. Cdr. A. H. Simmonds attacked shipping in Porsgrunn. The *Dione*, the *Kalmas*, the *Nordsjo* and the *Traust* were sunk. Two other ships were severely damaged. Two aircraft and crews failed to return.

On 19 April the Banff Strike Wing, consisting of 22 aircraft from No 143, 235, 248 and 333 Squadrons, attacked three U-Boats led by a minesweeper, a fourth submarine having dived. One No 248 Squadron aircraft was damaged and diverted to Sweden and another was hit over Denmark and force-landed there. U-251, a type VIIc commanded by Oberleutnant zur See Franz Sack, was sunk, U-2502, a type XXI commanded by Leutnant zur See Heinz Franke was damaged and U-2335, a type XXIII commanded by Leutnant zur See Karl-Dietrich Benthin was also damaged. The minesweeper was left burning. On 2 May, 35 Mosquitoes from Nos 143, 235, 248, 333 and 404 Squadrons led by Sqn. Ldr. A. G. Deck ranged over the Kattegat. They found, attacked and sank the type XXIII U-Boat U-2359 commanded by Oberleutnant zur See G. Bischoff and damaged another type XXIII in position 5729N01124E. Nos 333 and 404 Squadrons acted as top cover. A minesweeper was also sunk. One aircraft was damaged but landed safely in Sweden.

On 4 May, 43 Mosquitoes from Nos 143, 235, 248 and 333 Squadrons with an escort of Mustangs visited the port of Aarhus, Denmark. They were led by Wg. Cdr. C. N. Foxley-Norris, OC 143 Squadron. They sank the *Wolfgang L. M. Russ* and severely damaged the *Angamos* and the *Gunther Russ*. Three aircraft were damaged but they landed safely in Sweden.

DALLACHY STRIKE WING
On 10 January Sqn. Ldr. W. R. Christison led 22 Beaufighters from Nos 404, 455, 489 Squadrons and two Mosquitoes from No 333 Squadron in an attack against an anti submarine vessel and a minesweeper, causing severe damage. Two Search and Rescue Warwicks of No 279 Squadron from Fraserburgh and ten Mustangs of No 315 Squadron from Peterhead were present. Two Beaufighters were lost.

NORTH COATES STRIKE WING
On 17 January, 32 Beaufighters led by Wg. Cdr. D. L. Cartridge, OC 254, escorted by two squadrons of Spitfires, attacked the hull of a Hansa ship in the anchorage of Marsdiep. The hull, two of the four minesweepers and a flak ship were left on fire. Heavy flak was encountered from the escorts and shore batteries. Four Beaufighters were shot down and two more collided. Nine aircrew were killed.

No 119 squadron re-equipped with Swordfish IIIs in January 1945, disposing of its Albacores in February, when it moved to Knocke le Zout. It returned to Bircham Newton on 22 May 1945 and disbanded the same day.

No 143 squadron joined in with Nos 235 and 248 Squadrons on 9 April 1945 in an attack on U-804 and U-1065, sinking both. The Squadron disbanded at Banff on 25 May 1945, being renumbered No 14 Squadron and leaving the Command.

No 144 Squadron disbanded at Dallachy on 25 May 1945.

No 235 Squadron Mosquito HR434, flown by Flt. Lt. J. R. Williams and navigator A/Flt. Lt. J. T. Flower, located and attacked U-249 off the Norwegian coast on 24 March 1945. The aircraft was shot down and there were no survivors. The U-Boat however, had to return to Bergen. On 19 April 1945 the squadron joined with Nos 143, 248 and 333 Squadrons in an attack on U-251, U-2502 and U-2335. The squadron disbanded on 10 July 1945 at Banff.

No 236 Squadron with 13 Beaufighters and 17 from No 254 Squadron were on an anti-shipping search on 3 May 1945 with an escort of Mustangs from Nos 65 and 118 Squadrons. A surfaced U-Boat was sighted in position 5537N 01000E. Five Beaufighters of No 236 Squadron attacked with rockets and six from No 254 attacked with cannons. This was U-2503, a type XXI commanded by Kapitänleutnant Karl Jurg Wachter. It was hit, caught fire and then exploded. Out of control, it ran aground. The following day 12 Beaufighters of No 236 Squadron and 10 of No 254 Squadron, with an escort of Mustangs, gained sightings of three surfaced U-Boats in position 5520N 00950E with two escort vessels. These were U-2338, a type XXIII, commanded by Oberleutnant zur See Karl E. Kaiser, U-393, a type VIIc commanded by Oberleutnant zur See Friedrich Herrle and U-236 and a type VIIc commanded by Oberleutnant zur See Herbert Mumm. One aircraft from No 236 Squadron attacked the lead boat with cannons and it dived. Three aircraft from No 254 Squadron attacked the second boat and then all boats and escorts were attacked. The third U-Boat was seen to explode. All three U-Boats were sunk, as was one escort, and the other was damaged. Most of the crews survived. The squadron disbanded at North Coates on 25 May 1945.

No 248 Squadron joined in with Nos 143 and 235 Squadrons in a successful attack on U-804 and U-1065 on 9 April 1945. On 19 April 1945 the Squadron joined with Nos 143, 235 and 333 Squadrons in an attack on U-251, U-2502 and U-2335. The Squadron moved to Chivenor in July 1945 from Banff. It spent a few days at Ballykelly in December but returned to Chivenor the same month.

No 254 Squadron added some Mosquito XVIIIs to its inventory in March 1945 but disposed of them in May. On 3 May 1945, 13 aircraft in company with 17 from No 236 Squadron attacked and sank U-2503. On 4 May 1945 10 aircraft together with 12 from No 236 Squadron sank U-2338, U-393 and U-236. The squadron moved from North Coates to Chivenor in June and then to Langham in November.

No 333 Squadron joined with Nos 143, 235, and 248 Squadrons in an attack on U-251, U-2502 and U-2335 on 19 April 1945. "B" Flight moved to Fornebu in June 1945 and was transferred to Norwegian control in November.

No 334 Squadron formed out of No 333 Squadron with Mosquito VIs on 26 May 1945 and moved to Oslo Gardemoen on 8 June. It transferred to Norwegian control 21 November.

No 404 Squadron Royal Canadian Air Force re-equipped with Mosquito VIs in March 1945 moving to Banff in early April. It was disbanded on 25 May 1945.

No 455 Squadron Royal Australian Air Force disbanded at Dallachy on 25 May 1945.

No 489 Squadron Royal New Zealand Air Force moved to Banff in June 1945, re-equipping with Mosquito VIs and disbanding in August.

On 9 April, 1945 the Banff Strike Wing consisting of 34 Mosquitoes from Nos 143, 235 and 248 squadrons led by Sqn. Ldr. H. H. Gunnis DFC, attacked two U-Boats in position 5805N 01110E. On 19 April 1945 the Banff Wing, consisting of 22 Mosquitoes from Nos 143, 235, 248 and 333 Squadrons led by Wing Commander A. H. Simmonds, attacked U-251, U-2502 and U-2335. The results from this attack are shown under the Banff Strike Wing above.

On 4 May 1945, as stated above, the North Coates Strike Wing Beaufighters attacked and sank U-236, U-393 and U-2338 north of Flensberg Fjord in position 5455N 01007E. These were en route for Fredicia in Denmark through the Lille Belt. Other boats attacked were U-155 commanded by Oberleutnant zur See Friedrich Altemeier, U-680 commanded by Oberleutnant zur See Max Ulber and U-1233 commanded by Oberleutnant zur See Heinrich Niemeyer. No 126 squadron Mustangs were providing escort and attacked a Sperrbrecher. Major A. Austeen, DFC R. No. AF, the CO, was shot down, probably by U-155.

Second Tactical Air Force aircraft joined the attack on U-Boats. On 2 May 1945, Typhoons of No 245 Squadron attacked and destroyed by beaching one U-Boat. No 175 Squadron damaged one U-Boat. On 3 May No 175 Squadron sank one and damaged two U-Boats. No 184

Squadron sank one and No 245 Squadron damaged one. On 4 May No 184 Squadron damaged two U-Boats and No 245 Squadron damaged one. All the aircraft involved were Typhoons. The U-Boats were U-1210, U-2540, U-3030 and U-3032.

MEDITERRANEAN 1945

No 38 Squadron received Wellington XIVs and moved to Foggia Main with detachments at Rosignano and Hal Far in January 1945. In April it moved to Falconara and in July it moved to Luqa, where it added Warwick ASR 1s to its inventory. Detachments were at Elmas, Benina and Hassani.

No 221 Squadron moved to Idku in April 1945 with detachments at Aqir, El Adem and Benina. It disbanded 21 August 1945.

No 252 Squadron moved to Aboukir, Gianaclis and Hassani in February 1945 and to Araxos in August.

No 272 Squadron moved to Falconara in March 1945 and to Gragnano in April, where it disbanded on 30 April.

No 624 Squadron had detachments at Foggia and Hassani in January but moved to Foggia in February, adding further detachments to Falconara and Rosignano. In April the squadron moved to Falconara with more detachments at Treviso, Hal Far and Sedes. In July it moved to Rosignano and reduced its detachments to Hal Far and Sedes. While maintaining these detachments the squadron moved to Littorio and disbanded in November 1945.

MEDITERRANEAN AIR SEA RESCUE 1945

On 10 March a Mosquito was ditched off the Northern

Coast of Italy, which was still occupied by the Germans. ASR aircraft using flares tried to rescue the pilot and navigator, but heavy anti-aircraft fire forced them to give up. The next afternoon a Walrus and a Warwick escorted by Spitfires located a survivor on a beach near the wreckage of the Mosquito, which was in a minefield. The Walrus landed outside the field and tried to reach the crew member in a dinghy. Strong currents stopped this endeavour. The Warwick then dropped an airborne lifeboat alongside the Walrus. The two Walrus crew boarded the lifeboat and manoevoured it through the minefield, picked up the pilot, the navigator being dead, and brought him back to the Walrus, which then took off and returned safely to base.

No 283 Squadron was still at Hal Far with Warwick Is.

No 284 Squadron moved to Pomigliano in April 1945 and disbanded 21 September 1945.

No 293 Squadron, still with its Warwicks and Walruses, moved to Foggia in March 1945 with detachments at Cesenatico and Udine. In June the squadron moved to Pomigliano. On 2 April 1945 Lieutenant Veitch, South African Air Force, flying a Thunderbolt from No 260 Squadron was forced to ditch having received flak in his engine. A Catalina from the American No 1 Emergency Rescue Squadron found him in a minefield, which prevented the Catalina from landing. A No 293 Squadron Warwick arrived and dropped an Airborne Lifeboat which Veitch boarded and sailed clear of the mines. The Catalina then rescued him. On 5 April Veitch was again hit in a Thunderbolt and ditched in the Gulf of Trieste. An enemy torpedo boat tried to rescue him but a Mustang opened fire on it and it turned away. A Warwick dropped an Airborne Lifeboat and the pilot boarded it. Shore batteries opened fire on him and German naval craft approached with a view to pick him up. The Warwick's fighter escort fired its cannon across the enemy's bows, but this failed to deter it and a Mosquito was forced to sink it. Again there was a minefield which Veitch had to negotiate, and he was then picked up by a Catalina. Although it has nothing to do with the RAF rescue squadrons, Veitch on 30 April again ditched into a minefield and an American Flying Fortress dropped an Airborne Lifeboat to him. He sailed through the minefield and was then taken in tow by a HSL. He was awarded a DFC.

No 294 Squadron moved from the Mediterranean to the Middle East, namely Basrah in June 1945 with its Wellington XIIIs and Warwick Is. The Wellington XIs were disposed of in June.

No 459 Squadron returned to Chivenor in March where it was equipped with Wellington XIIIs only to be disbanded the following month.

MIDDLE EAST 1945

No 8 Squadron remained at Khormaksar with Wellington XIIIs and disbanded on 1 May 1945. However, it reformed at Jessore, north east of Calcutta on 15 May 1945 as a renumbering of No 200 Squadron. It was equipped with Liberator VIs and moved to Minneriya with a detachment to Sigiriya later in the month. It would disband in November.

No 244 Squadron disbanded on 1 May 1945 at Masirah.

No 621 Squadron was still at Khormaksar with its Wellington XIIIs but added Mark XIVs to the establishment in January 1945. In November it moved to Mersah Matruh. In December it disposed of its Wellingtons and converted to Warwick Vs.

WEST AFRICA 1945

No 95 Squadron was still at Bathurst with Sunderland IIIs but disbanded on 30 June 1945.

No 343 (French) Squadron was at Dakar with Sunderland IIIs. It disbanded on 27 November 1945, being transferred to French control.

No 344 (French) Squadron was also at Dakar with Wellington XIs and XIIIs with a detachment at Port Etienne. The squadron disbanded on 27 November 1945 being transferred to French control.

No 270 Squadron, still at Apapa with Sunderland IIIs, disbanded in June 1945.

No 490 Squadron Royal New Zealand Air Force was at Jui with Sunderland IIIs and disbanded 30 June 1945.

WEST AFRICA SEARCH AND RESCUE

Between March 1943 and February 1945 there had been 44 incidents and the Command had taken part in 32 of them. It had rescued 201 aircrew out of 270 and, with the aid of the Command's aircraft and boats, 649 merchant seamen had been rescued.

SOUTH AND EAST AFRICA 1945

No 209 Squadron remained at Kipevu, Mombasa with its Catalina IIAs but in February 1945 it started to re-equip with Sunderland Vs. The Catalinas were disposed of in June and in July the Squadron moved to Koggala in Ceylon.

No 259 Squadron re-equipped with Sunderland Vs at Dar-es-Salaam in March 1945 disposing of its Catalinas in April. In May the squadron disbanded.

No 262 Squadron at Congella disbanded in February 1945, renumbering as No 35 Squadron South African Air Force.

No 265 Squadron was still at Diego Suarez with Catalina Ib's and disbanded on 1 May 1945.

FAR EAST 1945

No 22 Squadron moved to Joari, near CoXs Bazaar south of Chittagong on January 1945 with Beaufighter Xs. It moved to Chiringa in April and Gannavaram north of Madras in June. The squadron disbanded on 30 September 1945.

No 160 Squadron moved to Minneriya in February 1945 disposing of its Liberator Mark VIs. In September it received Liberator VIIIs. In October 1945 it disposed of its Mark IIIs and moved to Kankesanturai. In November it disposed of its Mark Vs. After the Japanese surrender the squadron was engaged on transport duties.

No 191 squadron moved to Koggala in April 1945, re-equipping with Catalina IBs while retaining its Catalina IVBs. There was a detachment at Korangi Creek. The squadron disbanded in June.

No 200 moved to Jessore on 1 April 1945 with its Liberator VIs and disbanded on 15 May 1945, being renumbered as No 8 Squadron.

No 8 Squadron had disbanded in the Middle East on

1 May 1945, only to reform on 15 May with Liberator VIs and moved to Minneriya with a detachment at Sigiriya, Ceylon. It would disband in November 1945.

No 203 Squadron and its Liberator VIs moved to Kankesanterai, North Ceylon with detachments at Akyab and Cocos Island.

No 205 Squadron at Koggala disposed of its Catalina Is in February 1945, receiving Sunderland GR5s in June. It disposed of its Catalina IVbs in September. It had a detachment at Iwakuni.

No 209 Squadron arrived at Koggala in July from East Africa and in September moved to Kai Tak, Hong Kong.

No 212 Squadron added Catalina Ibs to its inventory in February 1945, but these and the Mark IVs were disposed of in June. The squadron moved to Red Hills Lake in May with detachments at Akyab and Bally. In July the squadron disbanded, renumbering as No 240 Squadron.

No 217 Squadron moved to Gannavaram with its Beaufighter Xs in June 1945 and in September it disbanded.

No 230 Squadron received Sunderland GR Vs in February 1945 and disposed of its Mark IIIs in April when it moved to Akyab with detachments at Red Hills Lake. In May the squadron moved to Rangoon and in July to Red Hills Lake with a detachment at Seletar.

No 240 Squadron was at Red Hills Lake with Catalina IVs when it was disbanded on 1 July 1945. It reformed on the same day at Red Hills Lake with personnel from No 240 and No 212 squadrons equipping with Catalina Is, IVs and Sunderland GR5's. It had detachments at Rangoon, Bally, China Bay and Penang.

No 321 Squadron Royal Netherlands Navy was at

China Bay with Liberator VIs and Catalina IVb's on loan from No 205 Squadron. These were handed back in February 1945. In April the squadron received some Catalina IVbs of its own. There were detachments at Kemajoran, Cocos and Soerabaya. The squadron was handed over to Dutch control in December.

No 354 Squadron moved to Cuttack in January 1945 with a detachment at Kankesanturai. The Squadron disbanded in May 1945.cx

No 618 Squadron moved to Narromine north west of Sydney, Australia in February 1945 receiving Mosquito VIs. In July the squadron disbanded.

FAR EAST AIR SEA RESCUE 1945

Despite the Admiralty's estimation that 40 Fairmile launches would reach the theatre by March 1945, due to delays in delivery and equipment no vessels were available for despatch and delivery was postponed until July 1945. Neither the Air Ministry nor the Admiralty was satisfied that these launches were suitable for the area and docking facilities remained a problem. The Air Council asked the Admiralty to provide naval rescue vessels. In the meantime two Fairmiles had set out on the voyage to South East Asia. By the time they had reached the Mediterranean, the Admiralty had agreed to provide naval rescue craft and the two boats were stopped. Commander in Chief East Indies had agreed to provide twelve Flower Class corvettes for long range rescue work. On 4 August ACSEA was informed accordingly and then, on 15 August Japan surrendered.

The Americans provided support in the form of two flights of the First Emergency Rescue Squadron being sent to the theatre from Italy. They became No 7 Emergency Rescue Squadron, with Catalinas and Flying Fortresses (B17s), equipped with airborne lifeboats.

No 292 Squadron moved to Agartala, North East India, in February 1945 with detachments at Kankesanterai and Chittagong. On 15 June it disbanded, being split into Nos 1347, 1348 and 1349 Flights. The Warwicks and Liberators were based at Agaterla and Kankesanturai and Sea Otters were at Akyab, Ratmalana and Mingaladen. In July, Warwick Mark Is specially treated with aluminium dope to counter the fabric dope problem, were sent to the Squadron.

As stated above No 212 squadron was disbanded in July but reformed as No 240 squadron. This squadron was equipped with Catalina Is until October 1945 and Catalina IVs until August 1945. It was also operating Sunderland GR Vs until March 1946 when it disbanded.

It had been decided that all GR flying boat squadrons should be re-equipped with the Sunderland as it was easier to maintain and had better seaworthiness. It could not, however, carry the airborne lifeboat.

Before June 1943 no records had been kept about rescue operations in the Far East. From that date to the end of the Far East war 150 aircraft involving 700 aircrew were in distress over the sea. In 88 incidents successful rescues were carried out. That is, 327 aircrew were saved, a 50 percent success rate. Most of these rescues were performed by operational aircraft and ships rather than dedicated ASR assets. The GR Catalinas, naval and merchant ships saved 1304 mariners between 1 May 1943 and 31 July 1945.

METEOROLOGICAL CALIBRATION 1945.

No 517 Squadron was at Brawdy and received Halifax IIIs in March. It disposed of its Halifax Vs in June 1945.

No 518 Squadron at Tiree also received Halifax IIIs in March 1945, disposing of its Mark Vs in June. It had detachments at Wick and Tain. In September the squadron moved to Aldergrove, adding Hurricane IIcs and Spitfire VIIs to its inventory.

No 519 Squadron disposed of its Hudson IIIs in March 1945 and moved to Tain in August. In this month it received Halifax IIIs and disposed of its Fortress IIs in September.

No 520 Squadron was still at Gibraltar. In January 1945 it received Hudson IIIs and in May it exchanged its Halifax Vs for Halifax IIIs. In July it added Warwick Is to its inventory.

No 521 Squadron received Fortress IIIs in May 1945.

PHOTGRAPHIC RECONNAISSANCE UNITS

No 540 Squadron moved to Coulommiers in March 1945 with a detachment at Trondheim. In June it disposed of its Mosquito VIs and of its Mark XXXIIs in August. In September it moved to Mount Farm, still with a detachment at Trondheim. In November it moved to Benson and added Mosquito XXXIVs to its inventory. It disposed of its Mosquito XVIs in December.

No 541 Squadron disposed of its Spitfire Xs in April 1945 and its Mustangs IIIs in June. In October it received some Meteor F3s.

No 542 Squadron disbanded in August 1945.

No 544 Squadron disposed of its Mosquito IXs in February 1945, its Mark XVIs in August and its Mark XXXIIs in October. It had received Mark XXXIVs in April. The squadron disbanded in October 1945.

CHAPTER TWENTY FOUR

COASTAL 1946

Now that the war was over, the process of reducing the armed forces had begun in 1945 and carried on into 1946.

UK MARITIME PATROL

No 53 Squadron disbanded in February 1946.

No 59 Squadron disbanded in June 1946.

No 86 Squadron disbanded in April 1946.

No 120 Squadron reformed at Leuchars from No 160 Squadron with Lancaster GR 3's and Liberator VIIIs.

No 160 Squadron had returned from the Far East to Leuchars in June and in August converted to Lancaster GR 3s. In October the squadron disbanded, being renumbered No 120 Squadron.

No 179 Squadron was split into No 179X Squadron and No 179Y Squadron in February 1946 and re-equipped with Lancaster ASR 3's. In June No 179Y Squadron was renumbered as No 210 Squadron and No 179X dropped its suffix. In September it was absorbed into No 210 Squadron.

No 201 Squadron was still at Pembroke Dock with

Sunderland GR 5's but in March it received some Seaford Is which it disposed of a month later. In April it moved to Calshot with a detachment at Finkenwerder.

No 203 Squadron added Liberators VIIIs to its inventory in January 1946 while in the Far East and returned home to Leuchars in May. In July it began to convert to Lancaster GR 3's and disposed of its Liberators in October 1946.

No 206 Squadron disbanded in April 1946.

No 210 Squadron reformed at St.Eval in June being No 179Y Squadron renumbered. No 179X Squadron joined in September to form "B" Flight.

No 220 Squadron disbanded in May 1946.

No 224 Squadron split into No 224X and No 224Y Squadrons in February 1946. In June 1946 No 224Y was renumbered No 228 Squadron and No 224 X Squadron dropped its suffix, In October the squadron exchanged its Liberators for Lancaster GR 3's.

No 228 Squadron reformed at St Eval in June 1946 with Liberators VIIIs only to disband in September.

No 230 Squadron returned from the Far East in August, moving to Castle Archdale in Northern Ireland and then in September to Calshot with a detachment at Finkenwerder, near Hamburg.

No 269 Squadron disbanded in March 1946.

No 304 Squadron exchanged its Warwick IIIs for Halifax VIIIs in May 1946 but was disbanded in December.

No 311 Squadron was disbanded in February when it was transferred to Czech control.

UK SEARCH AND RESCUE
No 279 Squadron disbanded in March 1946, the Lancasters at Pegu being absorbed into No 1348 Flight. No 280 Squadron disbanded in June 1946.

UK STRIKE WINGS
No 36 Squadron was reformed at Thorney Island from No 248 Squadron in October 1946 with Mosquito FB6's.

No 42 Squadron was reformed at Thorney Island from No 254 Squadron in October 1946 with Beaufighter TF 10's.

No 248 Squadron moved to Thorney Island in May and was disbanded in October being renumbered No 36 Squadron.

No 254 Squadron moved to Thorney Island in May 1946 and was disbanded in October, being renumbered as No 42 Squadron.

MEDITERRANEAN MARITIME PATROL
No 38 Squadron added Lancaster GR 3s to its inventory in July 1946, disposing of its Warwicks in November. It had a detachment at Ein Shemar, south of Haifa, to which base it moved in December.
No 252 Squadron disbanded in December 1946.

MEDITERRANEAN SEARCH AND RESCUE
No 283 Squadron disbanded in March 1946.
No 293 Squadron disbanded in April 1946.

MIDDLE EAST
No 621 Squadron moved to Aqir, south of Tel Aviv, in

April, where it added Lancaster ASR IIIs to its inventory In June it moved to Ein Shemar and disbanded in September, being renumbered as No 18 Squadron. This squadron then received Lancaster GR 3s in the same month and was then disbanded on 15 September 1946 being absorbed into B Flight of No 38 Squadron.

No 294 Squadron disbanded in April 1946.

FAR EAST

No 88 Squadron reformed at Kai Tak, Hong Kong in September 1946 by renumbering No 1430 Flight and was equipped with Sunderland GR 5's. This squadron had been a Boston light bomber squadron in Europe until it was disbanded in April 1945. There were detachments at Iwakuni and Seletar.

No 160 Squadron returned to Leuchars in June 1946. In August it added Lancaster GR 3's to its inventory. The Liberators were disposed of in October when the squadron was disbanded and reformed as No 120 Squadron.

No 203 Squadron added Liberator VIIIs to its inventory in January 1946 and in May returned home to Leuchars retaining its Liberators.

No 205 Squadron was at Koggala with Sunderland GR Vs. There was a detachment at Iwakuni.

No 209 Squadron moved to Seletar, Singapore in April 1946 with its Sunderland GR Vs.

No 230 Squadron returned home to Pembroke Dock, Wales in April 1946 with Sunderland GR Vs.

No 240 Squadron moved to Koggala in January 1946 and was then disbanded in March.

METEORLOGICAL CALIBRATION

No 202 Squadron was reformed at Aldergrove, Northern Ireland in October 1946 being No 518 Squadron renumbered. At the same time it received Halifax GR 6s.

No 517 Squadron was disbanded in June 1946.

No 518 Squadron added Halifax VIs to its inventory in March 1946. Its Hurricanes and Spitfires were disposed of in October. In October the Squadron was disbanded being renumbered No 202 Squadron at Aldergrove.

No 519 Squadron disbanded in May 1946.

No 520 Squadron disbanded in April 1946.

No 521 Squadron disbanded in March 1946.

PHOTOGRAPHIC RECONNAISSANCE

No 540 Squadron disbanded in October 1946, being renumbered No 58 Squadron and leaving the Command.

No 541 Squadron received some Lancaster PR1s in February 1946 and had detachments at Yudum, Takoradi, Kano and Accra. In October it disbanded the Lancaster Flight, being renumbered No 82 Squadron, and left the Command. It still retained its PR role.

The total number of squadrons left in Coastal Command and Maritime Forces overseas at the end of 1946 was now thirteen. These were:

UNITED KINGDOM

No 36 Squadron at Thorney Island with Mosquito FB6s.

No 42 Squadron at Thorney Island with Beaufighter TF 10s.

No 120 Squadron with Lancaster GR3s at Leuchars.

No 201 Squadron at Calshot with Sunderland GR 5s.

No 202 Squadron in the Meteorological Calibration role at Aldergrove with Halifax GR VIs.
No 203 Squadron at Leuchars with Lancaster GR 3s.
No 210 Squadron at St.Eval with Lancaster GR 3s.
No 224 Squadron at St Eval with Lancaster GR 3s.
No 230 Squadron at Calshot with Sunderland GR 5s.

MIDDLE EAST
No 38 Squadron with Lancaster GR3s at Ein Shemar, Palestine.

FAR EAST
No 88 Squadron at Kai Tak.
No 205 Squadron at Koggala with Sunderland GR 5s.
No 209 Squadron at Seletar with Sunderland GR 5s.

CHAPTER TWENTY FIVE

THE STRIKE WINGS

The Strike Wings did not exist at the beginning of the War in 1939. Coastal had the responsibility for attacking enemy surface shipping but the only aircraft available were two squadrons of Vildebeestes. Thus on 3 September 1939 a Blenheim of No 139 Squadron, Bomber Command, on a reconnaissance and photographic sortie, found enemy warships entering the Schillig Roads from Wilhelmshaven. The temperature at 24000 feet was so low that the radio was frozen and the aircraft had to return to base to pass on the information. The following day the same pilot, Flying Officer McPherson, took off and located enemy warships in the Schillig Roads, Brunsbüttel and Wilhelmshaven. A radio message was sent but it was received in a corrupt form. On returning to base five Blenheims each of Nos 107 and 110 squadrons were despatched to attack independently. No 139 squadron also took part, but failed to find the enemy. One of the ships was the Admiral Scheer and this was hit, but the bombs failed to explode. The fusing was set for 11 seconds and the bombs probably bounced overboard. One Blenheim crashed on the fo'c'sle of the Emden.

While this attack was going on fourteen Wellingtons of Bomber Command's Nos 9 and 149 squadrons were attacking Brunsbüttel. Two battleships had been reported in the harbour, but bad weather and heavy anti-aircraft fire defended the targets. Two Wellingtons failed to return.

Twenty-nine aircraft took part in these raids and seven were lost. The raids illustrate the unpreparedness of the British, the ineffective weapons and the lack of navigation aids. It also shows the courage and determination of the crews.

It was decided that awaiting the report of the enemy from a single aircraft on patrol was ineffective. By the time the attacking force arrived the ships would be back in port. Accordingly, the reconnaissance in force was designed whereby nine armed aircraft would sweep the Heligoland Bight and attack any enemy warships they might find. However, the crews were not to seek out or attack the enemy in their bases, nor were they to infringe Danish or Dutch territorial waters, nor were they to attack warships escorting merchant ships if there was any risk of damaging the merchantmen.

The first of these sorties occurred on 26 September and was uneventful. On the 29 September eleven Hampdens attacked two destroyers but lost five to fighters. The reconnaissance in force was then unpopular, but nevertheless Bomber Command had twenty-four aircraft on standby every day at the call of Coastal Command.

In 1940 there was a change. Coastal began to re-equip with the Bristol Beaufort and changed the role of Nos 48 and 217 squadrons from Maritime Patrol to Torpedo Bomber. Nos 53, 235, 236, 248 and 254 squadrons were transferred from Fighter Command to Coastal. No 53 had Blenheim IVs, No 235 had Blenheim IVFs converting to Mark IFs, No 236 had Blenheim IFs converting to Mark IVFs , No 248 had Blenheim IFs converting to Mark IVFs and No 254 had Blenheim IFs converting to Mark IVFs.

Again in 1940, Germany invaded Norway. This guaranteed the supply of iron ore from Sweden which was transported by two routes. The most important one was by rail to Narvik, then by sea through the islands and over the North Sea to Holland and then by barge up the Rhine. Germany exported coal and coke by the same route. Norway had nickel, molybdenum, iron pyrites and aluminium, which Germany needed for its armaments.

Strikes against shipping were not effective in UK waters. Post-war records show that all Commands sank only 107 enemy vessels from 1940 to March 1943. Nevertheless the crews were honing their skills but taking casualties. In June 1940 nine Beauforts of No 42 Squadron attacked the Battlecruiser *Scharnhorst* with bombs shortly after she had sunk the carrier HMS *Glorious*. No hits were scored and three Beauforts were shot down.

In April 1941 the Battlecruisers *Scharnhorst* and *Gneisenau* were in Brest harbour after a successful sweep. Bomber Command put in an attack. An unexploded bomb lay near the *Gneisenau*, which caused the Kriegsmarine to move her to deeper waters while the bomb was removed. This was observed by a PRU Spitfire and No 22 Squadron at St Eval was ordered to attack on 6 April. Six aircraft were available. The first three were to attack with bombs and the second with torpedoes. Two bombers failed to take off and the third failed to find Brest in the low cloud. Of the torpedo bombers only Flying Officer Ken Campbell and crew attacked. In the intense anti aircraft fire the aircraft was shot down and the crew killed. Flying Officer Campbell was probably killed early in the attack as it was the navigator, Sergeant James Scott, a Canadian, who was found in the pilot's seat. The torpedo struck the *Gneisenau*, causing her to be rushed into dry dock, where she remained until February 1942. Flying Officer Campbell was awarded the Victoria Cross. These two ships were scheduled to join the *Bismarck* to raid convoys in the Atlantic. At the end of May 1941 the *Bismarck*, accompanied by the *Prinz Eugen*, had broken out into the Atlantic. In an operation of co-operation between the Royal Navy and Coastal Command the *Bismarck* was sunk and the *Prinz Eugen* escaped to Brest to join the *Scharnhorst* and the *Gneisenau*.

In June 1941 the *Lutzow* (ex-*Deutschland*) was torpedoed by a Beaufort from No 42 squadron and the ship had to stay in dock in Kiel for six months.

On 11th February 1942 the three ships *Scharnhorst*, *Gneisenau* and *Prinz Eugen* sailed for Germany from Brest. They initially put to sea at 1930 but an air raid forced them to turn back in case their absence was noted. They set sail again at 2245. A Hudson on patrol covering the exits to Brest turned away at this moment on the next leg of his patrol and missed them. The next sortie fitted with ASV radar should have sighted them on radar but there was no return on the set. The next patrol, on a line from Ushant to Jersey, failed to detect the force as the radar had become unserviceable and the aircraft had been ordered to return to base. The next patrol along the Channel, from Cherbourg to Boulogne, was recalled to base due to a forecast of fog at the airfield. There were no further maritime patrols after this third patrol line. There were however, fighter patrols up to the River Somme, but still nothing was sighted. Radar stations picked up enemy air activity and when these patrols seemed to move up Channel at around 20 knots two Spitfires were sent to take a look. They found a number of small warships in the deteriorating weather, but no large warships. Then shore radar found two contacts near Le Touquet, which at that range meant they had to be large ships. Group Captain Victor Beamish, Station Commander of RAF Kenley and the Wing Leader of the Kenley Wing, Wing Commander R. F. Boyd, were airborne and located the capital ships and hurried back to Kenley with the sightings.

The Beauforts of Nos 42, 86 and 217 squadrons were put on standby, together with the Swordfish of No 815 Squadron of the Fleet Air Arm. However, not all the aircraft were in range as No 86 and a detachment of No 217 were at St Eval while No 42 was just landing at Coltishall. Six Swordfish made an attack against heavy fire and all were shot down. Five out of eighteen crew survived. The CO, Lieutenant Commander Eugene Esmonde, who was not one of the survivors, was awarded the Victoria Cross. Not one of the torpedoes hit the ships. Four Beauforts from Thorney Island were sent to attack, but due to errors in communication failed to make the rendezvous with the fighter escort. No 16 Group had forgotten that while the usual frequencies were on R/T for fighters and W/T for the Beauforts, the Beauforts had changed to R/T. Thus the inflight briefing was not received by the torpedo bombers and they did not know the nature of their targets.

Two Beauforts set out for the French coast, found nothing and returned to Manston. The other two had landed at Manston, been briefed and headed towards the targets. These two sighted what they thought to be the *Prinz Eugen* and in bad weather launched an attack, dropping their torpedoes at 1000 yards but missing. Meanwhile Bomber Command attacked with 242 aircraft. Thirty nine succeeded in bombing and 15 were lost, being either shot down or flying into the sea in the bad weather.

No 42 squadron were now at Coltishall, a fighter station and not at North Coates, a Coastal station, which was snowbound. Coltishall had no facilities for the Beauforts and a Mobile Torpedo Servicing Unit had been ordered from North Coates. However, that unit was unprepared and reached Coltishall too late to be of any service. Nine of the Beauforts were already loaded with torpedoes and they took off to rendezvous with fighters at Manston and some bomber Hudsons. Again, communication difficulties caused delays and the Beaufort leader decided to head out with his nine aircraft for the enemy based on his briefed intelligence. Six of the Hudsons followed him. The Hudsons sighted the enemy and made an attack, losing two aircraft. No hits were achieved. Six of the Beauforts now sighted the capital ships and attacked, but to no avail. Shortly after, two Beauforts of No 217 Squadron made an attack, but no hits were made.

The detached flights of Beauforts from Nos 86 and 217 Squadron at St Eval were moved to Thorney Island.

They refuelled and were ordered to meet a fighter escort at Coltishall. Again the rendezvous was not achieved and the aircraft set course for a position given to them while airborne. They found some enemy minesweepers and what one pilot thought to be a capital ship. He could not release his torpedo due to flak damage. The Beauforts returned to Coltishall having lost two aircraft. Coastal Command continued to shadow the force and Hampdens and Manchesters laid mines in the Elbe estuary. The *Scharnhorst* and the *Gneisenau* were damaged by mines laid earlier by aircraft.

This episode illustrated the shortcomings of the communications and the dangerous tactics employed by the torpedo bombers. They were required to fly low and slow and in a straight line to enable the torpedo to be dropped without it breaking up. There were insufficient aircraft and insufficient firepower to swamp the defences. Despite these problems, the Command had sunk 15 ships in the last quarter of 1941 but lost 46 aircraft. In the next four months it sank six ships but lost 55 aircraft. No 18 Group Hudsons, together with the Hampdens of Nos 144, 415, 455 and 489 Squadrons, were attacking shipping off Norway and those of No 16 Group, that traffic between the Elbe estuary and the Hook of Holland. In April 1942, Nos 144 and 455 Squadrons were detached to North Russia for strike operations. In May 1942 the Command sank 10 ships but at a cost of 43 aircraft.

The low level bombing by these crews was successful, but that meant in turn that the Germans were arming their ships more heavily, causing losses to the Hudsons and Hampdens in the order of 25 per cent. Joubert therefore ordered that bombing should be from medium level. This was not so accurate, mainly because there was no adequate bombsight. The Hampden was not fast enough and two of the four Beaufort Squadrons were sent to the Middle East.

The Luftwaffe was employing a tactic off North Norway in 1942 known as the 'Golden Zange' or Golden Comb. A low-level torpedo attack was supported by medium-level bombers and dive bombers. The idea was to fragment the defences and allow the torpedo bombers to attack under the radar. The Germans operated Heinkel 111H-6 and Junkers Ju88A-17 torpedo bombers as well as the usual Ju88 bombers from Banak and Bardufoss in occupied North Norway. The convoy was located by a Blohm und Voss BV138 or a Focke Wulff Fw200 Kondor. These aircraft shadowed the convoy and homed in the attacking aircraft. However, while this tactic may have fragmented the defences, it did not saturate them.

Then the AOC-in-C, Air Chief Marshal Joubert, found the Bristol Beaufighter. This was a twin-engined fighter with a crew of two, a pilot and a navigator. It was very fast, adaptable and well armed with six .303 machine guns and four 20mm cannon. He had previously suggested that some of these aircraft should be equipped with torpedoes and this version of the Beaufighter became known as the Torbeau. Joubert now proposed that Torbeaus and conventionally armed Beaufighters be combined into a Strike Wing which would saturate the defences of a convoy and allow a torpedo attack to be made. In September 1942 a decision was taken to form five Beaufighter squadrons by the following April. No 143 Squadron of Beaufighters, No 236 Squadron of bomber Beaufighters and No 254 of

Beaufighters and Torbeaus were stationed at North Coates (No 16 Group) in November 1942 for operations against shipping off the Frisian coast. Later that month, Nos 236 and 254 squadrons were ordered to attack a convoy heading for Rotterdam. It was protected by Focke Wulff 190s and the weather was bad. A large merchant ship and two escorts were hit, but three Beaufighters were shot down and four crashed or made forced landings on arrival back at North Coates. Joubert decided that the squadrons were insufficiently trained and withdrew them from the front line.

In the spring of 1943, training had been completed. On 18 April a force of nine Torbeaus from No 254 Squadron, six Beaufighter bombers from No 236 Squadron and six Beaufighters from No 143 Squadron covered by Spitfires and Mustangs attacked a convoy off the Dutch coast. Two "M" class minesweepers and an armed trawler were left on fire and the largest merchant was left on fire and listing badly. All 21 Beaufighters landed safely back North Coates. Some slight damage was sustained by two or three aircraft and no casualties were incurred.

In February 1943 Joubert was succeeded as AOC-in-C Coastal Command by Air Marshal Sir John Slessor. The Wick Wing was formed in March 1943, but no operations took place until November. The Hampdens attacking shipping off Norway were now escorted by Beaufighters. Slessor had intended to form three more Wings by April 1943. However, there was a shortage of Beaufighters, these being wanted as escorts for the maritime patrol aircraft over the Bay of Biscay and for the Mediterranean. In April 1943, No 1477 Flight, Norwegian Detachment began operations with six Mark II Mosquitoes from Leuchars.

The following month this unit became No 333 Squadron. Meanwhile No 236 Squadron was having their aircraft fitted with rockets, but the tactics took time to develop.

In the course of the year Rover patrols, that is single aircraft or formations of five or less looking for targets, were maintained by No 144 Squadron and No 455 Squadron RAAF from Leuchars and No 489 Squadron RNZAF based at Wick. The Strike Wing at North Coates became more powerful with the addition of Beaufighters armed with Rockets. A salvo of rockets from one of these aircraft was apparently equivalent to a broadside from a cruiser. By the end of 1943 the shortage of aircraft had eased and there were three Strike Wings, Wick, Leuchars and North Coates in operation. Nos 455 and 489 Squadrons had received the Beaufighter Xs and began to operate as a Strike Wing from Leuchars. No 333 Squadron was at Leuchars with Mosquitoes but it also had a Flight flying Catalinas at Woodhaven, near Dundee. This unit carried out reconnaissance of the Norwegian fjords for the Strike Wings and also flew in agents.

No 18 Group was responsible for the Wings operating off Norway and No 16 Group for operations along the German and Dutch coasts.

In June 1943 the mode of operation of the North Coates Wing changed. A formation of twelve Torbeaus was to attack the merchant ships and sixteen rocket and eight cannon-armed Beaufighters were to attack the escorts. If within range, fighters of Fighter Command were flown as well. These attacks, combined with minelayers and the light surface ships of the Royal Navy, put the port of Rotterdam out of use as far the Germans were concerned.

The Swedish iron ore carrier captains using the port now demanded high bonuses. In May 1943 the amount of shipping in Rotterdam was 37000 tons. A year earlier it had been 106000 tons. Bremen and Emden were no substitute for the Dutch port as they lacked the necessary unloading equipment.

An unrecognised (at that time) weapon was the mine. Bomber and Coastal Commands had laid 16000 mines, losing 329 aircraft. The number of ships sunk was 369. In the same period all the Commands had sunk 107 ships in 3700 attacks losing 648 aircraft. This was not realised at the time.

By the beginning of 1944 several Strike Wings had been set up. At North Coates, No 254 Squadron had Beaufighter Xs together with No 236 Squadron. They were joined by No 143 Squadron also with Beaufighter Xs who moved to Manston in May returning in September 1944. No 143 re-equipped with Mosquitoes in September, moving to Banff in October. Thereafter, the North Coates Strike Wing consisted of Nos 236 and 254 Squadrons until the end of the war.

At Langham Nos 455 Squadron RAAF and 489 Squadron RNZAF arrived in April 1944 with Beaufighter Xs both leaving in October 1944 to go to Dallachy. After this there were no Strike Wings at Langham.

Wick was the home of No 404 Squadron RCAF with Beaufighter Xs until May 1944. No 618 Squadron moved there for a month in July with Mosquitoes. After this, Wick ceased to be a Strike Wing base.

No 455 Squadron had been at Leuchars since April 1942. In December it re-equipped with Beaufighter Xs, leaving for Langham in April 1944. No 489 Squadron went to Leuchars in October 1943 when it exchanged its Hampdens for Beaufighter Xs. It left in October 1944 for Dallachy. Leuchars was also the home of No 333 Squadron RNoAF with Mosquito VIs until it moved to Banff in September 1944. After October 1944 Leuchars ceased to be a Strike Wing base.

In Cornwall, Portreath and Predannack were two Strike Wing bases. No 248 Squadron had been at Predannack since January 1943 with Beaufighter VIC's. These were exchanged for Mark Xs in June 1943 and were used until December 1943 when the squadron began converting to Mosquito VIs and XVIIIs. The Squadron moved to Portreath in February 1944 and to Banff in September.

No 235 Squadron had been at Portreath since August 1943 and moved to St Angelo in February 1944 for a month, when it returned to Portreath, joining No 248 Squadron. In April 1944 it received Beaufighter XIs but turned these in for Mosquito VIs in June 1944. Both Nos 235 and 248 Squadrons left Portreath in September for Banff and both Cornish bases were no longer Strike Wing bases.

Davidstow Moor was used by Nos 144 and 404 Squadrons in May 1944 when they left Wick. Both squadrons left in July 1944 for Strubby and Davidstow Moor had no further connection with the Strike Wings.

Beccles was used for two months by No 618 Squadron from August 1944 until September when it moved to Dallachy. It left a month later for Australia.

In the autumn, the Wings were concentrated on the Moray Firth at Dallachy and Banff and one at North Coates in Lincolnshire. Banff was the home of the

Mosquito Strike Wing, consisting of Nos 143, 144, 404, 333, 235 and 248 Squadrons. Dallachy was the home of the Beaufighter Strike Wing, consisting of Nos 144 and 404 (both moved from Banff), 455 and 489 Squadrons. Nos 144 and 404 Squadrons had Beaufighters and were moved to Dallachy in October 1944.

There is a Memorial to the Dallachy Wing on the roadside to Spey Bay at Bogmoor and there is a Memorial to the Banff Wing on the A98 road to Fraserburgh near Boyndie.

Search and Rescue was provided by Nos 279 and 281 Squadrons operating from detachments at Banff, Wick, Fraserburgh and Dallachy. Fighter escort was provided by Mustangs from Banff and Peterhead.

In summary it can be said that the following bases were used by the Strike Wings:

Portreath with Nos 143, 235 and 248 Squadrons from September 1943 to March 1944.

Predannack with Nos 248 and 618 Squadrons from January 1943 to February 1944.

Davidstow Moor with No 144 Squadron from May 1944 to July 1944.

Tain with No 144 Squadron from April 1943 until May 1943 when the squadron sent detachments to Wick, Tunisia and Algeria. It moved to Benson in July, returning to Tain in August 1943 remaining there until October 1943.

Wick with No 144 Squadron until it moved to Davidstow Moor in May 1944.

Manston with No 143 Squadron from May 1944 until September 1944 when it moved to North Coates.

Leuchars with Nos 235 Squadron from January 1943 to August 1943, No 333 Squadron from May 1943 to September 1944. Thus there was only a Wing in residence from May to August. No 489 Squadron moved in to fill the gap from October 1943 to April 1944.

Langham with Nos 455 and 489 Squadrons from April 1944 to October 1944.

North Coates with No 143 Squadron from August 1942 to August 1943 when the squadron went to Cornwall, No 236 Squadron from September 1942 and No 254 Squadron from November 1942. These last two units remained until the end of the war.

Dallachy with Nos 144 Squadron from September 1944 and Nos 404, 455 and 489 Squadrons from October 1944. Nos 144 and 404 Squadrons had been initially moved to Banff in September but it was decided to keep Beaufighters at Dallachy so they were moved to Dallachy. No 404 Squadron converted to Mosquitoes in March 1945 and was moved to Banff. No 618 Squadron was there for a month in September/October 1944 before moving to Australia.

Banff with Nos 143 Squadron from October 1944, and Nos 333, 235 and No 248 Squadrons from September 1944. These units were all equipped with Mosquitoes and remained at Banff until the end of the war.

Strike operations were very dangerous sorties and consequently terrifying, exciting and demanding. Flying to the target involved a low level profile probably at 50 feet in order to avoid alerting the defences. This, of course, is a bad weather zone, but if the sea is visible the wind velocity can be observed from the whitecaps and the wind lanes and Dead Reckoning navigation carried out. Initially, Gee would have been available, but on closing the enemy coast either it would be out of range or jammed. Consol would have been used, but it was not a quick fixing aid and was not so accurate. Approaching a coastline in bad visibility has its dangers, particularly one that is mountainous, like the coast of Norway. Consequently, precise navigation was required and a climb before reaching the coast was necessary in order to establish position and identify targets.

The size of the Strike force depended on the target. The majority consisted of anti flak aircraft, on the basis of three aircraft to each escort and around half a dozen torpedo aircraft for each main ship in the group. In order to confuse the enemy and to limit their avoiding action it was necessary to have as many torpedoes running in the water as possible. A basic form of daylight attack consisted of three waves of torpedo carriers approaching from ahead of the target force. When about eight to ten miles short of the target, the formation would split into three sections, one moving to the right, one to the left to be about four miles on each flank of the force and the third would continue straight ahead. Thus, even if the force took avoiding action, it still presented a target to the torpedo bombers. Anti flak aircraft would mix in with this, keeping up an incessant fire.

A night attack involved fewer aircraft, as the collision risk was too great. Radar was necessary and if there was moonlight, the attack would be made up-moon. On a dark night where there was no moonlight, a shadowing force, an illuminating force and a strike force would be required. The illuminator would normally be the Warwick ASR aircraft. Similar principles applied when rockets were used. In this case the chances of a ship avoiding these weapons were lessened as the projectiles were much faster than torpedoes.

Strike Wings could not fly in tight formation at night and the Germans realised this. Accordingly, they sailed their convoys at night, laying up by day. To counter this, No 18 Group adopted a technique named the Drem system, which was named after the airfield in East Lothian where it was developed. It was perfected by the North Coates Wing. This involved a Warwick taking off early in the morning, before twilight, flying to a suitable point off the Norwegian coast and laying there a number of marine markers Mark II and Mark VI together with flame floats and drift lights in a circle of radius around three miles. The Strike Wing would then take off in darkness, form up in a loose formation and rendezvous at the marked area. Here the Wing would form up into battle order and head for the target attacking in twilight.

Fighter escort for the Dallachy and Banff Wings was provided by the Mustangs of No 65 Squadron. These arrived at Peterhead on 3 October 1944, but the day after they returned to Matlask, north of Norwich and then to Andrews Field, north east of London, ten days later. However, the squadron came back to Peterhead on 16 January 1945 and thence to Banff on 26 January. The squadron went back to Peterhead on 1 February 1945. No

19 Squadron with Mustangs arrived at Peterhead on 13 February. No 315 Squadron Mustangs were at Peterhead from 1 November 1944 to 16 January 1945, when it returned to Andrews Field.

CHAPTER TWENTY SIX

THE OPERATIONAL TRAINING UNITS

◉

In order to fly operational aircraft it is necessary to train the aircrew on them. Therefore Operational Training Units (OTU's) were established.

No 1 OTU was formed at RAF Silloth in Cumberland on 1 January 1940 with Lockheed Hudsons, Bristol Blenheims, Bristol Beauforts, Vickers Wellingtons, Armstrong Whitworth Whitleys and Airspeed Oxfords. It moved to Thornaby, Yorkshire on 24 March 1943, where it operated Fortresses, Halifaxes, Liberators, Westland Lysanders and Miles Martinets. It disbanded on 19 October 1943.

No 2 OTU was formed at Catfoss, Yorkshire on 1 October 1940 operating Blenheims, Avro Ansons, Bristol Beaufighters, Oxfords, Beauforts, Lysanders and Martinets. It disbanded on 15 February 1944.

No 3 OTU was formed at Chivenor, Devon on 27 November 1940 operating Ansons, Beauforts, Whitleys, Oxfords and Wellingtons. It disbanded on 4 January 1944.

No 4 OTU was formed at Stranraer, Wigtownshire on 16 March 1941 operating Supermarine Stranraers, Short

CHAPTER TWENTY SIX

Singapore IIIs, Saro Londons, Saro Lerwicks, Consolidated Catalinas and Vickers Warwicks. It moved to Invergordon, Ross on 15 June 1941 and then down the road to Alness on 10 February 1943, Evanton on 1 September 1944, Tain on 10 December 1944 and then Pembroke Dock on 15 August 1946. It disbanded on 31 July 1947, becoming No 234 OCU (Operational Conversion Unit). It had a Target Towing Detachment at Evanton until 10 December 1942 and subsequently at Tain which it left on 15 August 1946.

No 5 OTU was formed at Chivenor on 1 August 1941 operating Ansons, Beauforts and Oxfords. The intention had been to form at Turnberry, but the airfield was not ready. However, on 16 May 1942 it moved to Turnberry, Ayrshire, where it added Handley Page Hampdens to its strength. On 29 December 1942 the unit moved to Long Kesh, Northern Ireland, where it operated Lockheed Venturas and Hudsons. On 15 February 1944 it moved back to Turnberry, where it operated Beaufighters, Warwicks and Wellingtons. The Warwicks were taken over from the ASR Training Unit. The unit was redesignated No 235 OCU on 1 August 1945 and the Warwick training was passed to No 6 OTU, which became No 236 OCU.

No 6 OTU was formed at Thornaby on 19 July 1941 operating Hudsons, Ansons, Oxfords and from October 1942, Wellingtons. On 10 March 1943 the Unit moved to Silloth and added Martinets to its inventory. This was more of a name change with No 1 OTU as that unit moved to Thornaby 14 days later. The unit moved to Kinloss on 18 July 1945 and transferred to No 18 Group from No 17 Group on 1 September 1945. In July 1946

516

the unit took over Lancaster training and redesignated No 236 OCU.

No 7 OTU formed at Limavady, Northern Ireland with Wellingtons, Ansons, Oxfords, Lysanders and Martinets. It disbanded on 16 May 1944.

No 8 OTU formed on 18 May 1942 with Spitfires, de Havilland Mosquitoes, Miles Masters, Oxfords and Ansons. The unit moved to Dyce, Aberdeenshire on 8 February 1943, to Haverfordwest, Pembrokeshire on 3 January 1945, to Mount Farm, Oxfordshire on 21 June 1945, to Chalgrove, Oxfordshire on 4 July 1946 and then to Benson, Oxfordshire on 19 October 1946 and became No 237 OCU on 31 July 1947.

No 9 OTU formed at Aldergrove, Northern Ireland on 7 June 1942 with Beaufighters, Beauforts and Oxfords. It moved to Crosby in Eden, Cumberland on 6 September 1942 adding Lysanders and Martinets to its inventory. The unit disbanded 11 August 1944.

No 111 OTU formed in Nassau, Bahamas with B24 Liberators and B25 Mitchells on 20 August 1942. The Mitchells operated out of Oakes Field and the Liberators from Windsor Field. On July 1945 the unit moved to Lossiemouth, Scotland under the control of No 17 Group, Coastal Command. Control was passed to No 18 Group on 1 September 1945 and the unit was disbanded on 21 May 1946.

No 131 OTU formed on 20 July 1942 at Killadeas, Fermanagh, Northern Ireland with Catalinas, Sunderlands, Oxfords, Martinets and Hurricanes. It disbanded on 28 June 1945.

No 132 OTU formed at East Fortune, East Lothian

on 24 November 1942 from No 60 OTU, operating Beaufighters, Blenheims, Oxfords, Lysanders, Martinets and Beauforts. Macmerry was used as a satellite airfield. There was a detachment at Haverfordwest from 11 February 1945 with Mosquitoes until 17 June 1945. The unit disbanded 15 May 1946.

No 235 OCU was formed in July 1947 from No 5 OUT to train crews on Sunderlands and Short Seafords at Calshot. It was later redesignated the Flying Boat Training Squadron.

No 236 OCU was formed out of No 6 OTU in July 1947, training crews on Lancaster maritime patrol aircraft. In June 1951 the School of Maritime Reconnaissance (S of MR) was formed out of this OCU and went to RAF St Mawgan, operating Lancaster MR3's while No 236 OCU took over the training of Shackleton crews. In 1956 No 236 and the S of MR formed the Maritime Operational Training Unit (MOTU) based at Kinloss. The Lancasters were struck off inventory. In 1965 MOTU moved to St Mawgan and disbanded on 30 June 1970. On the same day No 236 OCU was reformed at St Mawgan to train crews on the new Nimrod MR1. On 1 April 1982 the unit moved to Kinloss to train crews on the Nimrod MR2. It moved back to St Mawgan on 1 November 1983 returning to Kinloss 31 July 1992 where it disbanded. However, No 42 Squadron had disbanded and reformed as No 42(R)Squadron and took over the role of No 236 OCU.(R= Reserve).

CHAPTER TWENTY SEVEN

PHOTOGRAPHIC
RECONNAISSANCE

◉

Photo reconnaissance was used in the First World War, but the birth of modern photographic reconnaissance, or more specifically, long-range photo reconnaissance, was the innovation of the stripped down, unarmed and blue-painted Spitfire. This was largely due to Flying Officer M. V. Longbottom, who suggested that small, light, unarmed fast aircraft were better suited to air reconnaissance than the bombers that had been in use up to then. In 1938 Wing Commander Fred Winterbottom was authorised to form a special PR flight using a civilian registered Lockheed 12A with hidden cameras. This was the first of two Lockheeds and was registered G-AFKR. It was later handed over to the French. The second was registered G-AGTL. Sidney Cotton, an Australian businessman, flew sorties into Germany photographing military and industrial installations. He was given the rank of Squadron Leader in the RAF and organised an efficient air reconnaissance system called the Photographic Development Unit (PDU). The unit was equipped with Bristol Blenheim aircraft, but these proved not to have the performance required.

In November 1939 the unit was lent two Spitfires which were stripped of their armour and guns and fitted with extra fuel tanks. Detachments were sent to France under the cover name of Special Survey Flights. Squadron Leader Cotton was the last of the unit to leave France. In the summer of 1940 the PDU was renamed No 1 Photographic Reconnaissance Unit (PRU) under the command of Wing Commander G. W. Tuttle. It was placed under the overall command of Coastal Command, even though it was used by units outside that Command. Hudsons had now joined the Spitfires and these aircraft kept watch on the European ports. Operations were flown from Heston, Wick and St Eval. In the second week of August their photos showed the existence of barges which might be used in an invasion of the UK. Pilot Officer Suckling found the *Bismarck*, which initiated the Royal Navy hunt to sink her. Flight Lieutenant Dicing photographed the Freya radar at Bruneval, which led to the commando raid to capture components of the radar.

By the autumn of 1942 the PRU had become so large that it was disbanded and five squadrons were formed. These were Nos 540, 541, 542, 543 and 544 Squadrons.

No 540 Squadron was formed in October 1942 from "H" and "L" Flights at Leuchars with detachments at Gibraltar and Benson. The squadron disbanded in October 1946 being renumbered as No 58 Squadron, which also had Ansons. No 540 squadron reformed at Benson from the Mosquito section of No 58 Squadron at Benson in December 1947. Its PR 34s were reinforced with PR34As in April 1951, disposing of its PR34's in October 1951. (Mark numbers were now given in Arabic numbers instead of Roman). The squadron entered the jet age in December 1952 when the crews converted to Canberra PR3s, retaining the Mosquitoes until September 1953. The squadron moved to Wyton in March 1953 and received Canberra B2s three months later. In June 1954 Canberra PR 7s were added to its inventory, the B2s being disposed of in September 1954 and the PR 3s a month later. In March 1956 the squadron was disbanded.

No 541 Squadron formed in October 1942 from "B" and "F" Flights with Spitfire D's and IVs. The squadron disbanded in October 1946, being renumbered as No 82 Squadron. In November 1947 the squadron reformed from the Spitfire PR19 element of No 82 squadron. These aircraft were retained until May 1951, but in December of the previous year, it had received Meteor PR 10's. The squadron spent its time in Germany until it was disbanded in September 1957.

No 542 Squadron formed in October 1942 from "A" and "E" Flights at Benson. It disbanded in August 1945 but reformed at Wyton in May 1954 with Canberra PR 7s. It disbanded again in October 1955 but reformed a month later from No 1323 Flight as a Canberra bomber squadron.

No 543 Squadron formed in October 1942 from some of the remaining elements of No 1 PRU. Having been disbanded in October 1943, it reformed in April 1955 with Valiant B(PR)1s. In November 1955 it moved to Wyton. In December 1964 all Valiants were grounded, but in May 1965 the squadron received Victor B.2 (SR)s. In May 1974 the squadron disbanded.

No 544 Squadron formed in October 1942 at Benson

from the other remaining elements of No 1 PRU. It disbanded in October 1945 and was never reformed.

No 1 PRU was reformed in 1982. However, in July 1992, No 39 Squadron which had been a PR unit since July 1958 on its reformation but was disbanded in June 1982, reformed as No 39 (1PRU) Squadron. No 1 PRU was accordingly disbanded.

CHAPTER TWENTY EIGHT

THE FLEET AIR ARM SQUADRONS

A number of Fleet Air Arm Squadrons were attached to Coastal Command.

No 812 Squadron, flying Fairey Swordfish, was shown based at North Coates under No 16 Group in the Order of Battle for November 1940.

The Order of Battle of 15 June 1941 shows that a flight of No 816 Squadron operating Swordfish was based at Detling and another at Thorney Island, both under No 16 Group. No 812 Squadron had moved to Hatston and was under No 18 Group control.

The Order of Battle for 15 June 1942 shows no FAA Squadrons attached.

The Order of Battle for 15 October 1942 shows No 811 and No 812 Squadrons at Bircham Newton with Swordfish under No 16 Group control. Nos 816 and 818 Squadrons are shown at Thorney Island also with Swordfish under No 16 Group control.

The Order of Battle for 15 February 1943 shows Nos 833 and 836 Squadrons at Thorney Island under No 16 Group control.

The Order of Battle for 1 March 1943 shows that Nos 833 and 836 Squadrons were still at Thorney Island. No 834 with Swordfish was at Exeter under No 19 Group control.

The Order of Battle for 1 January 1944 shows no FAA Squadrons under Coastal control.

The Order of Battle for 1 April 1945 shows Nos 810 and 822 Squadrons both operating Fairey Barracudas based at Thorney Island under No 19 Group control.

CHAPTER TWENTY NINE

THE AMERICAN SQUADRONS

◉

When the United States of America entered the war, a number of their squadrons were attached to Coastal Command. These were numbered differently to the British. A United States Navy Maritime Patrol squadron was given the prefix "VP". VP84 means Patrol Squadron number 84.

In the Order of Battle of October 1942, VP73 of the US Navy is shown as based at Reykjavik in Iceland operating Catalina PBY 5As. VP84 was later detached to Reykjavik.

20 August 1942: Lt. R. B. Hopgood and crew from VP 73 was tasked to escort a minelaying force SN 73. About 10 miles from this force a visual sighting was gained of a U-Boat in position 6125N 01440W. An attack was made from 100 feet with a stick of five USN depth charges, giving a good straddle. The boat was U-464, a type XIV supply boat commanded by Kapitänleutnant Otto Harms. The boat sank, leaving 53 survivors in the water, who were rescued by HMS *Castletown*.

On 1-2 September 1942 a Catalina from VP 73 attacked U-491 but no damage was caused.

5 October 1942: A Catalina from VP 73 gained a visual sighting of a U-Boat in position 5852N 02142W and attacked with a stick of four 650lb depth charges. Fresh oil was seen and this marked the end of U-582, a type VIIc commanded by Korvettenkapitän Werner Schulte.

1 November 1942: Lt. R. C. Child and crew from VP 84 were escorting convoy HX 212. A visual sighting was gained of a surfacing U-boat in position 5700N 02500W. Child attacked, diving from 2000 feet and dropped two 650lb and two 325lb depth charges from 100 feet in a salvo as opposed to a stick. This means that the charges were all dropped at the same time, landing in the same position. No results were observed but the boat, which was U-664, a type VIIc commanded by Kapitänleutnant Adolf Graef, had been damaged.

5 November 1942: Lt. R. C. Millard and crew from VP 84 gained a visual sighting of a U-Boat from four miles in position 6740N 01832W. Millard attacked with a salvo of two 625lb and two 325lb depth charges from 125 feet. This sank U-408, a type VIIc commanded by Kapitänleutnant Reinhard von Hynmen.

10 December 1942: Lt. L. Davis and crew from VP 84 were escorting convoy HX 217. The second pilot gained a visual sighting of a surfaced U-Boat from six miles in position 5809N 02244W. Gun fire was exchanged as Millard attacked with a 650lb depth charge. This sank U-611, a type VIIC commanded by Kapitänleutnant Nikolaus von Jacobs.

In the Order of Battle February 1943, the 1st, 2nd, 4th and 19th Anti-Submarine Squadrons of the US Army Air Corps are shown as based at St. Eval with Liberators. VP

84 of the US Navy is shown at Reykjavik with Catalina IIIs.

20 February 1943: 1st Lieutenant Wayne Johnson and crew were flying at 1600 feet over a rough sea. The navigator gained a visual sighting of a wake at three miles and then a surfaced U-Boat in position 4930N 02155W. This was U-211, a type VIIc commanded by Kapitänleutnant Karl Hause. An attack was made with a stick of six depth charges from 200 feet and the navigator firing the nose guns. The U-Boat dived, leaving a patch of oil and air bubbles. The boat had suffered serious damage and returned to Brest from whence she had come seven days earlier.

28 April 1943: Lt. W. A. Shevlin and crew were tasked to an area in which No 172 Squadron had made two sightings. A visual sighting of a U-Boat from four miles in position 6018N 02953W was gained. This was around 80 miles from convoy SC 127. Shevlin attacked with four depth charges from 150 feet. The boat was U-528, a type IXC/40 commanded by Kapitänleutnant Georg von Rabenau and was damaged, causing her to return to France. However, she was found by Plt. Off. J. B. Stark and crew from No 58 Squadron on 11 May 1943 and sunk.

14 May 1943: Lt.(jg) E. T. Allen and crew from VP 84 were escorting convoy ONS 7 together with another Catalina (PBY5) flown by Lt P. A. Bodinot and crew, also from VP84. They attacked a surfaced U-Boat in position 6010N 03152W. This was U-640, a type VIIC commanded by Oberleutnant zur See Heinz Nagel. Previously it was believed that U-640 had been sunk by another aircraft from VP 84 and that Allen and crew had sunk U-657. However, HMS *Swale* sank U-657 on 17

May 1943. Allen attacked two U-Boats on 13 June but without success. For all these attacks he was awarded the British DFC.

25 May 1943: Lt. R. C. Millard and crew from VP 84 gained a visual sighting of a surfaced U-boat and attacked with three 350lb depth charges from 100 feet. A follow-up attack was made when the boat dived. This sank U-467, a type VIIc commanded by Kapitänleutnant Heinz Kummer. Millard was awarded the British DFC.

20 June 1943: Lt. E. W. Wood and crew from VP 84 were supporting convoy ON 189. A visual sighting of a surfaced U-Boat was gained at 14 miles in position 5703N 03120W. In the face of flak, Wood attacked with three 325lb depth charges which undershot. A follow up attack was made with a Mark 24 accoustic homing torpedo. Bubbles and oil were seen and then the stern broke surface and it could be seen that it had been split open. The propeller and rudder had gone. The boat then sank. This was U-388, a type VIIc commanded by Oberleutnant zur See Peter Sues.

24 June 1943: Lt. (jg) J. W. Beach and crew gained a visual sighting of a surfaced U-Boat and attacked. However, the depth charges failed to release. A follow-up attack was made with two 325lb depth charges. The boat was U-194, a type IXC/40 commanded by Kapitänleutnant Hermann Hesse and it sank in position 5900N 02618W. .

20 July 1943: 1st Lieutenant C. F. Gallimeir and crew operating out of St Eval gained a radar contact which was converted into a visual sighting of two U-Boats in position 4530N 00945W. An attack was made with nose, dorsal

and waist guns and a stick of seven depth charges from 600 feet, which exploded close to the port side of one of the boats. This was U-558, a type VIIc commanded by Kapitänleutnant Gunther Krech. The boat returned fire, wounding one of the gunners. A follow-up attack was about to be attempted but the no. 2 engine was hit and the aircraft was forced to return to base, which it reached safely. The attack was taken over by a No 58 Squadron Halifax which sank the boat. Only Krech, his second lieutenant and three ratings survived, being rescued by HMCS *Athabascan* five days later.

28 July 1943: Major S. D. McElroy and crew of the 4th Squadron gained a radar contact which converted to a visual sighting of a U-boat which was U-404, a type VIIC commanded by Oberleutnant zur See Adolf Schoenberg. An attack was made but the depth charges failed to release. U-404 dived and escaped. However, McElroy waited in the area and gained a further sighting some three hours later. An attack was made with eight depth charges in the face of heavy flak which damaged the Number 3 engine. This caused McElroy and crew to return to base which they reached safely. Then 1st Lieutenant A. J. Hammar and crew, also from the 4th Squadron, arrived on the scene having intercepted the sighting report. U-404 was surfacing and Hammar attacked immediately with a stick of eight depth charges, giving a good straddle, and then made a follow-up attack. The aircraft was hit in the Number 1 engine and had to return to base, which it reached safely. The U-Boat was finished off by another Liberator from No 224 Squadron and sank in position 4553N 00925W. This was hit in the number 4 engine, but it too reached base safely.

VP 128 USN was detached later in 1943 to Reykjavik.

2 August 1943: 1st Lieutenant J. L. Hamilton and crew from the 4th Squadron, USAAC, arrived on the scene of the attack by Sqn. Ldr. Ruttan RCAF and crew from No 415 Squadron RCAF on U-706, a type VIIc commanded by Kapitänleutnant Alexander von Zitzewitz. Hamilton's radar operator had gained a contact at 20 miles and the crew homed in. Having sighted the Hampden and then U-706, Hamilton attacked out of the sun, dropping a stick of 12 depth charges from 50 feet. The boat sank by the stern, leaving around 15 survivors in the water. Hamilton dropped a dinghy to them and they were rescued by HMS *Waveney* of the 40th Escort Group, having been guided to the scene by a Catalina and a Sunderland.

4 October 1943: A Ventura from VP128 flown by Cdr. C. L. Westerhofen and crew gained a visual sighting of a submerging U-Boat in position 6040N 02630W. No results were observed and a gambit tactic was employed. This was U-305, a type VIIc commanded by Kapitänleutnant Rudolf Bahr, and it survived the attack with damage. Then a further sighting was gained of a surfaced U-boat in position 6100N 02653W. An attack was made in the face of flak with three depth charges which gave a good straddle. The aircraft turned for a follow-up attack but then noted the crew abandoning ship. This was U-279, a type VIIC commanded by Kapitänleutnant Otto Finke. There were no survivors, as the aircraft had suffered damage to its radio and could not summon help.

10 November 1943: Liberators from VP 105 USN, VP 103 USN and VP 110 USN took part in the action against

U-966. After the Wellington from No 612 Squadron had attacked, a Liberator from VP 105 attacked twice, unsuccessfully. Flak had damaged the bomb bay. A Wellington from No 407 Squadron attempted to join in but was shot down. 1st Lieutenant K. L. Wright and crew from VPB 103 acted on a message that the boat was in position 4439N 00908W. They sighted two Ju88s en route and altered heading to avoid them. Further messages indicated that U-966 was heading for Ferrol. Wright headed for Ferrol and then on reaching it turned for the last-known position. A radar contact was gained and converted into a visual sighting. An attack with a stick of five depth charges was made with a follow-up attack of a 600lb anti submarine bomb. Gunfire was exchanged. The boat was seen to be down by the stern.

Later, 1st Lt. J. A. Parrish and crew from VP 110 came upon the scene. In the face of heavy flak an attack was made with guns and a stick of six depth charges. This was a good attack which rolled the boat on to its port side, but it recovered and continued to head for Spain. A Liberator from No 311 Squadron joined the action when the boat was some three miles from the Spanish coast and attacked. The U-Boat was later blown up by the crew in 53 metres of water. On 12 November 1943, Lieutenant (JG) R. B. Brownell and crew from VP 103 sent a locating report, but nothing further was heard. The next day two oil slicks were found and it was assumed that the U-Boat had been sunk and the aircraft shot down by the boat. This was U-508, a type IXC commanded by Kapitänleutnant Georg Staats and was sunk in position 4600N 00730W. The USN crew were awarded posthumous medals.

The Order of Battle for 1 January 1944 shows that Dunkeswell was home for VPs 103, 105 and 110 of the US Navy with Liberators. However, VP 84 had been released from attachment to Coastal. VP 63 was at Port Lyautey in Morocco.

28 January 1944: Lt. C. A. Enloe and crew from VP 103 were escorting convoy SC151/ON221 at 2000 feet. In visibility of eight miles a wake was sighted and then a surfaced U-Boat in position 5315N 01552W. This was U-271, a type VIIc commanded by Kapitänleutnant Kurt Barleben. Enloe attacked with guns and a stick of six depth charges from 100 feet. This lifted the stern, which then began to settle. A follow-up attack with a 600lb anti submarine bomb was cancelled when it was seen that air bubbles surrounded the boat. The boat then sank, leaving no survivors.

29 January 1944: Lt. H. H. Budd and crew from VP 110 gained a visual sighting of a wake and then the associated U-boat. This was U-592, a type VIIc commanded by Oberleutnant zur See Heinz Jaschke. An attack was made with guns and a stick of six depth charges from 100 feet. This was an undershoot and the Liberator was hit as it overflew the target. The aircraft circled the boat until it dived. Shortly afterwards, two Liberators from VP 110 arrived. U-592 had been damaged and was forced to return to St. Nazaire, but did not arrive as she was sunk by HMS's *Starling, Wild Goose* and *Magpie* of the 2nd Escort Group in position 5020N 01729W.

24 February 1944: Two Catalinas (PBY 5A) from VP 63 at Port Lyautey gained a radar contact in position 3551N 00645W, in the approach to the Straits of

Gibraltar. This area was patrolled by, amongst others, MAD fitted PBY 5s and was not a favourite passage for the U-Boats. The crews were Lt. T. R. Woolley and crew and Lt. H. F. Baker and crew. The procedure was that on gaining contact, the crew dropped a flame float on the MAD mark. Going round again, they repeated the procedure and the flame floats then showed the boat's track. Flying along this track, and then gaining another MAD mark, retro bombs were fired. They were joined by a USN Ventura from VB127, two destroyers, HMS *Wishart* and HMS *Anthony*, and a No 202 Squadron Catalina. The boat was U-761, a type VIIc commanded by Oberleutnant zur See Horst Gelder. The boat surfaced and was attacked by one of the PBYs, the destroyers and the No 202 Squadron Catalina. Survivors were seen in the water and 48 rescued, including Gelder, and taken to Gibraltar. Five minutes later the submarine blew up.

16 March 1944: Three PBY 5As, Lt. R. C. Spears and crew, Lt. V. A. T. Lingle and crew and Lt. M. J. Vopacek and crew, all from VP 63, were barrier patrolling the Straits of Gibraltar. Vopacek was patrolling further east in case the U-Boat got through the first barrier. A periscope had been sighted by Lt. D. Hill and crew from VP 112 on 14 March. On 15 March a Gibraltar-based Wellington had gained a radar contact, believed to be the same U-Boat. Thus a trap was set. Spears gained a MAD contact and called the other two for a co-ordinated attack. These made contact, which was then lost. A French submarine and a French sloop then approached from the West. Spears regained contact in position 3554N 00542W and fired 24 retro bombs, followed by an attack by Lingle's crew. The

British destroyer HMS *Vanoc*, which was nearby, was then asked by Spears to attack his MAD mark. A hedgehog pattern was fired and then contact was lost save a slight trail of oil. Vopacek gained contact but then lost it. All three PBYs then went into a MAD trap to try to re-establish contact.

Then three British frigates of 1st Escort Group arrived and started a search in poor sonar conditions. This was rewarded by an ASDIC contact, which was attacked. There was a considerable underwater explosion and Vopacek's crew thought they saw part of a hull. HMS *Affleck* launched a boat, the crew of which found debris , identified as German. The boat was U-392, a type VIIc commanded by Oberleutnant zur See Henning Schumann and had indeed been sunk.

15 May 1944: Lt. M. J. Vopacek and crew and Lt. H. T. Worrell and crew from VP 63 were patrolling the Straits of Gibraltar. Vopacek gained a MAD mark at 130 feet. Both aircraft attacked with retro bombs while calling in HMS's *Aubretia, Blackfly* and *Kilmarnock*. Some wreckage was seen and noises were heard from the sonobuoy which had been dropped. HMS *Kilmarnock* then fired a hedgehog pattern and a large amount of oil came to the surface. This was the end of U-731, a type VIIc commanded by Oberleutnant zur See Alexander Graf Keller, which sank in position 3554N 00545W. There were no survivors.

These squadrons were still in place in the Order of Battle for 1 April 1945. VP's 107 and 112 US Navy were attached at Upottery together with a detachment from VP 63 US Navy with Catalina PBY 5As.

27 February 1945: Lt. O. B. Denison and crew from VP 112 gained a visual sighting of a periscope, but it had disappeared before an attack could be made. They then sighted an oil slick. As this was not an accurate datum they commenced gambit tactics in the hope that the U-boat would surface, thinking that the aircraft had gone away. This did not happen, but the aircraft homed in part of the 2nd Escort Group, which sank the U-boat in position 4946N 00547W in the vicinity of convoy ONA 287. The boat was originally thought to have been U-327, a type VIIC/41, but it is now believed to have been U-1208, a type VIIc commanded by Korvettenkapitän Georg Hagens. The credit for the sinking was shared between the Group and VP 112.

11 March 1945: Lt. R. N. Field and crew from VP 103 were on patrol off Land's End when a surfaced U-Boat was sighted in position 4953N 00631W. Field attacked immediately with a stick of eight depth charges from 100 feet. The aircraft was not in a good attack position, but the boat was starting its dive and speed of attack was of the essence. Nevertheless, it was a good straddle and sank the boat, which was U-681, a type VIIc commanded by Oberleutnant zur See Werner Gebauer. The survivors were rescued by one of three British ships, HMS *Loch Fada*, from 2nd Escort Group. Field was awarded both the American and British DFCs.

25 April 1945: Lt. D. D. Nott and crew from VP 103 were on an anti-submarine patrol and gained a visual sighting of smoke from a schnorkel and then a wake in position 4812N 00542W. An attack was carried out and a good straddle obtained, causing the boat to sink. It was

thought to have been U-1107, a type VIIc/41, but later it was believed to have been U-326, a type VIIc/41 commanded by Oberleutnant zur See Peter Matthes. Nott was awarded the American DFC and the rest of the crew Air Medals.

30 April 1945: Lt. F. G. Lake and crew from VP 63 were on a MAD patrol. A visual sighting was gained of a schnorkel at two miles in position 4800N 00630W. An attack was made from 100 feet. As the Catalina flew over the schnorkel and periscope a MAD mark was gained and 24 retro bombs were fired. The water appeared to be boiling and bubbles and an oil slick were seen. This was U-1107, a type VIIc/41 commanded by Oberleutnant zur See Fritz Parduhn. A sonobuoy pattern was laid but no results were gained. However, the boat had been sunk. At first it was believed that it had been U-1055 but this has been re-assessed to have been U-1107. Lake received the American DFC.

POSTWAR

Sunderland by Geoff Kirkman

42 Sqn in Aden, early 1957

Shack formation (author)

Shackleton MR2 with mid-upper turret (author)

RAF North Front Gibraltar (author)

Route Nav Station, Nimrod 2 (Andy Raglan)

VP International Memorial RCAF Greenwood (author)

Shackleton MR3 No 35 Sqn SAAF (author)

Nimrod 2 at Coventry (Andy Raglan)

Flight Deck Nimrod 2 at Coventry (Andy Raglan)

Norwegian Orion (author)

Shack 3s at DF Malan (author)

Dutch Navy Orion at Kinloss (author)

Flt Lt John Campbell with XW240 at Kinloss
(Photographer Colin Cameron)

Flt Lt John Campbell with No 120 Squadron Standard Bearer.
(Photograher Al Mackie)

CHAPTER THIRTY

COASTAL COLD WAR

◉

The Second World War now over, the new threat appeared to be from the Soviet Union. It was Winston Churchill who said that an "Iron Curtain" had been drawn across Europe. In 1949 the North Atlantic Treaty Organisation (NATO) was signed by the Western Allies whereby if one was attacked the others would come to its aid.

Coastal Command was left with a vast area of ocean to watch over with minimum resources. However, the United States, after talks under the Mutual Defence Aid Pact, lent the United Kingdom 52 Lockheed P2V5 Neptunes. These equipped Nos 36, 203, and 210 squadrons plus a flight of four aircraft, No 1453 Flight, for Airborne Early Warning trials, at Topcliffe. The trials were not a great success and the flight was disbanded after around three years. The APS 20 radar was later used as the radar for the AEW Shackleton Mk2. No 217 Squadron with Neptunes was at Kinloss. The Neptune MR 1 carried ESM and AN/APS 20 radar with a repeater for the navigator. The Neptune was a twin-engined medium-range aircraft.

STRIKE WINGS

Nos 36 and 42 Squadrons, the remnants of the Strike Wings, were disbanded in October 1947. However, the idea was kept alive in the tactics known as Light Strike, Link Up and Velocipede. These were mainly for use against coastal craft.

LIGHT STRIKE

The search would be established on a patrol between enemy bases and the Allied shipping to be protected. On detection the aircraft would report the enemy position, the Maritime Headquarters (MHQ) would call for strike aircraft and the search aircraft would home them in to the target.

LINK UP

This was similar to light strike, but this time the MHQ would call for surface attack units, probably Motor Gun Boats (MGBs) which a shore station would home in using shore radar.

VELOCIPEDE

This was similar to Link Up, but this time the search aircraft would home in the MGBs.

MARITIME PATROL - PRE EXPANSION

No 37 Squadron reformed at Ein Shemar from a nucleus of No 38 Squadron in September 1947 equipped with Lancaster MR3s. There were detachments at Ramat David and Shallufa. In March 1948 the squadron moved to Luqa, Malta.

No 38 Squadron moved to Luqa, Malta in March 1948 with Lancaster GR 3s.

No 88 Squadron and its Sunderland GR 5s moved to Seletar in June 1951 with detachments at Iwakuni and Kai Tak. It disbanded in October 1954.

No 120 Squadron moved to Kinloss in December 1950 with Lancaster GR 3s.

No 201 Squadron moved to Pembroke Dock with Sunderland GR 5s in January 1949.

No 202 Squadron added Halifax A.9s to its inventory of Halifax GR 6s in August 1949. It remained at Aldergrove with a detachment at Gibraltar.

No 203 Squadron and its Lancaster GR 3s moved to St Eval in January 1947.

No 205 Squadron with its Sunderland GR 5s moved to Seletar in September 1949 with detachments at Iwakuni, China Bay, Kai Tak and Changi.

No 209 Squadron and its Sunderland GR 5s remained at Seletar until it was disbanded in January 1955.

No 210 Squadron moved to Ballykelly near Londonderry in early September 1952 with Lancaster ASR 3s.

No 224 Squadron disbanded in November 1947, only to reform in March 1948 at Aldergrove with Halifax GR 6s. There was a detachment at Gibraltar, which became the squadron's home in October 1948. It maintained a detachment at Aldergrove.

No 230 Squadron moved with its Sunderland GR 5s to Pembroke Dock in February 1949 and disbanded in February 1957.

EXPANSION OF COASTAL COMMAND-THE NEPTUNES

Coastal Command began to re-equip with more squadrons and new aircraft from 1949 when the Shackleton first flew. It would take time for the required numbers to reach the squadrons and the Neptune P2V5s imported from the USA were to fill the gap.

No 36 Squadron reformed at Topcliffe in July 1953, equipping with Neptunes. It disbanded 28 February 1957.

No 203 Squadron moved to Topcliffe in August 1952 with its Lancaster GR3s. These were disposed of in March 1953 and the Squadron converted to Neptune MR 1s. It disbanded 1 September 1956.

No 210 Squadron moved to Topcliffe in September 1952 with its Lancaster ASR 3s. It disposed of them in December and began to convert to the Neptune. It was operational by February 1953. The squadron disbanded 31 January 1957.

No 217 Squadron was the first Neptune squadron, being formed at St Eval in January 1952 with that aircraft and then moving to Kinloss in April. It disbanded on 31 March 1957.

No 1453 Flight was formed at Topcliffe with four aircraft for trials in Airborne Early Warning.

THE SHACKLETONS

"Master cocks on, tanks selected, crossfeeds off, switches one-turn one" – in came the Shackleton in 1951 with No 120 Squadron. These were the words spoken on start up in an interchange between the First Pilot and the Flight Engineer.

No 37 Squadron converted to the Shackleton MR2 in July 1953 at Luqa. The squadron became the permanent colonial policing squadron (later called internal security) in August 1957 when it moved to Khormaksar, Aden. It disbanded on 7 September 1967 when the British left Aden.

No 38 Squadron converted to the Shackleton MR2 in September 1953 at Luqa, Malta. It moved to Hal Far, Malta in October 1965 and disbanded on 31 March 1967.

No 42 Squadron reformed at St Eval in June 1952 with Shackleton MR1As. In January 1953 the crews started to convert to the Mark 2, disposing of the MR1As by July 1954. In November 1965 the crews began the conversion to the MR3 and disposed of the MR2's by June 1966. In April 1971 the conversion to the Nimrod MR1 started. The Shackletons left by September 1971. The squadron converted to the MR 2 starting in June 1983. The squadron disbanded in October 1992 but reformed as No 42(R) Squadron. The OCU had disbanded but reformed as this squadron.

No 120 Squadron received Shackleton MR 1s in March 1951. It moved to Aldergrove in April 1952 and added Shackleton MR 2s to its inventory in April 1953. The conversion to the MR3 began in September 1958 and the squadron moved to Kinloss in April 1959. Conversion to the Nimrod MR1 began in October 1970. In April 1981 the squadron converted to the MR2.

No 201 Squadron reformed at St. Mawgan on 1 October 1958, being No 220 Squadron renumbered with MR3s. The squadron moved to Kinloss on 1 July 1965. It converted to the Nimrod MR1 in July 1970 and to the MR2 in January 1982.

No 204 Squadron reformed at Ballykelly in January 1954 with Shackleton MR2s. In May 1958 the squadron converted back to MR1As, which were retained until February 1960. In May 1959 it re-equipped with MR2Cs. The squadron disbanded on 1 April 1971, only to reform on the same day at Honington from the Majunga Detachment Support Unit. This was the unit that flew sanction patrols against Rhodesia.

No 205 Squadron moved to Changi, Singapore on 1 March 1958 and converted to MR1As. It converted to MR2Cs in February 1962 and disbanded on 31 October 1971.

No 206 Squadron reformed at St Eval in September 1952 with Shackleton MR1As. In February 1953 it converted to the MR2, only to convert back to MR1As in June 1954. In January 1958 the squadron moved three miles south to St. Mawgan and began the conversion to the MR3. In July 1965 the squadron moved to Kinloss and five years later in August 1970, converted to the Nimrod MR1. It converted to the MR2 in February 1980.

No 210 Squadron reformed at Ballykelly, being No 269 Squadron renumbered with MR2s. It disbanded on 31 October 1970 and reformed the following day at Sharjah, Trucial States of Oman with MR2s. It disbanded on 15 November 1971.

No 220 Squadron reformed at Kinloss in September

1951 with Shackleton MR1s and moved to St Eval in November. The squadron converted to the MR2 in March 1953, but these were disposed of to No 228 Squadron which reformed from a nucleus from No 220 Squadron in July 1954 and it continued to operate its MR1s until February 1958. The squadron operated MR2s from March 1957 until October that year. In August 1957 the crews began to convert to MR3s. The squadron was disbanded on 1 October 1958, being renumbered as No 201 Squadron.

No 224 Squadron began to re-equip with Shackleton MR 1s in July 1951, finally disposing of its Halifax GR6s in March 1952. It converted to MR2s in May 1953 and was disbanded on 31 October 1966.

No 228 Squadron reformed at St Eval from a nucleus of No 220 Squadron in July 1954 with Shackleton MR2s. In November 1956 the squadron moved to St. Mawgan and then back to St. Eval in January 1958. The squadron disbanded in March 1959.

No 240 Squadron reformed at Aldergrove in May 1952 from a nucleus of No 120 Squadron with Shackleton MR1s. It moved to St. Eval in May 1952 and then to Ballykelly the following month. It converted to MR2s in March 1953 while retaining its MR1s. The MR2s were disposed of in August 1954 to other units and the squadron disbanded on 1 November 1958, being renumbered No 203 Squadron.

No 269 Squadron reformed at Gibraltar from a nucleus of No 224 Squadron with Shackleton MR1s in January 1952. It moved to Ballykelly in March. It took some MR2s on strength in March 1953, disposing of them in August 1954, and continued to operate the MR1s until November 1958. Some MRs2s came on strength again for a month in October 1958 and the squadron disbanded on 1 December 1958, being renumbered No. 210 Squadron.

No 236 Operational Conversion Unit (OCU) at Kinloss received its first Shackletons in May 1951.

ASWDU (see below) at St. Mawgan received three Shackletons for weapon development and installation trials in early 1951.

The original power installation for this aircraft was four 2450hp Rolls Royce Griffon 57 engines. These were fitted to the first Shackleton MR1s, but shortly after initial production the engine was modified and called the 57A. These were fitted rapidly to the MR1s, which then were called MR1As.

The RAF need for a replacement for the Lancaster GR3 was acute and the introduction of the MR1A was rapid. Even before the first MR1A reached a squadron the MR2 was under development.

TRANING

The initial training of the crews was carried out at the School of Maritime Reconnaissance, which was established at St Mawgan in Cornwall a few miles south of St Eval in June 1951. This unit trained pilots, navigators, flight engineers, signallers and for a short period, gunners, in signals, codes, ship recognition, aircraft recognition, aircraft systems and Maritime Operations. The trade of gunner became redundant and the work was carried out by signallers. Pilots and navigators were also trained in maritime navigation and Maritime Operations in greater detail. Since maritime flying had begun pilots had been trained in navigation, because at that time there were no navigators. This training carried on until the school disbanded in 1956. After the three-month course at St Mawgan the students were sent either to Pembroke Dock for those bound for Sunderlands or to No 236 OCU at Kinloss for those bound for Neptunes or Shackletons. After 1956 the Neptunes were phased out, the S of MR closed and No 236 OCU became the Maritime Operational Training Unit (MOTU). The MOTU was based at Kinloss.

The Joint Anti-Submarine School (JASS), which in effect was a replacement for Commodore Stephenson's work up course at Tobermory, was founded in January 1947. It had its own aircraft, namely Lancaster GR3s, until they were replaced by Shackleton MR1s. The School itself was at HMS *Sea Eagle* on the outskirts of Londonderry and the aircraft were based at Ballykelly. The object of the course at JASS was to work up aircrews, surface warships and submarines to an operational capability. In the three-week course classroom lectures were given, followed by mini exercises at sea called CASEXs and then an exercise lasting several days.

Squadrons were sent to Malta for intensive anti-submarine training on a fair weather station every 18 months or so.

Crew members were also subject to the Coastal Command Categorisation Board (CCCB) which visited each squadron in turn to examine aircrew in the various subjects in their individual profession. Certain senior members of each squadron were examined and, if passed, were awarded a "T" category enabling them to examine locally and to award categories to aircrew. These categories were "D", "C" and "B", "B" being the highest. The "A" category was awarded only by the CCCB.

DEVELOPMENT
Coastal had its own development unit, the Anti Submarine Warfare Development Unit (ASWDU), which in 1948 was based at Ballykelly but moved in May 1951 to St Mawgan. It was equipped with various aircraft, including Lancaster GR3s and Grumman Avengers.

THE KOREAN WAR 1950-53
The Shackleton force took no part in this war, but Sunderland squadrons Nos 88, 205 and 209 were involved. Once that was over, No 88 Squadron disbanded in October 1954.

No 209 Squadron disbanded January 1955.

No 201 Squadron disbanded in February 1957.

No 205 Squadron continued to operate Sunderlands until May 1959.

OTHER TASKS
The Shackleton is remembered as a maritime patrol aircraft, but it had many other tasks. It was used for search and rescue, although this is perhaps a misnomer in that it could not actually rescue anybody. It was a very effective vehicle and was able to drop a Lindholme gear to survivors. This was a series of five containers, four of which held supplies and the fifth a multi-seat (MS) dinghy which could accommodate nine persons and was known as an MS9.

In the late 1950s, when RAF transport aircraft were at a premium, Shackletons were used as transports to carry soldiers to Cyprus. Initially troops were sent to Cyprus to fight against the Enosis terrorists who wanted union with Greece. Later Shackletons carried soldiers to fight in Egypt when Colonel Nasser nationalised the Suez Canal. A skeleton crew of six, two pilots, one navigator, one flight engineer and two signallers, was carried and a passenger load of 33 to 36 soldiers.

In 1956 there was a flight of Lincoln bombers in Aden at RAF Khormaksar which were used in the colonial policing role later to be known as Internal Security. These aircraft were becoming old and rusty and it was resolved to replace them. The Shackleton Mark 2 was chosen. As a temporary measure the flight was to be replaced by a detachment from the UK and No 42 Squadron was selected to be the first. In 1956 the squadron went into training to carry out medium-level bombing, i.e. up to around 10,000 feet, using the T1A bombsight which was the manual version of the Mark XIV sight used in the war. The Mark XIV had an analogue computer fitted into which height, true air speed and the terminal velocity of the bombs were entered. This was done manually in the Mark T1A. This role was in addition to its maritime patrol duties. In late 1956 one aircraft flew to Aden for a few days to obtain first-hand knowledge of the situation. In January 1957 four aircraft flew to Aden via Tripoli/Idris in North Africa, Kano in Nigeria, Eastleigh in Kenya and on to Khormaksar. Various patrols along the Yemen/Aden Protectorate border were carried out, plus escorts for road convoys. When in February 1957 an Army patrol was ambushed, a bombing raid was flown against the insurgents. For several days before the raid leaflets were dropped requesting that the insurgents surrender.

On another occasion several rebels had been captured and were held outside a village. British officers and political agents went into the village to negotiate terms. The rebels escaped, retook their weapons, which were laid out by an armoured car, and ran into the hills. They believed that while in the village the officers and agents were virtually hostages. A small battle ensued and the RAF Regiment Air Liaison Officer (ALO) and his section of Aden Protectorate Levies (APLs) were pinned down. He called the Shackleton flying top cover and requested a strafing run while he and his men withdrew. The two 20mm nose guns were unreliable, being prone to jamming after a few rounds. However, the aircraft made the run several times, firing 475 out of 600 rounds. The Regiment ALO and his APLs made good their escape. He later rendered his thanks to the crew in Khormaksar Officers' Mess.

Later in 1957 No 228 Squadron took over this role and flew operations from Khormaksar, Sharjah and Masirah. In the Oman, three insurgents, Talib, Galib and Suleiman and their followers rebelled against the Sultan. Four aircraft from No 228 Squadron went to Aden and then to Sharjah to assist No 37 Squadron in the fight against the rebels, who eventually retreated into the Jebel Akhdar.

In July 1958 King Feisal of Iraq was assassinated. No 42 Squadron, on a Sub/Air exercise flying from Aldergrove was recalled to St Eval. Crew members were equipped with either .38 revolvers or Sten guns and flew to El Adem in Libya. The concern may have been that the Egyptians would attack Libya and great caution was exercised before the Shackletons landed. In the event all was well in this respect and they arrived safely. They then flew on to Khormaksar, where the low-level bomb sights were exchanged for the medium level Mk 1As. Practice bombing sorties were carried out and the Mk 1A sights were calibrated. The squadron flew up to Sharjah and carried out bombing sorties in support of the Sultan's forces.

No 224 Squadron was a later colonial policing squadron.

Christmas Island in the Pacific Ocean was the base for all those who were involved in the United Kingdom's hydrogen bomb tests known as Operation Grapple from early 1957. No 206 Squadron provided the Maritime Patrol around Ground Zero in that year followed by No 240 Squadron in 1958.

BIBLIOGRAPHY

Burn A, *The Fighting Captain*, Leo Cooper 1993

Burn A, *The Fighting Commodores*

Richard Woodman, *Arctic Convoys 1941-1945*, John Murray

Timothy P. Mulligan, *Neither Sharks nor Wolves*, Chatham Publishing

Norman Franks, *Another Kind of Courage*, Patrick Stephens Limited

David Wragg, *The Escort Carrier in World War II*, Pen & Sword Maritime 2005

Paul Kemp, *U-Boats Destroyed*, Arms & Armour 1997

Norman Franks, *Search, Find and Kill*, Grub Street 1995

Norman Franks & Eric Zimmerman, *U-Boat versus Aircraft*, Grub Street 1998

Norman Franks, *Dark Sky, Deep Water*, Grub Street 1997

Norman Franks, *Conflict over the Bay*, Grub Street 1999

C. G. Jefford, *RAF Squadrons*, Air Life 2001

Chaz Bowyer, *Coastal Command at War*, Ian Allan 1979

Alfred Price, *Aircraft versus Submarine*, William Kimber 1973

R.D.Layman, *Naval Aviation in the First World War*, Caxton Editions 2002

Ralph Barker, *The Ship Busters,* Chatto & Windus 1957

Julian Thompson, *The War at Sea 1914-1918,* Sidgwick & Jackson in association with the Imperial War Museum 2005.

Roy Conyers Nesbitt, *The Battle Of The Atlantic*

David Wragg, *Second World War Carrier Campaigns*

David Ross, with Bruce Blanche and William Simpson, *The Greatest Squadron Of Them All*

Roy Conyers Nesbit, *The Strike Wings*

EPILOGUE

○

DEFENCE REVIEW 2010 MARITIME PATROL

1. I was a Coastal Command Navigator and crew captain on Shackleton aircraft in the Maritime Patrol role. Later, I converted to Nimrods. I was an Intelligence Officer at COMAIRNORLANT, finally retiring in 1984 after 31 years.

2. Anti-submarine and anti-surface patrol work is a highly complex business requiring a number of skills, including navigation over the sea and at high latitudes, sonics, radar, ESM, intelligence appreciation and tactics. These skills cannot be learned except over a long period. Dispose of the personnel of all aircrew categories who have these skills and it will take a long time to catch up. That means that in modern warfare we will have lost before the battle starts! In a similar way, the aircraft required is also complex and unlike in previous wars, cannot be built quickly, as I am sure the reader is well aware.

In 1939 the RAF had inadequate aircraft such as the Avro Anson to fly antisubmarine patrols. In fact, Tiger Moth biplanes had to be used as well, to try to force U-Boat commanders to submerge their boats. A submerged diesel boat loses its effectiveness unlike a nuclear boat. Diesels are still used and are becoming quieter. I like to think that the Royal Air Force and Commonwealth Air Forces were, and are, better at this work than most. The German Naval Air Wing 3 with its Breguet Atlantics, later replaced by P3C Orions, are good, as were the Dutch Navy with its Atlantics and later P3Cs, sadly no longer in existence. The French Navy now operate 22 Atlantique 2s. The Italian Navy now has only four ATR72s. Spain operates the CN235 and Portugal still has ex-Netherlands P3Cs.

3. Maritime Patrol Aircraft (MPA) carry out other tasks, such as Search and Rescue (SAR). Their long range and on-board avionics systems make them ideal for operating open ocean searches for ships and aircraft in trouble. Other tasks include information gathering for intelligence purposes over land areas such as Afghanistan. Currently we have no such ability, as the Nimrod MR2, our only MPA, has been withdrawn from service. It is possible that the C-130 Hercules can provide some help here amongst its other many tasks, but the aircraft is not ideal. Frankly, I regard this as disgraceful for a maritime nation.

4. It can be argued that in the 2010 Defence Review some tasks can be undertaken by Allied Air Forces, and indeed with a common enemy, that would be possible. However, the plight of the Falkland Islands springs to mind and should Argentina repeat her attack of 1982 then probably we would have no allies. Thus we would lose the Falklands.

5.   In the early part of the 20th Century, post 1918, the nation had a policy called the "Ten Year Rule" which meant that if in the year under review there was no threat for the next ten years, then no further change to our defences was required. That failed, and I would suggest that it would fail again should the Government adopt such a policy. We have no means of knowing of what the attitude of nations like Russia and China would be in ten years, although they are friendly enough now. Five years is probably a more realistic period and should be made statutory.

6.   Ballistic missile submarines (SSBNs) require the support of Long Range Maritime Patrol Aircraft (LRMPA). Thus if the nuclear deterrent is to be kept (which I think is right) LRMPA are needed. Aircraft carriers can carry short-range MPAs but their proximity to a SSBN is a bit of a giveaway! The Royal Navy protects our trade routes and shipping but it cannot do that without LRMPA. An enemy will attack our shipping and its escorts from the air as well from the sea. Land-based fighters cannot combat this, thus aircraft carriers are necessary. These in turn are high-value targets and need protection. Exercise Highwood in the 1970s comes to mind. This exercise tried to prove that shore-based aircraft could protect the Fleet. It failed and the RN received three carriers, HMS *Invincible,* HMS *Illustrious* and HMS *Ark Royal,* which originally were called through deck cruisers. If it had not been for the *Ark Royal* the Falklands War would have been lost.

7. I appreciate the need for plenty of soldiers, particularly for Afghanistan, but that war will eventually end and there may be different wars to fight. The five-year period referred to above then would be realistic. I also understand the lack of money but if defence is short-changed I would feel distinctly uncomfortable, as the country would be exposed to any potential enemy willing to exploit our weakness. A strong defence can prevent wars, as history shows. Wars cost more money - it is cheaper to prevent them.

8. I have heard suggestions that the Armed Forces should be merged. The Canadians did this in the 1960s and it did not work.

9. As is well known the primary task of the British Government is to defend its people, which task, in my opinion, the Governments up to 2010 failed to carry out. I am suspicious of the attitude of the new Government. That task cannot come under the category of "Can we afford it?". Defence must come before everything else. We must be able to afford it.

10. On 19 October 2010, the Prime Minister of the United Kingdom announced in the House of Commons that the Nimrod MRA4, the replacement for the MR2, had cost £3.5 billion, was several years late and the cost had increased by some 200% per aircraft. The order was thereby cancelled. With these dismissive words he destroyed the Long Range Maritime Patrol tradition of this country and left it undefended and without SAR cover.